MEDICINAL
MUSHROOMS

AN EXPLORATION OF
TRADITION, HEALING & CULTURE

by Christopher Hobbs

Foreword by Harriet Beinfield

Author's Disclaimer

The following recommendations are for educational and health-increasing use only and not meant to be a prescription for any disease. If you are experiencing symptoms, I always recommend contacting a qualified health practitioner or physician for a diagnosis and total health program.

The author encourages the use of human tests with oral application of natural products and whole herbal extracts as the most effective way to support the long clinical use and history of use of many herbal medicines.

Our Commitment

We at Botanica Press are dedicated in our personal and professional lives to environmental awareness. We are strongly committed to recycling, and we gladly contribute a portion of our profits to the Nature Conservancy and other conservation groups. This book is printed on recycled paper with a minimum of 10% post-consumer waste, and the entire text is printed using soy-based ink.

Etching from *Esculent Funguses of England* by Charles D. Badham, M.D., 1847.

♲ This book is printed on Simpson 60lb recycled paper with soy-based ink.

Other Books in the *Herbs and Health* Series by Christopher Hobbs

Echinacea, The Immune Herb

Foundations of Health

Ginkgo, Elixir of Youth

The Ginsengs, A User's Guide

Handbook for Herbal Healing

The Herbal Prescriber (software)

Kombucha, Manchurian Tea Mushroom

Milk Thistle, The Liver Herb

Natural Liver Therapy

Usnea, The Herbal Antibiotic

Valerian, The Relaxing and Sleep Herb

Vitex, The Women's Herb

by Christopher Hobbs

Michael Miovic, Editor

Beth Baugh, Project Manager

Ken Jones, Research Consultant

David Arora, Technical Editor

Cover art, © February 1995 D.D. Dowden

Illustrations, Fig. 1, 2, 3 © February 1995 Marni Fylling

Library of Congress Catalog Card Number: 95-60381

Botanica Press, 10226 Empire Grade, Santa Cruz, CA 95060

Botanica Press is an imprint of Interweave Press

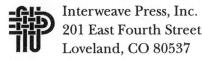 Interweave Press, Inc.
201 East Fourth Street
Loveland, CO 80537

TABLE
of
CONTENTS

Etching from *Our Edible Toadstools and Mushrooms* by W. Hamilton Gibson, 1895.

Foreword

Medicinal Fungi: Forest Friends

Western medicine celebrated the development of the single most valuable botanical of this century, penicillin, obtained in 1928 from a fungus. This spawned the entire class of life-saving antibiotics. There are over 100,000 species within the broad category of fungi, of which the penicillin mold is one, and there are 38,000 species of mushrooms. Clinical research today continues to document the health benefits of select fungi.

These fungi survive and thrive upon the decay of the forest floor through their dual power of self-protection and self-transformation. Over millions of years, mushrooms have successfully adapted to an environment replete with threatening microbial agents by developing natural substances that prevent bacteria and viruses from replicating inside their cells. Unlike other plants that, dazzling green with chlorophyll, synthesize nutrients from the radiant sun, the crimson, tawny, and inky mushrooms flourish by a different mechanism.

While plants absorb carbon dioxide and liberate oxygen, mushrooms mimic human respiration by captivating oxygen and exhaling carbon dioxide. In keeping with forest ecology, plants then reuse this carbon dioxide to manufacture their food. By discharging enzymes into the matter upon which they feed, fungi break down complex carbohydrates and proteins into simpler compounds. This process of decomposition enriches the soil and makes essential substances available to plants in a form they can absorb. But unlike humans who need light and fresh food, mushrooms feed on moist decaying organic matter in deep shade—they are the grand recyclers.

Within the body, a few medicinal mushrooms seem able to transmute metabolic waste and neutralize toxic accumulations without provoking eliminative catharsis as a consequence. They are a safe and effective medicament that has been valued over thousands of years of human civilization.

Taoist sages relied on their own observations to draw conclusions that today we test in laboratories. Twenty-two centuries ago, Emperor Ti instructed a fleet of ships to sail the Eastern seas in search of the Ganoderma (Ling zhi or Reishi) mushroom because it was believed to confer not only long life, but immortality. Chinese herbal texts suggest that the Ling zhi sharpens memory and mental capacity, awakens the spirit, calms the mind, opens the breath, strengthens the heart, protects the liver, increases stamina and endurance and helps the body resist falling prey to the demons of age and illness.

Mushrooms provide a link for us with these Taoist sages of ancient China who leaned on reishi-carved staffs and also used these mushrooms as spiritual aids—as foods presumed to foster enlightenment. In the mythic story, Alice in Wonderland, Alice ate one mushroom to make her larger, and another to maker her smaller, opening the windows of her imagination so that she could enter another dimension, a magical kingdom.

Paul Unschuld, scholar of Chinese medical history, informs us that fifteen centuries ago the classic pharmacopeia known as the Pen Tsao devoted its first monograph on a single herb to the Divine Fungus, Ling zhi. It was said to relieve the body of its material weight, prolong life, and transform the consumer into a supranatural being.

Today we can still share in the subtle, barely palpable mind-altering properties of reishi that attracted the Taoists. By analogy, just as young mushrooms feed on decomposing forest debris, so it seems that in the human body they assist in the neutralization of psychic waste and recycle such negativity into mental clarity and optimist. These mushrooms were regarded as sacred agents that elevate the spirit, helping people to transcend the gross material world and gain perspective on the grand scheme of the 10,000 myriad things.

Ingesting these mushrooms today can give us a taste of the state of mind whereby we experience illuminated detachment, enabling us to act on the stage and observe from the audience simultaneously—better realizing our destiny by remembering that the health of our spirit is not merely dependent on the vigor of our body or that spiritual purpose is not merely equated with material achievement. These mushrooms have not changed much over the millennia, nor has the human quest. We can experiment with them in our pursuit of physical and transcendent healing. They provide a way for us to commune with the Taoists, to taste the same flavors, and savor the same longings of our collective soul.

Harriet Beinfield
Co-author *Between Heaven and Earth: A Guide to Chinese Medicine*

Acknowledgements

In writing this book, I am delighted to share my personal experience in collecting, studying, eating, and using fungi as medicine for nearly 20 years. I have also combed the historical and modern scientific literature available in libraries throughout the U.S., such as the C.G. Lloyd collection on fungi at the Lloyd Library, the Boston Medical Library, and several University of California libraries, as well as a number of European libraries. I am grateful to the library staffs of these institutions for their invaluable help and insight.

A work of this complexity is, by necessity, a team effort. I want to express my heartfelt thanks to Michael Miovic, our super-editor, who has worked with us since 1988, until going on to medical school.

Many thanks also to Ken Jones, who made an important contribution to this work through his own knowledge of medicinal fungi, critical editing, and literature collection. It was a pleasure to work with him—his professionalism and attention to details are inspiring. Ken has the heart of a research warrior.

My dedicated research assistant, Patty Baker, has put many hours into this book, organizing literature, abstracting articles, checking references, and helping to move the project along when it got bogged down.

Heartfelt thanks to David Arora, Dr. Varro Tyler, and Dr. Subhuti Dharmananda for reading the manuscript and providing important insights and corrections.

I cannot put into writing what Beth, my partner, has contributed to this book—from editing to literature organization, help with literature acquisition, and especially moral support.

I translated articles and books from German with the help of my teacher, Shanti Coble, for whom I give many thanks for her patience and wonderful knowledge of scientific German.

Since I don't read Chinese, most of the Chinese studies quoted in this work were gathered from Chemical Abstracts, Abstracts of Chinese Medicines (Chang and But, 1986-1988), Pharmacology and Applications of Chinese Materia Medica (Chang and But, 1987), *The Fungi Pharmacopeia* (Bo and Yun-sun, 1980), and *Icones of Medicinal Fungi From China* (Ying et al, 1987), as well as on-line searches of the NAPRALERT database and MEDLINE. My admiration and heart-felt thanks to the researchers and translators who helped to make this information accessible. Also, my deep appreciation for the rich cultural experience and love of fungi that come from China, Japan, Russia, France, and all other countries where mushrooms are known and loved for their spirit, as well as their value as food and medicine. We have just begun to understand the riches they hold.

It is my responsibility to check and recheck the factual statements and references in this book, so any errors, as well as wild theories, are mine alone.

Sources, Historical and Scientific

A few words here are necessary about the quality and credibility of the various sources of information drawn upon in writing this book. As a reader of many herbal and health-related books, I am often frustrated when the writer does not mention the sources drawn upon. I hope this information is helpful when considering what personal value Medicinal Mushrooms may provide to you, the reader.

I extensively reviewed literature from the three following primary sources:

1. The historical record: written works from ancient Egyptian medicine and ancient Chinese medicine through the end of the 19th century, including folk uses and medical uses.

2. Clinical reports from the 20th century: written reports from clinicians of all types who have used medicinal mushrooms in their practices.

3. Scientific studies: organized laboratory studies *in vitro*, where various organisms (such as bacteria) or cells (such as human immune cells) were exposed to mushroom extracts to observe their influence, or *in vivo* laboratory or clinical studies with animals or humans, either controlled or uncontrolled.

It is sometimes difficult to judge the quality of these diverse reports and studies when one was not involved in the actual study or is unfamiliar with the credibility of the original observer or reporter. Thus, this present work does not pretend to offer a critical review of the literature in the sense of evaluating each report or study and commenting on its methodology or conclusions, except as it pertains to the possible use of a species.

As for the historical literature, I have chosen works from the Institute for Natural Products library which most epitomize the written record of herbal use throughout the ages. For instance, the works of Hippocrates, Dioscorides, the Pen T'sao, Gerard, Parkinson, and the Eclectics were reviewed for relevant information on medicinal mushrooms. Obviously many of the historical uses for mushrooms are very general and often based on a specific aspect of the appearance of a species (such as the phenomenally phallic stinkhorn). The theory that some morphological characteristic of a plant or other substance might give clues to its medicinal activity is called the "doctrine of signatures." A good example is the leafy lichen called lungwort that has the appearance of lung tissue and was said to be good for the lungs. It should be noted that some remedies, the activities of which may have been conceived under this doctrine, later proved to be active. The lungwort, *Lobaria pulmonaria*, for instance contains lichen acids that inhibit the growth of *Pneumococcus* organisms and mucilage to soothe inflamed membranes.

It has also happened that some purported uses of medicinal agents originated or amplified by superstition or rumor were subsequently passed on as fact. While traveling and teaching, I often hear ridiculous statements from unknown origins that appear to have been passed on by word of mouth. A good example is the notion that ginseng is for men only, and the blood-moving and tonifying herb dong quai is exclusively for women. According to Traditional Chinese Medicine or the age-old traditional use of these herbs, this idea is simply not true.

Scientific reports and studies on medicinal mushrooms come mainly from China, Japan, Germany, the United States, and Europe. As can be seen from a review of the bibliography of Medicinal Mushrooms, most of the laboratory and clinical studies were performed in China and Japan. The way in which these studies were designed, the care in which they were performed, and the data gathered and evaluated vary widely among research groups. In general, Japanese studies more closely follow accepted western protocols for scientific testing and evaluation, and the instrumentation available to the researchers is often of good design and quality. In China, the quality of the studies and instrumentation is much more variable. There the control group and the process of blinding and "crossing-over" the experimental groups, which attempt to eliminate the influence of the beliefs of the experimenters and volunteers on the results, are often not considered as important as in the West. This is beginning to change, but many of the studies on medicinal mushrooms performed in China are not controlled in any way. They are more like clinical reports, in that a group of researchers give mushroom extracts to a number of patients (sometimes many patients) and the overall results noted. The placebo effect is often not considered in evaluating the results of a study, perhaps because in China, the way in which the mind or emotions affect the body is accepted as a legitimate part of the results.

When evaluating a study, it is also important to note whether the experiment was performed *in vitro* or *in vivo*. If an *in vitro* study shows a plant extract to have activity, for instance a cancer-inhibiting effect, there is no certainty that the extract will be useful in treating or preventing human cancers. For one thing, the extract may be too toxic. Whether the study was performed on animals or humans, and whether the dose was orally administered (p.o.) or given by injection, intraperitoneally (i.p.), or intramuscularly (i.m.) is also relevant. It is not certain what the significance of many of the therapeutic results or toxicological effects noted in studies with animals have in human medicine, and if an herbal extract shows positive results when administered by injection, it does not necessarily mean that it will be active when taken orally.

Keeping the above discussion in mind, I invite the reader to use her or his own discretion and imagination when evaluating the possible uses and future potential, whether in medicine in general or for personal use, of the many species of mushrooms presented in this work. It is not my intention to raise false hopes that some of the species reviewed can cure any disease, especially serious chronic diseases such as hypertension, atherosclerosis, cancer, and AIDS. These diseases—in fact all diseases—are a result of the influences of one's lifestyle, diet, belief system, genetic predisposition, as well as many environmental influences. In my view, medicinal mushrooms show promise as part of an overall treatment plan for a number of ailments, but they are not magic bullets. They have a long history of use in many cultures and a fair amount of scientific investigation to their credit. I leave it up to the reader and to future investigation and experience to clarify more exactly what their role is in the treatment of disease.

In this book, I see my job as presenting the world's literature—which is vast—in an organized way, attempting to eliminate redundant and irrelevant information, so that the reader can gain an insight into the whole sweep and scope of the human record on medicinal mushrooms and what our healing relationship to them might be. I also will attempt to provide practical information that will enable the reader to try some of the species generally considered as safe for themselves. Each user of herbs is part of the tremendously long and valued association of plants and people.

Though of course vastly limited compared with the scope of human experience with medicinal mushrooms, I also add my own experience and insight throughout this work. For over twenty years, I have eaten or used as teas many of the species covered, as well as identifying them in the field.

My vision for future editions of this work is a process of continued gathering of new information from the literature, the addition of further clinical experience, and the addition of personal experience from other cultures who use medicinal mushrooms. My interest and love of mushrooms and healing is a lifelong passion that, if I am so blessed, I will continue.

The *Chanterelle,* from *An Encyclopedia of Gardening* by George Nicholson, circa 1887.

Introduction

Mushrooms have been valued throughout the world as both food and medicine for thousands of years. Throughout the world, many people enjoy hunting for wild mushrooms, delighting in the variety of shapes, sizes, and colors exhibited by these "flowers of the fall." Europeans have always appreciated the gastronomic value of wild mushrooms. In Japan, pushcart vendors on the streets still sell medicinal mushrooms to the average citizen who uses them to maintain health and promote longevity. Some Japanese people have even been said to travel hundreds of miles in order to collect wild mushrooms that only grow on very old plum trees—such as the Reishi—renowned as a cure for cancer and degenerative diseases. Likewise, for over 3,000 years the Chinese have used and revered many fungi for their health-giving properties, especially tonics for the immune system (Liu and Bau, 1980; Yun-Chang, 1985). To the Yoruba of southwestern Nigeria a number of fungi became an important part of their mythology and medical practice (Oso, 1977).

Mushrooms may also be the perfect food for staying trim and healthy. A recent "letter from the editor" in the *Nutrition Action* newsletter (September, 1994) from the Center for Science in the Public Interest mentioned that up to 1/3 of the U.S. population are overweight. Because fats occur in mushrooms in minor amounts, especially compared with protein and carbohydrates, and the fatty fraction consists predominantly of unsaturated fatty acids such as linoleic acid, they may be the perfect food for losing weight and maintaining a healthy heart and cardiovascular system.

When it comes to mushrooms, most Americans and inhabitants of the British Isles are rather ignorant. Many people in the United States have a distinct dislike, even a fear, of fungi—a phenomenon that may be called "fungophobia"—a term coined by Hay (1887). Rolfe and Rolfe wrote about the distinctly unsavory view of which the British view mushrooms and mushroom hunters, in their delightful *Romance of the Fungus World* (1925). Generally, the first association wild mushrooms bring to mind here is "poisonous." The principal edible mushroom most Americans know is the bland *Agaricus bisporus* (Lange) Sing., or "button mushroom" found in supermarkets. It has little flavor and negligible medicinal value compared with other wild species. In fact, it can even be unhealthful in the sense that it may be heavily sprayed with malathion and other pesticides (many commercially cultivated mushrooms are among the most heavily sprayed items in the vegetable section).

Happily, however, there are signs that these narrow-minded attitudes in the United States and England are changing and catching up with the rest of the world. The spreading popularity of natural foods is one factor that has helped re-awaken interest in mushrooms and mushroom-hunting. Another factor is the recent growth of the mushroom-export business, which has been boosted by troubles in Europe. Due to acid rain, sprawling development, and industrial accidents such as the one at Chernobyl, millions of acres of mushroom habitat in Europe and Russia have been disturbed, and many species of wild mushrooms are becoming scarce (Cherfas, 1991).

Europe imports thousands of pounds of chanterelles and boletus each year. The high price these traditional gastronomic delights bring creates a good supplementary income for knowledgeable gatherers in the United States. Indeed, wild or home cultivation may soon become viable cottage industries in the Pacific Northwest, which has the forest habitats and substantial rainfall needed for such ventures. Cultivation as a home business may be preferable to the recent problems that are surfacing in the Pacific Northwest among professional and itinerant pickers alike—namely squabbling over mushroom patches on public lands. A newspaper article told of teams of professional pickers using walkie-talkies to coordinate harvests and mentioned that they can become upset when other pickers stray into what they consider their turf. In response to the increased harvesting pressure, quotas were recently set in the Mt. Hood National Forest (McRae, 1993). For books and supplies for the cultivation of edible and medicinal mushrooms, see the appendix.

Finally, Japanese products containing LEM, a polysaccharide-rich extract from the shiitake mushroom, and similar extracts from maitake are currently undergoing trials in Japan and the U.S. to test their effectiveness in treating various forms of cancer. They show promise for treating people suffering from various forms of cancer and AIDS and are currently in strong demand in Japan. Commercial shiitake cultivators in the U.S., Canada, and in parts of Asia are decidedly interested in this new potential market and are starting large cultivation efforts, hoping the demand will continue to grow as further scientific studies are conducted. At present, pharmaceutical and nutraceutical products from mushrooms may be worth more than 1.2 billion dollars U.S.

I have written this book in the hopes that it will stimulate interest in the vital and fascinating field of medicinal fungi. Please note that this book is divided into two parts: the first part presents some general background about what fungi are, summarizes the history and use of medicinal fungi, and gives practical instructions on how to use them. It is written mostly in simple terms that should be understandable to the lay reader. For unfamiliar terms, see the Glossary of Terms on page 202. The second part, on the other hand, is detailed and technical, covering the botany, chemistry, pharmacology, clinical studies, indications, and dosages of medicinal fungi commonly available in the United States, Asia, Europe, and other parts of the world. It is intended primarily for researchers, writers, health practitioners and scientists, though it may also be useful for the lay reader with a strong interest in a particular mushroom. Here, one can find specific details on how to use many species of fungi for medicine and maintenance of health. In any case, whether you are new to the field of medicinal mushrooms, or a veteran mushroom-picker, there should be plenty of valuable information in this book that is appropriate for your needs and interests.

The Botany of Fungi

Many people feel a little uneasy when they first learn that a mushroom is a fungus. The word fungus often brings to mind unsalutary growths such as athlete's foot, the blue and green molds that grow on citrus fruits, the fuzzy white stuff on stale bread, or the mildew that thrives in dirty showers. Farmers and people who live in agricultural areas have also heard about the fungal parasites that can devastate food crops such as corn, rice, wheat, and rye. So what does the familiar umbrella-shaped mushroom have to do with these fearsome fungi, and how could fungi possibly be medicinal?

Actually, mushrooms are just one of the many kinds of fungi. The fungi are a unique group of organisms that occupy a kingdom all to themselves, the Kingdom Fungi. Scientists have named some 100,000 different species of fungi (plus many more have yet to be classified) and divided these into two major divisions, **Mastigomycota** and **Amastigomycota**. Mastigocycota are a large group of fungi that produce non-sexual motile *zoospores*, which make it possible for them to thrive and reproduce in damp or wet environments. The water molds that attack dead fish, plants, and insects in a pond environment are members of this division. These fungi are not used for medicine or food and will not be considered further here.

The other division of fungi, the Amastigomycota, is a large and diverse group that does not produce a motile stage and is not usually adapted to an aquatic environment. This group does contain all the edible and medicinal fungi, and consists of four subdivisions:

- the **Zygomycotina** are saprophytic, which means they grow on other plants and sometimes animals, rather than derive nutrients from a host as parasites do. Among this group is the genus *Rhizopus*, which includes black bread mold and the mold that grows on cooked soybeans to make the traditional Asian food tempeh. Other members are commercially important because they are used to produce alcohol, pigments, and steroids.

- the **Ascomycotina**, or "sac fungi", (ascomycetes) is the largest group of fungi, containing nearly 2,000 genera. Organisms such as yeasts, mildews, the cup fungi, ergot, and the edible and medicinal morels and truffles belong here. Many ascomycetes grow on decaying plant debris.

- the **Basidiomycotina**, or "club fungi" (basidiomycetes), consists of at least 15,000 known species. This important edible and medicinal group includes the jelly fungi, smuts, the polypores, puffballs, and the majority of the fleshy fungi that produce a visible "fruiting body" or *basidiocarp*.

- the **Deuteromycotina**, sometimes called the "imperfect fungi" or "Fungi Imperfecti" (deuteromycetes), is a miscellaneous group of about 15,000 species whose sexual phase (if any) is unknown. It is a somewhat haphazard assemblage of left-over taxa that are hard to place anywhere else. This group includes the famous *Penicillium* genus (Wallace, 1991).

See the excellent textbook *Fundamentals of the Fungi* (Moore-Landecker, 1990) for further information on the biology and taxonomy of the fungi.

The two subdivisions we will look closely at in this book are the Ascomycotina and the Basidiomycotina. The Ascomycotina are called "sac fungi" because they produce sac-shaped capsules that release spores, which are carried away by wind or water and eventually settle on the ground and grow into new mature organisms. Many tiny sacs are contained in the bowl-shaped fruiting body of an Ascomycete.

The Ascomycotina include the familiar truffles, green and blue citrus molds, ergot (a parasite of rye and other grains that we will discuss again later), and the *Cordyceps* genus, which is widely used in Traditional Chinese Medicine.

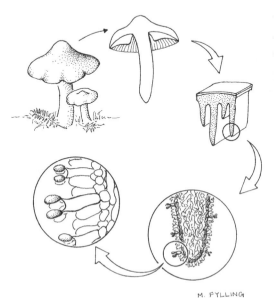

M. FYLLING

The Basidiomycotina, for their part, are called "club fungi" because their spores are attached to club-shaped structures named *basidia* (*basidium* means "club" in Latin). What are commonly called "mushrooms" are the *fruiting bodies* of Basidiomycetes and certain Ascomycetes. Fruiting bodies are reproductive structures that grow above ground to release spores. Many fleshy fungi release spores from flat, plate-like structures called gills (see Fig. 1), but polypores release them from hollow tubes or pores (see Fig. 2).

Fig. 1: Spore production in a Basidiomycete.

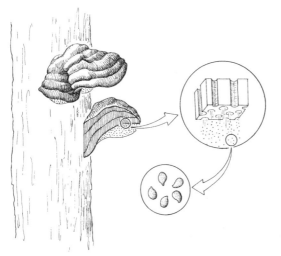

Fig. 2: Spore production in a polypore fruiting body

The main body of a mushroom, however, is a threadlike network called a *mycelium* that grows underground or in wood. It is the mycelium that breaks down complex molecules (like cellulose or lignan in trees) and absorbs food from the environment (see Fig. 3).

The Basidiomycotina contain many well-known medicinal genera, including *Boletus*, *Agaricus*, *Amanita*, and *Polyporus*. In scientific studies, many Basidiomycotina have demonstrated antitumor activity, and several have also been found to have antibiotic, antiviral, antiallergic, and immunostimulating properties, as well as the ability to lower blood sugar, blood lipids (such as cholesterol), and blood pressure (Lindequist et al, 1990).

Fungi resemble plants in that they cannot move on their own, and they have cell walls. Yet fungi are not really plants as we generally think of them—their cell walls are composed of chitin, not cellulose, and they do not carry out photosynthesis. Instead, fungi must absorb food and nutrients from their surroundings, similar to bacteria. They do this by secreting digestive enzymes into their environment and then absorbing the products of digestion. Saprophytic fungi are critical in nature, because they decompose and recycle dead matter such as trees, animals, and any other organic residues. This returns nitrogen, phosphorous, and other mineral nutrients to the soil.

However, many fungi are symbionts. For example, it has been found that fungi in the soil associate with the roots of about 90% of plants, helping them to obtain vital nutrients. This association is called *mycorrhizae* from *myco*= akin to fungus and *rhiza*= root. As the mycelia of fungi grow through the soil like a net of fingers, they absorb and concentrate nutrients, such as phosphorous, and water. Then, when the mycelia wrap around plant roots, even entering the plant's cells, the plant can absorb these concentrated nutrients straight from the fungus. Thus, the plants' absorptive capabilities are greatly increased. In return, the fungus can absorb complex compounds that the plant makes, such as sugars and amino acids. Thus both the plant and the fungus benefit. Significantly, studies have

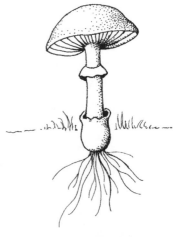

Fig. 3: Mycelium absorb food from the environment.

demonstrated that soil deprived of fungi produces stunted, weak plant growth or none at all (Wallace, 1991) and thus this association is extremely important for the health of the forest. Trees that are cultivated in sterilized soil (formerly a common forestry practice) have been shown to grow much more slowly and are not as healthy as trees growing in a soil rich with fungi and other microorganisms, which are naturally present with the recycling of old decaying wood from previous generations of trees. Thus the cycle of life goes on and is self-sustaining.

Fungi can also be helpful to people. Two species in the *Penicillium* genus, *P. roquefortii* and *P. camembertii*, are used to flavor the famous cheeses that bear those same names, and *Rhizopus oligosporus* grows through cooked soybeans to produce tempeh (Hesseltine & Wang, 1986). Of course the antibiotic penicillin is also made from the *Penicillium* genus, and *Aspergillus oryzae* is used to flavor soy sauce and help ferment saki. Yeasts, which are single-celled fungi, make ethyl alcohol and CO_2 as waste products. They manufacture the alcohol in beer and wine, and their CO_2 makes bread rise and gives some beverages their fizz. Cyclosporine, a product of the soil fungi, *Cylindrocarpon lucidum* Booth and *Trichoderma polysporum*, is an immunosuppressant that is widely used today in organ-transplant operations. By safely suppressing the immune response, it allows the body to "accept" a foreign organ that would otherwise be rejected (Reynolds, 1982).

One last fungus I will mention here is *Candida albicans*, which is a yeast-like imperfect fungi. It is notorious for causing overgrowth in the mouth of newborns (thrush) and vaginal infections. People often develop *C. albicans* infections after prolonged use of antibiotics, which destroy the many beneficial bacteria and fungi that live on and in the body. With these symbiotic organisms gone, the antibiotic-resistant *C. albicans* has no competition for food and starts to overgrow. That is one more reason to maintain a strong immune system in the first place, to obviate the need for antibiotics. Fortunately, many of the fungi in this book help strengthen the immune response and have been successfully used to treat *C. albicans* infections.

I have spent some time presenting general background information about fungi because these organisms are often poorly understood. As you can see, fungi come in an extraordinary variety of sizes and types, ranging from single-celled yeasts, to powder-like molds, to giant woody conks. And they affect plants and people in both beneficial and harmful ways. Let's take a look now at how fungi have been used in medicine in various cultures.

Please note that because the nomenclature or formal names (binomials) of mushrooms vary widely with the systems of classification followed by past authors, it is easy to become confused when reading older works on fungi. For the most part I have followed the system of nomenclature used in *North American Polypores* (Gilbertson and Ryvarden, 1986), and David Arora has kindly reviewed the nomenclatural assignments for this and all other groups of fungi used in this book. As an aid for deciphering older names in other works on fungi or medicinal herbs, I have included a taxonomic history with authorities (when available). The authority who first described a species is usually added to the end of the Latin binomial the first time the name occurs, but not with subsequent occurrences. In this book, the authorities are also included in the main headings for individual mushroom monographs, as well as in the comprehensive Table 12 on page 189.

History of Use

Western Medicine

Although fungi have been used medicinally in a variety of ways in the West, this use has not been as extensive as in Asia. The ancient Greeks used relatively few species as medicine, and that trend continued in Europe through the Middle Ages and the Renaissance. Nevertheless, in reviewing the writings of the ancients, there are a few mushrooms that were widely popular for food and medicine.

In this discussion, I will review the works of the four major ancient Greek writers on materia medica that have survived—those of Hippocrates, Pliny, Dioscorides, and Galen. Hippocrates, the renowned "father of medicine" who flourished around 455 B.C., mentions fungi as being used for moxa to stimulate specific points in serious chronic illness associated with the kidney, like dropsy (Potter, 133), and sciatica (Potter, 249), surprisingly similar to using moxa treatment on meridian points in Traditional Chinese Medicine (Potter, 133).

Pliny (ca. 23-78 A.D.), the great compiler of ancient lore on natural history, mentions a number of fungi in his writings, but it is difficult to determine what species he was talking about—most of them are simply placed under the general name "mushroom" or "*Agaricum.*" These are identified by Jones and Andrews (1956) as *Boletus igniarius* L. [=*Phellinus igniarius* (L.:Fr.) Quél.], *B. laricis* [=*Fomitopsis officinalis*], *B. hepaticus* (=*Fistulina hepatica* (Huds.) Fr. or "Boletus," which is said to be either *Agaricus caesarius* Scop. [=*Amanita caesarea* (Scop.:Fr.) Pers.:Schw.], *Boletus edulis* Bull.:Fr., or hog fungi (probably *Suillus* sp.). It is probable that fungi with similar appearance within the two groups were not well differentiated.

For instance, under the heading of *Agaricum,* a white fungus that grew on trees was taken in a dose of four obole (4.7 gram), crushed in oxymel (vinegar and honey) (Jones VII, 213). A similar species which was of two kinds (male and female) growing in Gaul was said to be weaker, tasting at first sweet and then bitter. These characteristics are similar to those of *Fomitopsis officinalis*, a likely suspect, given its singular popularity in the ancient world. As can be seen in Table 1 below, the *Agaricum* most definitely qualifies as a panacea! If even a fraction of the activity ascribed to it is true, modern science may find a fruitful area of research. Perhaps this fungi is a forerunner of the modern adaptogen, an herb which is reported to support adrenal function, build endurance, counteract the deleterious effects of stress, regulate body processes (such as blood sugar), calm the nerves, balance the hormones, and strengthen the immune system (Brekhman, 1980; Farnsworth et al, 1985).

Dioscorides, a physician in Nero's army (55 A.D.), was the author of the most widely used herbal of all times—*De Materia Medica*. This work stood the test of time—it was considered the absolute authority for over 1700 years! Dioscorides reflects the low esteem in which fungi seem to be often held in the ancient world—he says of them in general that they are difficult to digest, often poisonous, and he mentions that "they grow amongst rusty nails or rotten rags, or ye holes of serpents, or amongst trees properly bearing harmful fruits." The only fungus that seemed to have any kind of reputation as a healing medicine was the "Agaric" (Agaricon). The nature of this widely used species was not well understood in ancient times—Dioscorides places it first under the section entitled "Roots," though to his credit, he does mention that some observers thought it to "grow in the stocks of trees of rottennesse, as the mushrumps." Galen, the prolific late

The Origin of the Words
Mushroom, Fungus, and Agaric

The word *agaric* is generally thought to be derived from "Agaria," a region in S.W. Russia or Agarus—a town where an ancient culture, the Sarmatians, flourished along the Don river. Dioscorides (ca. 55 A.D.), the most famous herbalist of ancient times, used the name αγαρικον (*agarikon*) in his widely influential *De Materia Medica* (Gunther, 1934) to describe what is now thought to be *Fomitopsis officinalis* (Vill.: Fr.) Bond. et Sing., probably because the fruiting bodies were principally obtained from this region.

Throughout the Middle Ages and the Renaissance, the agaric was an important drug item and as such was often adulterated with other similar polypores. Subsequently, influential botanists like John Ray of the 17th and early 18th century, as well as the Renaissance herbalists, used agaric as a generic name for the entire group of bracket-like fungi with pores (instead of gills) that grow on trees. This trend was forever reversed when the great Swedish botanist, Linnaeus, single-handedly reformed systematic botany, placing thousands of species of plants and fungi into generic groups and applying specific names to each. Linnaeus mistakenly applied the name agaric to fleshy gilled fungi, and it remains so today (Cooke, 1862).

The word fungus is probably derived from spongia or sfggos (spoggos), a sponge, because of the sponge-like quality of some fleshy mushrooms (Murray et al, 1933). Mushroom probably originated in the 15th century or earlier. The French word *mousseron* from the old French *moisseron* is thought to be derived from *mousse* (moss), because many mushrooms grow closely in and around mosses (Murray et al, 1933).

Greek medical practitioner and writer (130-200 A.D.), mentions that mushrooms are "cold and moist" in nature, though *Fomitopsis officinalis* was said by Gerard to be hot and dry.

The influence of the Greeks was profound all through the Middle Ages and Renaissance, as can be seen in Gerard's *Herbal* (1633), a well-known compilation of many of the Herbals up to his time, (especially Dodoens, 1586). Gerard echoes the predominant English cultural bias in mostly dismissing fungi as "venomous and full of poison." This feeling is eloquently put by the great English poet Shelley:

And plants at whose name the verse feels loath,
Fill'd the place with a monstrous undergrowth,
Prickly and pulpous, and blistering, and blue,
Livid, and starr'd with a lurid dew,

And agarics, and fungi, with mildew and mould,
Started like mist from the wet ground cold;
Pale, fleshy, as if the decaying dead
With a spirit of growth had been animated.

Their mass rotted off them flake by flake,
Till the thick stalk stuck like a murderer's stake,
Where rags of loose flesh yet tremble on high,
Infecting the winds that wander by.

Gerard is quite specific about the health benefits of mushrooms, saying they are "cold and damp" and can damage the internal organs. And further, that they

"do approach unto a venomous and murthering facultie, and ingender a clammy, pituitous, and cold nutriment if they be eaten. To conclude, few of them are good to be eaten, and most of them do suffocate and strangle the eater. Therefore I give my advice unto those that love such strange and new fangled meates, to beware of licking honey among thornes, lest the sweetnesse of the one do not countervaile the sharpnesse and pricking of the other."

The last sentence was probably written to apprise the reader of the fact that among a number of edible and even delectable esculent fungi there lurks a few that are poisonous and even lethal. Gerard mentions three types of medicinal mush rooms, "Puffes-fists" or Wolfes fists (puffballs), the powdery spores of which were said to "dry without biting" when applied to "merigalls or kibbed heels (a recurrent localized redness and swelling, usually of the hands, feet or legs)." Because they have a hard crusty exterior shell enclosing the powdery spores, which will smolder when ignited, dry, mature puffballs were also recommended to carry the spark of fire from one location to another, long before matches were known. The second is "Jewes eare," (also called Judas' ear, because "...it was believed that when Judas hanged himself on an elder tree, these ear-shaped 'excrescences' were condemned to appear on elders thereafter") (Rolfe & Rolfe, 1925). This fungus is *Auricularia*, which Gerard recommends for soothing "the inflammations and all other soreness of the throat, being boiled in milk, steeped in beere, vinegar or any other convenient liquor." The third is the ubiquitous Agarick, which Gerard writes about in some detail under the section on the Larch Tree, upon which it was known to grow. See "The Panacea Mushroom" below and the section on *Fomitopsis officinalis* for more information.

After Gerard's time, the use of medicinal fungi in the West did grow to a certain extent. The eastern Europeans and Russians, especially, developed an interest in the gastronomic and medicinal uses of mushrooms (Redwood, 1857). During the last 100 years, Russian and Eastern European scientists have conducted many studies on the efficacy of medicinal mushrooms, but unfortunately this literature is generally not as available as western European research, partly because of translation difficulties. One exception is the Chaga, *Inonotus obliquus* (Pers.: Fr.) Pilat., a very prominent species used in Russian folk medicine, for which a number of scientific papers are available in English.

Medicinal mushrooms also found limited use in the young United States. Porcher (1854) summed up the situation adequately when he said, "The medical uses of fungi are probably of far greater importance than their present very limited application might lead us to suppose"—little did he realize what a prophetic statement this would be—today, 140 years later, a number of major pharmaceutical companies worldwide, including Merck, have mycologists (scientists who specialize in fungi) on staff and are actively extracting and looking for marketable compounds. Nonetheless, a number of species of fungi have been used medicinally at various times in Europe and the United States. The most important of these are discussed below according to their primary uses, that is, as panaceas, absorbents, for tuberculosis, and to affect the nervous system.

THE PANACEA MUSHROOM

Because of the implications from Chinese Medicine that some polypores, such as Reishi and Mu er, were revered as cancer cures and panaceas, any reference to similar uses for western species of polypores is notable. The only hints of this, however, come in reference to *Fomitopsis officinalis*, and I will spend some time on this species because it is the most written about by far in western medicine.

This polypore is the agaric, or agaricum, of the ancients and has subsequently been called *Agaricus albus*, White Agaric, Purging Agaric, Larch Agaric, and Quinine fungus. It was also used, along with several other polypores, as tinder, when it was called Touchwood, Spunk, and Tinder. According to Rolfe & Rolfe (1925), the Greeks and Romans believed in universal remedies (similar to the reverence for which the Chinese hold *Panax ginseng*). An example is the formula called the Mithridate,

Fig. 4: Larch Agaric from *The Theater of Plants*, by J. Parkinson, 1640.

which contained Agaric, as well as such interesting items as "skinks bellies". This formula, copied and recopied (with free additions of new ingredients by the copiers), was supposed to render the taker safe from any sort of poison, of both human and animal origin. The legend goes that a king (after whom it was named) took it for a period of time to safeguard himself against the possibility of being poisoned by his enemies. Later in life, after losing a decisive battle, he became depressed and tried to kill himself by drinking a virulent poison—and it didn't work (Watson, 1966)! *Fomitopsis* was included in the Mithridate formula since ancient times, and it was included in the formula given in the first *Pharmacopoeia Londenensis* of 1618 (Urdang, 1944).

Pliny was the first to write about the agaric; much of his information is summarized in Table 1.

Table 1

USES OF AGARICUM IN PLINY
(FROM THE TRANSLATION BY W.H.S. JONES)

Uses	Admixtures	Page number (Vol. VII)
Spider and scorpion bites	taken in 4 cyathi of wine	223
Protection against noxious drugs after vomiting as a component of the Mithridate formula	sometimes taken with centaury, aristolochia, cinquefoil, or betony seed	229
The stomach is strengthened	juice of scordotis, as well as centaury and gentian in water, plantain mixed in food (such as lentils or wheat gruel, betony, aristolochia, *Nymphaea heraclia,* or the juice of peucedanum	289
Eases breathing difficulties	or aristolochia taken in doses of three oboli in hot water or ass's milk	291
Benefits the kidneys	taken in drink	293
Relieves sciatica and pains in the spine	taken in drink	295
Acts as an aperient (mild laxative)	2 drachmae with a little salt, taken in water or in 3 oboli of honey wine	305
Good for disorders of the spleen	3 oboli in 1 cyathus of old wine	321
For troubles of the hypochondria and groin	with powdered fenugreek as a liniment	321
Diseases of the bladder and to eliminate stones	taken in wine	323
Cures stranguary	3 oboli doses in 1 cyathus of old wine	333
Cures injuries of the achilles tendon and shoulder pain	3 oboli taken in 1 cyathus of old wine	333
Helps cure tuberculosis	in raisin wine in 2 oboli doses	347
Helps indigestion	taken in hot water after food	349
Cures epilepsy	3 oboli in oxymel	349-50
Relieves the chills of fever	taken in hot water	351
Cures dropsy	2 spoonfuls taken in water	355

Cures jaundice	3 oboli doses in a cyathus of old wine	359
Helps heal bruises and bad effects of falls	2 oboli taken in 3 cyathi of honey wine	367
Relieves hysterical suffocations accompanied by delayed menstruation	3 oboli taken in a cyathus of old wine	379
Acts as an emmenagogue	taken in hydromel (honey and water)	381

Note: 1 cyathus = a small cup or ladle
    1 obolus = 1.12 grams

Dioscorides wrote that agaric was used for just about everything. Not only did he use it as a styptic (astringent) to stop bleeding, but he also used it for the following:

♦ injuries, bruises, falls, and fractured limbs

♦ kidney diseases with difficulty in passing urine

♦ menstrual insufficiency

♦ liver complaints and jaundice

♦ hysteria

♦ dysentery

♦ epilepsy

♦ sallow complexion (perhaps blood or heart deficiency)

♦ internal weakness of the organs

♦ asthma

♦ colic

♦ phthisis (wasting diseases with night sweats, e.g., tuberculosis)—give it in raisin wine

♦ pain in the hips, loins, and joints, poisoning, snake and animal bites

According to Dioscorides, *Fomitopsis* should be taken for the above complaints in amounts appropriate to one's strength and age—either by eating the plain herb with water (as in tea or soup) or in wine (as an alcoholic tincture). The average dose was 3 oboli (3 1/3 grams). For people with stomach weakness, he directed it to be chewed and eaten in its whole raw form (I use it this way in small amounts and find it to be quite palatable and effective). For people with spleen (assimilation) weakness, he recommended a warm tea with vinegar and honey.

He considered it at first sweet and then bitter as well as dry and warm. It is noteworthy that in the system of herbalism that is an integral part of Traditional Chinese medicine, many of the important tonics (such as ginseng) taste bitter and sweet and are considered warm in nature. Thus *Fomitopsis officinalis* may be an important first-class tonic (especially for enhancing immune strength and supporting adrenal function). This action has been disputed by one well-respected Chinese herbalist (Dharmananda, 1994), and it has not been proven by any scientific studies. See the monograph on this species for more details.

Fomitopsis was used as a panacea, according to Dioscorides' prescription, for the next 1600 years or so. Gerard (1633) reported that agaric was still used in his time to cleanse the intestines and for jaundice, menstrual difficulties, edema, asthma, chronic fevers, and to restore healthy complexion, among other things. For those who can harvest their own *Fomitopsis* (they are common on larch and pine, but also on spruce, fir, hemlock, and Douglas-fir throughout the Northern Hemisphere), Gerard also emphasizes that *"The best Agarick is that which is whitest, very loose and spungie, which may easily be broken and is light and in the first taste sweet."* Note that the secondary taste is decidedly bitter.

My own experience with this fungus suggests to me that this is indeed a very good tonic, when used in small amounts before meals. I have harvested it in the Pacific Northwest and in coastal California on old Douglas firs, especially ones that have been damaged by lightning or other natural catastrophies. The fruiting bodies often grow high up into the tree and are difficult to harvest but will sometimes grow within reach. In former times they were dislodged from on high by rifles. The taste is hard to describe, but it is at first sour and sweet, with an enjoyable mild lingering bitterness, reminiscent of some wild American ginseng I have tasted. If the tea is taken in substantial quantities, intestinal irritation, nausea, and vomiting can occur in sensitive individuals.

Gerard says of *Fomitopsis* that it is *"hot in the first degree and dry in the second degree,"* and that it *"cutteth, maketh thin, cleanseth, taketh away obstructions or stoppings of the intrailes, and purgeth also by stoole…and is "a sure remedie for cold shakings, which are caused of thicke and cold humors."* We might say it warms the mucous membranes, increases circulation, and helps to promote the uptake of nutrients and the elimination of excess mucus and toxic wastes. The bitter taste helps to activate the mobility and secretions of the digestive processes, about which Gerard says, "it comforteth the weake and feeble stomacke, (and) causeth good digestion."

Gerard also recommends agaric for menstrual difficulties, edema, asthma, chronic coughs, tuberculosis, to restore proper color, and cure long-standing fevers. He suggests a dose of 1-2 drams in powder form (could be taken in capsules) or 2-5 drams in decoction. He indicates that it "purges" (rids the body of toxins and mucus, speeds bowel transit time) and can cause nausea. For this reason, he reports that Galen recommends an infusion with ginger, carrot seed, or lovage seed. Ginger has been shown in modern studies to allay nausea. The very best way to take Agaric is supposed to be in a syrup of vinegar, with the addition of ginger.

From the 1600s, Agaric lost some of its magic, giving way to new and more specialized herbal medicines. In *A New English Dispensatory* (Alleyne, 1733), it is mentioned as a purging herb to be taken with aromatics (Ginger) and that a "purging pill" was official in the College Dispensatory, but that *"it is hardly at all in use, or to be met with in prescription."* From the 2nd *U.S. Dispensatory* (Wood and Bache, 1834) we read that the 'purging agaric' *"In the dose of four or six grains (up to a dram) is said to act powerfully as a cathartic. In this country it is scarcely employed, though we have met with it in the shops."*

Nonetheless, in the late 1800s, the *Agaricum* was incorporated into the famous "Warburg's Tincture," otherwise known as the "Antiperiodica Tinctura," also available in pill form. The *British Pharmaceutical Codex* from 1934 mentions its use, and a dose is given of 0.2 to 2 grams.

Warburg's tincture was used widely well into the 20th century for a variety of conditions, but mainly to check night sweats due to tuberculosis, reduce excess secretions, and as a digestive stimulant to be taken in cases of tuberculosis and malaria. If you are interested in trying this formula, which is probably the most famous Western herbal formula containing a fungus as a major ingredient, see the directions on the recipe card (modified from the *British Pharmaceutical Codex*, 1934). Although this formula was traditionally considered a "tonic" in western herbal medicine, it is more of a digestive warming stimulant formula in the view of TCM. As discussed below, western herbalism traditionally considered digestive stimulants strengthening to the entire bodily constitution. Cold and bitter herbs such as gentian and golden seal stimulate the production of digestive enzymes and if used chronically over several months, especially when combined with warming herbs such as ginger, can help strengthen the immune system, improve energy levels, and facilitate the healing process in people who are recovering from long-term chronic ailments (Maiwald, 1987). In TCM, sweet and warm herbs that provide nutrients, such as vitamins, minerals and immune-stimulating polysaccharides, are generally used to tonify and strengthen body systems and the overall constitution. My experience has led me to the integration of the two for optimum strengthening and sustaining effects. Strengthening the digestion is particularly important for

---

Modified Warburg's Tincture

Fennel, bruised	4.6 g	Saffron	4.6 g
Gentian, bruised	2.3 g	Cubeb, bruised	2.3 g
Cumin (zedoary)	2.3 g	Myrrh, crushed	2.3 g
Rhubarb root, bruised	9.1 g	Agaric, powder	2.3 g
Angelica fruit, bruised	9.1 g	Black pepper, bruised	.5 g
Elecampane, bruised	4.6 g	Cinnamon, bruised	.9 g

Directions: *Mix the herbs together, grind them to a powder in a blender or coffee mill, and add enough 100 proof vodka to provide about 1 inch of liquid over the final mass of soaked herbs. Shake this mixture every day for 2 weeks, then squeeze out the liquid through linen. You may also strain the liquid through cheesecloth to remove any debris or sediment, if desired. The usual dose is 4-16 ml, which is about 20 drops to 2 dropperfuls, 2-3 times per day, preferably just before meals.*

Note: *This formula is a slight modification of the original one—I have omitted opium, for obvious reasons, as well as quinine sulfate, for which agaric is supposed to be a substitute. This version has no aloe, as it is intended here more as a warming digestive stimulant than a purgative. However, you could add 2-5 grams of aloe for a more pronounced laxative effect.*

healing, because it is this organ system that supplies vitality and warmth from the food that we eat. For a further discussion of these issues, see my book *Foundations of Health* (Hobbs, 1992).

ABSORBENTS

Several species of polypores have been used for stanching and dressing wounds because of their fibrous, absorbent nature. Among these are *Fomes fomentarius* (L.: Fr.) Kickx., *Phellinus igniarius, Fomitopsis pinicola* (Swartz:Fr.) Karst., *Phellinus pomaceus* (Pers.:S.F. Gray) Maire, *Fomitopsis officinalis, and Piptoporus betulinus* (Bull.:Fr.) Karst. These were usually prepared by removing any crusty exterior surface, pulling the fibrous fruiting body apart or cutting it into strips, and then pounding the pieces to make them soft and pliable. Up through the early 1700s, it was thought that these polypores had some special power (what we would now call a pharmacological action) as a styptic, but later it was decided that their action is purely mechanical, working as a soft, absorbent mass. With the coming of modern scientific equipment and knowledge, we have confirmed anti-bacterial, anti-tumor, and immune-activating properties in many polypores, thus adding further credence to their use for wound-healing.

A number of puffballs, such as *Calvatia gigantea* (Batsch:Pers.) Lloyd and *Calvatia bovista* Batsch, were also quite well known for their ability to stanch wounds. They were used after they were mature and dry. Interestingly, some puffballs were reported to have anesthetic properties on humans and to stupefy bees so that their honey could safely be collected. For instance, a Native American Indian author reports that her people, the Ahnishinaubeg, used the smoke of puffballs for these purposes (Keewaydinoquay, 1978). The Maasai of Kenya and Tanzania sell dried puffballs for burning, to collect honey (Arora, 1994). This use may not be especially due to any chemical properties of puffballs *per se*, rather the phenomenon of smoke from any source causing bees to become less active outside of the hive. It is assumed that bees gorge on honey within the hive in response to its impending destruction due to fire (Tyler, 1977).

Fig. 5: Puffballs from *Our Edible Toadstools and Mushrooms* by W. Hamilton Gibson, 1895.

TUBERCULOSIS

Porcher (1854) commented on several mushrooms for treating tuberculosis. He reported that a French doctor, Dufresnoi, in the early 1800s, cured over 30 cases of tuberculosis using an electuary (a sweet herbal formula) that contained the fungus *Lactarius deliciosus* Fr., conserve of roses, spermaceti (substitute cetyl esters wax— synthetic spermaceti), washed sulphur, and syrup of yarrow with a dose the size of a grape during the day. Another French doctor recommended the powder of the mushroom be simply mixed with honey and given in small doses. The mushroom was reported to contain a soothing mucilage. Dr. Dufresnoi also prescribed *Lactarius piperatus* (L.:Fr.) S.F. Gray (its acrid taste may warm and stimulate the respiratory tract). Modern science has identified sesquiterpenes from a number of *Lactarius* spp., including the pungent isovelleral and velleral which have strong antibacterial (*Escherichia coli*) and antifungal (*Candida utilis*) activity, as well as the less active isovellerol and vellerol (Sterner et al, 1985).

One of the most widely used of medicinal fungi for tuberculosis was *Coriolellus suaveolens* (=*Trametes suaveolens* L.:Fr.), a polypore with an anise-scented fruiting body that grows in the United States from Idaho to the East Coast and in Europe and Asia as well. It was highly recommended by a number of French and German doctors of the time as a cure for this ailment; several cases were reported in Porcher that had been given up as incurable and then completely recovered. Two drams of the powder were given morning and evening to affect a cure.

NERVOUS SYSTEM

Three fungi that have been used in medicine are notable for containing compounds that strongly affect the nervous system—ergot (*Claviceps purpurea* (Fries.) Tul.), corn smut (*Ustilago maydis* DC), and fly agaric (*Amanita muscaria* (L.:Fr.) Pers.:Hook).

Ergot: *Claviceps purpurea* is a fungal parasite that attacks grains, especially rye. It does this by producing a *sclerotium*, or compact mass of hardened mycelia, that replaces the seed of the grain. "Ergot" is the common name for this sclerotium, and it is known to contain several alkaloids that cause smooth muscles in peripheral blood vessels to constrict, inhibiting blood flow. During the Middle Ages, people in Europe often unknowingly ate ergotized rye and contracted a condition called "St. Anthony's fire" characterized by burning hands and feet and hallucinations. Sometimes the restricted blood flow brought on gangrene and required amputation, and occasionally it even induced fatal respiratory and heart failure. Interestingly, some historians believe that the eccentric behavior of Salem's "witches" was induced by ergot poisoning (Wallace, 1991). Despite the fact that ergot is potentially toxic (it can cause vomiting, diarrhea, thirst, tachycardia, confusion, and coma), it was and is used medicinally. The *Merck Index* (1907) indicated ergot for stimulating labor, difficult menstruation, internal hemorrhages, nightsweats, whooping cough, migraine, diabetes, epilepsy, and chronic cerebral congestion. Today ergot derivatives are still used in a number of countries to induce abortions, to stop uterine bleeding after childbirth, for orthostatic hypotension, and especially for the treatment of cluster and migraine headaches (Wallace, 1991). Also, among ergot's alkaloids is a diethyl derivative of lysergic acid amide, the source of Dr. Hoffmann's discovery of LSD in 1934. See the Ergot monograph for more information.

Corn smut: *Ustilago maydis* is a common fungal growth that occurs on kernels of corn. It grows from the size of a marble to that of a child's head. It has been reported to contain alkaloids similar to ergot's (List & Hörhammer, 1979), but this has been disputed (Osol & Farrar, 1947; Watt & Breyer-Brandwijk, 1962). *Ustilago* does appear to have significant uterine stimulating and abortifacient effects, and a liquid extract of it is used in Europe in midwifery and gynecology (Watt & Breyer-Brandwijk, 1962).

During the 1880s, Ustilago was briefly popular in medicine in the U.S. as an oxytocic, and it was even official in the 6th *United States Pharmacopeia* (USP) in 1880.

It was also used in traditional North American medicine. The Ahnishinaubeg, a Native American Indian people, are known to have used *Ustilago maydis* to increase uterine contractions during childbirth (Keewaydinoquay, 1978); the Zuni used it to facilitate birth and to stop postpartum bleeding; and the Tewa eat the fungus with cold water for irregular menstruation (Youngken, 1925). However, due to the irregularity and weakness of the action of corn smut, this fungus has never enjoyed the same popularity in medicine as ergot. David Arora, in his *All That the Rain Promises and More*, extols the virtues of corn smut as a food; in Mexico, it is considered a delicacy. For recipes, consult *The Art of Mexican Cooking* by Diana Kennedy (New York: Bantam, 1989). See the monograph on *Ustilago* for more information.

Fly agaric: *Amanita muscaria* is the famous bright red mushroom with white dots sprinkled on its cap. It has a long history of use as an hallucinogenic mushroom with great religious and cultural significance in Siberia, Northeast Asia, and perhaps elsewhere (Saar, 1991b; Wasson, 1968). Extracts of the fungus have also been recommended for epilepsy, spinal irritations, and for killing flies (after infusing the fungus in milk). Homeopaths still use it today for chorea (ceaseless, rapid, jerky movements of the body) and skin afflictions. Scudder (Felter, 1922), a renowned Eclectic doctor, prescribed a tincture of the fresh fungus for "pain in the occiput and an inclination to fall backward," as well as for "involuntary twitching of the muscles of the face, forehead and eyes." The Eclectics were medical doctors who used primarily herbs and practiced clinical medicine during the first part of the 1900s.

People who drink the urine of *Amanita*-intoxicated individuals have been known to become intoxicated themselves, due to the presence of ibotenic acid and muscimol (Ramsbottom, 1953).

MISCELLANEOUS USES OF FUNGI IN THE WEST

A few other uses of fungi in Western folklore and medicine bear mentioning. According to Swanton (1915), in West Sussex, England, old men carried *Daldinia concentrica* (Bolt.) Ces. et de Not. (also known as "cramp balls" or "carbon balls") for protection against cramps. I have tried this numerous times and even seen some of my students carry them during their menstrual cycle, but to no avail—maybe there is something we don't know about the *way* in which they were carried. *Phellinus pomaceus* was used as a poultice for swollen faces, and in other English villages the charcoal of *Piptoporus betulinus* was used as an antiseptic and disinfectant.

Elaphomyces (a genus of truffles) were traditionally used in love potions in the 16th century (Rolfe & Rolfe, 1925) and recommended as aphrodisiacs by English herbalists in the 1700s (Berkeley, 1857) perhaps due to their resemblance to human testicles (Tyler, 1977). Native people in Mexico use *Elaphomyces* in divinitory rituals with the addition of *Psilocybe*.

Fomes fomentarius and other conks (*Phellinus*, *Fomitopsis*) were powdered and used as snuff by the Ostyacks on the Ob river, in western Siberia (Berkeley, 1857), while *Boletus edulis* Bull: Fr., the suillus or hog-fungus of Pliny (23-78 A.D.), was used for bowel complaints, sore eyes, ulcers on the head, and for dog bites (Rolfe & Rolfe, 1925).

Table 2 summarizes the major uses of fungi in Western medicine. If you would like further historical information, two notable works on the subject are Porcher's *On the Medicinal and Toxicological Properties of the Cryptogamic Plants of the United States* (1854) and R.T. Rolfe's *The Romance of the Fungus World* (1925).

Table 2

FUNGI USED AS MEDICINE IN EUROPE

Species	Synonym	
Agaricus campestris L.:Fr.	—	nerve tonic (it contains potassium)
Amanita muscaria L.:Fr.P Pers.:Hook	—	as a hallucinogen; for epilepsy, ringworm
Auricularia auricula (Hook.) Underw.	*Hirneola auricula-judae*	sore throat
Boletus edulis Bull. ex Fr.	*Suillus* (of the Greeks)	bowel complaints
Bovista nigrescens	—	sedative; spores used as styptic
Calvatia gigantea (Batsch ex Pers.) Lloyd	*Lycoperdon giganteum*	styptic, anaesthetic
Claviceps purpurea	—	ergot used for migraine, stimulating labor, difficult menstruation, cerebral congestion, diabetes, epilepsy, hemorrhages
Coriolellus suaveolens	*Trametes suaveolens*	tuberculosis; also as an aphrodisiac
Daldinia concentrica (Bolt.) Ces. et de Not.	—	cramps
Dematium giganteum	—	dressing for ulcers
Elaphomyces granulatus Fr.	—	aphrodisiac, galactagogue
Fomes fomentarius (L.: Fr.) Kickx	*Polyporus fomentarius*	styptic; also as tinder to start fires
Fomitopsis officinalis	*P. officinalis, Boletus laricis*	panacea

Fomitopsis pinicola (Fr.) Karst	*Polyporus pinicola*	dysentery, chronic diarrhea, nervous headache, neuralgia, increased flow of urine, ague cake, bilious remittent fever (King, 1985)
Lycoperdon caelatum	—	styptic
Phallus impudicus (L. Pers.)	—	applied to sore limbs
Phellinus igniarius (L. Fr.)	*Polyporus igniarius*	same as above
Phellinus pomaceus	*Fomes fulvus, Polyporus fulvus*	poultice for swollen face
Piptoporus betulinus (Bull.: Fr.) Karst.	*Polyporus betulinus*	styptic, antiseptic (as charcoal)
Ustilago maydis (DC.) Corda	—	similar to *Claviceps purpurea*, above

NATIVE AMERICAN INDIAN USES OF FUNGI

Many Native American Indian tribes did not regard fungi as an important food, and some thought them entirely unfit for consumption. Other peoples, such as the Ahnishinaubeg, the Tewa, and the Iroquois, did eat them, some with relish (Keewaydinoquay, 1978; Burk, 1983). Nonetheless, many Native American Indians did use fungi medicinally for rheumatism, pain in the joints, congested organs, sciatica, and gout. Interestingly, they used fungi in much the same manner as the Chinese use moxa, that is, by employing ignited, smoldering polypores to blister, or even burn, the skin over the affected area. Early Europeans learned of these uses from Native American Indians who called dried polypores used in this way "spunk" or "touchwood" (Lawson, 1714; Josselyn, 1860).

Beverly (1947) described this practice as it was done among the native peoples of Virginia:

"....they take Punk, (which is a sort of soft Touchwood, cut out of the knots of Oak or Hiccory Trees...) this they shape like a Cone...and apply the Basis of it to the place affected. Then they set fire to it, letting it burn out upon the part, which makes a running Sore effectually."

Another author reported that Native Indians of Manitoulin Island, in Canada, did much the same (Winder, 1846).

Puffballs (*Calvatia* and *Lycoperdon* spp.) and earthstars (*Geastrum* spp.), in particular, were almost universally used by the Native American Indians—both medicinally and in other ways. The Blackfoot called them *ka-ka-toos*, or "fallen stars," and, according to legend, these fallen stars were an indication of supernatural events. Various Native American Indians used puffballs as tinder to start fires and as incense to keep away unwanted spirits. Some wore them as magical charms, and puffballs were also dried, filled with gravel, and used as rattles. Medicinally, puffballs were frequently used as a styptic. The soft, interior portion of the immature puffball was dried, ground, and applied to wounds to stop bleeding. In some cases, puffball spores were mixed with spiderwebs to make a hemostatic dressing. Tribes as diverse as the Cherokee, Chippewa, Kiowa, Kwakiutl, Makah, Menomini, Pawnee, Omaha, and Navaho all used puffballs in this way. For an excellent review of the uses of puffballs by the Native American Indians see Burk (1983). The Blackfoot drank an infusion of puffball spores to stop internal bleeding, while the Arikara combined the spore mass with the pulverized root of red baneberry to make a poultice for inflamed and abscessed breasts (in women). Puffballs were also used to soothe burns and itching. Dried, mature puffballs were used as a remedy for earaches and broken eardrums, while the mycelia were used to help heal bone fractures in animals (Burk, 1983). The Okanagan-Colville Indians of British Columbia and Washington used the spores like talcum powder to treat diaper rash and if the rash was very serious, alum root (*Heuchera cylindrica*) was added. Sores were also treated with the spores (Turner, 1980).

Native American Indians used other species of fungi for medicine. For instance, the Ahnishinaubeg employed *Fomitopsis officinalis* as a powerful purgative, especially in cases where poisoning was suspected. However, only very small doses were prescribed, as too much was thought to cause paralysis. They also used *Fomes fomentarius* as a cauterizer and styptic, and *Lycoperdon caelatum* (also known as *Calvatia caelata* (Bull. ex DC.) Morg.) as a blood coagulant (Keewaydinoquay, 1978). The Cherokee put *Geastrum* (earthstars) on the navels of babies after childbirth and left them there until the withered umbilical cord fell off. This was done as both a prophylactic and therapeutic measure (Mooney and Olbrechts, 1932). The Okanagan-Collville Indians were known to bathe their babies in a broth of mushrooms with the idea that like mushrooms, which are so strong they move rocks as they grow out of the soil, babies subjected to the broth would grow up strong enough to move men (Turner, 1980). In British Columbia, the spores of a tree fungus known as "owl wood" (*Trichaptum abietinus* Fries) were collected from the trunks of fir trees to provide a powder that young men of the Thompson Indian tribe rubbed their skin with in conjunction with sweat bathing to impart strength (Turner, 1973).

The Use of Medicinal Mushrooms in Asia

Fungi have played an important role in Chinese culture for perhaps 7,000 years. Over the millennia, common mushrooms such as the wood ear and jelly fungus have been important food items. Various simple fungi were also utilized to make fermented food products such as wine, vinegar, soy sauce, and pickled vegetables (Wang, 1985). Fungi were utilized for their healing properties in Japanese and Malaysian cultures, but probably not to the same extent as in China, and there is far less written about these uses in English. In 1883, researchers (Batchelor & Miyabe, 1893) collected information about plants used by the Ainu from the Japanese island of Hokkaido. They reported on the uses of several fungi, but only two were conclusively identified to species. Spores of a puffball (*Lycoperdon* spp.) were said to be applied externally to heal scalds, burns, and "pains in the body," and *Fomitopsis officinalis* was used as a decoction for stomachache. The fungus was said to be "greatly prized by the old Japanese doctors."

The use of fungi such as hoelen, caterpillar fungus, and ergot in Traditional Chinese Medicine (TCM) was also recorded in the classic literature. TCM is over 3,000 years old and is now gaining popularity in the West. The two earliest great classics of Chinese herbal medicine are the *Shen nung Pen ts'ao king* or *Pen ts'ao king*, also called *Pen king*, generally translated to mean "Herbal Classic," and the *Ming i pie lu* or simply *Pie lu* which is thought to be a supplement to the *Shen nung Pen ts'ao*, written in the Wei dynasty (221-264 A.D.). Subsequent authors sometimes combine both works into either name, considered to be the "Herbal Classic." The *Pen King* is traditionally ascribed to the legendary Emperor Shen Nung (28 Century B.C.) but is now thought to be compiled from earlier manuscripts about 202-221 A.D. The *Pen king* mentions a number of medicinal mushrooms, specifically *Ganoderma lucidum* (W. Curt.:Fr.) Karst., *Wolfiporia cocos* (Schw.) Ryv. & Gilbn. [=*Poria cocos* (Schw.) Wolf], *Grifola umbellata* (Pers.) Pilát (=*Polyporus umbellatus* Fr.), *Polyporus mylittae* Cook. et Mass, *Calvatia lilacina* (Mont. et Berk.) Lloyd, and *Tremella fuciformis* Berk. (Yang & Jong, 1989). Earlier mention of the use of fungi in medicine outside of the main classics occurred as early as 26 B.C. in the "Book of Songs," a compilation of folk-songs and poems. In 300 A.D., several important medicinal mushrooms, such as the caterpillar fungus (*Cordyceps* spp.), ling zhi, zhu ling, hoelen, and *Mylitta lapidescens* (=*P. mylittae*), were mentioned. Shiitake was included in a work on herbal medicine first in 1309 in the *Materia Medica in Daily Use* (Wang, 1985).

A number of ancient Taoist works mention "*chi*" as a plant that brings happiness and immortality. In both the *Pen king* and the *Pie lu* the name *chi* is applied to various mushrooms, six of which are talked about in detail.

- ◆ *ts'ing* (green) *chi*, also called *lung* (dragon) *chi* is said to be sour and non-poisonous; it brightens the eye, strengthens the liver, quiets the spirits, improves the memory, and prolongs life.

- ◆ *chi* (red), also called *dan* (cinnabar) *Qi* tastes bitter but non-poisonous; acts especially on the heart; it has the same tonic and calming properties of *ts'ing chi*.

- ◆ *huang* (yellow) *chi*, also called *kin* (gold) *chi*, is sweet and non-poisonous; acts on the spleen—tonic and constructive.

- ◆ *pai* (white) *chi*, also called *yü chi*, is considered pungent and non-poisonous; acts on the lungs, opens the air passages.

- ◆ *hei* (black) *chi*, also called *hüan* (dark) *chi*, tastes saltish and non-poisonous; acts on the urinary tract, same tonic properties.

- ◆ *tsu'* (purple) *chi*, also called *mu* (wood) *chi*, considered sweet and non-poisonous; acts on the bones and ligaments.

(from Bretschneider, 1895 and Shih-Chen, 1973).

A number of sources conclude that the *chi* are different forms of *Ganoderma lucidum* or *ling zhi*, a name which first occurs in the *Ling yüan fang* from the 11th century A.D. (Bretschneider, 1895). Ling means either "effective" or "spirit" or "intelligence" (Jingrong, 1979).

Probably the most famous of all works on Chinese materia medica is the monumental *Pen Ts'ao Kang Mu*, which was compiled by Li Shih-chen and published in 1578. This herculean labor took Shih-chen 26 years and includes 1,892 species of animal, herbal, and mineral drugs, plus 8,160 prescriptions (Smith & Stuart, 1911). Although the work has never been translated into any western language in its entirety, there are two English summaries of various parts which include botanical, chemical, and herbal information about a limited number of species; these are *Chinese Materia Medica, Vegetable Kingdom*, (Porter F. Smith and rev. G.A. Stuart, 1911) and *Chinese Medicinal Plants from the Pen Ts'ao Kang Mu...A.D. 1596* (Bernard E. Read), first published in 1936 from smaller earlier editions. Smith and Stuart cover about 700 species and include some information on their historical uses. Read's work contains 867 herbal drugs but includes mainly bibliographic references from Europe and Japan (plus a few from China), as well as constituent lists for some herbs. The chief value of this work is a confirmation of the Latin names of some important traditional Chinese herbs which were included in the *Pen Ts'ao*, along with a historical bibliography listing early articles (from the late 19th century and early 20th century) concerning identification and trade of Chinese herbs.

These two works mention a number of fungi from the *Pen Ts'ao*, including the species mentioned in Table 3.

Table 3

MEDICINAL FUNGI OF THE PEN TS'AO

Reid's Name	Current Name	Chinese Name	Notes and Uses
Agaricus ostreatus Jacq. (W.)	*Pleurotus ostreatus* (Jacq.:Fr.) Quél.	tian hua xin	benefits respiratory tract and inhibits worms
Armillaria mellea Vahl.	*Armillaria mellea* (Vahl.:Fr.) Karst.	zao jai xin	honey mushroom (see monograph section)
Auricularia auricula-judae Schr. (Br. G.H. St.) *Auricularia polytricha* was mentioned as interchangeable	*A. auricularia* L.: Hook Underw.	mu er	"wood ear;" one of the most often used medicinal fungi in TCM; some authors believe the epiphytes listed below to be variants of mu erh; each kind was said to take on the properties of the tree upon which it was growing; makes the body light and strong, strengthens the will, cures hemorrhoids, prevents hemorrhages; che erh (grows on *Cudrania triloba*) is used to treat respiratory diseases like hemoptysis and fetid expectoration; yang lu erh (grows on *Diervilla versicolor*) used to disperse ecchymoses and move the blood; shan chün (grows on *Cunninghamia sinensis*) relieves cardiac pain; t'ao chi sheng (peach or *Gleditschia chinensis* epiphyte) aborts abscesses and treats diarrhea due to cold

Not given	Unknown	ti er; ti ta ku (popular name)	taste, sweet, cold nature, non-poisonous; eaten as food; brightens the eyes, improves respiration, and promotes fertility; mushrooms that grow on the ground
Not given	Unknown	shih er	edible; benefits gravel and virility; often used to treat bowel hemorrhages, rectal prolapse; said to resemble ling zhi in action
Clavaria corniculata Schaeff. (W.)	*Clavulinopsis corniculata*	qitsung	strengthens the stomach, invigorates the spirits, benefits hemorrhoids
Clavaria pistillarius L. (HM.)	*Clavariadelphus pistillaris* (Fr.) Donk	mo gu xin	acts on the intestines and stomach, dissolves phlegm, and improves respiration
Ithyphallus rugulosus Fisch. (M.J.)	*Phallus rugulosus* (Fisch.) D. Kuntze	qui pi	considered poisonous; used to treat skin problems, especially from parasites
Not given	Unknown	qui gui (yellow and white fruiting body), ti chin (ephemeral; fruits in the morning, fades by afternoon)	varieties of the common field mushroom, useful for treating nervous diseases in children
Not given	Unknown	huan chün, huan kün or kuan kün (heron mushroom)	taste salty; grows in ponds and marshes; said to be the transformed excrement of the heron by one ancient writer; slightly poisonous; valued for cardialgia, insect and snake bites, favus, as an internal remedy for colic; excellent for intestinal worms; appearance white, light, empty; should be sun-dried
Not given	Unknown	shu ko	a "prickly variety" of huan chün; used to treat fevers and menstrual problems
Lycoperdon boviste L. (BN. St.)	*Calvatia bovista* Batsch	ma bo	only mentioned
Mylitta lapidenscens	*Polyporus mylittae*	to cai	"thunder pills"; grows from rudders of old ships; treats goiter
Pachyma cocos Fr. (M. J. Br. St.)	*Wolfiporia cocos* (Schw.)	fu ling	indian bread, tuckaho (for uses, see monograph section)
Pachyma hoelen Rumph. (St. M.)	*Grifola umbellata* (Pers.) Pilát	zhu ling	"pig's dung" (see monograph section)
Polyporus arcularius Batsch: Fries	Same	shan shan	

Puccinia coricioides Berkl. et Br. (M.); *Stereostratum corticioides* Magn. (J.)	Unknown	zhu ru	grows on bamboo; considered a delicacy; used for treating poisoning from noxious gas
Not given	Unknown	sang er (epiphytic on mulberry), huai er (*Sophora* epiphyte), yu er (*Ulmus epiphyte*), tao Qisheng (peach or *Gleditschia chinensis* epiphyte), liu er (willow epiphyte), chu er (*Broussonetia* epiphyte)	all classed in the *Pen T'sao* under the heading "dwellers on wood;" likely to be species of *Loranthus* or *Viscum*; Bretschneider, Smith & Stuart call them variations of mu er—auricularius fungi (see above); sang er is considered slightly toxic
Taphrina deformans (BN.)	*Irpex* spp.?	tao qisheng	epiphytic on peach
Not given	Unknown	shi tz'u mu	grows on wood, woody
Ustilago carbo Tul. (BN.)	Same as ergot? (Watt)	mai nu	

*Notes: Chi er (mushrooms growing on wood), chun (growing on hard ground), and xin (growing on soft ground) are all general names for mushrooms (Smith & Stuart, 1911).

A number of medicinal mushrooms, such as ling zhi (*Ganoderma lucidum)*, bai mu er (*Tremella fuciformis*), cordyceps (*Cordyceps ophioglossoides* [Ehrenb.] Link), and hoelen *(Wolfiporia cocos)*, along with ginseng and astragalus (*Astragalus membranaceus*), are deemed to belong to the highest class of medicines, i.e., tonics, which are said to impart strength, vigor, and longevity. They fall into the category of remedies called "fu zheng", or "supporting the normal" (maintaining homeostasis), and are still widely used in China and Japan, now often in conjunction with Western medicine.

Some of the most commonly used fungi in the history of Traditional Chinese Medicine (TCM) include ling zhi, cordyceps, zhu ling, and hoelen. As a group, the polypores are all thought to possess superior healing properties. I will only present some highlights on a few of these fungi here, because the volume of information that has developed about them over the years is indeed vast. If you would like to learn more about these or related fungi, I invite you to look them up in the second half of this book. A great deal of scientific work has been done on them and, since TCM is a living tradition, they are still widely used today much as they have been in the past.

Ganoderma lucidum is, without doubt, one of the most famous medicinal mushrooms. It is known as *ling zhi* in China and *reishi* in Japan. It has been used for thousands of years to treat liver disease (such as hepatitis), nephritis (kidney inflammation), high blood pressure, arthritis, neurasthenia, insomnia, bronchitis, asthma, and gastric ulcers (Kabir et al, 1988). It is also said to benefit the heart (Ying et al, 1987). In the past, *G. lucidum* was very expensive, because it only grew in the wild, but cultivation techniques developed in the last 20 years have now made it accessible and affordable (Willard, 1990). Today this king of fungi is used especially for aging-related and degenerative conditions, such as cancer, and as an immune stimulant.

Some members of the genus *Cordyceps* have the unusual distinction of fruiting on caterpillars, which is why they are known as "winter worm, summer herb" (Bensky and Gamble, 1986). They were very rare in ancient China, so only the Emperor had the luxury of using them. Because these fungi were deemed to have tonic properties similar to those of ginseng, they were used to build stamina and restore vital energy after exhaustion or prolonged illness. Today *C. ophioglossoides* is used in TCM to stimulate blood circulation and treat menstrual disorders, while *C. sinensis* (Berk.) Sacc. is used as a lung and kidney tonic and a nutritional supplement to build vital energy in the elderly. An article in *Newsweek* (Sept. 27, 1993, p. 63) reported on the female Chinese long-distance runners who shocked the sports world by sweeping the distance events at the World Outdoor Track and Field Championships in Stuttgart, Germany. Shortly after, Wang Junxia broke 3 world records in 6 days of competition, and Qu Yunxia broke another long-standing record in China's National Games. These remarkable performances led the international athletics community to voice accusations that the women might have been taking outlawed performance-enhancing drugs. So far there is no evidence of wrongdoing, and the athletes' coach has said emphatically that these substances were not used. He credits the success to a hard training and a special diet which includes a "mineral-rich soup" containing dong chong xia cao (*Cordyceps sinensis*)! This may be in question, after 11 Chinese swimmers tested positive for dehydrotestosterone, a performance-enhancing substance that is banned by the International Olympic Committee (Reuter News Service, 1994).

Lentinula edodes (Berk.) Sing., better known to the general public as "shiitake," is another superstar fungus with a delicious taste and texture. It is the second most produced mushroom in the world, after *Agaricus bisporus*, about 14% of the total world mushroom production of 4.3 million metric tons (as of 1991) valued at 8.5 million dollar U.S., compared with 56% for *Agaricus*. See the excellent review, *Nutritional and Medicinal Value of Specialty Mushrooms* by Breene (1990) for further information. Historical records indicate that the Japanese used it at least as far back as 199 A.D. It was said to be praised by the Emperor Chuai who was given the mushroom by the Kyusuyu, a native tribe. In ancient China, it was known and revered even before that (Scientific Consulting Service). In the past, as in the present, shiitake was used for any and all conditions where the immune function needs a boost, from colds to cancer and everything in between. Numerous scientific studies have been conducted on *L. edodes*, showing it to be antiviral and cancer-protective, among other effects.

In Japan, a preparation of "turkey tail," or *Trametes versicolor* (L.:Fr.) Pilát, is used as a health food. Modern laboratory tests show it to have cholesterol-lowering as well as immune-enhancing activity (Mitomo et al, 1980). I will review some of the key findings on shiitake, *Cordyceps,* and reishi in the next section. If you are interested in further information on the history and use of Chinese medicinal fungi, a beautifully-illustrated work on the subject is *Icones of Medicinal Fungi from China* (Ying, 1987). See the Resources section for ordering information.

Besides the use of single mushrooms in teas and soups in folk medicine and in hospitals, there are many products in tablet form that combine a number of herbs in one formula. They are often made by freeze-drying a tea of the herbs, creating a powder which is then made into small pills and packed into glass bottles. There are a number of well known products manufactured in China and prescribed by acupuncturists and herbalists which contain a combination of several medicinal mushrooms. As an example, Wu Ling San is a traditional Chinese formula that was first recorded in the classic Chinese work, *Discussion of Cold-induced Disorders.* The uses of this are detailed in the monographs on the Chinese herb *Grifola umbellata* below.

Finally, using modern fermentation technology, active compounds such as large molecular weight polysaccharides and protein-bound polysaccharides are being removed from the fruiting bodies, spores, and mycelium of the most popular medicinal mushrooms (Wang, 1985; Yang & Jong, 1989). At the present time, there is information on 300 species of wild and cultivated edible fungi and 117 species for medicinal use. Because of increased use pressures and the difficulty of obtaining popular species at different times of the year, many species are currently being cultivated in China and other countries. This is an increasingly important economic force in many parts of the world.

Illustration from Matthiolus, 1578

The Medicinal Value of Visionary Mushrooms

Laboratory and clinical experiments, especially in the 1950s and 1960s, showed lysergic-acid diethylamide (LSD) to be a valuable tool in brain research and experimental psychiatry (Abramson, 1959; Freedman, 1967; Caldwell, 1968; Soskin, 1973; Pollock, 1976; Schultes, 1978; Grof, 1980). A number of these clinical trials and reports have suggested that LSD has potential for treating chronic alcoholism (Freedman, 1967; Abramson, 1967; Fadiman, 1967; Smart et al, 1967; Mottin, 1973; Ludwig, 1970).

In light of these early promising results, it is interesting to note that research on the clinical usefulness of psychedelic substances has dwindled considerably over the last 30 years and lags behind basic neuro-pharmacological work (Crisp Data Base, N.I.H.). For instance, a search of Medlars, the world's largest medical database, reveals that in the 9-year period from 1966 to 1975, there were 262 published papers on psilocybe and psyilocybin and in the last 10 years, only 48—and as a percentage, many more of the older studies were related to clinical application. This reduction in scientific interest is probably due mainly to regulatory and political pressures.

Through this research, as well as through massive popular use, one might suggest that by altering the brain chemistry and shaking one's firm footing in fixed everyday life-reality, positive healing changes subsequent to "expanding the consciousness" might be possible. On the other hand, the use of psychedelic substances has the potential of amplifying an existing emotional imbalance, leading to anxiety and adverse physical symptoms. Hallucinogenic substances purchased "on the street," from unknown sources are unstandardized and hold the possibility of adulteration with toxic solvent residues or impure hallucinogens from "kitchen chemists." For this reason, naturally-occurring mind-altering substances such as *Psilocybe* (Fr.) Quél. mushrooms have been preferred by many seeking to explore their more healing aspects (Pollock, 1975).

Besides LSD, the science and practice of psychiatry has also benefitted from the discovery and subsequent research on hallucinogenic mushrooms (Guzman, 1980; Hofmann, 1967). At least one active compound responsible for the psychoactivity of *Psilocybe* species, psilocybin (the other 3 are psilocin, baeocystin, and norbaeocystin), has been synthesized and has provided insight into how the brain works, as well as the process of such mental disorders as schizophrenia (Singer, 1978; McDonald, 1980). Several researchers have commented on the potential usefulness of psilocybin in psychiatric work (Schultes & Hofmann, 1973). After over a thousand controlled sessions with psilocybin, it was proposed to be more useful than LSD, because it is shorter-acting and has less potential for side effects, such as fewer flashbacks and less post-session depression (Fischer & Goldman, 1975; Leuner, 1968; Pollock, 1976). Because people who ingest *Psilocybe* mushrooms often experience a feeling of profound detachment from the everyday world and its problems and vicissitudes, they might be able to open up and discuss problems with the therapist without excessive emotional baggage. Several controlled clinical studies and clinical reports support further research with psilocybin in this vein (Delay et al, 1959; Ruzickova et al, 1967; Leonard and Rapoport, 1987).

Pollock (1975) has suggested that *Psilocybe* active compounds may be very useful for helping the alert terminally ill go through their dying process, based on previous work in this area with LSD, and because of the use of the mushrooms in medico-religious rites may "be a more natural, psychologically aesthetic medicinal sacrament in the preparation of these patients for a death with dignity."

When one ponders the possible medicinal effects of *Psilocybe* spp. and other hallucinogens, the question arises how can one profoundly affect the mind and consciousness without gaining insight into the spiritual nature of health and disease as well? It is well known that many indigenous peoples have used hallucinogenic and visionary plants for healing disease, divining the future, and as a gateway to converse with nature or God (Guzman, 1983; Schultes and Hofmann, 1979), but also for their euphoric effects (Singer, 1958). A common belief is that God gave the sacred mushrooms to the people for their inner development (Davis, 1981). Many Native American Indian healers made use of Datura (Jimson weed), those from Mexico, peyote and *Psilocybe*, and a number of plants are used in Central and South America, notably ayahuasca. Excellent popular accounts of the uses of visionary plants for healing include Schultes & Hofmann (1979), Emboden (1979), and Ott (1976, 1994).

Psychedelic mushrooms have been used for gaining insight into the disease process by shamans and healers for probably thousands of years (Hofmann, 1978; McDonald, 1980). In less industrialized societies, disease is associated with spirits and other influences closely related with one's general mental, emotional, and spiritual health. Schultes (1983) has pointed out the urgency in preserving the rich cultural knowledge of native peoples worldwide in regard to the use of hallucinogenic mushrooms for spiritual and healing purposes, "in view of the rapid disintegration and disappearance of indigenous cultures in many parts of the world, including, especially, Mexico." "To neglect (these cultural uses of hallucinogenic mushrooms) would be tantamount to the closing of a door, forever to entomb a peculiar kind of native knowledge with the culture that gave it birth."

In many western countries, *Psilocybe* mushrooms are illegal, but in other countries they are entirely appropriate—the context and culture are the key elements. In the 1970s, the widespread use of these mushrooms was not ideal because of the lack of guidance from spiritual healers and curanderas trained in their appropriate use.

In my experience, psychedelic mushrooms, such as *Psilocybe semilanceata*, a widespread native species, have the potential, if used carefully with knowledge and awareness, to be useful for developing a sensitivity to the cycles of nature, to learn how we can be in harmony with its processes. The experience can help to guide a receptive person through the often-held attachment of inhabitants of industrial societies to controlling nature, rather than enjoying the stay on mother earth as a caretaker and cohabitant with all the other animals, plants, and living beings. I have experienced their healing powers to break addictions, as a catalyst in learning how to eat more healthfully, and even heal specific ailments. Of course, one could say that these feelings and experiences are merely a reflection of my personal nature—that others taking them would experience as many different visions of their usefulness as a healing or enlightening agent as there are people, and this is probably true. Yet I have often seen an increased reverence for life and a heightened sensitivity to the beauty and mystery of nature as a common theme among people who have used these mushrooms. Other researchers have stated that experiences after ingestion of *Psilocybe* vary with the individual's expectations, beliefs, setting, presence of an experienced guide, and amount and species ingested, and this is undoubtedly correct.

In a practical way one must be aware that *Psilocybe* and other hallucinogenic fungi can also be powerful agents for change and are not to be taken without awareness of the potential risks. Some people, especially if they are psychologically disturbed, emotionally unstable, or simply unhealthy, may become quite agitated and experience very unpleasant feelings of both body and mind. To be used as an agent of psychological and physical healing, it is best to work with a qualified wise woman or shaman experienced in their use. Unfortunately, this person and setting may not be easy to find.

Although *Psilocybe* may precipitate an acute reaction in rare individuals, or in those who overdose (one person was said to have jumped off a balcony), the health consequences of the long-term use of *Psilocybe* is unknown. Wasson (1957) has said that there are no cumulative effects on humans, citing the curandera, Maria Sabina, who took the mushrooms for 35 years in substantial doses, without any known side effects, although this obviously does not preclude adverse effects in others. Death from hallucinogenic mushrooms is virtually unknown, even after an overdose, and most of the danger lies in misidentification of species during collection and consumption—a very real possibility (Ott, 1978). For instance, acute renal failure has been reported from toxic *Cortinarius* species in a 20-year-old woman who thought she was buying and ingesting "magic" mushrooms (Raff et al, 1992).

It must be remembered that *Psilocybe* mushrooms may act as a liver toxicant, and that the long-term mutagenic, carcinogenic, adverse effects on the immune system, and other toxic effects have not been studied and are at present unknown. Of related interest is a 1994 study (House & Thomas) which shows that immune cells are affected by LSD *in vitro* at blood concentrations that can be achieved after oral ingestion.

Today, there is probably a wide spectrum of beliefs about psychedelic mushrooms in different societies. Some undoubtedly feel that they are dangerous and should be strictly regulated, while others argue they should be freely available. On one side of the spectrum, Pollack (1975) had this point of view about the government regulation of natural hallucinogens.

> *"One would need only to become acquainted with the wealth of ethnobotanical knowledge pertaining to natural hallucinogens to readily perceive that legislation prohibiting possession and use of these naturally occurring materials must be in fundamental violation of certain extremely basic aspects of human behavior, not to mention cherished human rights."*

Throughout history, humans have sought to alter their consciousness through natural and artificial means. Witness the popularity of alcoholic beverages in most parts of the world. A number of prominent researchers have concluded that *Psilocybe* spp. are neither addictive nor particularly toxic in contrast to the widely used tobacco products—in fact, a preliminary comparative overview of the dependence-inducing potential and acute physical toxicity of 20 psychoactive substances was published in 1993 (Gable), based on an extensive literature review and work of the Committee on Problems of Drug Dependence and the National Institute of Mental Health, on-going since 1948. The review reported that of the 20 substances, oral use of psilocybe mushrooms was by far the least toxic (highest safety margin) and had the lowest potential for inducing physical or mental dependence. Alcohol, tobacco and coffee were reported to have small to moderate safety margins and moderate to high dependence potentials.

So why all the fuss over psilocybe? Perhaps there are frightening aspects to traveling within inner psychic realms that are peculiarly disquieting to many. Daniel Freedman from the Department of Psychiatry, University of Chicago put it this way.

> *"It has been remarked that tradition-bound scientists will predictably conclude that the proper use of hallucinogens is for research and medical application; the illicit abuse is for kicks and cults. Our puritanical ethics are said to prohibit us from even exploring whether the use of hallucinogens could improve the healthy, or possibly transform Western society into a Zen elysium.*
>
> *"Whatever scientists may think, history does indeed record our unceasing urge to transcend limits and escape dreary reality or anxiety with the aid of magic, drugs, drama, festival rites, and ....through dreams."*

The other side of the spectrum regarding the use of psychoactive mushrooms by non-researchers is epitomized by the view of Dr. Varro Tyler, a respected pharmacognocist with many years of research experience on medicinal plants and psychedelic mushrooms, who states emphatically that given our present state of knowledge, the use of *Psilocybe* mushrooms should be avoided altogether (Tyler, 1994). Some potential objections to the practice have been previously mentioned, namely the possible negative impact on the user's brain chemistry, mental health and immune system. For instance, hallucinogenic mushrooms have been reported to lead to panic reactions, acute psychosis, mental depression and even convulsions (Schwartz & Smith, 1988: Musha et al, 1986), as well as nausea, vomiting and tachycardia (Peden et al, 1982), though some of these effects may have been due to psilocybin interacting with other recreational drugs (Schwartz & Smith, 1988). Severe symptoms such as vomiting, myalgia, and temporary hepatotoxic and nephrotoxic effects after injection of an extract of Psilocybe mushrooms has also been reported (Curry & Rose, 1985; Sivyer & Dorrington, 1984). Misidentification or the inadvertent substitution of assumed psychoactive species with toxic or even lethal species of fungi from other genera (Raff et all, 1992; Tebbett, 1984; Rold, 1986), or from substitution from commercially purchased street drugs has also been reported from the literature (Raff et al, 1992). Young or inexperienced users are likely to take several mind-altering or euphoriant drugs at one session, increasing the possibility of additive or synergistic effects producing harmful side effects (Schwartz & Smith, 1988).

No matter how far out or unfathomable one perceives the use of LSD, *Psilocybe* spp., and other mind-altering hallucinogens to be, what may be even more of a cultural challenge is the promise of "designer personalities" through prescription drugs such as Prozac®, which may have the ability to permanently alter one's brain chemistry (Kramer, 1993).

For a more detailed account of the chemistry, ethnohistory, toxicology, and pharmacology of *Psilocybe* and other hallucinogenic species of mushrooms, see pp. 152-157.

Note of Caution: Although I have personally not experienced side effects from the use of *Psilocybe* mushrooms, I realize that they are powerful agents capable of producing toxic symptoms in suceptible individuals. I am in no way recommending the use of hallucinogenic mushrooms, and I am not suggesting that they are safe or healthful, especially *Amanita* species. They stress the liver and have other toxic properties, especially when used chronically.

It is **essential to note** that some species of *Amanita* (*A. phalloides* (Vaill.:Fr.) Secre., *A. virosa* Lam.:Secr. (=A. verna (Bull.:Fr.) Pers.:Vitt., *A. ocreata*, etc.), as well as members of other mushroom genera, contain **potentially lethal** liver toxins, even when taken in small amounts. They **could kill you!**

The possession, use, or sale of hallucinogenic mushrooms is also illegal under the provisions of Public Law 91-513, Section 202, Schedule 1(c) and Schedule 3(b).

A fascinating insight into the promise of hallucinogens in the healing process can be seen in the current research with ibogaine, an indole alkaloid from the African shrub *Tabernanthe iboga* Baill. in the same subclass of compounds as psilocybin, which shows some promise for eliminating difficult addictions to cocaine and other drugs (Jetter, 1994; Ousley, 1993; Sershen, 1994). Preliminary animal experiments with the substance are encouraging, but controversial due to a possible neurotoxic effect of ibogaine (O'Hearn and Molliver, 1993). The alkaloid is extracted from the plant, and clinical trials are underway at the University of Miami.

THE HALLUCINOGENIC PROPERTIES OF AMANITA MUSCARIA AND A. PANTHERINA

Gordon Wasson, a banker who became the world's most renowned ethnomycologist (1968), claimed in his meticulously researched and presented book *Soma, The Divine Mushroom of Immortality*, that *Amanita muscaria* is the sacred Soma of the Rig Vedas, the writings which contain over a thousand hymns to soma, and upon which the Hindu religion is based. That may or may not be true, but in any case, this fungus is well-known as an inebriant and hallucinogenic mushroom in Russia and other parts of Europe (Saar, 1991b); it also grows in Central America, North America, Tibet, and North Africa. Some writers have put forth the doctrine that the Maya knew of *A. muscaria*, considering it sacred, and that Christianity may have been originally founded upon a mushroom cult, the Bible being a euphemistic work talking about the effects of the mushroom to avoid persecution by the Romans, though there is little evidence to support these hypotheses (Cooke, 1977; Tyler, 1994).

Fig. 6: *Amanita muscaria* from *The Illustrated Dictionary of Gardening* by George Nicholson, circa 1887.

Years ago, a close friend of mine, now a naturopathic physician, experimented with *Amanita* ingestion; his experiences are written in the following account.

SOMA—A somewhat Divine Experience?

In the early 70s I happened across a copy of Gordon Wasson's book, *Soma, The Divine Mushroom of Immortality* in the library at Oregon State University. His contention was that *Amanita muscaria* was Soma, the source of inspiration for the Vedic scriptures. I was living on a rural hippie commune at the time. We were, in that culture, ever alert to any new possibilities for exploring the boundaries and depths of our consciousness. The Amanita, a mushroom of preternatural beauty, is ubiquitous in western Oregon during the fall. It had an ineluctable draw to persons of our world view.

Under the influence of some forgotten authority, we attached significance to the ritual of taking the mushrooms in multiples of seven. Both whole mushrooms and pellicles were eaten. We first ate them fresh in small numbers, then dried. The most I ever tried was twenty-one.

The experience could not be described as pleasant or enlightening (except as a demonstration of the extremes people will go to alter their awareness). In the caution of age I would discourage anyone from trying Amanitas.

Within less than an hour of ingesting the mushrooms I would begin to perspire profusely. I clearly remember huddling next to my blazing wood stove, soaked with sweat, but feeling an unreachable coldness to the core of my body. With larger doses, nausea and vomiting would overcome me. I attached no great significance to this message of toxicity since other valued substances also had this effect. Shortly after purging, I would fall into a deep sleep. I never had any clear remembrance of spectacular dreams or revelatory visions occurring during this phase, but I seldom do even after normal sleep.

I awakened after 2 or 3 hours. My state then would be best described by the word equanimity. Whatever needed to be done—daily chores, fixing meals, dealing with an unwelcome guest—was accomplished with an easy detachment. The sense was (though never tested) that if disaster were to befall, the world come to an end, I would have been imperturbed, though not unobservant or incapacitated. It was a not unpleasant state that I optimistically likened to the desired state of nonattachment purportedly achieved by certain religious practices. This condition would fade over a few hours time.

One day, a feline member of the commune where I lived ate half of an Amanita button that was drying above the stove. The attraction was puzzling. The drying fungus was redolent of stale vomit. After realizing what had happened, we paid close attention to Blue, as the cat was named. He became glassy eyed and lay drooling on the walkway outside. After about an hour, his head drooped in what appeared to be the sleep stage. It was a sleep from which he never awakened. He was dead less than two hours after consuming the mushroom.

Sobered by Blue's demise and from reports of liver damage caused by *Amanita muscaria*, our experimentation came to an end. I have not eaten any since. My feeling is that either the chemistry of the Eurasian mushrooms is different from that of North American varieties, or the chemistry of Vedic poets is different from the chemistry of Oregon hippies. Perhaps if I could remember the experiences of my mind during periods of Amanita induced stupor, I would be penning paeans to the glory of the mushroom, but, I have my doubts.

Stephen Brown, N.D.

For more information about the cultural and medical uses of *A. muscaria*, see the monograph on page 64.

Modern Uses of Medicinal Fungi

As I have been hinting at all along, far from being curiosities of the past, medicinal mushrooms are gaining an ever-wider popularity today. This new interest has been greatly stimulated by the large number of scientific studies that have been conducted on medicinal mushrooms. These modern studies have confirmed the traditional uses of many fungi and have even found new applications for them in some cases. Let's take a brief look at some of the findings. For complete summaries, see the monographs on individual species in the materia medica section.

SCIENTIFIC FINDINGS ON MEDICINAL FUNGI

One of the key results that has come out of both laboratory and human clinical studies conducted on fungi is that a number of compounds in fungi can stimulate immune function and inhibit tumor growth. In particular, compounds called *polysaccharides*, which are large, complex branched chain-like molecules built from many smaller units of sugar molecules, have been intensively studied since the 1950s. Again and again they have been shown to have antitumor and immunostimulating properties, not only from many of the medicinal mushrooms reviewed in this book, but also from lichens (such as usnea), bacteria, and even from the cell wall of a yeast (called zymosan) (Chihara et al, 1970b).

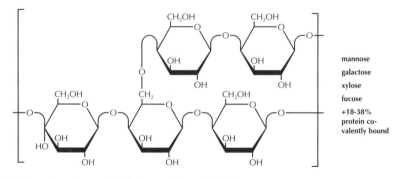

mannose
galactose
xylose
fucose
+18-38%
protein co-
valently bound

Fig. 7: High-molecular weight heteropolysaccharides

Recently, German researchers have demonstrated that immune-activating poly-saccharides similar to those found in many fungi are also found in higher plants, such as the widely popular *Echinacea* and *Astragalus*, an important Chinese herb (Wagner and Proksch, 1985). These giant molecules are similar to ones found in the cellular membranes of bacteria, and thus may "fool" our immune system into mounting an immune response to them, while posing no actual threat. This response has been shown to activate a variety of immune effector cell responses, including an increase in macrophage and killer T-cell activity. Since these het-eropolysaccharides are considered to be among the most important of the active compounds in medicinal mushrooms, it is useful to look at them in closer detail for a moment.

In fungi, polysaccharides are often molecularly bound to various proteins. Proteins are molecules that closely represent the unique identity of organisms, and thus often activate the immune system as they enter the body. They can sometimes initiate an immune response which does not act as a beneficial stimulant or tonic but can induce a powerful immune overreaction—leading to an allergic response, for instance as in casein from milk products or gluten from wheat or grass pollens. This response can even be life-threatening, such as in a bee or wasp sting. I know of no reported cases of people having such extreme immunological responses to proteins in the medicinal mushrooms covered in this book; however, some people are known to have idiosyncratic (highly individualized) reactions to such usually safe mushrooms as *Boletus edulis*. It is unknown what the allergenic compound(s) are. On the flip side, a number of mushrooms are said to *increase* the beneficial immune-activating response of the body.

There are several questions that come up when one considers exactly what role the polysaccharides or protein-bound polysaccharides play in the overall benefits ascribed to the herbs and mushrooms that contain them.

Many existing scientific studies on medicinal mushrooms and their active com-ponents are performed with test animals such as rats and mice, where extracts of various kinds are injected, rather than given orally. It is pertinent to ask how this applies to humans using fungi for food and medicine. Do the polysaccharides, which are large molecular weight molecules, make it past the highly acidic environment of the stomach and the alkaline environment of the duodenum? Do the polysaccharides work when taken orally, or do they have to be injected? Also, when a tincture is made from the mushrooms (extracted with alcohol and water), how does the alcohol affect the polysaccharides or proteins? Are they destroyed by the alcohol, or partially broken down so that their activity is reduced? What aspects of the immune system do they activate (T-cell function and growth, macrophage activity, etc.), and how long does the activity last? While we do not know all the answers to these questions, there is some evidence to support the positive activity of polysaccharides orally, and a low (below 25%) percentage of alcohol does not seem to destroy all their beneficial effects. For instance, the world's oldest echinacea product that is still manufactured today is made from the freshly-pressed juice of *Echinacea purpurea* (L.) Moench and then stabilized with about 24% ethanol. Because no other active compounds have been demonstrated (such as alkylamides), the manufacturer points to the polysaccharides as the immune-activating principle. Other studies have shown that while very large molecular-weight polysaccharides (about 800,000) activate a wide variety of immune functions, after reducing the size of the molecules by heating, the range and strength of the activity is proportionately reduced (Adachi, 1990). Small compounds with a molecular weight of about 6400 show only the ability to activate glucose consumption (possibly lowering blood glucose) and synthesis of lysosomal enzyme (an anti-bacterial protective function).

Various polysaccharides and protein-bound polysaccharides (i.e. they occur naturally bound to protein molecules) have shown strong antitumor and immune-enhancing effects.

I have summarized a number of representative studies about active polysaccharide-containing fractions from medicinal mushrooms in Table 4. More detailed information can be found in the individual monographs.

Table 4

ACTIVE POLYSACCHARIDES FROM MEDICINAL FUNGI

Polysaccharide/ Protein	Activity	Subjects	Ref.
Shiitake **_Lentinula edodes_**			
lentinan (a polysaccharide containing no protein; must be administered by injection)	accelerates degeneration of tumor cells	animals and humans	Kosaka, 1986
	increases T-lymphocytes improves health of chronic hepatitis patients	animals	Liu, 1988
	inhibits HIV virus, benefits AIDS patients	humans	Lin, 1987; Iizuka, 1988, 1990a,b)

| LEM (a protein-bound polysaccharide) | benefits chronic hepatitis sufferers liver-protectant, anti-viral, and immune stimulating | humans animals | Izuki, 1986 Mizoguchi, 1987b; Lin, 1987 |
| | hiv inhibitor | animals | Aoki, 1984a |

Turkey Tail
Trametes versicolor

psk/krestin (a water-soluble, protein-bound polysaccharide)	inhibits binding of HIV with lymphocytes	*in vitro*	Tochikura, 1987a
	immunopromoter	animal	Zhu, 1987
	antioxidant activity	animal	Nakamura, 1986
	interferon and antitumor activity	animal	Ebina, 1987a
	many chronic ailments improved with administration orally and by injection	human	see monograph, p. 161
	cancer patients show increased life span	human	see monograph

Oyster Mushroom
Pleurotus ostreatus
(Jacq.:Fr.) Quél

| acidic polysaccharide fraction | 95% tumor inhibition rate against sarcoma-180 from doses of 5 mg/kg | animal | Yoshioka, 1972 |
| polysaccharide | 4% addition to a normal diet was found to lower serum and liver levels of cholesterol after 2 months' feeding | animal | Bobek, 1991b |

Hen of the Woods
Grifola frondosa

| fraction-D etc. from Grifola | tumor growth inhibition, orally | animal | Nanba, 1993 |

Of course polysaccharides are not the only active constituents found in fungi, nor do they show only antitumor activity. Smaller compounds, such as terpenes and steroids, have also been found, and some of these have shown antitumor activity. And a great number of polysaccharides and protein-bound polysaccharides have been shown to have antibiotic and antiviral properties, as well as the ability to lower blood pressure and reduce blood levels of lipids (that is, fatty acids) and sugar (Lindequist, 1990). These active compounds make many fungi useful for treating infections, flu, diabetes, heart conditions, and perhaps even AIDS.

Following is a summary of research on the three fungi discussed above in the section on Chinese medicine. These fungi are by no means the only ones studied, but two of them, ling zhi or reishi (*Ganoderma lucidum*) and shiitake (*Lentinula edodes*), are perhaps the best-known and most extensively studied mushrooms in the world. For more complete information on their chemistry and pharmacology, as well as literature references to document all of the uses, please refer to the monographs in the second half of this book.

Reishi, Ling Zhi

In numerous clinical trials conducted on humans over the last 20 years, *Ganoderma lucidum* has been used to treat a wide variety of disorders, including:

◆ neurasthenia, dizziness, insomnia, rhinitis, and duodenal ulcers

◆ retinal pigmentary degeneration, leukopenia, progressive muscular dystrophy, and osteogenic hyperplasia

◆ mental disease caused by environmental stress, Alzheimer's disease, hyperlipidemia, and diabetes

◆ hepatitis and symptoms associated with anorexia

◆ high-altitude sickness (by oxygenating the blood)

Of special note are reishi's action on the heart and lungs. In patients with coronary heart disease and hyperlipidemia, reishi has been studied for its ability to alleviate symptoms such as palpitations, dyspnea (sudden difficulty in breathing), precordial pain, and edema, and it seems to lower blood cholesterol and blood pressure. *G. lucidum* has also been used to treat heart arrhythmias. As for reishi's effect on the lungs, in one study of over 2,000 patients with chronic bronchitis, reishi brought about marked improvement in 60-90% of the patients. The older patients, especially, seemed to benefit the most (Chang & But, 1986). Bronchial asthma has also been reported to respond well to treatment with *G. lucidum*, as do several other allergic diseases. Although the antiallergic compounds in *G. lucidum* are not yet clearly understood, scientists have shown that *G. lucidum* inhibits the release of histamine, a compound that causes blood vessels to dilate and is responsible for swelling, inflammation, and other allergic reactions.

Cordyceps

Dong Chong Xia Cao

In the clinic, *C. sinensis* has been studied for the treatment of chronic obstructive liver disorders, high cholesterol, and other aging disorders, including loss of sexual drive, and has shown positive effects. *C. sinensis* has also been reported to be effective in the treatment of heart arrhythmias, lung carcinoma, and chronic nephritis and kidney failure.

Shiitake

Note: "The shiitake mushroom is now *Lentinula edodes*; this separates it from a number of other *Lentinula* spp. that are not closely related. DNA studies support this separation. Many other *Lentinula* species are more closely related to the genus *Polyporus* (Arora, 1994)."

Two types of shiitake preparations have been studied extensively: lentinan, an active polysaccharide extracted from the fungus, and an extract preparation of the mycelium of *Lentinula edodes* called LEM (an acronym for "*Lentinula edodes* mycelia"). In animal studies, lentinan and/or LEM have shown antitumor and antiviral activity, and a distinct stimulation of killer T-cells, which are involved in the immune response. They have also stimulated the production and function of white blood cells, as well as the production of both antibodies and interferon (an antiviral protein), while they have inhibited the synthesis of prostaglandins, which are locally-acting hormones that regulate blood vessel size, mediate inflammation (a protective immune response) and smooth muscle reactivity. Another active constituent of shiitake, eritadenine, may lower levels of cholesterol in the blood (Yamamura and Cochran, 1974a). Table 5 summarizes the important potential uses of shiitake based on studies conducted on both animals and humans.

Table 5

SUMMARY OF RESEARCH ON SHIITAKE

Action	Type of Test	Extract or Form	Dose (Amount, Oral or iv)	Reference
Antitumor	*in vivo*— Mice	Lentinan	10 doses of 1mg/kg body weight (I.p.)	Chihara et al. 1970b
Antiviral	*in vitro* Mice	LEM Cultured mycelia	10 mg/ml	Sorimachi, et al. 1990 Fujii et al. 1978
Immune enhancement	*in vivo*— Mice	Cultured cells	I.p.	Zheng et al. 1985
	Human	Lentinan	Injected	Miyakoshi & Aoki, 1984b
Lowers blood pressure & cholesterol	*in vivo*— Human	Shiitake powder	oral	Kabir et al, 1987
Protects liver from immunological damage	*in vitro*	LEM	animals	Mizoguchi et al. 1987b.
Helps produce antibodies to hepatitis B and improves liver function	*in vivo*— Mice	LEM	—	Harada, 1987
Protects physically active people from overwork and exhaustion; builds vitality in the elderly	*in vivo*— Human	Lentinan	—	Aoki,1984b
Inhibits growth of HIV	*in vitro*	LEM	0.4mg/ml	Tochikura et al. 1987b
Reduces bronchial inflammation	*in vivo*— Human	Fruiting body	6-16 g, dry	Liu and Bau, 1980
Regulates urinary incontinence	*in vivo*— Human	Fruiting body	6-16 g, dry	Liu and Bau, 1980
Anti-cholesteremic	*in vivo*— Human	Fresh dried	90g/day 9g/day	Suzuki & Oshima, 1974

In human clinical trials, lentinan has shown antitumor activity and has been reported to increase the survival rate and length of life of women with various cancers in hundreds of patients (Aoki, 1984). Today it is commonly used for treating cancer, often in conjunction with chemotherapy. It has also been reported to be useful in treating chronic hepatitis and pulmonary tuberculosis, as well as gastric cancer, pancreatic cancer, leukemia, lymphosarcoma, and Hodgkin's disease.

LEM has inhibited HIV infection of cultured human T-cells *in vitro* and in clinical trials (Iizuka, 1988, 1990a,b). A symptomatic patient with antibodies to the AIDS virus and a T4 cell count of $1,250/mm^3$ was given a freeze-dried tea of shiitake mycelium orally at 6 g/day. The T4 cell count improved to 2,045 after 30 days and $2,542/mm^3$, and the symptoms were much improved after 60 days. The extract also inhibited the production of AIDS virus particles by infected T4 lymphocytes *in vitro* and increased the production of interleukin 1 by peritoneal macrophages.

LEM may also be beneficial for non-insulin-dependent diabetics because of its reported ability to lower blood sugar levels. In Japan, lentinan is currently classified as a drug, while LEM is considered a food supplement. Note that LEM or other concentrated extracts are probably preferable to raw shiitake for medicinal purposes because they are more concentrated and are easily absorbed in the digestive tract, but using the mushrooms in cooking and in teas may also be effective. It is known that large overdoses of 10 to 50 times the normal clinical dose can lead to immune suppression, or it simply will not have any immunopotentiating effect. Otherwise, side effects are few, except for skin rashes that clear up shortly after discontinuing the extract.

Adaptogens and Immune Stimulants

Now that we have explored some of the ways in which modern science views medicinal fungi, I would like to explain a bit about how modern herbalists and natural health practitioners classify and use fungi. Fungi are, by and large, used as adaptogens and immune stimulants. An adaptogen is any substance that meets three criteria, as defined by the Russian doctor and researcher, I.I. Brekhman, who, with his teacher, N.V. Lazarev, first defined the category of natural plant-derived "biological response modifiers." These are as follows:

◆ It should cause no harm and place no additional stress on the body;

◆ It should help the body adapt to the many and varied environmental and psychological stresses; and

◆ It must have a nonspecific action on the body, supporting all the major systems, such as the nervous system, hormonal system, and immune system, as well as regulating functions (such as the blood sugar); if they are too high, an adaptogen will lower it; if too high, reduce it.

Through various scientific studies, it is known that the pharmacological effects of many adaptogenic herbs are complex—they apparently support adrenal function (Farnsworth, 1985), and they are especially noted for their ability to build endurance and reduce fatigue.

Adaptogens also stimulate the immune system indirectly, building the body's resistance to non-specific stresses such as novel chemicals in the environment, noise, pathogens, overwork, and emotional factors, among others. Immune stimulants, on the other hand, stimulate the immune system directly, boosting its resistance to specific stresses such as pathogens, like viruses and bacteria.

If you have any doubt that people today need adaptogens and immune stimulants, perhaps even as regular dietary supplements, just take a look around. The modern environment is full of many new biological challenges created by the industrial and electronic revolutions. This is especially true given that most of these new challenges have popped up during the last hundred years, which is quite sudden in terms of the time it takes for the human body to evolve defense mechanisms.

One sign that our bodies are not yet fully adapted to these new changes and challenges is the recent proliferation of immune-based disorders such as AIDS, *Candida* infections, Chronic Fatigue Syndrome, and cancer. All of these continue to elude the standard methods of modern scientific medicine, despite massive efforts to stop them. For example, the American Cancer Association has spent billions of dollars over the last 20 years in search of a cure for the many forms of cancer—but to no avail. One out of three Americans is now expected to contract cancer at some point in their lives. After seeing the cancer rates rise in spite of all the money poured into cancer research, the American Cancer Association recently announced that there may not be any hope of finding such a cure and that perhaps prevention is the only answer.

Fortunately, TCM has been interested in preventive medicine for thousands of years, and modern western medicine is also taking a closer look. Looking at traditional medicine as a model, I have identified three separate classes of immune-active herbs or herbal programs—adaptogens, surface immune stimulants, and immune tonics. Each of these has a different application and works in a different way.

ADAPTOGENS

Adaptogens boost immunity mainly by supporting and balancing the endocrine (or hormonal) system. More specifically, laboratory tests have shown that they can support adrenal function, help the cells of the body utilize oxygen more efficiently, and increase the efficiency of cellular respiration. Scientists are now discovering that the nervous, hormonal, and immune systems are all interconnected and strongly affect each other (Locke and Hornig-Rohan, 1983). It is well-known, for instance, that excess cortisol (a hormone released from the adrenals in response to stress) can depress the immune system. And even more interesting, exciting new work suggests that attitudes and moods really *can* cause biochemical changes in the body that either enhance or depress the immune response. Thus, it is entirely plausible that adaptogens which stabilize the hormonal balance in the body can consequently enhance the functioning of the immune system.

Another way in which a number of adaptogens (such as eleuthero, reishi, and *Panax ginseng*) might work is through the element germanium, which is reported to increase the uptake and utilization of oxygen in body tissues, while at the same time protecting against damage from free radicals generated by this extra oxygen. Free radicals are highly reactive molecules (such as —OH radicals) that have at least one unpaired electron. Because they like to "grab" electrons from nearby molecules to complete a pair (paired electrons are always more stable than single ones), they tend to react with important substances in the body, such as DNA, and are thus capable of causing widespread damage. Since more free radicals are produced during periods of increased immune-system activity (as during infections or stress), it is especially important to add adaptogens and antioxidant supplements to the diet at these times The most effective and tested nutrient antioxidants to add to an herbal regime are vitamin E and vitamin C.

It is highly significant, then, that some mushrooms and other adaptogenic herbs contain high amounts of germanium, which has been shown to have immunomodulating activity (Reynolds, 1993). For instance, in a recent analysis of 24 Chinese herbs, it was found that Reishi and *Panax ginseng* contained much higher levels of germanium than the others (Chiang and Wann, 1986). Many other medicinal mushrooms may contain large quantities of germanium, as well as polysaccharides and protein-bound polysaccharides, which have also been found to directly stimulate the immune system (Hung-Cheh & Mieng-hua, 1986). It is relevant that some reports indicate that it may not be wise to take purified germanium supplements due to possible kidney toxicity (Reynolds, 1993).

IMMUNE STIMULANTS

Immune stimulants work mainly by increasing *macrophage* activity. Macrophages (macro=big, phage=eater) are a kind of white blood cell that "eats up" and destroys pathogens such as bacteria, yeast cells, virus-infected cells, etc.—a kind of garbage-disposal system. They reside in great numbers in the mucous membranes of the body—especially throughout the digestive, urinary, and respiratory tracts. They also play a role in the reticuloendothelial system, which is a system of immune cells (including macrophages) centered in the spleen, liver, and lymphoid tissues that engulf and store wastes and toxic chemicals, taking them out of action. Macrophages and other phagocytes (like neutrophils) are like the body's protective shield; they are our first line of defense. Stimulating this aspect of our immune system helps protect us against colds, flu, and infections of any kind, because these immune "effector" cells do not allow pathogens to even gain a foothold.

Like muscles and other organs, the surface immune system needs constant exercise to keep it fit and ready to do its job. It gets natural exercise as a result of foreign organisms which we regularly ingest and inhale, as well as from minor illnesses (such as colds), bee stings, and other environmental influences. Since this exercise keeps it ready and able to fight off more serious illnesses, such as cancer, the next time you get a cold, be grateful that your surface immune system is getting a good workout!

Currently, it is known that *Cordyceps* (Zhang et al, 1985), lentinan and LEM from shiitake (Ladanyi et al, 1993), and protein-bound polysaccharides from *Trametes versicolor* (PSK, PSP) (Yang et al, 1993; Nguyen & Stadtsbaeder, 1979) have shown an ability to stimulate macrophage activity and strengthen our immune system's fight against infection from bacteria and viruses.

Herbs and other natural remedies that activate the immune system include echinacea, eastern white cedar (*Thuja occidentalis* L.), wild indigo (*Baptisia tinctoria* (L.) R. Br. ex Ait. f.), osha (*Ligusticum porteri* J. M. Coulter & J. N. Rose), cold-water and hot-water baths/showers, and physical exercise. Note that echinacea is really an all-star in this class. See my book *Echinacea: The Immune Herb!* for more information.

IMMUNE TONICS

Immune *tonics*, (spleen, kidney, or lung "chi" tonics as they are called in TCM) work by supporting the bone marrow reserve, from which macrophages, all other immune effector cells (such as T-cells), and red blood cells are made. Reishi is a good example of a medicinal mushroom which has been shown in laboratory tests to build up the bone marrow (Jia et al, 1993b; Guan & Cong, 1982), possibly acting a little like an "herbal bone-marrow transplant." Many fungi are deep immune tonics, such as reishi, *Cordyceps* spp., hoelen, and shiitake. Ginseng, too, is a spleen Qi tonic, which is one reason it is so prized in TCM.

An interesting case history that illustrates the difference between the surface and deep immune systems involves a group of young cancer patients who were given a surface immune stimulant combination containing *echinacea, thuja*, and *baptisia* during radiation therapy to help maintain their levels of white blood cells. In many of these children the depressed white blood cell count climbed quickly back to normal levels after taking the herbal formula for a week or ten days. However, some of the children did not respond. Upon investigating this lack of response, it was found that these children had such low bone marrow reserves that they no longer had the resources to create more white blood cells, even though this immune function was stimulated. After these children rested and ate an extra nourishing diet for a period of several weeks, a number of them were able to respond positively to the immune-stimulating herbal treatment (Chone and Manidakis, 1969).

The best way to take immune tonics is to eat them as part of one's regular diet, allowing them to provide the nutrients and vital substances the body needs to build superior immunity. This is a tradition in China and Japan, where food and medicine are not so artificially separated. If you would like to make an excellent immune tonic, try my recipe for "Wei Qi Soup." The body's immune vitality is called *wei Qi* in TCM. This soup is very strengthening and building. It contains large quantities of vitamins and minerals in a readily assimilable form, as well as substances (such as polysaccharides) that the body can use to rebuild a weakened immune system. This recipe also provides a great opportunity to try some of the mushrooms mentioned in this book. Try adding shiitake, turkey tail, common poria (such as *Oxyporus corticola* (Fr.) Ryv.), *Cordyceps*, or any sweet-tasting polypores, such as *Fomitopsis pinicola*, available in your local area.

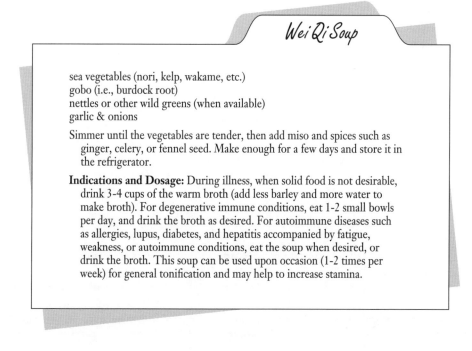

Wei Qi Soup

Directions: Fill a pot 2/3 full with purified or spring water, then add:

Astragalus membranaceus, 5-7 sticks

Ganoderma lucidum (i.e., reishi) 1 medium

(any other tonifying mushrooms), 2-3 small fruiting bodies

Slightly sprouted beans, 1/4-1/2 cup (aduki, black, etc.)

Bring water to boil, simmer for 20 minutes, then add:

Organic barley, 1/2-1 cup (choose amount depending on thickness desired)

Simmer another 20 minutes, then add favorite vegetables such as:
    carrots & celery
    beet tops (or chard, collards, mustard greens, etc.)
    cabbage
    potatoes (optional)

continued...

Wei Qi Soup

sea vegetables (nori, kelp, wakame, etc.)
gobo (i.e., burdock root)
nettles or other wild greens (when available)
garlic & onions

Simmer until the vegetables are tender, then add miso and spices such as ginger, celery, or fennel seed. Make enough for a few days and store it in the refrigerator.

Indications and Dosage: During illness, when solid food is not desirable, drink 3-4 cups of the warm broth (add less barley and more water to make broth). For degenerative immune conditions, eat 1-2 small bowls per day, and drink the broth as desired. For autoimmune diseases such as allergies, lupus, diabetes, and hepatitis accompanied by fatigue, weakness, or autoimmune conditions, eat the soup when desired, or drink the broth. This soup can be used upon occasion (1-2 times per week) for general tonification and may help to increase stamina.

A Guide to Using Medicinal Fungi

W ell, enough theory. At this point you probably have a number of practical questions about how to use fungi as medicine. For your convenience, I have compiled a table that lists the most commonly used medicinal fungi generally available in natural food stores, herb shops, Chinese herb dealers, or sometimes local acupuncturists (see the appendix for source addresses and phone numbers), along with indications for use and recommended dosages. This section will include information on making home products such as tinctures and other extracts with fungi, as well as evaluating and choosing commercially-available products.

GATHERING YOUR OWN MEDICINAL MUSHROOMS

I could not write a book on medicinal mushrooms without saying something about collecting wild mushrooms. An exciting aspect of medicinal mushrooms is that many of them grow commonly throughout the world. Some, such as *Trametes versicolor* (turkey tail), *Ganoderma applanatum* (artist's conk), *Ganoderma lucidum* (ling-zhi or reishi), and *Schizophyllum commune* Fr. (split-gill), may be growing right in your backyard or in a local wooded area. I like to encourage those who are interested to develop an active interest in mushroom hunting (and home growing to preserve our wild resources), for not only is eating wild mushrooms beneficial to our health but so is the activity of roaming through the woods.

The rich smells of the earth (abundant with fungal mycelium), the splashes of fall colors, and the soothing greens of mosses and ferns enliven one's spirit and senses. I often walk down creek beds, fording small brooks here and there to check brightly-colored spots, in case they might be a chanterelle or sulfur shelf, rather than another dying leaf among a thousand. I splash through pools, picking up sticks tufted with Usnea and other lichens for later use. I climb up on banks thick with leaf-litter and twigs, run my hand down the length of smooth alder logs, checking for tiny Pleurotus buttons.

One of my greatest joys is filling my daypack with paper bags of various sizes, as well as wax paper (to protect delicate mushrooms), a basket, and a good field guide or two, and going on a mushroom foray. Stalking wild mushrooms seems to satisfy a deep instinct for the hunt and allows me to pick food and medicine that are entirely renewable, as long as I remember to be conscious about the gift of the earth that is being offered and pick carefully and respectfully. Here are a few helpful suggestions for conservation of useful fungi.

- ◆ Slice fungi that have stalks at the base, or carefully twist and pull them up. Try not to disturb the mycelium.

- ◆ When pulling conks from live or dead trees, always leave one or two to encourage the distribution of spores. The mycelium is a perennial growth, insuring that the fungus will continue to flourish inside trees or decaying logs, until the work of breaking down molecules such as cellulose is complete. To insure that specific fungi can continue to spread through areas of the forest eco-system where they are needed, some spore-producing conks must be preserved. Also remember that when we remove one conk, we are removing years of growth rather than days.

- ◆ The less we disturb the forest duff while walking or picking, the better; remember to walk lightly so no one can tell that you passed there. Cover over any holes where mushrooms are cut with dirt, duff, or leaves. This shows respect for the earth as well as for other pickers—there is nothing more depressing than seeing holes where mushrooms once were.

Besides the walking, bending, crawling, and climbing that is necessary in a good mushroom hunt, the solitude and close contact with nature is a healing connection that soothes the soul and calms the spirit. So many times I have felt the turbulence of the human world in my mind and body and have gone out into the woods and found the serenity that comes when a contact is made with our higher intelligence through nature. I find nibbling on wild mushrooms such as the Turkey Tail (*Trametes versicolor*) to be very energizing.

The first thing that may come to mind when it comes to picking wild mushrooms is the possibility of eating a poisonous one—and a healthy respect for this potential is good. Though it is true that some mushrooms are poisonous, most are not. There are plenty of unmistakable medicinal mushrooms that you *can* gather safely—and if you are ever in doubt about a particular one, just play it safe. It is best for beginners to learn two or three easily identified mushrooms found in one's local area, as well as how to distinguish them from potentially poisonous mushrooms. Local community colleges or city adult education programs often offer good mushroom-hunting classes. Weekend seminars can also be found in the fall in many areas, and these provide an invaluable opportunity to learn from the experts.

As for mushroom guidebooks, there are several good ones that have color photographs, detailed descriptions, and pointers to aid the novice and experienced hunter alike. My favorite is David Arora's *Mushrooms Demystified* (1986), which offers a wonderful mixture of good scholarship, the experience of many years of field work, humor, a meticulous attention to details, and the best keys to the identification of the fungi of the western United States available (though it is useful for other areas as well). This book has much valuable information about American, and especially West Coast, species of fungi. See the Resources section in the Appendix for other choices.

You will also want to learn how to prepare tasty wild mushroom dishes. Where I live, in Santa Cruz, California, one of the highlights of the fall season is the "Fungus Fair," sponsored by the city museum and the Fungus Federation, where exotic mushroom dishes are sampled by thousands of eager fungiphiles. I've included a few mushroom recipes here to get you started. For more, see *Wild Mushroom Cookery* (eds. Wells, Rogers, and Piekenbrock, 1987) and *A Passion for Mushrooms* by Antonio Carluccio. You may be surprised to learn that mushrooms can be highly nutritious, in addition to being medicinal and tasty (see the section on the nutritional value of fungi). So there's one last reason to get interested in mushrooms. Now go out there and experiment. Remember, fungi are fun!

OTHER SOURCES OF MEDICINAL FUNGI

There are an increasing number of people dealing in medicinal mushrooms and their products in the U.S., Europe, and Australia. In Asia, where they have been popular for centuries, mushrooms are increasingly being recognized as useful in medicine. This increased use is partly driven by modern research showing how valuable compounds such as lentinan can be for supporting the immune systems of people with cancer while they are undergoing treatments with chemotherapy, and partly because the art of cultivation of many medicinal species has reached a point where growers can supply the increasing market demand (Stamets, 1994).

There are currently a number of growers of shiitake, reishi, and other medicinal species in the U.S. Here is a list of the most promising ways of obtaining medicinal mushrooms and their products. See the Appendix for a list of suppliers and growers.

Table 6

SOURCES OF MEDICINAL FUNGI

Type of Product	Source
Bulk mushrooms	Natural food stores (reishi, shiitake)
	Markets (shiitake, pleurotus)
	Chinese herb dealers (reishi, cordyceps, zhu ling, hoelen, auricularia, etc.)
	Herb shops (reishi)
	Home grown—logs, supplies (shiitake, pleurotus, reishi, others)
	From the wild (pleurotus, reishi, turkey tail, auricularia, tremella, honey mushroom, chanterelles, and many others)
Powdered concentrates (capsules, tablets, granules)	Natural food stores (reishi, shiitake, maitake, cordyceps) Chinese herb dealers (formulas, freeze-dried granules to make instant tea, reishi tea cubes) Herb shops (same as natural food stores) Selected drug stores (reishi)
Liquid extract products (tinctures, ampules— extract in honey base)	Natural food stores (reishi, shiitake, cordyceps, rarely others) Herb shops (same as above) Chinese herb dealers (reishi, shiitake, cordyceps)

STORING MEDICINAL MUSHROOMS

When storing fleshy mushrooms, such as shiitake or *Pleurotus*, it is usually best to dry them. Small food driers are readily available at many department stores for under $50 and are well worth the investment. Any mushrooms I pick during the fall and winter seasons that I don't eat are dried for use throughout the rest of the year. Heavy, conk-like polypores such as *Ganoderma applanatum* are perennials and will readily dry, maintaining (even for years) the same appearance and medicinal properties as the day they were picked. Besides their medicinal use, they make great conversation pieces and desk ornaments. I have several brightly-colored red-belted polypores that have been on my desk for several years and they still look as fresh as the day I picked them! More delicate polypores, such as *Trametes versicolor*, should be quickly dried in a food drier or even the oven on low heat (there are no active volatile substances to worry about), as they will soon be turned to sawdust by fly larvae if left in the open air to dry on their own.

MAKING PREPARATIONS:
POWDERS, POWDERED EXTRACTS, PILLS, ENCAPSULATION

Since the scientific literature seems to point to whole mushroom fruiting bodies as being especially active as antitumor agents and immune enhancers, I recommend taking dried and powdered mushrooms by the teaspoon, either in a cup of ginger tea, or even sprinkled into soup or on stir-frys and rice, etc. Some conk-like fungal fruiting bodies such as artist's conk or red-belted polypore cannot be powdered because they are too tough and fibrous. These can be sliced (or sawed) into thin slices and dried for tea or tincturing. Softer and thinner polypores or dried fleshy fungi can easily be powdered and encapsulated. When placed in "00" capsules, the average amount of powdered mushroom/capsule is about 400 mg. For mild to moderate immune support I recommend 2 capsules morning and evening. For specific immune-suppressed conditions, take 2-3 capsules 3 times a day.

To make a mushroom extract that is stronger and more readily assimilated, try simmering the mushrooms (as many fruiting bodies or pieces as can be covered by the water in a pot) for about an hour. Strain off the dark tea and replace the liquid with fresh water to cover the mushrooms and simmer for another 30 minutes. Strain the new tea and add it to the first decoction. Throw the soggy, spent fruiting bodies away. Combine the first and second decoctions and begin simmering. Reduce this liquid to a thick paste, which might take as much as several hours. Take this paste off the heat, scrape it out with a cake spatula, and knead it with an organic rice or wheat flour to a dough-like consistency. Pack small pieces of this dough into "00" capsules and take 1 of them morning and evening. The dough can also be dried in a food drier or oven with low heat. The dried extract pieces can then be powdered in a blender or coffee grinder. The powder can be packed into capsules, sprinkled on food, or try adding a half-teaspoon to one cup of warm water or ginger decoction for an instant immune-supportive tea. In my experience, these extracts are stronger than simple mushroom powders, and the preparations retain the polysaccharides, or their breakdown products and nutritional qualities in a readily-assimilable form, though there is little scientific data available on what effect the heat has on the efficacy of these compounds.

TEAS AND SOUPS

Teas are a good way to use medicinal mushrooms, and they should be simmered until the tea is somewhat dark and strong-tasting—about 40 minutes to an hour. Add ginger or other flavorful herbs (1/8 part by weight of the mushrooms) and a little licorice (1/16th part) to help improve the taste, which might be somewhat bitter in its native state.

For soups, add a variety of vegetables, such as broccoli, carrots, potatoes, beets, greens, garlic, onions, and a little seaweed and barley (to thicken) to the mushroom tea stock. Fish, chicken, or a little red meat can be added for certain deficiency conditions. Drink the broth (1-3 cups a day) and eat the vegetables. Tender fleshy fungi, such as shiitake and oyster mushrooms, can be eaten with enthusiasm, but it is best to push tough and fibrous fungal fruiting body chunks such as reishi, artist's conk, and turkey tail aside—the essence has already permeated the broth, and they are far too tough to chew, even after boiling (unless you are a 3 or 4 pack of gum a day fan and have very well-developed jaws).

PREPARING A TINCTURE; MAKING A LIQUID EXTRACT

Making tinctures is a time-honored method of extracting and preserving the active ingredients of medicinal herbs and mushrooms. When making a tincture, use either 190 proof clear grain alcohol, if available (called Clear Spring in some places) diluted 50-50 with distilled water for most fungi, or if it is not available, 80 or 100 proof vodka. To determine the percentage of ethanol (ethyl alcohol) in a given proof product, divide by two. In other words, a common 80 proof vodka will contain 40% ethyl alcohol. This strength of liquid solvent, which is called the menstruum, is fine for tincturing many medicinal mushrooms. The process is simple. Place the chopped up dried mushroom pieces in a blender and cover with the menstruum. Blend until the consistency is similar to that of a fruit smoothie and pour into a quart or half-gallon canning jar. After half an hour, a clear one inch of menstruum should appear, and the blended mushroom fibers and particles should sink into a solid mass at the bottom. Make sure that there is at least an inch of clear menstruum after settling, so that none of the actual mushroom material sticks up above the top of the liquid, because fermentation can take place leading to off-flavors in the finished tincture. Shake the bottle every day and keep it in a warm place out of the direct sunlight. After two weeks, squeeze as much of the liquid from the mushroom mass as possible and bottle the mostly clear tincture. This liquid can then be stored in a canning jar or other suitable glass container for future use. It will retain its potency for two to three years. This type of tincture is a simple single liquid extraction, and it should contain a good amount of the major active constituents.

My favorite method of creating a liquid extract of dried mushrooms for tonic long-term use is to make a double extraction. For this, the first liquid extract is separated from the extracted (or "spent") herb mass, which is called the "marc." Set the alcoholic tincture aside and then simmer (decoct) the marc in five times its volume of distilled water for an hour. Let the brew cool and then filter and squeeze as much of the water from the marc as possible. Compost this last marc, and begin simmering the watery decoction under low heat. Evaporate this to about one-fifth its original voume, and add enough of this concentrate to the first alcoholic tincture so that the final concentration of alcohol is at least 20-25%, which is needed to preserve the preparation. Some measuring is needed, but this can be calculated by knowing the approximate alcoholic percentage in the first tincture. I feel, based on my experience, that this "double extraction" is richer in the immune-activating and anti-tumor polysaccharides, as well as the protein-bound polysaccharides and will be more tonifying than the original alcoholic preparation. Simmering the herb in water may soften and break down cell walls, releasing immune-strengthening high molecular-weight polysaccharides.

DOSES

It is best to take any tonic herbs, such as medicinal mushrooms, for at least three months, up to nine months. This is a general course for any "constitutional remedy" taken for its general tonic and strengthening effects.

Take 1/2 to 1 tsp of the homemade tincture morning and evening in a little water or ginger tea as a good average dose. Also follow the suggested dosages in the sections on individual mushrooms.

Split-gill
Schizophyllum commune (Arora)

Shiitake
Lentinula edodes (Arora)

Corn smut
Ustilago maydis (Arora)

Jew's ear
Auricularia auricula (Arora)

Chaga
Inonotus obliquus (Arora)

Maitake
Grifola frondosa (Arora)

Chaga
Inonotus obliquus (Arora)

Oyster mushroom
Pleurotus ostreatus (Hobbs)

Qunine conk
Fomitopsis officinalis (Hobbs)

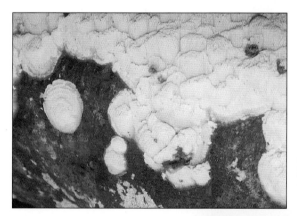

Poria
Poria corticola (Hobbs)

Stone fungus
Polyporua tuberaster (Arora)

True tinder polypore
Fomes fomentarius (Hobbs)

Birch polypore
Piptoporus betulinus (Hobbs)

Gilled polypore
Lenzites betulina (Hobbs)

Gilled polypore
Lenzites betulina (Arora)

Artist's conk
The author with Ganoderma applanatum
(Hobbs)

Red-belted polypore
Fomitopsis pinicola (Hobbs)

Turkey tail
Trametes versicolor and
False turkey tail
Stereum hirsutum (Hobbs)

Turkey tail
Trametes versicolor (Hobbs)

Pine tree fungus
Ganoderma tsugae (Hobbs)

Pine tree fungus
The author with
Ganoderma tsugae

Reishi
Ganoderma lucidum (Arora)

Fly agaric
Amanita muscaria (Arora)

Honey mushroom
Armillaria mellea (Arora)

King bolete
Boletus edulis (Arora)

Blewit
Lepista nuda (Arora)

Puffball
Calvatia bovista (Arora)

Witch's butter
Tremella mesenterica (Arora)

Stinkhorn mushroom
Phallus impudicus (Hobbs)

Bladdercup
Peziza domestica (Hobbs)

Nutritional Value of Fungi

Although fresh, undried mushrooms are 85-95% water, they do have signficant nutritional value. A number of reliable laboratory analyses of edible and medicinal mushrooms are available, especially on commercially important species such as *Agaricus bisporus* (button mushroom), *Lentinula edodes* (shiitake), *Volvariella volvacea* (Bull.:Fr.) Sing. (straw mushroom), *Flammulina velutipes* (Curt.:Fr.) Sing. (enokitake), and *Pleurotus spp.* (oyster mushroom) (Crisan & Sands, 1978; Breene, 1990; Kurtzman, 1993; Garcha et al, 1993).

It has been estimated that of approximately 38,000 species of fungi worldwide, as many as 2,000 may be edible. My feeling is that this figure is very conservative. Fungi may be one of the world's greatest natural food resources, because they are able to transform nutritionally poor substances into foods rich in fat and protein. Edible fungi can be grown on cheap food by-products such as molasses, vegetable scraps, potatoes, and even sulfite waste liquids from the wood-pulping industry.

The potential nutritional value of mushrooms ranking the highest on several internationally-accepted tests compares with meat and milk, whereas the least nutritive mushrooms are similar to common vegetables such as carrots and turnips (Crisan & Sands, 1987). It is also interesting to note that a number of wild mushrooms are consistently more nutritious than their cultivated relatives. For instance, the straw mushroom, *Volvariella volvacea*, the cepe (*Boletus edulis*), and the parasol mushroom (*Macrolepiota procera* [Scop.:Fr.] Sing. (=*Lepiota procera*) rated high on the nutrition scale, while various morels (*Morchella esculenta* [L.] Pers., *M. deliciosa*

Fr.), the cultivated oyster mushroom (*Pleurotus ostreatus*), and shiitake (*L. edodes*)—while tempting in texture and flavor—rated lower.

Although there is a wealth of information on the levels of important nutrients such as protein, carbohydrates (soluble and insoluble fiber), amino acids, vitamins, and minerals, it is often difficult to interpret the data. The two main problems are the lack of uniform procedures and techniques among laboratories and the different ways of reporting the data. Even when data between mushroom species is comparable, it is hard to determine the significance in human nutrition. This is because a lab value of the percentage of protein in shiitake, for instance, says little about how much protein we can actually utilize. This depends not only on our own individual digestive capacity—the effectiveness of our digestive enzymes to extract the nutrients and how the mushroom is prepared or cooked—but in the quality and composition of the protein, as well as how it is bound to other molecules, such as carbohydrates.

Mushroom protein digestibility ranges from 34-97%, taking either egg protein or casein (from milk) as a standard 100% (Crisan and Sands, 1978; Garcha et al, 1993), possibly because mushrooms are high in free essential and non-essential amino acids. In animal feeding experiments, the addition of mushroom pellets to the basal diet led to increased body weights. The rats increased food intake in the mushroom groups, especially when fed *Pleurotus florida*, but not as much when fed *A. bisporus*. Lipid peroxidation and organ weight tests revealed no toxic reactions even when the mushrooms were consumed in significant amounts (Garcha et al, 1993).

Imaki and his co-workers (1991) determined the digestibility of shiitake by measuring various components in the fecal output and comparing it to the nutrient levels in the fruiting bodies and the percentage of the diet. When shiitake was added to the diet of volunteers at 40g/day, the digestibility of protein (from the shiitake) was 85.5 +/- 23.8%. Digestibility of fat was 70.0 +/- 90.1%, digestibility of carbohydrate was 65.8 +/- 13.1%, and the ratio of the total available energy to intake energy (Net Energy Availability) was 67.4 +/- 25.9%. At 60 g/day, the digestibility of the above nutrients was somewhat reduced.

The range of nutritional content between mushroom species is wide, and different populations of mushrooms are known to vary considerably in their nutrient content and digestibility even within the same species (Crisan & Sands, 1978), possibly because of harvest during different stages of maturity and different growth substrates (Garcha et al, 1993).

Because of this, figures for the nutritional content of edible and medicinal species in Table 7 are given as a range of values, based on high and low figures from a number of published studies. The figures are based on mg/100 grams of dry mushroom weight, unless otherwise stated. Fresh mushrooms contain about 85-95% water, so divide figures by ten to approximate the nutrient amounts.

Generally, protein concentrations range from 1-4% of fresh weight, or about 10-45% of dry weight, a significant amount. It is also known that up to 40% of the amino acids in mushrooms are essential amino acids. The fairy ring mushroom (*Marasmius oreades* [Bolt.:Fr.] Fr.) has one of the highest protein contents at 50-

55%, while the chanterelle ranges from 11.8-24.3% and the king bolete (cep), 27-35.8% (Vetter, 1993).

Carbohydrates range from 3-28% of fresh weight and fiber from 3-32%, usually consisting of pentoses like xylose and ribose, hexoses like glucose, galactose and mannose, sugar alcohols like mannitol (particularly abundant) and inositol, to name only a few. Large polysaccharides commonly found in mushrooms include glycogen, which is the same energy-storage compound animals use, and chitin, the main compound of insoluble mushroom fiber.

Many classes of lipid compounds are represented in mushrooms, such as free fatty acids, mono-, di-, and triglycerides, sterols, sterol esters, and phospholipids. Fats usually range from 0.2-0.8% of fresh weight, or between 2-8% of the dry weight, with linoleic acid (an esssential fatty acid) being the most abundant lipid (Senatore, 1990). The content of this important fatty acid can be comparable to the amount in safflower seed oil, which is considered a rich source. When preparing mushrooms for the table, save the stem, which contains a higher content of linoleic acid than the cap. No one will gain weight when dining on fungi, except when they are sautéed in copious amounts of butter! And think of the calories you will burn hunting them.

Mushrooms are a good source of several vitamins, including thiamine, riboflavin, niacin, biotin, and vitamin C. Even beta-carotene, while not common in mushrooms, can be found in some species. The minerals phosphorus, sodium, and potassium are fairly high, while iron and calcium are present but tend to be low, with a few exceptions (Crisan & Sands, 1987). It is also notable that mushrooms may accumulate heavy metals (especially lead and cadmium) in some species, perhaps related to the environment in which they are picked (Breene, 1990).

Nutritional profiles of five common medicinal mushrooms are presented in Table 7. The figures are drawn predominantly from Crisan & Sands (1978), Bano & Rajarathnam (1988), Breene (1990), Ershow & Wong-Chen (1990), Kurtzman (1993), and Garcha et al (1993). Because fresh mushrooms vary considerably in water content, the figures are calculated on a dry-weight basis, which allows a greater consistency of data. To determine an approximate fresh-weight value, divide by 10 if the mushroom is very fresh (just picked), 9 if it has been in the refrigerator for a day or two, or 8 if purchased from the store.

Table 7

NUTRIENT CONTENT OF EDIBLE AND MEDICINAL FUNGI
(PER 100 GRAMS)

Nutrient	Shiitake	Agaricus [a]	Oyster m.	Wood Ear	Baked Potatoes[e]
Protein	9.6-17%	23.9-48.3% [b]	10.5-30%	2.1-10.6%	3.9%
Total Carbohydrates	54.0-82%	24.5-62%	60-81.8%	62.4-65.5%	31.7%
Calories (kcal)	296-375	175.5-337	80.8-367	279-356	136
Crude Fiber	6.5-8.5	6.0-7.4	7.5	4.2-7.0%	2.7%
Total Fat	0.6-8.0%	1-6.8%	1-7.2%	0.2-1.5%	0.2%
Vitamins (mg/100 g)					
Beta-carotene (µg)	—	—	0	0.03-20 mg	trace
Biotin	—	162	—	—	0.5
B6	—	2.4	—	—	0.54
C	40-60	13.5-82	36-58	—	14
Pro-vitamin D[d] (ergosterol)	0.06-0.27%	0.23%	0.13%	19	0
E	—	1.6	—	—	0.11
Folic acid (µg)	—	594-933	—	—	44
Pantothenic acid	—	22.8-27	—	—	0.46
Thiamine	0.07-0.4	.1-1.4	4.8	0.15-0.16	0.37
Riboflavin	0.2-1.3	4.2-5	4.3-4.7	0.48-0.55	0.02
Niacin	11.9-18.9	36.19-57	108.7	2.7-4.1	1.1
Minerals (mg/100 g)					
Aluminum	182	—	—	—	—
Calcium	11-126	23-131	5-292.9	210-357	11
Chlorine	73	690-931.5	—	—	120
Copper	—	7.2-9.7	1.6	—	0.14
Iodine	—	40.5	—	—	5
Iron	1.7-30	.2-8.1	5.0-19.2	56.1-185.0 [c]	0.7
Magnesium	130-247	121.5	174-292.9	—	32
Manganese	—	1.4	1.3-36.4	—	0.2
Phosphorus	171-650	718-1429	1212-1406	201-220	68
Potassium	380-1530	2590-4762	2130-3793	860	630
Selenium (µg)	—	121.5	30.3	—	2
Silicon	262	—	—	—	—
Sodium	13-1079	67.5	158-837	63	12
Sulfur	237	459	—	—	53
Zinc	—	5.4	9.1	—	0.5

Notes: [a] (*Agaricus bisporus*) the highest protein level for each species is probably based on total protein content. Kurtzman (1993) and other authors have mentioned that mushrooms contain more non-protein nitrogen than many animal products (such as chitin), and thus the true protein content should be about 20% lower than milk.

[b] the actual average range is 21.6-39.0.

[c] Ershow & Wong-Chen, 1990

[d] Huang et al, 1985

[e] Baked potato, fresh; for comparison

It is also interesting to note that the members of the Polyporaceae (polypores) had relatively low mineral contents, and the percentage of copper, zinc, manganese, and lead was lower in mushrooms that were growing on wood than on the ground (Kawai et al, 1990).

The levels of vitamin D2 in maitake, shiitake, and a number of other medicinal and edible mushrooms were determined by HPLC analysis and found to be in the range of 10 to 150 IU in 100 g of fresh fruiting bodies (Yokokawa & Takahashi, 1990). Ergosterol, a pro-vitamin D which is converted to vitamin D under the influence of sunlight, makes up more than 70% of the total sterol fraction in many mushrooms, and about 55-65% of it is in the free form. Shiitake mushrooms containing about 0.5% ergosterol (dry weight) were able to produce 400 IU of vitamin D per gram after being exposed to a fluorescent sunlamp (Breene, 1990).

How does cooking affect the nutrients in mushrooms? Some heat-labile nutrients such as vitamin C, thiamine, and other B-vitamins are obviously diminished (often up to 50-70%) or destroyed. Most minerals are unaffected and can actually become more available after cooking. Fiber is generally broken down to a degree, and protein is affected, though its value is probably not diminished.

Stir-frying or sautéeing lightly, a traditional way to use choice edible species, will obviously preserve more unstable nutrients than boiling. Medicinal species, especially tough polypore conks, are best well-boiled. Most of the active constituents are associated with cell wall structures and may be released, becoming more available to express their healing properties, after simmering for 45 minutes to over an hour. Other active constituents such as terpenes are also more soluble in very hot water and are relatively stable to heat. It is not known for certain whether vitamins and minerals play a significant role in the healing properties of medicinal fungi, but again, immune-enhancing minerals, such as germanium and zinc, are more accessible to the human system after cooking.

Antinutritional Properties of Mushrooms

It is important to consider anti-nutritional factors that may be present in raw mushrooms. For instance, it is known that *A. bisporus* and *P. ostreatus* contain hemagglutinins that have been shown to interfere with protein absorption in rats and have even produced lesions in the small intestine. After cooking at 100 degrees C for 1 hour they did not produce lesions. It is probably wise to cook most wild mushrooms that are eaten in any quantity. Besides just a taste to aid in identification of the species, I only eat three wild mushrooms raw—*Agaricus campestris*, the meadow mushroom, *Trametes versicolor*, turkey tail, and *Tremella spp.*, witch's butter. I find them mild and delicious and have never experienced abdominal discomfort after ingesting them. I have tried oyster mushrooms raw but found them distinctly unappealing, which is interesting, because they are one of my favorites when cooked properly.

Mushroom Recipes

Stuffed Shiitakes

1 dozen shiitakes

1 onion

1/2 cup celery

1 cup bread crumbs

1/2 dozen wild mushrooms (oyster, honey, etc.)

chopped parsley

2 tblsp olive oil

2 cloves garlic

1/2 tsp tamari

1/3-2/3 cups parmesan

paprika

Cut the stems off shiitakes and chop them finely. Chop the onion and celery (finely) and sauté (in a little olive oil) with the garlic. When onions turn transparent, add the shiitake stems, tamari, plus 1/2 dozen chopped honey or oyster mushrooms, and sauté with the bread crumbs and 1/3 to 2/3 cup of parmesan cheese for 3 or 4 minutes. Stuff the shiitakes with the filling, sprinkle with chopped parsley and paprika and place on a cookie sheet, and bake at 375 degrees for 15 minutes; then place under broiler for 1 minute and serve.

Breakfast Tofu– Mushroom Scramble

3 tblsp olive oil

1 green or red pepper

1/4 cup cabbage

1 cake tofu

1/2 cup cooked rice

2 tblsp nutritional yeast

1 tsp oregano

1 onion

1 stalk celery

1 cup shiitake or oyster mushrooms

2 tblsp tamari

2 handfuls chard or kale

1 tsp basil

parsley, cilantro, or green onions

In 3 tblsp olive oil sauté the chopped onion, diced green or red pepper, chopped celery, and chopped cabbage; lastly add the cup of sliced shiitake or oyster mushrooms. Cook until nearly tender, then add diced tofu and sprinkle with tamari. When tofu begins to brown, add the cooked rice, 2 handfuls chopped greens, nutritional yeast, basil, and oregano. When ready, top with chopped parsley, cilantro, or onion greens.

Mushroom Barley Soup

1/2 cup cooked barley

4 tblsp tamari

3 cloves garlic

1 lb wild mushrooms

1/2 tsp salt

1 1/2 cups stock or water

1 cup onion, chopped

3 tblsp olive oil

black pepper to taste

Cook barley in 1 1/2 cups stock or water until tender. Add 5 cups water and tamari. Saute chopped onion and 3 cloves minced garlic in olive oil. When onions are clear, add 1 pound sliced shiitake, cauliflower mushroom, honey mushrooms, or oyster mushrooms and 1/2 tsp salt. When tender, add to barley. Apply freshly ground black pepper liberally and simmer covered for 20 minutes.

Boletus Burritos

Steam 1 8-oz package of tempeh for 3 minutes. Sprinkle the tempeh with tamari and place it in a skillet brushed with olive oil; sauté lightly on each side for 2 minutes. When browned, cut the tempeh into 1/2" strips and set aside.

Steam 1 head chard and 1 thinly sliced red onion until chard is tender. Place it in a bowl with 3 tblsp Red Star yeast, 1 tblsp olive oil, 2 tblsp vinegar, 1/2 tsp tamari, and some crumbled feta cheese.

Sauté thinly-sliced *Boletus edulis* (you may substitute chanterelles, cauliflower, or honey mushrooms, etc.) in a small amount of olive oil and a generous amount of garlic.

Warm tortillas in a skillet and fill with the tempeh, mushrooms, and chard.

Mushroom Leek Soup

In 4 tblsp olive oil saute 1 cup chopped onion, 1 cup chopped leeks, 1 cup diced carrots, 1 cup chopped celery, 2 cups sliced shiitake or oyster mushrooms, and 6 medium diced potatoes until onions are transparent. Pour in 1 quart stock, 2 tsp salt, 1 tsp basil, 1 tsp dill seeds, 1 tsp caraway seeds, 1/2 tsp paprika, and simmer 50 minutes. Add 1 cup milk.

A modification of this recipe follows.

Christopher's Late Winter, Early Spring Nettles and Chanterelle Soup

Gingerly pick the nettle tops (about 3-5 pairs of leaves down the stem) with clippers. Use gloves to protect tender skin, though a few stings are part of the ritual of spring nettle-picking and actually have a healing effect, activating blood and preventing arthritis and neuralgia, according to traditional medicine. Place the nettles into paper bags. Nearby, neatly cut off about a dozen fresh chanterelles under oaks and brush leaves over the cut stems as a way of showing respect. Place into mushroom basket and give abundant thanks for the gifts of the earth. Note: chanterelles from the store are not quite as fun but will serve nicely.

continued...

Christopher's Late Winter, Early Spring Nettles and Chanterelle Soup

At home, cook a soup stock with chicken, or with stir-fried onions, garlic, seaweed, and herbs. Add the chanterelles sliced into pieces of desired size to the stir-fry, and when done, combine with about 3 quarts of water. Add a variety of fresh vegetables (such as carrots, potatoes, squash, burdock root, etc.), 2 medium-sized leeks, and simmer for about 20 minutes. Dip out about a quart of the soup stock and blend with enough fresh trimmed nettles to fill the blender to a puree. Add this back into the soup stock and simmer for another 15-20 minutes. Serve with good hearty bread if desired.

This soup is as nutritious as it is delightful to the palate. The nettles are thought by many herbalists to build the blood because of their high mineral content; the burdock is traditionally recommended to stimulate liver and digestive function and has been reported to have antimutagenic effects (Morita, 1985); and the chanterelles soothe and nourish the liver and the eyes according to TCM.

Mushroom Paté

Preheat oven to 350F. Toss together 3 cups wild mushrooms, sliced, 1 tblsp. chopped garlic, 1 tblsp. chopped green onions, and 2 tblsp. balsamic vinegar. Roast for 15 minutes.

Roast 1 cup of shelled walnuts for 5 minutes. In a covered saucepan, cook 1 cup of red lentils in 2 cups water until soft, about 20 minutes; drain.

In a food processor or blender combine mushrooms, lentils, herbs, 1/4 cup olive oil, and walnuts. Pureé until smooth. Serve with crackers

Polenta with Chanterelles and Feta

Bring 4 cups water to boil in a heavy pot. In a small skillet simmer for 3 minutes 2 cup coarsely chopped chanterelles, 1 tblsp. fresh parsley, 1 tblsp. fresh thyme, 2 cloves chopped garlic, and 1 tblsp. tamari. Add pepper to taste.

To boiling water slowly add polenta in a stream, stirring constantly to avoid burning. Turn heat to low, simmer for 15-30 minutes, or until polenta pulls away from sides of pan.

After polenta has cooked, add mushrooms and 1/2 cup feta cheese. Simmer 3 minutes more. Pour into a non-stick pan and cool. Cut into pieces and broil, toast, or grill. (You may hold it in a double boiler until ready to serve.

Medicinal Fungi Monographs

The following monographs and additional charts present information on some of the better-known species of medicinal mushrooms, including the traditional uses, chemical constituents, pharmacology, current uses, toxicology, and other relevant data. Most of the information comes from China, Japan, Europe, and published materials from other parts of the world. We have been comprehensive in our collection of material, and our search for information, especially on the historical and cultural uses, is on-going. This material will eventually be incorporated into a second edition. As can be seen from the bibliography, we consulted nearly 900 articles and books.

We have also gathered stories and information from practitioners of Traditional Chinese Medicine and others with experience with useful fungi. Finally, I have added my own personal experience with a number of species gathered over the last 20 years. I have identified, harvested, extracted, and eaten many of the following mushrooms, and used some in a clinical setting.

Most of the species are either available in natural food stores, from Chinese herb dealers (see resource section), or in the wild, and all have a history of human use, sometimes for thousands of years, and have shown positive physiological activity in scientific studies.

The chemistry of fungi is a fascinating area of research in itself. It is interesting to note that many steroid compounds have been isolated from genera such as

Amanita, Rhizopus, Polyporus, Hydnum, Fomes, and *Ganoderma.* For a review of these compounds, see the *List of Fungal Products* by Shibata et al (1964). Generally speaking, low molecular-weight compounds from Basidiomycetes, such as terpenes and steroids (which are more alcohol-soluble), have antitumor activity, while high molecular-weight compounds such as proteins, polysaccharides, and lipopolysaccharides (which are better extracted with hot water) may have antibiotic, cyctostatic, immunostimulating, virostatic, antiallergic, hypoglycemic, antilipemic, and hypotensive properties in addition to antitumor activity (Lindequist, 1990).

A list of terms used commonly in the ensuing monographs is given below in the Appendix on page 202. In order to avoid repetition, I shall define them in the Appendix rather than explain them in parenthetical statements throughout the text. An understanding of these terms will greatly enhance comprehension of the information presented on pharmacological activity.

A word about such information as "Taste and Energy" and traditional contraindications found in the individual monographs. This is included to help health practitioners and herbalists who use a traditional system of energetics to determine the correct use and dosage for a given individual patient. The information was gathered from Chinese works on medicinal herbs, such as Bensky & Gamble (1993), Liu and Bau (1980), Hsu (1986), and from the author's own experience.

Gifts of Forest and Field, from One Thousand American Fungi by Charles McIlvaine, 1902

AMANITA MUSCARIA (LINN.:FR.) PERS.:HOOKER

(musca=fly, amanita=Galen's name for an ancient edible species, perhaps after Mt. Amanus)

FLY AGARIC

Synonyms
Agaricus muscarius Pers.

Other Common Names
Fly amanita; in Japan it is called "beni-tengu-take" (scarlet long-nosed goblin mushroom) (Ott, 1976).

Description and Habitat
One of the most striking of fungi, it has a bright red cap scattered regularly with white (or sometimes yellow) dots. These are the most obvious identifying features.

Amanita muscaria stamp from Bulgaria.

Like other Amanitas, there is a ring on the stalk and a scaly, attached volval cup at the bottom. The spore print is white, and in mature fruiting bodies the gills are free from the stalk. Fly agaric grows in woods, usually mycorrhizal with pine, spruce, fir, birch, and aspen (Arora, 1986).

Range
Common throughout the northern hemisphere and abundant in pine plantations in the southern hemisphere (New Zealand, Australia, etc.).

History
A quote from a traditional legend of the Koryak tribe of Kamchatka, Siberia goes as follows: "Then the Big-Raven said, 'Let the Agaric remain on earth, and let my children see what it will show them.'" Fly agaric derives its name from the ancients who mixed it with milk to stupefy flies (Cooke, 1977). *Amanita* has traditionally been used for epilepsy and to soothe spinal irritations (Rolfe & Rolfe, 1925), and by the Russians and Vikings as a hallucinogen (Ramsbottom, 1953).

For centuries, the consumption of *A. muscaria* was practiced among native peoples of West Siberia, such as the Khanty, from the Taimyr peninsula, and nations on the continent east of a line drawn through the mouth of the Kolyma River and on the Kamchatka peninsula, including the Chukchi, the Koryak, the Eskimos, and Russians (Saar, 1991b). The custom is still practiced today, and the mushroom is considered a "supernatural being."

Although the use of *A. muscaria* to enter into the world of supernatural beings and communicate with them is often found among the highest and most sacred persons, it is also eaten by all classes, including the common people. The mushroom was also used in magical rites, associated with such activities as communication with the souls of the dead, discovery of the name of a newborn child, to aid in assessing a dangerous situation and overcoming it, for the interpretation of dreams, for predicting the future, seeing the past, and visiting other worlds (Saar, 1991b). *A. muscaria* was also used by healers to divine the nature of illness. In this case, it is thought that the spirit of the mushroom enters the shaman or wise woman who then speaks and acts through them. The consumption of the mushroom is said to give the eater ample courage to communicate with the awesome spirit world and to meet powerful spirits, just as the bear eats it in order to have courage during mating. Songs were often sung in order to make a connection with spirits. The following is a Khanty song which was reported by Saar (1991b).

> Oh you little gold-stiped fly-agaric, chao-chao-chao,
> Such tidings you brought me, chao-chao-chao,
> Little patterned-stiped fly-agaric, chao-chao-chao,
> Many messages, many words you have, chao-chao-chao,
> (An unknown word) is placed on golden grass, chao-chao-chao,
> Little duckling, little duck, chao-chao-chao,
> One half of you walks on the ground, chao-chao-chao,
> The other half of you walks on the ground, chao-chao-chao,
> So one must rock, chao-chao-chao,
> You are among fly agarics a little fly-agaric.

The mushroom was also eaten to increase physical endurance for working, hunting, resisting cold, and traveling long distances by foot.

A. muscaria was used in homeopathic and herbal practice in early 19th century European and American medicine. For instance, an extract of fly agaric was prescribed by the Eclectics in the early 19th century for night sweats due to debilitating disease as well as "profuse sweating during the daytime." The dose given was 5 drops of a 1% solution of extract (Felter & Lloyd, 1898). Culbreth (1927), another Eclectic doctor, reported that this fungus "reduces force and frequency of pulse, contracts muscles of intestines and bladder, increases abdominal secretions, causes dyspnea, paralysis, death." He also said that it is given "for intestinal torpor, duodenal catarrh, diabetes, antidote to atropine to replace physostigmine." As *Agaricus muscarius* it was introduced into the *Homeopathic Pharmacopeia* in 1828 (HPUS 8, 1978).

Chemistry
It is now known that *A. muscaria* contains a variety of potentially hallucinogenic and toxic compounds, and the closely-related *Amanita pantherina* produces them in even higher concentrations. It contains the isoxazole derivative, ibotenic acid, as well as its decarboxylation product muscimole (not present in the *fresh* fruiting body) and the related muscazone (Tyler, 1977). The quaternery compounds muscaridine and muscarine have also been identified, but the alkaloids bufotenine, atropine, hyoscyamine, and scopolamine reported in earlier studies are now known not to occur (Falch et al, 1984; Moore-Landecker, 1972; Tyler, 1965; Tyler & Gröger, 1964).

Pharmacology
The quaternery compound muscarine is found in trace amounts but probably does not have hallucinogenic properties; however, it can produce such unpleasant side effects as nausea, vomiting, diarrhea, perspiration, excess salivation, and tearing (Cooke, 1977).

Muscimol is another similar compound that may not be present in the fresh fruiting body but is a breakdown product of ibotenic acid produced in the body after its ingestion. Muscimol is also closely related chemically to GABA (gamma-aminobutyric acid), a major inhibitory neurotransmitter in the brain. Both of the compounds affect brain concentrations of other neurotransmitters, such as NE, 5-HT, and Dopamine in the same manner as LSD. Tests with humans have shown that a large amount of ibotenic acid taken orally could be detected in the urine within 90 minutes, and the breakdown product, muscimol, is probably excreted in this manner as well, possibly leading to a stronger effect from the urine products than the original mushroom. This seems to support stories of people in Siberia drinking the urine of *A. muscaria* ingestors in order to maximize or prolong the hallucinogenic effects (Ramsbottom, 1953). Reports from Siberia say that a dose of *A. muscaria* can be recycled through 4 or 5 people (Ott, 1976). Ott reports that because a higher concentration of the water-soluble toxins are concentrated in the skin on the cap, people often peel this off and parboil the remainder when preparing the mushroom for food, though this practice is not recommended. Muscarine has a cholinergic effect on the peripheral nervous system; however, it does not enter the central nervous system (Falch et al, 1984).

These compounds are also known to produce such unpleasant effects as nausea, vomiting, diarrhea, perspiration, tearing, and salivation (Cooke, 1977). It has also been theorized that the hallucinogenic effects of the two *Amanita* species might be based on the cyclic acid, muscimol, working synergistically with the two cyclic amino acids, muscazone and ibotenic acid. Variations in the vision-producing effects that researchers have experienced might be due to differing levels of active compounds as well as the potential of the individual to "suspend belief" and allow the experience to unfold without the burden of the modern skeptical mind (Cooke, 1977).

It is interesting to note that studies show the ethanol extract of sporophore inhibits the growth of sarcoma 180 in mice, but it is quite toxic and kills insects (Ying et al, 1987).

Human Clinical Studies
No data.

Toxicity
Considered poisonous by many writers. Three undried fruiting bodies are said to be lethal by some cultures in Siberia and Eastern Russia, but among cultures who use them regularly, up to 21 fruiting bodies are reported to be eaten. Between 1 and 11 is more common (Saar, 1993). Among people who do not use *A. muscaria* culturally, the fungus should be considered potentially dangerous. Extreme caution should be exercised when ingesting even one-half of a fruiting body, and the author is not suggesting that the reader should experiment with them—I am simply reporting on the cultural and medical uses.

Uses in Traditional Medicine
The taste and energy is sweet and cool. In certain areas of Japan, quantities of *A. muscaria* are dried, pickled, then thoroughly washed prior to ingestion as a food (Ott, 1976), though this is not recommended due to its inherent toxicity.

This species is also used as a visionary and divinatory substance. The culture and attitude of the person taking it are said to be directly related to the quality of the experience. One should have reverence and humility, and it is important to tell the mushroom spirit the purpose of its use, even in a loud voice (Saar, 1991b).

Medical Uses

Homeopaths currently use *Amanita* (in homeopathic dilution only!) to treat chorea and skin afflictions; it is specific for bunions and sunstroke, and it is reported to clear up some types of cataracts (HPUS 8, Ramsbottom, 1953).

Preparation and Dosage

For medical use, in homeopathic dilution only (*Homeopathic Pharmacopoeia of the U.S.*, 8th ed. under "Bug Agaric," *Agaricus muscarius*).

Among peoples who used *A. muscaria* for the traditional uses detailed above, the young fruiting bodies picked before the caps were fully expanded were considered the most effective, particularly for increasing endurance, but older specimens were considered better to induce hallucinations or euphoria (Saar, 1991b). The fungus is eaten in a variety of forms, and which one is best depends on the local customs of the people who are using it. Saar (1991b) mentions fifteen ways of administration—namely eating it raw, fried, cooked, dried, in the form of an extract or tea, drinking the urine of a person who has already ingested the mushroom, or eating the flesh of a reindeer who has eaten it. The most common way of eating *A. muscaria* was after drying, because it is thought that fresh mushrooms were more poisonous. Over the last 20 years, I have often heard this idea in speaking with people who have experience with the mushrooms in the western part of the U.S. Fireweed (*Epilobium angustifolium* L.) was sometimes added to the mushroom preparation to reduce toxicity or potentiate its action.

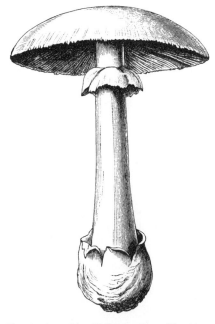

The number of fruiting bodies consumed at one session varies, but it is generally reported to be between 1/2 to 11 (Saar, 1991b). For hallucinations, 3-11 mature fruiting bodies are recommended; for facilitating work, 3-5 young mushrooms; for simply inducing a pleasant state, 3 fruiting bodies are sufficient.

Related Species

Amanita pantherina (DC:Fr.) Secr. has a similar chemistry but is reported to contain more ibotenic acid and muscimol than *A. muscaria* (Ott, 1976). Amanita is a dangerous genus to experiment with! Some of its members, such as *A. phalloides*, *A. ocreata*, *A. bisporigera* Atkinson, and *A. verna* are **deadly**. Learn to recognize these before experimenting with any gilled fungi for edible or medicinal purposes.

Fig. 6: *Amanita phalloides* from *The Natural History of Plants* by Kerner & Oliver, 1896.

Procurement
Amanita muscaria is available in homeopathic dilution where homeopathic remedies are sold, e.g. natural food stores and some pharmacies. The fresh fungi can be
picked in the summer and fall under conifers and birches in many parts of the
world.

ARMILLARIA MELLEA (VAHL.:FR.) KUMMER

(armilla=a ring; mellea=honey-colored)

HONEY MUSHROOM, MI HUAN JUN

Synonyms
Armillariella mellea (Vahl.:Fr.) Kar.

Other Common Names
It is called oak root fungus in California because of its affinity for oaks (Arora, 1986) and is also known as honey-tuft fungus (Ramsbottom, 1953). Other names include honey fungus, honey agaric, halimasch, shoeshing fungus, and honey cap (Liu and Bau, 1980).

Description and Habitat
This honey-colored mushroom is actually a group of very similar species collectively called the honey mushroom (Arora, 1994). It is extremely variable in color and habit and often grows in clusters on dead wood (sometimes submerged, giving the appearance that they are growing on the ground), and it has dark fibers on its cap that tend to concentrate towards the center. It also has a white or honey-colored ring toward the top of the stalk, though this may be absent. The yellow-capped variety is most often found on hardwoods, while the pinkish-brown variety grows on conifer wood (Miller, 1979; Arora, 1986). In Asia, the fungus forms an interesting symbiotic relationship with the medicinal orchid, *Gastrodia elata* Blume in parts of Asia.

Range
Honey mushrooms are cosmopolitan, widely distributed throughout the northern hemisphere. They are among the most common mushrooms, often occurring in large numbers in the late summer and fall.

History
No data.

Chemistry
The major constituents isolated to date include the sesquiterpenoid aromatic esters, armillaricin, armillarigin, armillarikin, armillarilin, armillarinin, armillaripin, armillaribin, armillaritin, armillarivin, and armillarizin; and the nor-sesquiterpenoid esters, armillasin and armillatin (Yang & Cong, 1988; Yang et al, 1989a,b; 1990a,b,c; 1991a,b). A group of antibacterial and antifungal sesquiterpene aryl esters melleolide, armillol, 4-0-methylmelleolide, and judeol, have been isolated from this species, as well as the sesquiterpene aryl esters, armillyl everninate and arnamiol (Donnelly et al, 1985; Donnelly et al,1986; Junshan et al, 1984; Yang et al, 1984.) In the mycelium extract, armillane (Donnelly & Hutchinson, 1990) is present. The volatile organic acids found in *A. mellea* consist of mostly propionic, valeric, isocaproic, and caproic acids, with valeric being the most abundant of them. Isobutyric, butyric, isovaleric, and heptanoic acids are minor constituents (Hong et al, 1990).

The nutritional value of honey mushrooms is significant, and because of their abundance, may be a good dietary supplement. I have dried them for use throughout the winter and early summer months. Published analyses show that the protein content varies from 11.4-29.2%, total carbohydrate, 75.9%, calories 384 (kcal), crude fiber, 5.8%, calcium 0.27-0.4 mg/100 g, phosphorus 8.4-12.5 mg/100g, and potassium 32.6-43.4 mg/100 g.

Pharmacology
A. mellea has shown antibiotic action (*in vitro*) against the pathogenic bacteria *Staphylococcus aureus, Bacillus cereus*, and *B. subtilis* (Richard, 1970). Armillaric acid, recently isolated from *A. mellea*, inhibits Gram-positive bacteria and yeast (Obuchi et al, 1990), while a polypeptide dextran exhibits antitumor activity (Ying et al, 1987). *In vitro* studies with the mycelial extract of *Armillaria mellea* also showed significant antibacterial activity against Gram-positive bacteria (Donnelly, 1986).

Animal studies on *A. mellea* reported that it decreases heart rate, reduces peripheral and coronary vascular resistance, increases cerebral blood flow (Chang & But, 1986), exhibits a cerebral-protective effect with AMG-1 (a compound isolated from *A. mellea*) (Watanabe et al, 1990), and increases coronary oxygen efficiency without altering blood pressure (Zhang et al, 1985; Chang & But, 1986). In addition, it has demonstrated sedative and anticonvulsant activity (Chang & But, 1986). Polysaccharides from *A. mellea* have helped to protect animals against the negative side effects of exposure to ionizing radiation (Wang et al, 1989).

Human Clinical Studies
A. mellea has been reported to reduce symptoms of essential and renal hypertension, as well as neurasthenia (Chang & But, 1986).

Toxicity
May cause nausea especially if not well-cooked or consumed with alcohol; poisonings may also be related to host (e.g. buckeye) (Arora, 1994). In some people the fungus may cause diarrhea (though I have not observed it), reflected in the German name Hallimasch, said to be a contraction for "Hell im Arsch" (Tyler, 1977).

Uses in Traditional Medicine
In TCM, it is considered sweet and cold and is recommended as a nutritive tonic (Liu and Bau, 1980). The herb is most active in the liver, lung, stomach, and large intestine systems (Liu and Bau, 1980). A tablet product of the mycelia is produced in China and is said to affect the nervous system (anti-convulsant, analgesic effect), similar to the plant Rhizoma Gastrodia, with which it forms a symbiotic relationship. It is also said to strengthen the lungs, intestines, and stomach; prevents dry skin; and aids leg pains, lumbago pain, rickets, and epilepsy (Liu and Bau, 1980; Ying et al, 1987).

Medical Uses

In TCM, *A. mellea* is said to prevent some respiratory and digestive tract conditions, including gastritis and painful digestion, if taken on a regular basis. It is used in China to improve vision and to counteract ophthalmia and night blindness (perhaps due, in part, to its high vitamin A content). In China, tablets of *A. mellea* are said to increase the blood flow to the brain and heart and are recommended for treating dizziness, neurasthenia, insomnia, tinnitus, epilepsy, and numbness of the limbs (Yang & Jong, 1989).

Preparation and Dosage

Use the whole mushroom *ad lib* in stir-frys, soups, stews, tea, etc. Or take 30-90 grams of the dried powder in capsules (2 "00" caps 3 x daily), or 30-90 grams sprinkled on food, or as a tea. Of the specially-produced tablets (250 mg), which are created by a "deep layer" fermentation process, 3-5 tablets are taken daily. For home use, make a powdered extract as described on page 49-50, and take about 400 mg/day—about 2 "00" capsules filled with the powder, one morning and one at night.

Preparations and Recipes

The honey mushroom can be preserved in oil or vinegar (Liu and Bau, 1980), or dried and then frozen (to stop insect damage). It should be dried quickly and thoroughly, for it has a tendency to turn powdery from insect damage when left sitting in a semi-fresh state.

Related Species

A. tabescens (cop.:Fr.) Sing. of Europe and Eastern North America; it is similar but lacks a ring (Arora, 1994), and the European species *A. bulbosa*, is closely related, but its medicinal qualities are unknown. In China, tablets are made from an extract of the mycelia from this species, which is said to contain the coumarin derivative armillarisin A. Pharmacologically, it is reported to decrease the tension of the sphincter of Oddi, the duodenal sphincter, and increases bile flow (Yang & Jong, 1989).

Notes

It was not possible to cultivate the highly prized medicinal orchid, Tian Ma, until the symbiosis with the honey mushroom was discovered.

Procurement

Honey mushrooms grow commonly and abundantly on ornamental trees, fruit trees, and on live and dead trees in the forest throughout the world. It is best to pick any mushrooms at least 100 feet away from a busy road, and to avoid areas like parks that can be sprayed with toxic chemicals to control weeds or the mushroom itself. I recently spoke with the horticulturist at the UCLA botanical gardens in Southern California, where there is a problem with *Armillariella* attacking valuable trees and shrubs. His method of controlling the fungus was to withhold all water or at least use only a minimum of water, especially on native trees and shrubs which are drought-tolerant, depending mainly on natural rainfall.

Dried honey mushroom fruiting bodies, and possibly tableted products, are not generally available through commercial channels. They can be ordered through some Chinese herb dealers under the name mi huan jun.

AURICULARIA POLYTRICHA (MONTAGNE) SACC.
AURICULARIA AURICULA (L.:HOOK.) UNDERW.

(auricula=ear) [Both species were mentioned under mu erh in the *Pen T'sao*, according to Read (1936), and they are used interchangeably today.]

MU ERH (WOOD EAR), JEW'S EAR

Synonyms
A. polytricha—Hirneola polytricha Fr. (Bn. Samp.); *A. auricula—A. auricula-judae* Schrot., *A. sambucina* Mart., *Tremella auricula* L., *Hirneola auricula-judae*, *Tremella cyathiformis* (Linn.).

Other Common Names
Jew's ear (a contraction of Judas' ear), wooden ear, or tree ear (Liu and Bau, 1980); in Germany, Judasohr. In Japan *A. polytricha*

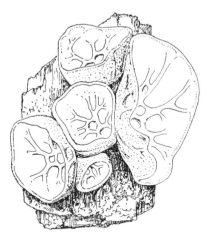

Fig. 7: *Auricula auricularia* from *British Basidiomycetes* by W. G. Smith, 1908.

is called *kikurage*, meaning an edible mushroom (Misaki et al, 1981), and in China it is known as *Yung Nge* or *Muk Nge* (Miller, 1979). In TCM, it is called *Mu erh* (wood ears) or *yun-erh* (cloud ears) (*Barefoot Doctor's Manual*, 1977); also known in China as Liu er and Mo-er (Ying et al, 1987; Agarwal et al, 1982).

Description and Habitat
This jelly fungus grows mostly on wood (either live or dead), often in broadleaf tree groves or on fir trees. The fruiting body is semi-translucent, brown, cup or ear shaped, and rubbery in texture (except when dry, in which case it turns quite hard).

Range
A. auricula is common throughout the United States. *A. polytricha* has been reported from Louisiana south to Argentina. Also throughout Asia and Europe. Widespread.

History
Both have been used for thousands of years in China (McIlvaine, 1973), frequently to treat hemorrhoids and as a stomach tonic (Ying et al, 1987). Traditionally, there are 5 kinds of mu erh that are used, which are detailed in Table 3, page 22 (Bretschneider, 1895).

In European tradition, *A. auricularia* was boiled in milk, beer, vinegar, or any other convenient liquid and taken for inflammations of the throat (Rolfe & Rolfe, 1925), as well as applied locally for eye irritations because of its high mucilage content and ability to hold medicated eye water (Cooke, 1862; Dragendorff, 1898). The appearance of the fungus, which is similar to the fauces of the throat may have played a role in its eventual acceptance as a throat medicine. Linnaeus mentions wood ear in his *Materia Medica* (1749) as being refrigerant, drying, and astringent, and says that it is used in eye complaints, inflammations, and heart pain (angina). The name *Judas' ear* derives from a legend that holds these ear-shaped fungi appeared as a sort of curse on the elder tree on which Judas hanged himself (Rolfe & Rolfe, 1925).

Chemistry

The nutritional content of 100 g of dry *A. auricula* is as follows: 10.6 g protein; 0.2 g fat; 65 g carbohydrates; 7.0 g course fiber; 5.8 g ash; 375 mg calcium; 201 mg phosphorous; 185 mg iron; and 0.03 mg carotene (Ying et al, 1987). Various active polysaccharides such as heteropolysaccharide glucans (Misaki et al, 1981) and acidic heteroglycans have been isolated (Ukai et al,1983).

Pharmacology

Polysaccharides from *A. auricula* have stimulated DNA and RNA synthesis by human lymphocytes *in vitro* (Xia et al, 1987); this provides some support for the fungus' traditional use as an immune tonic. *A. auricula*'s polysaccharides have also shown the following effects and activities in studies on mice and rats: antimutagenic but not antihepatitis (Zhou et al, 1989b); anti-ulcer, with little effect on the gastric acid secretion and pepsin activity (Xue et al, 1987); anticoagulant (Sheng & Chen, 1987); lowered total cholesterol, triglyceride, and lipid levels (Sheng & Chen, 1989); possibly antidiabetic and might have a cytoprotective effect on cells of pancreatic islets in mice (Xue et al, 1989); also reported to be anti-aging, by decreasing the lipofuscin content of the heart muscles, increasing SOD activity of the brain and liver (thus clearing free-radicals and possibly reducing tissue damage), and inhibiting monoamine oxidase B (MAO inhibitor) in the brain (Zhou et al, 1989a); immunostimulatory, antiradical, antileukocytopenic, and anti-inflammatory (Xia & Chen, 1989); prevention of egg implantation in animals, thus terminating early and mid-pregnancy (He & Chen 1991.); and antitumor action on implanted sarcoma 180 (Misaki et al, 1981; Tobata et al, 1981); anti-aggregatory activity on blood platelets, which might make it beneficial for coronary heart disease (Agarwal et al, 1982); antibiotic (Brian, 1951).

Human Clinical Studies

No data.

Toxicity, Contraindications

May cause allergic reactions in susceptible individuals, but this is rare. One case history reports that after consuming 250 g of the fresh fruiting body of *A. auricula*, a human male experienced "solar dermatitis," i.e., upon exposure to sunlight he developed flushing on the exposed parts of his body, with significant swelling, blisters, and exudation. He recovered and was discharged ten days later after treatment with pharmaceutical medications (Gu, 1986). Owing to possible anti-fertility effects (He & Chen, 1991), *A. auricula* should not be taken by pregnant or lactating women and those planning to conceive.

Uses in Traditional Medicine

In TCM, mu erh is considered mild and sweet; it activates the blood, stops pain. It is used to increase physical and mental energy. It is considered specific for bleeding—especially excessive uterine bleeding, and bleeding hemorrhoids, as well as abdominal and tooth pain (Hanssen & Schädler, 1982).

Medical Uses
It is beneficial for lumbago, debility after childbirth, pains, muscle spasms, poor circulation, dysentery with blood, leukorrhea (white vaginal discharge), excess mucus, nausea, slow healing of wounds in the aged, and for mushroom poisoning (Liu and Bau, 1980). In the *Barefoot Doctor's Manual* (1977) it is said to strengthen the lungs.

A. auricula is used to treat hemorrhoids, as an anticoagulant, to stimulate bowel movements, and to help build energy (Ying et al, 1987).

Preparation and Dosage
Take 15 g of the dried mushroom in decoction as tea 2X/day. Or mix the powder with honey to make pills and take them twice daily. You may also add 60 g to the recipe for "Wei Qi Soup" given on page 45.

PREPARATIONS AND RECIPES:

◆ For excessive leukorrhea, powder well-dried fruiting bodies, mix 9 g of fine powder in boiling water and drink 2X/day (Liu and Bau,1980). Add honey or other sweetener to taste.

◆ As a postpartum tonic, soak 30 g *A. auricula* in vinegar and drink 5-6 g, 3X/day (Liu and Bau, 1980; Ying, 1987).

◆ For excessive phlegm and nausea, concoct 7-8 large wood ears by simmering and drink 2X/day (Liu and Bau, 1980).

◆ For bloody feces, uterine bleeding, or bleeding piles, boil the fungus (15 g) in water with 15 g sugar (or substitute 1 tsp honey) over low heat and take 2X/day, 1 cup at a time (Liu and Bau, 1980). For piles of the elderly that won't heal—mix the powder with water to make a paste, spread on gauze and apply on the spot (Ying, 1987).

◆ For hypertension, vascular sclerosis, and ophthalmic bleeding, soak 3 grams of mu erh overnight in water, then steam it for 1-2 hours. Add honey to taste (optional) and drink 1 cup before bed (Ying, 1987).

Related Species
A. polytricha and *A. auricula* (Liu and Bau, 1980) are used interchangeably and both are cultivated in China. *A. polytricha* has a tradition as a folk medicine in the Orient for coughs and for the improvement of the general physical condition (Pacioni, 1981). Studies on mice have shown that *A. mesenterica* (Dicks.) Pers. contains polysaccharides that inhibit the growth of both sarcoma 180 and Ehrlich carcinoma (Ying et al, 1987).

Procurement

Wood ear can be commonly purchased in grocery stores that emphasize Chinese food products. I have seen packages of dried fruiting bodies throughout Chinatown in San Francisco. A number of tableted products are available through Chinese herb dealers under the name mu erh. A few western herb products may contain this species as a minor component.

BOLETUS EDULIS (Bull:Fr.)

(boletus=the best kinds of mushrooms;
edulis=edible)

CEPE, KING BOLETE

Synonyms
none

Other Common Names
Steinpilz, cepe.

Description and Habitat
B. edulis grows under conifers as well as
hardwoods and broadleaf trees (Arora,1986).

Range
China, Europe, Russia, and throughout
North America.

Fig. 8: *Boletus edulis*, from the *Illustrated Encyclopedia of Gardening* by George Nicholson, circa 1887.

History
Although various species of Boletus grow in the Bohemian Forest area and the people of Bohemia and Bavaria collect great quantities of them for food, the only species they accredit with cancer preventive properties is *B. edulis*. The folklore appeared to have proved out when studies at Sloan-Kettering Institute for Cancer Research in the U.S. found that among the species they had collected from Bohemia and screened for antitumor activity, only *B. edulis* was active (Lucas, 1960; Lucas, 1957).

Chemistry
No data.

Pharmacology
Extracts of the fruiting bodies have shown antitumor properties in mice (100% inhibition rate against sarcoma 180 and a 90% inhibition rate against Ehrlich carcinoma) (Ying et al, 1987; Lucas et al, 1957), which might be attributable to a peptide or protein. The mycelium of *Boletus edulis* does not appear to have anti-tumor properties (Lucas et al, 1957). Polysaccharides from *B. edulis* produced an antagonizing and neutralizing action on inflammation mediators. Administered to rats (10 or 25 mg/kg), polysaccharide A (a glucan) and B (a glucogalactomannan) showed membrane stabilizing and phlogistic exudate formation-inhibiting activity in the pleural cavity. In peripheral blood, eosinophils and neutrophiles increased and when administered in saline, the polysaccharides caused lymphocyte counts to decrease while lymphocytes increased in pleural fluid (Grzybek et al, 1992).

Human Clinical Studies
No data.

Toxicity
No data.

Uses in Traditional Medicine
In TCM, this fungus is considered to have a mild and salty taste. When used in "Tendon-easing pills," it has a positive effect on lumbago, leg pain, numbness in limbs, bone and tendon discomfort, tetany, and leukorrhea (Ying et al, 1987).

Medical Uses
None.

Doses
The fruiting body is considered a gourmet food and is eaten in quantity by mycophagists in soups, stews, and stir-frys whenever available. Taken 9 g, 3X daily, the powder is followed with "gauliapng" wine.

Preparations and Recipes
In China, the dried, unopened mushroom (93 g) is cooked with pork to treat leukorrhea (1 X/day X 7). The unopened mushroom baked with *Acanthopanax spinosua* Harms. provides a powder used by women in China to conceive (Liu and Bau, 1980).

Notes
B. edulis also contains 8 essential amino acids and is said to promote good health if taken regularly (Ying et al, 1987).

Related Species
B. speciosus Frost is used in TCM to treat flatulence and indigestion. The dried mushroom (6 g) is taken two times daily in the form of a simmered decoction. *Suillus cavipes* (Opat.) Kalchbr. is used in TCM to ease "tendons and veins," and to dispel cold and wind. This species is a major component of Tendon-easing Powder (Liu and Bau, 1980). *B. satanas* Lenz contains a toxic glycoprotein (Kretz et al, 1991).

Procurement
Dried or canned Cepes can be found in markets, especially ones specializing in gourmet foods. They grow commonly along the Pacific coast of the U.S., in Europe, and other parts of the world, fruiting in the summer and early to late fall. Commercial products for medicinal use are not available.

M. FYLLING

CLAVICEPS PURPUREA (Fr.) Tul.

(clav=club, ceps=head; purpurea=purple)

ERGOT

Synonyms
none

Other Common Names
Holy fire, *Siegle cornu, Secale cornutum*, spurred rye, Mutterkorn, Womb grain, St. Antony's fire, St. Martial's fire, and clavus (Liu and Bau, 1980; Arora, 1986).

Description and Habitat
The genus *Claviceps* includes 12-50 species, depending on the source consulted. *C. purpurea* is the source of ergot, the sclerotium that forms when this fungus parasitizes the ovaries of plants, usually grasses and cereal crops. Although *C. purpurea* has many hosts, medicinal ergot is obtained only from rye grain (Sastri et al, 1950).

Range
Worldwide.

History
Until the advent of modern agricultural practices, *C. purpurea* often invaded rye fields in Russia and eastern Europe, producing ergot, which was harvested with the grain. Animals and humans who consumed this contaminated grain frequently suffered from ergotism, a disease that produced either convulsions or gangrene. Large doses of ergot were known to induce nausea, vomiting, diarrhea, loss of consciousness, and even fatal respiratory collapse and heart failure, while ingesting smaller doses over a long period of time is thought to have produced gangrenous and/or convulsive ergotism (Sastri et al, 1950). During the Middle Ages, people unknowingly ate ergotized rye and suffered from a condition called *St. Anthony's fire* characterized by burning sensations in the hands and feet (produced by restriction of peripheral blood vessels) and hallucinations. Indeed one historian has suggested that the "voices" Joan of Arc heard and the Salermo witch trials were both products of ergot poisoning (Wallace, 1991). For a provocative yet classic discussion of ergot's use as a visionary drug in Europe, see Aldous Huxley's *The Doors of Perception* (1954). Today, the potential for ergot poisoning, known as ergotism, is understood, and therefore uncommon.

Despite its potential toxicity, ergot has been used medicinally both in Europe and China. It entered into the *London Pharmacopeia* in 1836 and was subsequently official in most pharmacopeias. It was official in the *U.S. Pharmacopeia* from 1820 until 1942. The 1907 *Merck Index* indicated its use for stimulating labor, difficult menstruation, internal hemorrhages, night-sweats, whooping cough, migraine, diabetes, epilepsy, and chronic cerebral congestion. For a discussion of further uses, see Felter and Lloyd (1898). Ergot fluid extract was still official in the *National Formulary* of the U.S. in 1965, but has largely been replaced with ergotamine tartrate, which is still official (Osol et al, 1955).

Chemistry

A number of alkaloids have been isolated from ergot, three of which are oxytocic and have important therapeutic actions—ergotamine, ergotoxine, really a mixture of 3 alkaloids (Reynolds, 1993) and ergometrine (Evans, 1989; Sastri et al, 1950; Ying et al, 1987). Lysergic acid is the nucleus of a number of the cited alkaloids, and lysergic acid diethylamide (LSD), the most potent hallucinogenic compound known, is a derivative of *C. purpurea* (Barron, 1967; Richards, 1969).

Pharmacology

The various physiological effects of ergot, let alone the purified alkaloid, are complex. Ergotamine has peripheral vasoconstrictor action, affects central serotonergic neurons, and in therapeutic doses potentiates epinephrine and norepinephrine, inhibiting the re-uptake of these amines after nerve stimulation (AMA, 1983). As early as the 16th century in Europe, and possibly much earlier in China, ergot was known for its ability to promote uterine contractions (Osol, 1955; Evans, 1989; Madaus, 1938).

Human Clinical Studies

A number of studies have been performed with various ergot derivatives, especially dihydroergotamine mesylate, which is used in the treatment and prophylaxis of migraine and with heparin in the prophylaxis of postoperative deep-vein thrombosis, as well as ergotamine tartrate and methysergide maleate for the treatment of migraine attacks and cluster headache (Reynolds, 1993).

Toxicity

Ergot is a very strong abortifacient and thus should be strictly avoided during pregnancy, except the third stage under the supervision of a practitioner trained in its use (Osol, et al, 1955; Liu and Bau, 1980; Ying et al, 1987).

Ergot and ergot liquid extract are considered less toxic than purified derivatives in small doses taken for short periods, except in susceptible individuals, particularly those with sepsis, hyperthyroidism, or impaired liver function (Osol, 1955). When taken in large doses (more than an ounce of the fluid extract), it may provoke vomiting, diarrhea, thirst, tachycardia, confusion, and coma. Taken chronically, it is dangerous, even though at first there are no symptoms. There are two forms of epidemic toxicity that have been described: (1) a gangrenous form causing agonizing pain in the extremities and (2) a more unusual nervous type causing convulsions (Reynolds, ed., 1993).

Uses in Traditional Medicine

C. purpurea has a sweet taste, followed by acridicity and a strong odor (Liu and Bau, 1980). In TCM, natural ergot alkaloids and their derivatives are used in the treatment of the ears (especially inner auditory tubes), eyes (corneas), lips, nose, and tongue. It is also used in the treatment of certain hyperthyroid diseases and as a preventive for dizziness due to motion sickness (Ying et al, 1987).

Medical Uses

In modern medicine ergot derivatives, especially ergotamine tartrate, are still used to induce abortions (by promoting uterine contractions), to decrease postpartum uterine bleeding, and for the treatment of migraine headaches (Zurich, 1993; Wallace, 1991). Dermatologists have used ergot to treat diseases that involve problems in regulation of the autonomic nervous system (Ying et al, 1987). Ergot itself is still official in the pharmacopeias of Austria, France, Romania, Russia, Turkey, and Australia (Reynolds, 1993).

Preparation and Dosage
150 mg to 500 mg—daily dose depends on type of condition being treated (Osol, 1955; Liu and Bau, 1980). Liquid extract, 0.6-1.2 ml (*British Pharmaceutical Codex*, 1954). Not recommended without the supervision of a practitioner trained in its use.

Notes
None.

Related Species
None.

Procurement
I have seen ergot growing in wild grass in England. It can be found in commercial fields of grain in Europe, Asia, and North America, and other parts of the world, especially where rainfall is plentiful. Extracts of ergot are available in homeopathic dilution, and isolated, purified alkaloids are sold as prescription drugs, e.g. ergotamine.

CORDYCEPS SINENSIS (BERK.) SACC. LINK
C. OPHIOGLOSSOIDES (EHR.:FR.)

(cord=club, ceps=heads; sinensis=from China);
(cord=club; ophi=snake, gloss=tongue)

CATERPILLAR FUNGUS, DEER FUNGUS PARASITE

Synonyms
none

Other Common Names
C. sinensis is commonly called caterpillar fungus or summer-plant, winter-worm, while *C. ophioglossoides* is known as club-head fungus (Liu and Bau, 1980; Pereira, 1843).

Description and Habitat
C. ophioglossoides is a small (2-6 cm), club-shaped parasite on the fruiting bodies of the truffle genus *Elaphomyces*. It is found in the soil of bamboo, oak, and pine woods (Arora, 1986; Ying et al, 1987).

C. sinensis is slightly larger (4-11cm) and is club- or finger-shaped. It is found on mountain tops above 3,000m high in cold and snowy grass marshlands of China (Ying et al, 1987; Liu and Bau, 1980).

Cordyceps spp. grow by infecting insect larvae, mature insects, or truffles with spores that germinate, sometimes before the cocoons are formed, thus preventing further growth of the larvae. The fruiting body of the *Cordyceps* eventually emerge from the

Cordyceps taylori from *The Natural History of Plants* by Kerner and Oliver, 1897.

anterior end of the dead host. *C. sinensis* grows on the larvae of Lepidoptera, especially the *Hepialus armoricanus* (Bat moth) (Ma et al, 1986; Liu and Bau, 1980). The Chinese consider this fungus to be a vegetable during the summer and an animal during the winter, giving it the name "summer-plant, winter-worm" (Pereira, 1843). Various methods of cultivating *Cordyceps* spp. have been studied in China, including submerged fermentation culture (Zhang et al, 1986; Liu and Bau, 1980).

Range
C. sinensis grows throughout Asia. *C. ophioglossoides* occurs fairly commonly in the eastern United States but is rare on the west coast; it also occurs in Asia and Europe. The related species *C. militaris* (L.:Fr.) Link and *C. capitata* grow on submerged caterpillars and are fairly common in parts of North America and Asia (Arora, 1986).

History

In ancient China, *Cordyceps sinensis* was used exclusively in the Emperor's palace, because it was very scarce. It was prepared by stuffing five drams of the fungus into the stomach of a duck and slowly roasting it over a fire until it was well cooked. Then the *Cordyceps* was removed, and the duck was eaten twice a day for 8-10 days (Pereira, 1843; Rolfe & Rolfe, 1925). Pereira (1843) reported in the *New York Journal of Medicine* that *C. sinensis* has properties similar to those of ginseng, being used to strengthen and rebuild the body after exhaustion or long-term illness. It was also used traditionally for impotence, neurasthenia, backache (Huang, 1993), and as an antidote for "opium poisoning" and to cure the habit of opium eating (Uphof, 1968).

Chemistry

C. sinensis contains 10.84% water; 8.4% fat; 25.32% coarse protein; 18.53% coarse fiber; 28.9% carbohydrates; and 4.1% ash. Its fat content consists of 13% saturated and 82.2% unsaturated fatty acids (31.69% oleic, 68.31% linoleic) (Ying et al, 1987). Uracil, uridine, adenine, and adenosine have been extracted from *C. sinensis* (Zhang & Li, 1987). From the water-soluble fraction of both species, cordycepic acid has been isolated and from *C. ophioglossoides*, the antibiotic compound, ophiocordin (Furuya et al, 1983). Also from this species three anti-tumor protein bound polysaccharides, CO-N, SN-C, and CO-1, have been identified (Ohmori, 1988a,b).

Pharmacology

C. sinensis caused a significant increase in erythroid progenitor cells and erythroid colony-forming units in the bone marrow of mice and given before (150 mg/kg X3) administration of an anticancer drug (harringtonine) that causes dramatic depletion of these erythroid cells, it prevented the decrease. While macrophage stimulation is a proposed cause of the increase in red blood cells, *C. sinensis* also caused erythroid cells to increase *in vitro* (Yu et al, 1993). A number of studies have demonstrated that *C. sinensis* has a range of immunostimulating and immunoregulating activities (Liu & Xu, 1985; Zhu, 1987). Notably, its polysaccharides have been found to stimulate phagocytotic functions and macrophage activity (Gong et al, 1990), particularly that of peritoneal macrophages (Zhu, 1987). Likewise, *Cordyceps* preparations and extracts have been shown to increase phagocytic activity (Tang et al, 1986), especially in the peritoneal macrophages (Zhang et al, 1985). A water-soluble extract of *C. sinensis* fruit-body administered to mice (50 mg/kg) by the oral route provided a significant prolongation of lifespan against lymphoma. This effect was also found against lymphoma in mice that had received an immuno-suppressing chemotherapy agent (cyclophosphamide, i.p.) in addition to the extract (orally). B-lymphocytes were strongly stimulated, and IgM and IgG responses in cyclophosphamide-treated lymphoma-bearing mice could be restored to normal with *C. sinensis* extract (oral), as well as levels of macrophage activity (Yamaguchi et al, 1990). However, although immunostimulatory effects have been observed in immunosuppressed animals, one study found no such effect on humoral immunity in normal mice (Tang et al,1986). Another study found that normal rat T-cells were not enhanced by *C. sinensis*, while defective T-cells were (Chen & Zhang, 1987). Thus, *C. sinensis* may boost depressed immune function but not enhance normal function to the same degree. Significantly, wild and cultivated *C. sinensis* have demonstrated equal levels of immune activity, neither being superior to the other (Chen et al, 1987b; Zhang et al, 1985). True to the actions of other immunostimulants, a high dosage of *C. sinensis* (4 g/kg) produced an immuno-suppressive effect in mice comparable to that of cyclosporin A (5 mg/kg) by prolonging skin allograph survival. *C. sinensis* proved highly active in mice against Ehrlich ascites carcinoma, causing an 80% survival 60 days following tumor cell implantation. *C. sinensis* warm water extract was without antitumor activity *in vitro*, indicating that the major action of the fungus against Ehrlich tumor cells is mediated through the host immune system (Yoshida et al, 1989). In addition, *C. sinensis* has been reported to have antitumor activity against lung cancer in both mice (Zhang et al, 1987) and humans (Xu & Peng, 1988).

In vitro, *C. sinensis* extracts and culture broths have shown positive inotropic and negative chronotropic effects as well as causing a relaxation of aorta and bronchus (Furuya et al, 1983; Naoki et al. 1994). In animals, *C. sinensis* also shows bronchodilatory, sedative, and hypnotic actions (Chang & But, 1986); a sedative action due to the amino acids glutamic acid, tyrosine, and L-tryptophan (Zhang et al, 1991); inhibition of monoamine oxidase obtained from brain tissue (Xu et al, 1988); increased platelet formation, with normal platelet ultrastructure (Chen et al, 1987b); and prevention of spleen and liver atrophy, as well as of thymus hypertrophy in mice given cyclophosphamide (Chen et al, 1985). A fraction of a mycelial extract inhibited the formation of thrombi and platelet aggregation (Zhao, 1991). Finally, *C. sinensis* has demonstrated antibacterial actions *in vitro* against *Streptococcus*, *Bacerium mallei*, *Bacillus anthracis*, *Pasteurella suiseptica*, and *Staphylococcus*, as well as *Microsporum gypseum* and *Microsporum lanosum* (Chang & But, 1986; Ying et al, 1987).

Two protein-bound polysaccharides extracted from *C. ophioglossoides*, CO-N and SN-C, have been reported to have antitumor activity in animal studies. SN-C also appears to stimulate the immune system. Both CO-N and SN-C are galactosaminoglycans (Ohmori, 1988a,b; 1989a,b). CO-N has "mainly" a direct cytocidal action on tumors (MM46 carcinoma, Ehrlich carcinoma, and P388 leukemia) (Ohmori, 1989a). CO-N is a water-insoluble amino acid bound sugar (glycan) derived from the liquid cultured mycelium (1 g/liter) (Yamada, 1984a). Against tumors in mice, CO-N is highly active in small doses. Against sarcoma 180, a single dose of 0.5 mg/kg (i.p.) inhibited tumor growth by 98.7% (Ohmori, 1989). SN-C is active against a larger range of tumor systems than PSK or lentinan (Ohmori, 1988). The antitumor action of SN-C is from both a direct cytocidal activity and immunostimulation. SN-C, derived from liquid cultured mycelia (2-4 g/liter), is reported to be the first immunomodulating protein-bound polysaccharide found that displays both kinds of antitumor activity (Ohmori et al, 1986). The primary polysaccharide component of SN-C that holds the immunostimulating action is CO-1, a glucan with a structure similar to lentinan and some other polysaccharides (Kawaguchi and Yamada, 1987). Although insoluble in water, SN-C is soluble in lactic, acetic, or citric acid (Ohmori, 1988). *C. ophioglossoides* has also shown strong anti-fungal (due partly to the compound ophiocordin), immunostimulant, and anticancer activity in animal trials (Kneifel et al, 1977; Liu & Xu, 1985). Like *C. sinensis*, it appears to activate the peritoneal macrophages (Zhang et al, 1985). Another active polysaccharide, called CO-1, shows strong inhibition against sarcoma 180 tumor (Yamada et al, 1984a), but not from oral administration (Ohmori et al, 1988b).

Human Clinical Studies

Clinical studies have been performed with *C. sinensis*, and based on these, it is reported to have therapeutic value in the treatment of chronic obstructive hepatic diseases, hypercholesterolemia, and other aging disorders, including loss of sexual drive (Chang & But, 1986; Chen & Zhang, 1987). For instance, in 155 cases of sexual hypofunction, 64.15% of the patients showed improvement when treated with cultured *C. sinensis*, and 23.68% showed improvement with wild *C. sinensis* grown on bath-moth larva, versus improvement in 31.57% of patients treated with a placebo. One capsule was given 3 times daily (330 mg/capsule) for 40 days, with 46 of the patients able to continue a normal sex life. An increase in 17-hydroxycorticosteroid and 17-ketosteroid levels was demonstrated in these patients (Yang et al, 1985).

These trials with human volunteers are supported by animal studies in which *Cordyceps* lowered total cholesterol, plasma triglycerides, LDL-C, and VLDL-C, and increased plasma HDL-C and HDL-C/TC in both normal and hyperlipemic rats (Xu & Zhang, 1987), as well as increased spermatogenesis in mice and rabbits (Huang et al, 1987).

The effects of cultivated cordyceps, a product of strain Cs 4 isolated from *Cordyceps sinensis*, were studied in a double blind, randomized placebo controlled study, which lasted for 2 months. Out of 273 patients with hyperlipidemia, the total cholesterol blood level decreased by 17.5% and the triglyceride level by 9.9%. No serious side effects were observed (Geng et al, 1985).

In addition, significant improvement (77.2%) was obtained in 87 cases of arrhythmia using 0.25 g of encapsulated *C. sinensis* mycelia 3X/day for 3 weeks (Yu, 1985). Three cases of lung carcinoma were treated with *C. sinensis* over a 3-month period with excellent results (Chang & But, 1986), while 18 cases of chronic nephritis showed significant improvement after treatment with cultivated *Cordyceps* (Shen & Chen, 1985). Wild *Cordyceps* and cultured mycelia of *C. sinensis* both significantly benefitted patients with chronic kidney failure. The cultured mycelia dosage was 2 g, 3 times daily for 30 days (Chen et al, 1986).

In a human study involving 51 patients with chronic renal failure, the administration of 3-5g per day of *Cordyceps sinensis* to 28 of the patients improved renal and immune function (Guan et al, 1992).

In a study with 33 chronic hepatitis B patients, cultured *Cordyceps sinensis* mycelia was reported to improve liver function, raise plasma albumin, and adjust protein metabolism (Zhou et al, 1990). In 45 patients treated for post-hepatic cirrhosis with *C. sinensis* and extract of semen Persicae, the improvements found compared to an untreated group of patients, were in NK cell function, T-cell ratio and numbers, immunoglobulin levels, serum complement levels, and liver function (Zhu and Lin, 1992).

Finally, in twenty-three cases of tinnitus treated with an infusion of *Cordyceps*, eight were reported as cured and nine significantly improved, while six found no improvement. The researchers concluded that *Cordyceps* was effective for tinnitus caused by fluid accumulation in the middle ear, while it was ineffective in cases with a long history of auditory nerve disorder (Zhuang & Chen, 1985).

Toxicity

Animal studies show the extract of *C. sinensis* is low in toxicity (Chang & But, 1986), and the LD50 was 27.26 ±4.38 g/kg I.P. in mice. When a preparation was given p.o. daily for 3 months to rabbits, no abnormalities were seen in the blood tests, or in liver or kidney functions (Huang et al, 1987).

Uses in Traditional Medicine

In TCM, *C. sinensis* is said to be sweet and acrid in taste and warm in nature. Therapeutically, its action is related to the lung and kidney channels (Chang & But, 1986; Liu and Bau, 1980). *C. ophioglossoides* is mild and slightly acrid (Liu and Bau, 1980). In China the herb is used as a tonic to the lungs and kidneys, to increase sperm production, increase blood production (counteracting some types of anemia), and reinforce Qi. It is often prescribed as a tonic to be cooked with duck meat (Huang, 1993). In China *C. sinensis* cooked with duck is particularly recommended as a nutritional supplement for the elderly; indeed, a meal of this type is thought to be as potent as 50 g of ginseng (Ying et al, 1987).

Medical Uses

Cordyceps sinensis is known as an antiasthmatic and anticancer agent which causes smooth muscle relaxation and can potentiate the effects of epinephrine. It has been used to stimulate the endocrine system, as an antibacterial agent, and for patients suffering from chronic renal failure.

In China, *C. sinensis* is used to regulate and support the gonads and as a lung and kidney tonic. It is used specifically for excessive tiredness, persistent cough, impotence, debility, and anemia. It is also used as a tranquilizer, to build the bone marrow, and reduce excess phlegm (Liu and Bau, 1980; Ying et al, 1987). *C. sinensis* is official in the *Chinese Pharmacopoeia* (Tu, 1988) and is used as a hemostatic for treating phthisis, as a mycolytic, antiasthmatic, and expectorant for treating chronic cough and asthma and for "impotence and seminal emissions with aching of loins and knees;" it is also listed as a tonic.

C. ophioglossoides stimulates blood circulation and regulates menstruation. In some parts of China, the above-ground parts of the fungus are used for treating metrorrhagia and abnormal menstruation (Ying et al, 1987; Liu and Bau, 1980).

Preparation and Dosage

For weakness and debility and for use as a tonic, use 3-9 g *C. sinensis* twice daily (Liu and Bau, 1980), or 1 gram of an extract. For menorrhagia and irregular menstruation, simmer 3-6 g *C. ophioglossoides* in chicken soup and take twice daily, or take a water decoction of 6 g each *C. ophioglossoides* and garden burnet, twice daily (Ying et al, 1987). For treating anemia and impotence, another Chinese source text recommends taking 25 to 50 grams stewed with pork or chicken (Hanssen & Schädler, 1982).

Notes

Cordyceps spp. show higher anticomplementary activity than krestin, an immunostimulant extracted from Japanese *Trametes versicolor* (Jeong et al, 1990).

Related Species

C. shanxiensis, a newly discovered species, is regarded in Shanxi, China as having
greater medicinal value than any other type of *Cordyceps*. It is called "Jinbangbang
Chongcao" in China (Liu et al, 1985).

C. cicadae contains two galactomannans, CI-P and CI-A, which show potent
hypoglycemic activity in normal mice (Kiho et al, 1990), and its polysaccharides
have shown significant antitumor activity (Ukai et al, 1983). A number of species
grow in the United States, among them *C. capitata*, which is common in northern
California and the Pacific Northwest; also several undescribed neotropical species
exist (Arora, 1986). Like *C. sinensis*, *C. barnesii* (Xiangbang Chongcao) contains D-
mannitol, alkaloids, steroids, and inorganic elements. It has the same amino acids,
though twice the amount (Guo et al, 1985). *C. militaris* contains cordycepin, b-
sitosterol, ergosterol, adenine, adenosine, and D-mannitol (Liu et al, 1989).
Cordycepin is a reverse transcriptase inhibitor (Penman et al, 1970) and antitumor
compound not found in *C. sinensis*. Cordycepin was dropped as a clinical agent for
cancer due to toxic side effects (Shiao et al, 1989). *C. hawkesii* Gray has alkaloids,
sterols, amino acids, vitamins, and trace elements similar to those found in *C.
sinensis* (Guo et al, 1990).

C. capitata (Fr.) Link growing on *Elaphomyces* is reported by the ethnomycologist
Singer (1958) "to be collected as a remedy for various diseases." Traces of an
indole alkaloid were also found in this species according to Tyler (Tyler, 1994;
Wasson, 1961).

Procurement

Though expensive, cordyceps can be purchased in bulk through Chinese herb
dealers. It is also a component of a number of tableted formulas, of both Asian and
western origin. Species of cordyceps grow throughout the world; they are uncommon and of scattered occurrence, at least in temperate climates.

FOMES FOMENTARIUS (L.: Fr.) KICKX.

(fomes, foment=tinder)

TRUE TINDER POLYPORE, AMADOU

Synonyms
Pyropolyporus fomentarius (L.:Fr.) Teng, *Polyporus fomentarius* Fr. (Gilbertson and Ryvarden, 1986), *Boletus igniarius*, Fungus chirurgorum.

Other Common Names
Surgeon's fungus, zunderpilz.

Description and Habitat
F. fomentarius is hoof-shaped, grey to grey-brown or grey-black in color, and has a hard, thick crust. It grows on both living and dead hardwoods, especially birch, maple, and poplar (Arora, 1986; Phillips, 1991).

Range
Very common in most parts of the world.

History
Various *Fomes* species were traditionally used in Europe and America as tinder to start fires and as absorbent "pads" to stop bleeding and dress wounds. See the beginning of this book, page 10, for more details. Amadou is called Tsuriganetake in Japan.

Chemistry
F. fomentarius was able to synthesize small quantities of prostaglandins from linolenic acid and arachidonic acid (Kapich et al, 1992). The lipid fraction contains ergosterol, fungisterol, and isoergosterone (Singh & Rangaswami, 1965; Yokoyama et al, 1975), and ergosta-7,22-dien-3-one (Arthur et al, 1958).

Pharmacology
A lignin from *F. fomentarius* completely inhibited the growth of *herpes simplex* virus in cultures (Sakagami & Kawazoe, 1991), while the liquid extract of sporophore reached an 80% effective rate against sarcoma 180 in mice (Ying et al, 1987). Isolated polysaccharides from a mycelium culture proved to be tumor-inhibiting in mice (Ito et al, 1976).

Human Clinical Trials
No data.

Toxicity
No data.

Uses in Traditional Medicine
In TCM, *F. fomentarius* is considered slightly bitter and mild. It is recommended for reducing stasis of digestive vitality (Liu and Bau, 1980; Ying et al, 1987).

F. *fomentarius* was used by the Okanagan-Colville Indians of British Columbia and Washington State and by the Shuswap to cure rheumatism. A piece of the fungus (after pounding and softening) was put on the skin over the affected area with spittle and ignited. This is also the possible species of fungus used by the Okanagan-Colville for arthritis, though Turner describes the fruiting body as "small and flat and grows on birches." This species is not flat, but often taller than wide and more hoof-shaped. It is more likely the fungus in question is *Piptoporus betulinus*, the birch polypore. This species fits the description, and it grows on birches, as stated in Turner (1980). The fungus, called "ktikwmn", was pounded until "mushy" and put "in a cloth" to make a fungal poultice for arthritic areas. In European folk medicine, F. *fomentarius* was used internally for bladder complaints (List & Hörhammer, 1977).

Medical Uses
In China, it is used for indigestion and to reduce stasis of digestive vitality, as well as for esophageal cancer and gastric and uterine carcinomas (Liu & Bau, 1980; Ying et al, 1987). In Europe, it has been used as an external application to stop bleeding in small wounds (List & Hörhammer, 1977).

Preparation and Dosage
As a decoction, 13-20 g, 2x/day.

Related Species
Fomes hornodermus Mont. is used in China as a folk-remedy as a sedative hemostatic and to clear endogenous wind for stopping itch (Ying et al, 1987.)

Procurement
Amadou is not available commercially in bulk or tablet form. It grows commonly throughout parts of North America, Asia, Europe and elsewhere.

FOMITOPSIS OFFICINALIS
(VILL.: FR.) BOND. ET SING. (=FOMES OFFICINALIS VILL.:FRIES) FAULL.

(fomes=tinder; officinalis=pharmaceutical use)

QUININE CONK

Synonyms
Boletus officinalis Vill., *Polyporus officinalis* Vill.:Fr., *Fomes laricis* Jacq.:Murr. (Gilbertson and Ryvarden, 1986).

Other Common Names
White agaric, agarick, purging agaric, and larch agaric. When used as tinder, it has been called "touchwood," "spunk," and "tinder" (Rolfe and Rolfe, 1925). These last names have been shared by other polypores, especially *F. fomentarius*.

Description and Habitat
White and knob-shaped when young, it becomes convex, then cylindrical, hard, and tough; it is more friable than most other polypores and not as fibrous. The surface

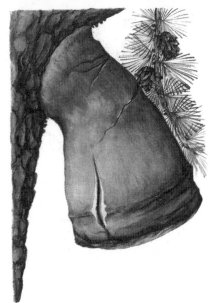

Fomitopsis officinalis

becomes cracked as it ages, and the color changes from white or yellow to gray. Grows on larch, pine, spruce, fir, hemlock, and Douglas fir.

Range
Common year-round throughout much of the Western U.S., from the Sierra Nevada north and east; the great lakes region. Also found in Europe and Eurasia.

History
Quinine conk, or "Agaric" as it was called by the ancients, has had a long history of use in the West (see sidebar on page 8 for history of the word "agaric"). The Greeks and Romans used it in a formula which was alleged to be an antidote to any and all poisons (Rolfe and Rolfe, 1925). As the legend goes, the king Mithridate (after whom the formula was named) took this potion for a period of time to safeguard himself from being poisoned by his enemies. Then later in life he became depressed and tried to kill himself by drinking a virulent poison—but the poison didn't work, presumably because of the formula he had taken many years earlier.

Dioscorides, the noted Greek physician (c. 200 A.D.), thought of it as a panacea, saying that *"On the whole it is serviceable in all internal complaints when taken according to the age and strength of the patient; some should take it with water, others with wine, and others with vinegar and honey, or with water and honey"* (Gunther, 1934).

Gerard (1633), the English herbalist, used it in much the same way, suggesting a dose of 1-2 drams in powder form or 2-5 drams in decoction. Interestingly, Gerard felt that the best agaric would be white-colored, loose and spongy in texture, easily broken, and have a sweet taste; he considered heavy, blackish, and fibrous agaric to be poisonous. He also noted that since it is purgative and may cause nausea, the best way to take agaric is with syrup of vinegar and ginger, to prevent any negative reactions.

After Gerard's time, the medicinal use of agaric declined, replaced with more effective specific laxative and anti-malarial medicines. In the *New English Dispensatory* (1733), it is mentioned as a purging herb to be taken with aromatics (such as ginger), but the author reports it is rarely used and recommends that it be allowed to fall into disuse. Linnaeus, in his *Materia Medica* (1749), says that it is warming, mildly laxative, carminative, and anthelmintic. In the second edition of the *U.S. Dispensatory* (1834), the authors state that agaric *"is scarcely employed, though we have met with it in the shops."* The use of this fungus refused to fade completely, however, and in the later 1800s, it was incorporated into the famous "Warburg's" or "Antiperiodica" tincture (see page 14 for recipe and uses), and the *British Pharmaceutical Codex* of 1934 includes it.

It is said to have been successful in malarial fevers in India; the recommended dose was 1/2 ounce of the tincture, and after 3 hours, another 1/2 ounce. "Soon after the second dose, a violent, aromatic perspiration comes on, and the fever is usually broken." As far as I know, there are no modern clinical reports or studies to substantiate this use. The tincture was also recommended for general collapse, because of its stimulant properties, in cases where there was no apparent organic disease present. Warburg's Tincture was official in the *U.S. National Formulary* from 1888 to 1926 (Osol et al, 1955). The agaric is not much known or used by modern herbalists and the risk of side effects, such as bowel irritation, may outweigh its benefits (Dharmananda, 1994).

Chemistry
According to the *Merck Index* (1983) and *Hager's Handbook* (List & Hörhammer, 1977), agaric contains agaricic acid, agaricinic acid, which is 2-hexadecylcitric acid sesquihydrate (14-16%), cetyl alcohol, ricinolic acid, eburicolic acid, dehydroeburicolic acid, dehydroeburiconic acid, agaricol, phytosterin, ricinoleic acid, cetyl alcohol, glucose, oxalic, malonic, succinic acid, maleic acid, 7 polyacetylene, dehydromatricaria ester, octadien-(1,7)-diin-(3,5)-dicarbonic acid-(1,8), octene-(1)-diine-3,5-dicarbonic acid-(1,8) and decen-(7)-diin-(3,5)-diol-(1,2)-carbonic acid-(1), ergosta-4,6,8(14),22-tetraenon-(3), gum, wax, and carbohydrates; also ergosterol (Valentin & Knütter, 1957). Agaric acid was still official recently as an astringent and purgative in the Austrian and Portuguese Pharmacopoeias (Reynolds, 1982). Graf and Winckelmann (1960) report on early chemical analyses of *F. officinalis* and the possibility of extracting sterols from this species and others for use in human steroid synthesis.

Pharmacology
Shows an inhibition against sarcoma 180 of 80% (Ying et al, 1987). An observed laxative effect from the fruiting body was said to be due to agaricin, water-soluble salts, and mannitol (Jaretzky & Breitwieser, 1944).

Human Clinical Studies
None.

Toxicity
On the basis of experience in TCM, *F. officinalis* should not be used in doses of more than 1 g per day (Liu and Bau, 1980). In England (1965) agaric acid was recommended to be prohibited as a flavoring agent in foods because animal studies showed that in sufficient quantities, it could produce skeletal muscle weakness and CNS depression (Reynolds, 1982).

Uses in Traditional Medicine
According to traditional European practice the energy of agaric is slightly sweet, bitter, and slightly acrid (Linnaeus, 1749); neutral to slightly cool. See page 10 for further traditional uses.

Medical Uses
Prescribed prior to the mid-20th century as a purgative, bitter tonic, for bronchial asthma, night sweats from tuberculosis (List & Hörhammer, 1977); also a powder of the fruiting body, and later, agaricic acid, is used as an anhidrotic (agent that reduces sweating) (Windholz et al, 1976). The mushroom itself was still official in the Swiss Pharmacopeia in 1967 (Todd, 1967), and agaric acid in the Austrian and Portuguese pharmacopeias in 1982 (Reynolds, 1982).

Preparation and Dosage
200 mg-2 grams decocted as a tea (List & Hörhammer, 1977), or taken as a powder in "00" capsules, usually with other herbs. One dropperful of the tincture (1:5, 50% menstruum), 3 x daily.

Related Species
Currently in the same genus with *F. pinicola*, the red-belted polypore and *F. cajanderi* (Karst.) Kotl. et Pouz., the rosy conk, but these taste nothing like quinine conk, as they are not friable and do not have the same medicinal effects.

Notes
Still in trade, especially in Europe, but may be adulterated with *Laetiporus sulphureus* (Bull.:Fr.) Murr. (=*Polyporus sulfureus* Bull.:Fr.), which is not as bitter or friable (List & Hörhammer, 1977).

Procurement
The bulk fruiting bodies are still in European herb trade. I have seen large fruiting bodies on Douglas fir in the Pacific Northwest, south to the San Francisco bay area in California, though it probably grows further south. It is common in other parts of North America, Europe, and Asia.

FOMITOPSIS PINICOLA (Swartz:Fr.) Karst.

(fomit=tinder; pin=pine, col=inhabitant)

Red-Belted Polypore

Synonyms
Boletus pinocola Swartz, *Polyporus pinicola* Swartz:Fr., *Fomes ungulatus* Schaeff.:Sacc., *Fomes pinicola*, *Ungulina marginata*, *Polyporus ponderosus* von Schrenk (Gilbertson and Ryvarden, 1986; Arora, 1986; Overholts, 1977).

Other Common Names
Red-belted conk (Arora, 1986); tsugasaruno-koshikake (Yokoyama, 1975).

Description and Habitat
F. pinicola is a beautiful, varnished, orange to red to brown shelf fungus. It has white pores, which are scarcely visible underneath its cap, that do not bruise and a lighter belt around the margin of the top cap. It has a very tough, cork-like or woody flesh and is usually found on dead conifers, less often on hardwoods (on the West Coast, I have seen it mostly on Douglas fir). *F. pinicola* is known to feed on the heartwood and sapwood of its host, and it is a major decomposer of dead timber (Arora, 1986).

Range
Throughout Canada and in the states of North Carolina, Arizona, California, and Ohio (Lincoff, 1981). Also found in Eurasia.

History
The red-belted polypore was also known as Mech quah (red touchwood) by the Cree in Eastern Canada. They dried and powdered the fruiting body, making a paste with water and applying it to excessively bleeding wounds as a styptic. A half teaspoon of the powder was also steeped in water and taken internally as an emetic for purification (Beardsley, 1944).

In King's *American Dispensatory* (1895), *F. pinicola* was recommended for persistent, intermittent fevers; chronic diarrhea and dysentery; periodic neuralgia and nervous headache; excessive urination; jaundice; and chills and fevers in consumptive patients.

Chemistry
The triterpenes ergosterol, 3 compounds closely related to trametenolic acid, polyporenic acid C, ergosterol, ergosta-7,22-dien-3β-ol, fungisterol, eburicoic acid, lanosterol, inotodiol (Schmid & Czerny, 1953; Yokoyama et al, 1975), 21-hydroxylanosta-7,9(11)-24-trien-3-on, 21-hydroxylanosta-7,9(11)-24-trien-3β,21-diol, 3α-oxylanosta-8,24-dien-21-oleic acid, and pinicolic acid, which may be a mixture of triterpenes (List & Hörhammer, 1977).

Pharmacology
F. pinicola has shown moderate tumor-inhibition against sarcoma 180 (Ito et al, 1972-73; Ikekawa et al, 1968; Shibata et al, 1968). Mice given crude polysaccharides extracted from *F. pinicola* orally showed significant retention of

Bromsulphalein and elevation of serum glutamic pyruvic transaminase induced by carbon tetrachloride (Zhang, 1987), which suggests an effect on liver enzymes.

Human Clinical Studies
No data.

Toxicity
No data.

Taste & Energy
Sweet, tonic.

Uses in Traditional Medicine
Use daily as a tonic to reduce inflammation of the digestive tract and increase general resistance, or as a cancer-preventative, though this use is not supported by scientific studies with humans. The tea is sweet and mild-tasting with a little bitterness. It is one of the most common polypores in many parts of the world. I have enjoyed it as a tonic beverage with the addition of ginger or licorice for a number of years.

Medical Uses
Used in homeopathic medicine for fevers with headache, yellow tongue coating, nausea, epigastric weakness, and constipation (Boericke, 1927).

Preparation and Dosage
20-30 g 2X/day in soups or as a tea. Note that this fungus must be simmered for at least an hour to extract its active constituents. Before cooking, saw up the dry carpophore into 1/2" slices and break up into pieces. When fresh and small, they can simply be cut up with a serrated knife to increase surface area for extraction.

Related Species
F. cytisina shows weak tumor inhibition (Ikekawa et al, 1968).

Notes
Fiberboard made from wood chips pretreated with the extract of *F. pinicola* shows excellent flexibility, high tensile strength, and little swelling tendency (Wagenfuehr et al, 1989).

Procurement
The red-belted polypore is not available in commercial trade but is one of the most common polypores throughout north temperate regions of the world.

GANODERMA APPLANATUM (PERS.) PAT.

(gan=shiny; derm=skin; applanatum=flattened)

ARTIST'S CONK

Synonyms
Boletus applanatus Pers., *Polyporus applanatus* Pers.:Wallr., *Polyporus megaloma* Lév., *Effvingia megaloma* (Lév.), (Overholts, 1977; Gilbertson and Ryvarden, 1986), *Fomes applanatus* Pers.;Wallr.) Gill, *Elfringia applanata* (Blum. et Nees:Fr.) Kuntze, *G. tornicatum* (Fr.) Pat. (Yokoyama et al, 1975).

Other Common Names
G. applanatum is also known as "red mother fungus" (Liu and Bau, 1980) or "the ancient ling zhi" (Willard, 1990). In North America it is known as "artist's conk."

Description and Habitat
G. applanatum often grows on the trunks of broadleaf trees, as well as on bamboo and conifers (Ying et al, 1987). It tends to cause decay in its host and may release over 5 trillion spores annually (Arora, 1986). In California, the fungus often grows on bay laurel (*Umbellularia californica*) (Hook. & Arn.) Nutt., and I have found these to be more bitter and acrid than ones growing on other trees. Another similar *Ganoderma* known only from California, *G. brownii* (Murr.) Gilbn., also grows on bay laurel and is distinguished from *G. applanatum* by having a distinctly yellow pore surface, rather than white (Gilbertson & Ryvarden, 1986).

Range
Common throughout the United States.

History
The name *applanatum* means "flattened" in Latin and refers to its flat bracket-shape. The Athabaskans of Alaska burn the fungus to provide a mosquito repellent smoke, and they scratch pictures on the white underside of the fresh fungus. The Alaskan Indian name "k'vajeghetl'a" indicates use of this fungus for "playing catch." The Susitna Dena'ina Indians of Alaska hold that in the area of Alexander Creek, a "giant k'adatsa" (*G. applanatum*) once grew to around a quarter mile in width (Kari, 1977).

Chemistry
Like *G. lucidum*, this species contains various steroidal compounds (Pettit and Knight, 1962; Ripperger and Budzikiewicz, 1975), such as ergosterol, ergosta—7,22-dien-3β-ol, fungisterol (Yokoyama et al, 1975), alnusenone, friedelin, and other triterpenes (Protiva, 1980). Ganoderenic acid, furanoganoderic acid, and ganoderic acid derivatives have been isolated from *G. applanatum* (Nishitoba et al, 1989). Because triterpenes such as ganoderic acid have been correlated with bitterness, flavor may be a good measure of quality for *G. applanatum*, *G. oregonense*, and other wild species (Shiao et al, 1994). This particularly holds true if one is interested in the pharmacological effects that are especially associated with these compounds, namely hepatoprotection, antihistamine, ACE inhibition, and hypolipidemic activity.

Pharmacology

G. applanatum has demonstrated immunostimulating properties in animal studies. RNA from *G. applanatum* caused the production of a substance with interferon-like properties in mice spleen, while i.v. doses of nucleic acids isolated from *G. applanatum* conferred protection against tick-borne encephalitis virus in mice (Kandefer-Szerszen et al, 1979). *G. applanatum* polysaccharides have been found to increase spleen cell proliferation *in vitro* and stimulate antitumor activity against sarcoma 180 in mice, as well as increase spleen cell primary antibody responses to sheep red blood cells (Gao & Yang, 1991). Single doses of polysaccharides (from 10-50 mg/kg) from the mycelium have produced 100% tumor inhibition ratios (Mizuno, 1982).

Human Clinical Studies

No data.

Toxicity

No data.

Uses in Traditional Medicine

In my experience, the energetic property of *G. applanatum* is warming and slightly bitter and sweet, depending on the host tree from which it is harvested. In TCM, *G. applanatum* is used to reduce phlegm, eliminate indigestion, stop pain, and remove heat.

Medical Uses

In China, it is considered useful for rheumatic tuberculosis and esophageal cancer (Ying et al, 1987). It also has antibiotic properties and shows activity against other types of cancer as well (Kim et al, 1990).

Preparation and Dosage

30 g a day in tea or water-based extract.

Related Species

Also see the entry on *G. lucidum* (pages 96-107).

Procurement

Artist's conk is available in commercial products and in bulk through Chinese herb dealers. I have seen it as the major ingredient in "Ling Zhi" extracts made in Taiwan. It is also an extremely common fungus, growing on a variety of hosts throughout the world.

GANODERMA LUCIDUM (W. CURT.: FR.) KARST.

(gan=shiny; derm=skin; lucidum=shining)

LING-ZHI, REISHI

Synonyms
Boletus lucidus Fr., *Polyporus lucidus*, *Ganoderma sessile*, *Polyporus polychromus*, *Ganoderma polychromum* (Gilbertson and Ryvarden, 1986).

Other Common Names
G. lucidum is commonly known as "ling zhi" ("ling chih or ling qi" are variant spellings) in China and "reishi" in Japan. The name *ling zhi* means "spirit plant" (Huang, 1993) and first appears in the 11th century *Ling yuan fang* (Bretschneider, 1895). Other common Chinese names include "plant of immortality," *shi rh* ("mushroom which grows on stone"), "ten-thousand year mushroom," and "herb of spiritual potency" (Liu

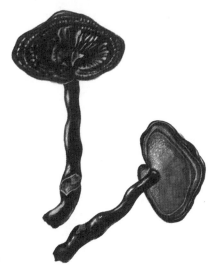

Reishi

and Bau, 1980; Bretschneider, 1895). Because of the difficulty in obtaining it, reishi was often referred to as the "phantom mushroom" in Japan (Matsumoto, 1979). It is also called varnished conk (Arora, 1986).

Description and Habitat
The Latin *lucidum*, meaning "shiny" or "brilliant," refers to the appearance of the fungus' fruiting body, which has a modeled, varnished look. *G. lucidum* frequently infects trees, especially oak trees, causing their wood to rot. This has an unfortunate impact on the wood industry (Kac et al, 1984).

The fruiting bodies of *G. lucidum* are reddish-orange to black, usually delicate, slender, and have a definite stalk which usually attaches to the cap from the side, though stalkless (sessile) specimens have been found. The annual fruiting bodies of *G. oregonense* and *G. tsugae* (species which may have similar medicinal uses), on the other hand, are larger and fatter, with less of a well-defined stalk (or none at all). *G. oregonense* occurs from British Columbia south to northern California and apparently intergrades there into *G. tsugae*, which has a similar stature. Both commonly grow on fir (*Tsugae* spp.) and hemlock (*Abies* spp.), while *G. lucidum* grows exclusively on hardwoods, especially oaks (*Quercus* spp.) (Gilbertson & Ryvarden, 1986).

In Japan, 99% of reishi growing in the wild are found on old Japanese plum trees. Nonetheless, they are so rare that only a few reishi are generally found per 100,000 plum trees (Matsumoto, 1979).

Range

Ganoderma spp. grow throughout the United States, Europe, South America, and Asia. In North America, *G. lucidum* occurs most commonly on the East Coast, especially the Gulf Coast and the Southwest.

History

G. lucidum has been used in the folk medicine of China and Japan for 4,000 years (Zhao & Zhang, 1994), especially in the treatment of hepatopathy, chronic hepatitis, nephritis, hypertension, arthritis, neurasthenia, insomnia, bronchitis, asthma, and gastric ulcer (Kabir et al, 1988). In the *Ben Cao Gang Mu* (A.D. 1578), China's most famous natural history book, it is explained that "continued use of Ling Zhi will lighten weight and increase longevity" (Huang, 1993). It was once thought that the pharmacological effect of *G. lucidum* was due to its color; in actuality, ling zhi possesses many different properties depending on the stage and environment of its growth (Jong and Birmingham, 1992). During the Ming Dynasty (1368-1644) it was called Qi *zhi*, or "red fungus". It was said to benefit the heart (Yeung, 1985). In TCM, ling zhi is considered to be in the highest class of tonics, promoting longevity. There are many Chinese and Japanese stories of people with cancer and other degenerative diseases traveling great distances to find it.

In the past, reishi grew only in small quantities in the wild, so it was very expensive. In the last 20 years, however, successful cultivation of *G. lucidum* has made it more accessible and affordable (Willard, 1990). The cultivation of the reishi was pioneered by Shigeaki Mori, a Japanese man who spent 15 years developing an elaborate method of culturing wild-grown reishi spores in specially treated old plum tree sawdust. Mori's process takes about two years from start to finish, and it is designed to cultivate *akashiba* (red reishi). The "antlered reishi," which is traditionally the rarest and most highly valued of the reishis (Matsumoto, 1979), is produced by growing reishi in a controlled environment high in carbon dioxide.

In addition to its medical indications, Reishi has been used in the Orient as a talisman to protect a person or home against evil (Matsumoto, 1979).

Chemistry

The sporophore, or spore-bearing structure, of *G. lucidum* contains carbohydrates (both reducing sugars and polysaccharides), amino acids, a small amount of protein and inorganic ions, steroids, triterpenes, lipids, alkaloids, a glucoside, a coumarin glycoside, volatile oil, riboflavin, and ascorbic acid (Ying et al, 1987). Regarding the inorganic ions, specifically, the horn-shaped carpophore (stalk) contains Mg, Ca, Zn, Mn, Fe, Cu, and Ge, while the pileus (cap) contains the same except no Cu (Shin et al, 1986). The spores themselves contain choline, betaine, tetracosanoic acid, stearic acid, palmitic acid, ergosta-7, 22-dien-3β-ol, nonadecanoic acid, behenic acid, tetracosane, hentriacontane, ergosterol, and β-sitosterol (Hou et al, 1988). One of the lipids isolated from *G. lucidum* is pyrophosphatidic acid (Sugai et al, 1986).

The fruiting body of *G. lucidum* contains, in addition, ergosterol, fungal lysozyme, and acid protease (Chang & But, 1986). A hot-water extract of the fruiting body was found to consist of 51% polysaccharide and 5% protein (Shin et al,

1986), while water extracts of the sclerotium produced soluble proteins, amino acids, polypeptides, and saccharides (Chang & But, 1986).

The mycelium of *G. lucidum* contains sterols, lactones, alkaloids, and polysaccharides (Chang & But,1986), as well as triterpenes. Indeed, some 100 different triterpenes can be found in the fruiting body and/or mycelium of *G. lucidum* (Shiao et al, 1994). These include highly oxidized lanostane-type triterpenoids such as ganoderic acids C,D, E, F, G, H, I (Hirotani et al, 1985; Kikuchi et al, 1985a,b; Komoda et al, 1985), L (Nishitoba et al, 1986), R, S, T (Hirotani & Furuya, 1986), U, V, W, X, Y, and Z (Toth et al, 1983a); ganoderenic acids A, B, C, and E (Komoda et al, 1985); ganolucidic acids A, B (Kikuchi et al, 1985b) and D (Nishitoba et al, 1986); lucidenic acids D, E, F (Kikuchi et al, 1985a), and G (Nishitoba et al, 1986); and lucidone C (Nishitoba et al, 1986).

Pharmacology
Animal studies have shown the active constituents of *G. lucidum* to have a variety of pharmacological activities and effects (summarized in Table 6). A number of its polysaccharides have demonstrated antitumor and immunostimulating activities. For instance, Beta-D-glucan, also called G-I, shows potent action against sarcoma 180 (Willard, 1990), as does GL-1, an arabinoxyloglucan (Miyazaki & Nishijima, 1981). A polysaccharide-enriched fraction of *G. lucidum* has demonstrated the ability to stimulate macrophages to produce more tumor-necrosis factor (TNF-α) and a number of interleukins (Wang et al, 1994). The polysaccharide portion of these protein-bound polysaccharides has been found to consist of glucose, galactose, mannose, and traces of xylose and fucose, while the protein portion contains some 17 amino acids (Kim et al, 1990). In addition to having antitumor effects, *G. lucidum*'s polysaccharides have been shown to increase DNA synthesis of spleen cells in mixed lymphocyte culture (Lei & Lin, 1991) and increase both RNA and DNA synthesis in the bone marrow of mice.

The sterols in *G. lucidum* are reported to act as hormone precursors, while adenosine (a derivative of RNA) has been found to inhibit platelet aggregation (Shimizu et al, 1985). Ganoderans A & B, glycans of the fruit body of *G. lucidum*, significantly reduced plasma sugar levels in hyperglycemic mice (Hikino et al, 1985).

Another major class of compounds in *G. lucidum*, the triterpenes, are reported to have adaptogenic and antihypertensive, as well as anti-allergic effects. (It is interesting to note that *Ganoderma* is a rich source of these bitter triterpenes, as a bitter taste has long been associated with some of its therapeutic properties) (Jong and Birmingham, 1992). Ganoderic acid C appears to be the most active anti-allergic constituent, followed by ganoderic acids A and D. Ganoderic acid B is the least active; however, ganoderic acids B and D are reported to be anti-hypertensives. The precise mechanisms of the ganoderic acids' anti-allergic actions are still unknown (Jones, 1992b). Also, ganoderic acids T through Z show antitumor activity against hepatoma (liver-tumor) cells (Toth et al, 1983b), and A through D inhibit histamine release (Khoda et al, 1985).

Oleic acid, an unsaturated fatty acid, and cyclooctasulphur are known to inhibit the release of histamine, thus preventing allergic reactions and inflammations

(Tasaka et al, 1988), though oleic acid is a common element of a balanced diet. The polypeptide Ling Zhi-8 (or LZ-8), too, has shown activity against several type I allergic hypersensitivity reactions. Ironically, however, *G. lucidum* may be a source of an allergen itself: some people have demonstrated allergic reactions to the fruiting body, others to the spores, and some to both. In areas where *Ganoderma* grows in abundance, the extremely high number of spores released into the air (*G. applanatum* produces about 11 billion spores per week from a single fruiting body) frequently cause reactions in susceptible individuals (Tarlo et al, 1979).

Table 6

ACTIVE CONSTITUENTS OF *G. LUCIDUM*.

Compound	Type	Action
Cyclooctasulphur		Inhibits histamine release
Unknown	Alkaloid	Cardiotonic
Unknown	Glycoprotein	Tumor inhibitor
Adenosine	Nucleotide	Inhibits platelet aggregation; muscle relaxant; analgesic
Ganoderans A,B,C	Polysaccharide	Hypoglycemic
Unknown	Polysaccharide	Cardiotonic
Unknown	Polysaccharide	Antitumor; immunostimulating
Beta-D-glucan	Polysaccharide	Antitumor; immunostimulating
GL-1	Polysaccharide	Antitumor; immunostimulating
FA,FI,FI-1a	Polysaccharide	Antitumor; immunostimulating
Beta-D-glucans D-6	Polysaccharide	Enhances protein synthesis and nucleic acid metabolism
LingZhi-8	Protein	Broad spectrum antiallergic; immunomodulator
Ganodosterone	Steroid	Anti-hepatotoxic
Ganoderic acids		
A,B,C,D	Triterpene	Inhibit histamine release
R,S	Triterpene	Anti-hepatotoxic
B,D,F,H,K,S,Y	Triterpene	Anti-hypertensive, ACE-inhibiting
Ganoderic acid B	Triterpene	Inhibits cholesterol synthesis
Ganoderic acid Mf	Triterpene	Inhibits cholesterol synthesis
Ganodermadiol	Triterpene	Anti-hypertensive, ACE-inhibiting
Ganodermic acid	Triterpene	Inhibits cholesterol synthesis
Oleic acid	Unsaturated fatty acid	Inhibits histamine release

Without focusing on specific active constituents, researchers have also reported the following activities and effects (*in vivo* and/or *in vitro*) in studies using *G. lucidum*, generally in the form of watery or ethanolic extracts. Keep in mind that most of these results are uncontrolled clinical or laboratory studies or reports, mostly from China.

PHARMACOLOGICAL EFFECTS OF WHOLE REISHI EXTRACTS *IN VIVO* AND *IN VITRO*

◆ **Analgesic** (Chang & But, 1986)

◆ **Anti-allergic** activity

◆ **Bronchitis**-preventative effect, inducing regeneration of bronchial epithelium (Chang & But, 1986)

◆ **Anti-inflammatory** (Lin et al, 1993; Stavinoha et al, 1990)

◆ **Antibacterial**, against *Staphylococci*, *Streptococci*, and *Bacillus pneumoniae*, (perhaps due to increased immune system activity) (Hsu, 1990)

◆ **Antioxidant**, by eliminating hydroxyl free radicals (Wang et al, 1985; Chen & Zhang, 1987)

◆ **Antitumor** activity

◆ **Antiviral** effect, by inducing interferon production

◆ Lowers **blood pressure**

◆ Enhances **bone marrow** nucleated cell proliferation (Jia et al, 1993b)

◆ **Cardiotonic action**, lowering serum cholesterol levels with no effect on triglycerides, enhancing myocardial metabolism of hypoxic animals, and improving coronary artery hemodynamics (Chang & But, 1986; Chen & Zhang, 1987)

◆ **Central depressant** and **peripheral anticholinergic** actions on the autonomic nervous system reduce the effects of caffeine and relax muscles (Chang & But, 1986; Kasahara & Hikino, 1987)

◆ Enhanced **natural killer cell** (NK) activity *in vitro* in mice (Zhang & Yu, 1993)

◆ **Expectorant and antitussive** properties demonstrated in mice studies (Hsu et al, 1986; Chang & But, 1986)

◆ General **immunopotentiation** (Shin et al, 1986; Chang & But, 1986)

◆ **Anti-HIV** activity *in vitro* and *in vivo* (Kim et al, 1994)

◆ Improved **adrenocortical function**

◆ Increased production of **Interleukin-1** by murine peritoneal macrophages *in vitro* (Jia et al, 1993a)

◆ Increased production of **Interleukin-2** by murine splenocytes *in vitro* (Zhang et al, 1993)

- **Liver-protective and detoxifying** effects (Chang & But, 1986)

- No effect on type **B monoamine oxidase** obtained from mouse brain *in vitro* (Dai & Yin, 1987)

- Protection against **ionizing radiation** when treated with *G. lucidum* both *before* and after exposure (Chang & But, 1986; Hu & But, 1987)

- Slight **anti-ulcer** activity, perhaps due to the central depressant effect (Kasahara and Hikino, 1987)

- Increase **white blood cells** and **hematoglobin** in peripheral blood of m i c e (Jia et al, 1993)

Human Clinical Studies

In the last 20 years, *G. lucidum* has undergone a number of clinical studies with humans and is thought to be beneficial for a wide variety of disorders, including neurasthenia, dizziness, insomnia, rhinitis, and duodenal ulcers (Ying et al, 1987); liver pain (hepatodynia), symptoms associated with anorexia, maldeveloped brain, retinal pigmentary degeneration, leukopenia, progressive muscular dystrophy, atrophic nyotonus, and osteogenic hyperplasia (Chang & But 1986; Chang et al, 1984; Huidi & Zhiyuan, 1982); and mental disease caused by environmental stress, Alzheimer's disease, liver failure, hyperlipidemia, and diabetes (Tamura et al,1987a,b,c,d,e). The clinical effectiveness of ling zhi extract and its components in this wide range of disorders is still largely unsubstantiated by *modern* internationally-recognized scientific standards, but it is currently being used in clinics and tested extensively throughout Asia and other parts of the world.

G. lucidum has also shown favorable results in treating hepatitis, especially in cases *without* severe impairment of liver function (Chang & But, 1986). For example, in a study of 355 cases of hepatitis B treated with Wulingdan Pill, which includes the fruiting body of *G. lucidum*, 92.4% of the patients had positive results (Yan et al, 1987). In a clinical report from the MARA Institute of Technology, Malaysia, a lyophilized extract of the mushroom was said to be beneficial in alleviating the symptoms of patients suffering from hepatitis B by significantly reducing the SGOT and SGPT levels and leading to seroconversion in 1 case after 3 months of administration (Teow, 1994). Positive results were also seen in patients with diabetes, acute myeloid leukemia (AML), and recurrent nasopharyngeal carcinomas.

Of special note are reishi's action on the lungs and heart. In clinical studies conducted in China during the 1970s, over 2000 patients with chronic bronchitis were given a tablet form of reishi syrup. Within 2 weeks, 60-90% of the patients showed marked improvement, including increased appetite. The older patients, especially, seemed to benefit the most, and those with bronchial asthma, in particular, responded well (Chang & But, 1986).

As for its action on the heart, reishi has been reported to benefit patients with coronary heart disease and hyperlipidemia, bringing about varying degrees of improvement in symptoms such as palpitations, dyspnea, precordial pain, and edema (Chang & But, 1986). In one controlled study, a reishi extract showed the ability to reduce blood viscosity and plasma viscosity in hypertensive patients with hyperlipidemia, some of whom were recovering from an episode of cerebral thrombosis (Cheng et al, 1993). In another study, reishi extracts were reported to reduce blood cholesterol and lower blood pressure (Kanmatsuse et al, 1985). *G. lucidum* is said to act as a cardiotonic and has also been used to treat arrhythmia (Ding, 1987a).

Another key action of *Ganoderma* spp. is found in its anti-allergic effects. Fructificatio Ganodermae (FG), a formula of the fruiting bodies of several *Ganoderma* spp., including *G. lucidum*, *G. japonicum*, and *G. capense*, has been used in China as a tonic for over 2,000 years. Recent studies on FG have reported it to be effective in the treatment of chronic bronchitis, bronchial asthma, and several other allergic diseases. Although the effective principles responsible for this action have not been identified, it is known from animal studies that FG inhibits the mediator release and, at high concentrations, suppresses the mediator activity. Although FG can regulate the immune response, there are no reports of its effects on IgE antibody synthesis (Qiu & Wu, 1986). We do know, however, that in animals, *G. lucidum* inhibits the release of histamine, thus preventing or alleviating types I, II, III, and IV allergic sensitivity reactions. Reishi has been observed clinically to stabilize immunoglobulin levels, reducing the number of excess antibodies and boosting low levels. Since this effect includes stabilizing levels of IgE, IgM, IgA, and IgG antibodies, reishi may help alleviate food sensitivities (Kohda et al, 1985).

Finally, reishi has been found to be effective for two unusual applications. First, it alleviates high altitude sickness by oxygenating the blood. Chinese mountain climbers given *G. lucidum* before ascending mountains as high as 4,000-5,000 m (13,200 to 17,000 ft.) felt minimal reactions to the climbs (Chang & But, 1986). Second, and most unusual, *G. lucidum* has been found to be surprisingly effective in treating myotonia dystrophica, a rare hereditary disease characterized by muscular atrophy which begins in the face, neck, and larynx, and progressively affects the musculature of the entire body. Eventually even the skin and many glands such as the pituitary, thyroid, parathyroid, adrenal, and gonads atrophy as well. There is no known cure for this disorder. Although reishi is not a cure, it can help alleviate symptoms. In one study, patients with myotonia dystrophica were given 400 mg/day of water-soluble *G. lucidum* spores administered i.m. Many showed marked improvement in muscle strength, improved sleeping and eating patterns, and weight gain within 1-2 weeks. Patients unable to lift their heads before treatment were able to do so after treatment, and their speech and walking ability improved as well. Indeed, in three cases the disease even ceased to progress (Fu & Wang, 1982).

Toxicity
In animal experiments, reishi extracts have shown a very low toxicity. (Chang & But, 1986). There is little reported data on the long-term adverse effects of reishi and its derivatives.

Uses in Traditional Medicine
In TCM, *G. lucidum* is considered warming and acts to nourish, tonify, remove toxins, astringe, and disperse accumulation (Hsu et al, 1986; Chang & But, 1986). Different types of reishi have different tastes and thus affect different organs.

There are thought to be six different types of *G. lucidum* (classified according to color), each with a different use. For a summary of these types as they are named and used in Japan, see Table 8. The red-colored variety is generally regarded as the most potent and medicinal (Hsu et al, 1986; Matsumoto, 1979). The Japanese have used reishi as a folk remedy to help cure cancer, heart disease, liver problems, high blood pressure, joint inflammation, ulcers and other diseases (Matsumoto, 1977), which may be due to the ability of the aqueous extract to increase fibrin degradation products and inhibit blood platelet aggregation (Kubo et al, 1983).

Medical Uses

In China and other parts of Asia, *G. lucidum* is used for many aging-related diseases, such as coronary heart disease, chronic bronchitis, hypertension, and cancer (Chen & Zhang, 1987), and also as a diuretic, laxative, sedative, and tonic (Liu and Bau, 1980). In China, numerous preparations are made for daily use to promote health, inducing sound sleep and increasing resistance to infections and heart disease, and are also recommended for a wide range of ailments such as neurasthenia, chronic bronchitis, and coronary heart disease (Yang & Jong, 1989). The Japanese government has officially listed reishi as an adjunct herb for cancer (Willard, 1990). Preliminary clinical reports and practitioner experience seems to indicate that its immunostimulating polysaccharides may make it useful for people who are HIV positive, as well as for those who have Epstein Barr Virus (EBV), an infectious virus that causes mononucleosis (Dharmananda, 1988). Because of a high adenosine content (e.g.150 mg%), reishi was not advised for use by hemophiliacs, but a pilot study in five HIV-positive hemophiliacs given reishi extract (adenosine intake, 1.35 mg/day) found no changes in blood aggregatibility, and it was concluded that the extract could be safely used by these patients (Gau et al, 1990). It is important to note that the adenosine content of various strains of *G. lucidum* varies greatly, and that a number of other species of medicinal mushrooms also contain adenosine in significant quantities, namely, *Cordyceps sinensis, Auricularia polytricha,* and *Lentinula edodes* (Shiao et al, 1994).

Other uses of *G. lucidum* include as an antidote for poisonous mushrooms (Ying et al, 1987) and as an ingredient in skin lotions for protecting against UV radiation (Naeshiro et al, 1992b,d). It is also used for nervous disability, dizziness, hepatitis, nephritis, gastric ulcer, leukopenia, and as an expectorant and antitussive (Chang and But, 1986; Liu and Bau, 1980; Ying et al, 1987; Huang, 1993).

Reishi extract is being used with favorable results in a Moscow cancer research center for treating cancer patients according to reports given at the First International Conference on Mushroom Biology and Mushroom Products held in Hong Kong, August 23-26, 1993 (Chilton, 1994). A clinical report from China (Lui, 1994) details a clinician's work with "*Ganoderma* detoxification and softening liver soup," which was given to 70,000 patients with a success rate in toxipathic hepatitis of 90%, according to the author.

In my experience, it is especially suitable as a calming herb for people with anxiety, sleeplessness, or nervousness accompanied by adrenal weakness or general neurasthenia or deficiency syndromes. In this regard, it is to be much preferred to traditional western sedative herbs such as valerian, which could be too warm and actually stimulating for some individuals.

Table 8

THE SIX TYPES OF REISHI

Color	Taste	Japanese Name	Use
Blue	sour	aoshiba	improves eyesight and liver function; calms nerves
Red	bitter	akashiba	aids internal organs; improves memory; enhances vitality
Yellow	sweet	kishiba	strengthens spleen function; calms the "spirit" (shen)
White	hot (or pungent)	shiroshiba	improves lung function; gives courage and strong will
Black	salty	kuroshiba	protects kidneys
Purple	sweet	murasakishiba	enhances function of ears, joints, muscles; helps complexion

Note: Information from *The Mysterious Reishi Mushroom* (Matsumoto, 1979). The original source of these attributes is apparent from the *Ben Cao Gang Mu* wherein various "Chih" or tree fungi are discussed from the earlier writings of the alchemist Ko Hung. The black or purple are today identified by Chinese authorities as *Ganoderma sinense* and the red as *G. lucidum* and *G. capense*. To date, these are the only species to which any of the Japanese color designates above have been matched (Jones, 1994).

Preparation and Dosage

G. lucidum may be taken in a variety of forms—in syrups, soups, teas, injections, tablets, and tinctures, or as a bolus containing powdered medicine and honey. The dose in tincture form (20%) is 10 ml 3x/day; in tablet form (for insomnia) the dose is 1 g tablets, 3 tablets 3x/day. The syrup dose is 4 to 6 ml per day (Huang, 1993).

As an antidote for poisonous mushrooms, make a decoction of 120-200 g of dried *G. lucidum* in water (Liu and Bau, 1980; Ying et al, 1987), and drink 3-5 cups a day.

Notes

The polysaccharides extracted from *G. lucidum* have shown higher anticomplementary activity than Krestin® (PSK), an immunostimulant extracted from Japanese *Trametes versicolor* (Jeong et al, 1990). Also, an analysis of the relationship between chemical structure and antitumor activity in the glucans of *Grifola umbellata*, *Ganoderma lucidum*, *Trametes versicolor*, and *Omphalia lapidescens* revealed that the common unit of these active glucans is a C-6 branched (1-3)-b-D-glucopyranosyl-(1-3)-b-D-glucopyranosyl residue. Branching frequency appears to be important in determining activity (Miyazaki, 1983).

Some products containing *Ganoderma* include a melanin-inhibiting skin preparation, a hair-growing extract which includes Japanese horseradish, a bath preparation, and a sake drink (Jong and Birmingham, 1992).

RELATED SPECIES

The Genus *Ganoderma* Karst. contains a number of species that have been used medicinally, or may prove to be useful in the future (Zhao & Zhang, 1994). For instance, *G. oregonense* grows in the western U.S., and has no particular history of use but is currently being harvested and substituted for reishi by some herbalists (personal observation). Though this species may prove to be identical with *G. tsugae* which does have a history of use in China, this kind of substitution should be carefully evaluated, because there may be significant differences in activity between species. For instance, Wang et al (1993) have said that the active high molecular weight polysaccharides of the mycelium and fruiting bodies of *G. applanatum, G. lucidum,* and *G. tsugae* "showed marked qualitative and quantitative differences in the component sugars, the protein-moiety content and average molecular weight."

Ganoderma capense

Another of the red Ganodermas used in China is *G. capense* (Lloyd) Teng, which might belong in *G. tenue* Zhao, Xu et Zhang (Zhao & Zhang, 1994). Water extracts of *G. capense* contain adenine, adenine nucleoside, uracil, uridine, and D-mannitol (Chang & But, 1986). From a liquid mycelial culture, two anti-inflammatory alkaloids were isolated and named Ganoderma alkaloid A (1-isopentyl-2-formyl-5-hydroxymethylpyrrole) and Ganoderma alkaloid B (phenylethyl-2-formyl-5-hydroxymethylpyrrole) (Yang, 1990). Other alkaloids from the mycelium are ganoline, ganodine, and ganoderpurine (Yu, 1990). Animal studies with *G. capense* show it has sedative (on the CNS), peripheral anticholinergic, liver-protective, and detoxifying actions (Chang & But, 1986). It has also increased immunocytes in mice (Xu et al, 1985), and other animal studies show *G. capense* can potentiate the effects of some sedative drugs, including chloropromazine and respirine (Chang & But, 1986).

Chinese physicians report success using an injectable preparation of the mycelia of *G. capense* (the formula is called "Bao gai ling zhi") to treat collagen-related diseases such as dermatomyositis (a condition involving decay of muscle fibers accompanied by inflammation of muscles, subcutaneous tissue, and skin), lupus erythematosus, scleroderma, and alopecia areata (Jones, 1992a). In one study involving dermatomyositis and multiple myositis, patients received 4 ml intramuscular injections of *G. capense* 1X/day for 1 month, or 2 g of a tablet preparation orally 3X/day for 2 months. The results were 6 cases cured, 6 markedly improved, and 7 significantly improved (Chen et al, 1987). In a study involving 232 cases of alopecia areata (hair loss) treated with *G. capense*, 30.17% of the patients were cured, 21.98% significantly improved, and 26.72% improved. The course of the treatment was from 20 days to 10 months, with the best effects appearing in 2-4 months (Cao et al, 1986). *G. capense* has also been found beneficial in hereditary cerebellar ataxia (Wang & Fu, 1981), which was more effective if treatment was initiated in the early stages of the disease (Zhiyuan & Huiti, 1981).

Ganoderma japonicum (Fr.) Sawada

A water-soluble glucan, with the structure of an alkali-soluble polysaccharide, isolated from *G. japonicum* has demonstrated significant antitumor activity (Ukai et al. 1983). Animal studies have shown *G. japonicum* to improve cardiac function by increasing myocardial blood flow and microcirculation and to protect and detoxify the liver (Chang & But, 1986). Also, as with *G. lucidum*, treatment *before* exposure has been found to significantly increase the survival rate of irradiated mice (Hu & But, 1987). The fruiting body of *G. japonicum* contains ergosterol, organic acids, glucosamine, and polysaccharides (Chang & But, 1986). A water extract strongly inhibited a-glucosidase, a key enzyme in glycoprotein processing of viruses (Fung, 1993).

Ganoderma oregonense Murr.

As previously mentioned, this species may be identical with *G. tsugae*, but this has not yet been determined. *G. oregonense* holds a "crystalline substance" which has shown a high degree of activity against acid fast and Gram positive bacteria (Brian, 1951). I have experimented with fruiting bodies of this species. It has a taste similar to reishi and produces very large fruiting bodies. I displayed several in mushroom exhibits that were about 24" long and 8" wide with a thick lateral stalk.

Ganoderma sinense

G. sinense Zhao, Xu et Zhang is considered by some taxonomists to be synonymous with *G. japonicum* ; however, much controversy surrounds the distinction of *G. japonicum* (Zhao & Zhang, 1994). It is commonly known as "zhi chih" or "zi zhi," the purple type of ling zhi, and is sweet and warming. *G. sinense* was traditionally used to treat deafness, afflictions of the joints, and to strengthen the "shen," or spirit. It is also said to improve the complexion, increase agility, and impart longevity (Jones, 1992a), and it may be used as an anti-inflammatory, diuretic, and to improve stomach function (Liu and Bau, 1980). Both the mycelium and fruitbody have shown analgesic and anti-inflammatory activity in arthritis models in mice and the mycelial extract promotes the phagocytic ability of the immune system (Wan, 1992).

Ganoderma tsugae

Another species is *G. tsugae* Murr., some forms appearing similar to *G. lucidum*, though it grows mainly on conifers instead of hardwoods. Its common Chinese name, Song shan ling zhi, means "pine tree fungus" or "pine wound" (Jingrong, 1979), but though it is common in the U.S. and other parts of the world, it is more often found on fir and hemlock than pine (Gilbertson & Ryvarden, 1986). *G. tsugae* is today one of the major cultivated species of *Ganoderma* in Taiwan.

Three of the same triterpenoids, lucidone A, ganoderic acid B, and ganoderic acid C2, that occur in reishi have been identified from this species. Significant hepato-protective activity from carbontetrachloride-induced liver toxicity was seen from ganderic acid B from *G. tsugae* when administered to mice (Su et al, 1993). The fruit-body also contains seven polysaccharides which have shown "strong" antitumor activity against sarcoma 180 in mice. The more potent are water-soluble polysaccharides which produced tumor inhibition ratios of 95.1-100.0% and prolonged life span by 236.3-267.5% (Wang et al, 1993). Mycelial extracts administered to mice (i.p.) significantly increased serum interferon levels and augmented splenic NK cell activity, but only at doses of from 1-50 mg/kg (Won et al, 1992).

In North America, *G. tsugae* is found on dead conifer trees in the midwestern states, the Southwest, California, Maine, N. Carolina, and eastern Canada, typically on hemlock (Lincoff, 1981).

Some of my students found a 16 pound fruiting body of this species or *G. orego-nense* high in the Sierra range in California on old hemlock. When fresh, it easily separated into tender strips like cooked chicken. The taste was sweet, mild, and slightly bitter. We all sampled it extensively and everyone pronounced it delicious. We packed the massive fruiting body (there is a picture in the color section) out of the wilderness area for several miles wrapped in a sheet. A word of warning about this species, though. If harvested before full maturity, it must be prepared as a tincture fresh or sliced and dried within 12 hours, or it will mold and take on an unpleasant taste. We are currently experimenting with the tincture and tea of this species.

Procurement
G. lucidium is arguably the most common medicinal mushroom found in tableted and liquid products throughout the world. It is available in herb stores, natural food stores, Chinese herb dealers in bulk, and including drug stores in a wide array of prepared products to boost energy levels, improve sexual vigor, counteract aging, and for general health improvement. Various *Ganoderma* species grow throughout the world, including the Amazon.

(geo=earth, astr=star; triplex-three-fold)

EARTHSTAR

and other *Geastrum* species

Synonyms
G. indicum is a synonym for *Geastrum triplex* (Arora, 1986).

Other Common Names
G. triplex is commonly known as "saucered earthstar" (Arora, 1986).

Description and Habitat
The mature outer wall of *G. triplex* splits into 4-8 rays, each of which is 3-10 cm broad when expanded. This fungus is usually seen when its rays unfold and bend under the spore case, opening the apical pore so that the spores may be released (Arora, 1986; Miller, 1979).

Geastrum triplex from *The Illustrated Dictionary of Gardening* by George Nicholson, circa 1887.

Hygroscopic (water-absorbing) earthstars are so named because they open their rays in rainy weather exposing their spore cases to moisture, facilitating spore release, and then close up again to retain them when it is dry. Many other species of *Geastrum* are not hydroscopic (Arora, 1986).

Range
Geastrums are common throughout the United States (Arora, 1986), Europe, and Asia.

History
In North America, the Cherokee applied the powder of several *Geastrum* species to the umbilical cord after childbirth, perhaps as both a hemostatic and antibiotic (Mooney and Albrechts, 1932).

Chemistry
No data.

Pharmacology
No data.

Human Clinical Studies
None.

Toxicity
None known; said to be inedible because they are so tough (Arora, 1986).

Uses in Traditional Medicine
In TCM, *G. triplex* is pungent, detoxifying, and tonic to the lungs and throat (Liu & Bau, 1980); it also clears internal heat and fever (Ying et al, 1987). It is said to reduce inflammation in the respiratory tract. Decoct it with licorice for sore throat, coughs, and laryngitis. It is used to stanch bleeding and reduce swelling (Ying et al, 1987). The Maya use the spores of *Geastrum* species to treat wounds (Arora, 1994).

Medical Uses
Not known.

Preparation and Dosage
Decoct 3 g for a batch of tea (about 5-6 cups of water) and take twice daily.

Related Species
The use of *Geastrum* in various cultures is probably not species-specific—any available species is apparently useful. *Astraeus hygrometricus* (Pers.) Morg. (said to be unrelated to *Geastrum* but superficially similar), also called the "hygroscopic earthstar", has also been used traditionally in Chinese folk medicine as a hemostatic (Liu and Bau, 1980; Ying et al, 1987). The spore dust of *A. hygrometricus* is applied externally to stop bleeding of wounds and watery chilblains (a swelling associated with coldness and dampness) (Liu and Bau, 1980). In India, the spore mass is blended 1:1 with mustard seed oil and applied to burns, 4-5 times daily (Rai et al, 1993). The related *Geastrum fornicatum* (*Geaster fornicatus* Huds.) had a reputation in West India as a styptic (Dragendorff, 1898).

Procurement
Earthstars are not available commercially, except on occasion by special order through Chinese herb dealers. They grow commonly in many regions of the world.

GRIFOLA FRONDOSA (DICKS.:FR.) S.F. GRAY.

(grifola=braided fungus; frondosa-leaflike)

MAITAKE, HEN OF THE WOODS, SHEEP'S HEAD

Synonyms
Boletus frondosus, Polyporus frondosus (Gilbertson and Ryvarden, 1987).

Other Common Names
G. frondosa is called "maitake" in Japanese, which means "dancing mushroom." Some say it is so named because in ancient times people who found the mushroom danced with joy since it could be exchanged for its weight in silver. However, others feel the name "maitake" derives from the fact that the fruiting bodies of adjacent fungi overlap each other, looking like butterflies in a wild dance (Nanba, 1992; Harada, 1993). It is also called hen of the woods and sheep's head (Arora, 1994).

Description and Habitat
Small overlapping tongue- or fan-shaped caps with stalks that are often fused together occurring in masses at the base of stumps and on roots.

Range
It is common in parts of the Eastern U.S., Europe, and Asia; also reported (rarely) from the western half of U.S.

History
Maitake collectors in Japan traditionally guard their hunting grounds with hatch marks on trees bordering the trove and keeping others out of the marked areas. Even so, maitake hunters always forage alone and never divulge the location of their treasure, even to their own family. Until cultivation techniques were developed in 1979, maitake was only available as a wild harvested mushroom. In 1990, Japanese cultivators produced nearly 8,000 tons of maitake, and production is expected to increase with expanding exports to the West (Harada, 1993).

Chemistry
Both α- and β-D-glucans have been detected from maitake, with β-D-glucans predominating. They appear to occur in two forms—the native form (laminaran type) and the helix (curdlan) type (Ohno et al, 1987). Other identified polysaccharides include a β-D-glucan and a D-glucan (Kato et al, 1989; Kato et al, 1990; Mizuno et al, 1988; Wei et al, 1991), grifolan (Oikawa et al, 1987), grifolin-LE (Ohno et al, 1986a; Aduchi et al, 1989), MT-2 (Adachi et al, 1987), LELFD (Suzuki, I. et al, 1989) and grifolan NMF-5N (Takeyama et al, 1988), as well as metal-bound proteins known to act as carriers of metals in intestinal absorption (Shimaoka et al, 1990), and an N-acetylgalactosamine-specific lectin (Kawagishi et al, 1990).

Dried maitake was found to be relatively rich in 5'-nucleotides (106-366 mg/100g), including GMP (Sekizawa et al, 1988; Sekizawa et al, 1989). The total lipid content of *G. frondosa* is 3.4%, with octadecenoic and octadecadienoic acids being the major unsaturated fatty acids (Endo et al, 1981), and phosphatidylcholine, phosphatidylethanolamine (mycelium) and phosphatidylinositol, phosphatidylserine, and phosphatidic acid (fruiting body) the major phospholipids (Kojima et al, 1991). Ergosterol (vitamin D2) is the major sterol, at the concentration of 50-150 IU in 100g wet material (Yokokawa and Takahashi, 1990).

Pharmacology

Maitake reduced blood pressure in rats without changing plasma HDL levels. *Lentinula edodes* (shiitake) also lowered blood pressure but in addition reduced plasma free, VLDL-, and HDL-cholesterol levels (Kabir and Kimura, 1989). Refer to the main entry on *Lentinula edodes* for further information about shiitake's pharmacological activity.

Adachi and co-workers (1988) found a blood-pressure-lowering effect with the powder of maitake fed to hypertensive rats in their normal chow. The effect was of rapid onset, short-lived, and dose-dependent and was noted in a low-molecular subfraction from the ether-extracted fraction. There was no activity reported from the water-soluble fraction, which may indicate that the tea of maitake is not effective in lowering blood pressure, unlike reishi and shiitake, whose water-soluble fraction has demonstrated this effect. However, an aqueous extract of maitake reduced serum cholesterol levels in rats (Yagishita et al, 1977).

A hepatoprotective effect was found from an extract of *G. frondosa* (300 mg/kg) in rats in a hepatitis model (paracetamol-induced). With the exception of shiitake extract, extracts of five other edible mushrooms (*Auricularia auricula, Flammulina velutipes, Tremella fuciformis,* and *Volvariella volvaceae*) failed to protect the rats (Ooi et al, 1993). In another report, a number of popular medicinal fungi were tested for hepatoprotective protective effects (*in vitro*), showing maitake to be among the active species (Lee et al, 1992).

Feeding maitake fruiting body powder (20% of the diet for 21 days—1 gram/day) to genetically diabetic rats has also lowered blood glucose levels in a non-insulin dependent diabetes mellitus model (Kubo et al, 1994). The blood glucose-lowering effect was said to be both due to a high (150,000) molecular-weight glycoprotein from the hot water decoction and from compounds of an ether-ethanol extract. Nanba (1991, 1994c) reported at the Japan Pharmaceutical Conference that when maitake powder was orally administered to rats, the water weight in the excrement increased by about 120%.

Powdered maitake orally administered, enhanced the activities of macrophages, N-killer-cells, and cytotoxic T-cells (by 1.4, 1.86, and 1.6 times respectively) and induced an 86% tumor growth inhibition compared with those of non-treated tumor-bearing mice (Mori et al, 1987).

Various isolated polysaccharide and protein-bound polysaccharide fractions and sub-fractions from maitake, which are both water-soluble and -insoluble, have also been tested for antitumor and immune-enhancing effects *in vivo* (with animals) and *in vitro* (Wu & Zou, 1994; Ohno et al, 1988, 1986a, 1987, 1984; Suzuki et al, 1987, 1985; Adachi et al, 1987; Mizuno et al, 1986; Iino et al, 1985). Nearly all (the "D-fraction" mentioned below seems to be the exception) of these fractions are active by injection only and not orally (where tested in this dose form) (Ohno et al, 1986a), varying only in the type of tumor it is most active against and the dose and regime with which it is most effective. While scientists look for the most active fractions, which may be effective at low doses and possibly patentable, these studies may also support the use of whole fruiting body teas, extracts, and dietary additions, where one receives the benefit of the synergy of all of the fractions. Whole powdered fruiting bodies *have* been shown to be active orally, and unfortunately, there is little if any data on the chronic daily use of this (as well as other) species and their effect on the immune system and general health. However, the testing of isolated fractions and sub-fractions may be useful in pointing the way to the production of very active and safe preparations that can help people overcome chronic immune diseases such as AIDS and cancer.

Recently, a number of studies have been performed with the so-called D-fraction (a 3-branched b-1,6-glucan with about 30% protein) from maitake which has shown an interleukin-1-stimulating effect. This may be partly responsible for its anti-tumor effect (implanted MM-46 carcinoma and IMC carcinoma) when given to mice by injection and also orally (Nanba, 1993). Nanba (1994b) has also reported that D-fraction administered to tumor-bearing mice along with the chemotherapeutic agent mitomycin C, markedly enhanced tumor inhibition, and that the extract inhibited the growth of MM-46 breast cancer cells in mice when administered orally, even after the tumors were well formed. The researcher also found the extract to be effective in the formation of new tumors and slowing metastasis of existing cancer cells to the liver of mice.

See Table 9 for a complete review of anticancer and immune-potentiation effects of maitake.

Recently, murine monoclonal antibodies (Mab) were isolated by injecting mice with a proteoglycan fraction derived from maitake and subsequent hybridization and culturing of spleen cells (Hirata et al, 1994). The authors predict that the antibodies may "recognize" the type of immunologically-active b-D-glucans that are found in maitake, shiitake, and other similar fungi, thus acting as a means to identify active polysaccharides.

A sulfated proteo-glucan from maitake also shows anti-HIV activity and apparently prevents HIV from killing T-cells *in-vitro* (Nanba et al, 1992), though the National Cancer Institute chose not to follow up with subsequent studies (Japanese NIH, 1990, 1991; National Cancer Institute, 1991) because of the toxicity posed by sulfation, and also because of its high molecular weight, which makes it difficult to study as an injectable (Shirota, 1994). Researchers have suggested that maitake extract, as well as schizophyllan, may stimulate the immune system in people with chronic fatigue syndrome (Ostram, 1992).

A group of researchers in Japan have identified a peptide that can enhance the absorption of copper from the small intestine by increasing the level of soluble copper (Shimaoka et al, 1993).

Table 9

LABORATORY STUDIES WITH MAITAKE EXTRACT: ANTICANCER EFFECT AND IMMUNE-POTENTIATION

Effect	Form of Administration	Dose	Duration	Animal and #	Authors	Year
tumor inhibition of sarcoma 180 over 90% from treatment at day of tumor inoculation; no inhibition from oral route, nor from GF-1 given before or after tumor; also active against meth-A fibrosarcoma and MM-46 carcinoma	GF-1	i.p., i.v., 0.5-5.0 mg/mouse/day	10 days	mice	Suzuki et al	1984
tumor inhibition of sarcoma 180 by 99%; ineffective orally at all doses and at 1mg	grifolan LE (b-1,3 glucan) from mycelium	i.p., i.t. (intra-mural), oral 100-200 mg/mouse/day	5 days	mice	Ohno	1986a
tumor growth-rate was inhibited by 43.3% and 86.3% and complete remissions in 2/8 mice in a second experiment (dose not given)	dried, powdered fruiting bodies of maitake were added to mouse feed	oral, 20% of feed	31 days	10 mice in each group	Mori, et al.	1987
antitumor effect against syngeneic tumors (MM-46 and IMC carcinomas); immune-potentiating (directly activates macrophages and stimulates production of interleukin-1, activates natural killer cells, killer T cells)	a polysaccharide sub-fraction isolated from the water-soluble fraction of the fruiting body of maitake (MT-2), containing about 0.6% protein	i.p., 1 mg/kg/day	5-10 days	# of mice not given	Adachi, et al.	1987
antitumor effect against syngeneic, allogenic tumors; immune-enhancement (IL-1) production increased, delayed-type hypersensitivity response increased	similar to MT-2, but called fraction-D (containing about 30% protein), isolated from hot-water (100 deg. for 10 hours) extract	orally, 0.2 mg	every other day for 10 days	10 mice in each group?	Hishida, et al.	1988
delayed-type hypersensitivity response of macrophages and T-cells is increased in tumor-bearing mice, leading to tumor inhibition	fraction-D	orally, 0.5 ml	every other day for 10 days	5 mice in each group	Yamada, et al.	1990
tumor-inhibition is 86.6% compared with PSK (from *Trametes versicolor*) (-7.1%) and lentinan (54.4%)	fraction-D	injection, 1.0 mg (fraction-D), 300 mg (PSK), 1.0 mg (lentinan)	daily for 10 days	# of mice not given	Nanba	1993

Note: Grifola fruiting bodies contain acid insoluble, alkali soluble, and hot water extractable D-fraction, which is a polysaccharide bound to a protein in the ratio of 70:30. Oral dosages of fraction-D (0.4% of maitake, dry weight), that is effective in mice at inhibiting tumors and restoring immune functions suppressed due to the growing cancer, are about 0.75 milligrams/kilogram of mouse weight. Although it is difficult to compare the activity in mice with humans, assuming a 1:1 activity ratio would mean that a comparable dose of D-fraction, found in the quantity of 4 mg/g of fruit body, is 47.25 mg for a 140 pound person—the amount contained in about 11.81 grams of maitake fruiting body—assuming a laboratory extraction similar to those in Hishida (1988) and others. However, the usual dose recommended by doctors using maitake in cancer treatment is 3-7 grams/day (Shirota, 1994; Nanba, 1994a).

In Mori et al (1986), it was found that including dried maitake powder in the mouse chow as 20% of their feed seemed to activate the immune response as well as stimulate a strong antitumor response.

The dose of fraction-D that proved effective in mice was administered every other day for 10 days. The hot-water extract of *Grifola* fruiting bodies was fractionated to create fraction-D by successive precipitations and purification using several solvents: first ethyl alcohol, then other solvents. The tumor-inhibition rate for the whole hot-water fraction ("Pre-A" fraction) only was 2%, as compared with 58% for fraction-D (29 times as strong). Whether a longer administration of weeks or months of the hot-water extract (and perhaps in a higher dose than given in the experiment—0.5 ml every other day X 10/mouse) would lead to significant antitumor and immune-enhancing effects is not clear (Hishida, 1988). It is interesting to note that Hishida claimed to have found a substance in the pre-A fraction that "inhibited immune stimulation," which may have led to the very low tumor-inhibition rate of 2%. Later purification may have eliminated those substances responsible.

Human Clinical Studies
A maitake D fraction-containing extract is being studied in medical clinics in the U.S. for patients with breast and colorectal cancers (Miller, 1994). In China a *Grifola* extract demonstrated an anticancer effect in 63 patients with lung, stomach, hepatocellular cancers, and leukemia (Zhu et al, 1994). The extract was given orally, 4 capsules three times daily before meals for 1-3 months. Nanba (1994a,b) reports that he has "seen a lot of advanced cancer patients recovered from severe side effects from chemotherapies" (with fraction D). Maitake extracts with D fraction may also prove to be an effective therapy for patients with AIDS. Dr. Joan Priestley, MD reports that her patients with Kaposi's sarcoma and other symptoms of AIDS show improvement when administered the extract, and Dr. David Hughes, MD has had positive results with Kaposi's sarcoma lesions (Nanba, 1994a). These reports are encouraging, but keep in mind that they are preliminary clinical reports, not controlled studies.

A prospective uncontrolled, non-randomized study was undertaken at the Ayurvedic Medicine Center of New York (Gerson, 1994). Eleven volunteers with documented essential hypertension were given three 500 mg caplets of maitake mushroom extract (Grifron™) two times daily in the morning and evening. Blood pressure (BP) was measured weekly for an average of six weeks. There was a mean decrease in systolic BP of 14 mm Hg and 8 mm Hg in diastolic BP, which was about a 7% and 9.4% average drop respectively. The drop was steady and consistent. Some of the patients in the study were taking medication during the test, and of course, the possibility of the patients getting used to the testing procedures and technician during the test leading to a gradual decrease in blood pressure cannot be overlooked. The results do suggest that a follow-up controlled study would be desirable.

A concentrated polysaccharide extract of *G. frondosa* was used in a randomized controlled clinical trial with 32 chronic hepatitis B patients. The recovery rate was reported to be 72% in the *Grifola* group and 57% in the control group. Seroconversion from HBeAg positive to negative was 44% in the *Grifola* group and 13% in the control group (Wu & Zou, 1994).

Toxicity
No data.

Uses in Traditional Medicine
The closely-related *G. umbellata* (sclerotium) has a sweet, bland taste and mild energy (Chang and But, 1986).

Medical Uses
When used consistently (3-5 times weekly) as a food or tea, it possibly aids in cancer-prevention, immune-stimulation in people with cancer, support for people with cancer undergoing chemotherapy (which is immunosuppressive), and people infected with the AIDS virus. It potentially benefits diabetics (lowering blood glucose) and people with hypertension.

Preparation and Dosage
3-7 grams a day in supplement form, in tea, or in cooking (soups, etc.).

Related Species
Grifola umbellata, reviewed below.

Procurement
Maitake can be found in gourmet restaurants (I recently enjoyed a dish featuring them in Maine), dried and packaged in gourmet grocery stores, occasionally through Chinese herb dealers, and increasingly, in prepared products in Japan, throughout other parts of Asia, the U.S., and Europe. It grows commonly in Europe and Asia and in the eastern U.S.

GRIFOLA UMBELLATA (PERS.:FR.)

(grifola=braided fungus; umbellata=umbrella-like)

ZHU LING

Synonyms
Polyporus umbellatus Fries.

Other Common Names
Polyporus sclerotium, China sclerotium (Liu and Bau, 1980); choreimaitake (Yokoyama et al, 1975).

Description and Habitat
Whitish to gray circular caps with central stems. The fruiting bodies arise from sclerotia, or "tubers" (Arora, 1986).

Range
Eastern North America and Asia.

History
Zhu ling is first mentioned in the *Divine Husbandman's Classic of the Materia Medica*, also known as the *Classic of the Materia Medica*, which was the first book that focuses on descriptions and uses of individual herbs (Bensky & Gamble, 1993). This important work was said to be written by the legendary "Divine Husbandman," who is considered the father of herbal medicine in China, but is known to originate from the first century A.D., later reconstructed from several manuscripts on herbal medicine by the famous Taoist, Tao Hong-Jing (452-536 A.D.).

Chemistry
The sclerotium of *G. umbellata* contains ergosterol, α-hydroxy-tetracosanoic acid, biotin, soluble polysaccharide I (Gu-I), and crude protein (Yoshioka & Yamamoto, 1964; Yokoyama et al, 1975; Chang and But, 1986). According to Suzuki et al (1982), its mineral content (ppm) is as follows:

Na	K	Ca	Mg	Fe	Mn	Zn	Cu
103	1,010	23,400	520	1,800	43	16	13

Studies on 1-, 2-, and 3-year-old *G. umbellata* have determined that total sugar, polysaccharide, and ergosterol content is highest in the 2-year-old fungus (Guo et al, 1992).

Pharmacology
The most important use of zhu ling in TCM is as a diuretic in cases of edema, scanty urine output, and damp heat conditions such as jaundice, vaginal discharge, and diarrhea. A number of modern studies, mostly from China, have supported this traditional use. For instance, zhu ling has produced increased urine output and elevated excretion of sodium and chloride in rats, after an injection (i.p. of the acetone extract, apparently by inhibiting active transport of chloride and blocking sodium reabsorption in the ascending loop of Henle) (Huang et al, 1985). The effect was similar in strength to ethacrynic acid, a commonly used diuretic drug with significant side effects, such as depletion of potassium, an important elec-

trolyte (Reynolds, 1993). The zhu ling extract did not increase the excretion of potassium. In an older study by Shen and coworkers in 1957, a decoction (8 grams administered 4 times as a decoction) increased the 6-hour urine output by 62% and chloride output by 54.5% in healthy volunteers, which was stronger than that seen with *Akebia quinata* or hoelen (*Wolfiporia cocos*). The water decoction may be stronger than an ethanolic extract (tincture), which did not increase the urine output in healthy human subjects, but did in another study with dogs (Chang & But, 1986). The zhu ling extract did not lead to thinning of blood or a change of the glomerular filtration rate, so the diuretic effect was thought to be due to inhibition of electrolyte and water reabsorption by the renal tubules (Chang & But, 1986).

In a number of *in vitro* and *in vivo* studies, *G. umbellata* and its crude and refined hot-water extracts (Ueno et al, 1982; Miyazaki et al, 1979; Chang and But, 1987; Ying et al, 1987, Yu et al, 1985), as well as the ethanolic extract (Chang & But, 1987), have demonstrated marked antitumor activity against sarcoma 180 and hepatoma, plus a number of other types of experimentally-induced cancers (Ito et al, 1973). The extracts accelerate the production of IgM and strengthen the phagocytic power of the monocytes (Li, 1985; Chang & But, 1986), while improving cellular immunity (macrophage proliferation and activity) in normal and liver-compromised mice (Zhang et al, 1991). A number of polyporusterones, A-G have been isolated and determined to be cytotoxic on leukemia 1210 cells *in vitro* (Ohsawa et al, 1992). However, the fungus shows no effect on leukemia L615 (Chang and But, 1987). A special zhu ling extract "757" showed DNA synthesis inhibition in mouse sarcoma 180 (Chang & But, 1987). Zhu ling polysaccharides, especially, have been shown to be antineoplastic *in vivo*, and this effect may be due to a nonspecific immunostimulant or immunopotentiating action (Chang and But, 1986). For example, although a polysaccharide extracted from this fungus has shown antitumor activity (*in vivo*), increased formation of antibody cells in the spleen, and increased phagocytosis of the peritoneal macrophages in mice, *G. umbellata* extract was not directly effective on the tumor cells *in vitro* (Zhu, 1987). Also, in mice with hepatoma H22 given *G. umbellata*, restoration of liver carbohydrate metabolism and adrenocortical function took place, which suggests that the antitumor properties may also be attributed to a metabolism-restoring action (Wei et al, 1983). Zhu ling purified hot water extract has also demonstrated a mitogenic effect *in vitro* (Yadomae et al, 1979b). Mitogens are high-molecular weight compounds often associated with bacterial cell walls and are known to modulate the immune response.

Tumor-necrosis factor (TNF), which may be produced by macrophages associated with the reticuloendothelial system (RES), is also known to reduce tumor size and increase the survival time of animals with various cancers. Zhu ling spray-dried water extract was fed to mice and showed no TNF-releasing activity, whereas the Chinese herbs bupleurum, angelica, cnidium, and cinnamon had strong activity in the same assay (Haranaka et al, 1985).

An alcoholic extract of *G.umbellata* has demonstrated antibiotic actions *in vitro* against *Staphylococcus aureus* and *Escherichia coli* (Chang & But, 1986), and a polysaccharide derivative demonstrated hepatoprotective effects in mice (Lin and Wu, 1988). The polysaccharides have also been found to confer protection against ionizing radiation (Hu and But, 1987). In this study, the survival rate for mice given *G. umbellata* 2 hours before exposure was 35.5%, while the survival rate of mice treated 48 hours before exposure was 75%. The control group's survival rate was only 2.5%.

In a screening of 80 different Chinese herbs for hair growth promoting activity, *G. umbellata* placed third among the five most active species. One of the constituents responsible for this action was identified as 3,4-dihydroxybenzaldehyde, a compound with anti-inflammatory activity (Inaoka et al, 1994).

Human Clinical Reports

Grifola umbellata was shown to increase diuresis, stimulate the immune system, and act as an anticancer agent. This fungus is used to treat edema, increase vaginal secretion, and promote urination. The dose is 6 to 15 g made into a decoction. It is one of the major ingredients in the Chinese formula, Wu Ling San, which has been reported from clinical trials to radically improve cirrhotic ascites (Huang, 1993).

G. umbellata's polysaccharides have been used in the treatment of cancer patients since the mid-1970s, with varying degrees of improvement reported, including better appetite, weight gain, and greater mental alertness (Zhu, 1987). The clinical symptoms associated with lung cancer (10 cases studied) and chronic hepatitis (170 cases) were improved with the administration of a polysaccharide from *G. umbellata* (Li, 1985). Clinical studies on a new *G. umbellata* extract named "757" show that this fungus could help reduce the side effects of chemotherapy and strengthen the immune system (Chang & But, 1986). For example, when 757 was used in combination with chemotherapy, an 86% rate of symptomatic improvement was noted in subjects with lung cancer, while those who were treated with just *G. umbellata* had only 62.5% rate of improvement in symptoms. Tumor stability was 70% in the combined therapy group, as compared to 25% for the use of the extract alone. The "757" extract seemed to protect immune system functions in 13 patients who had esophageal cancer and were concurrently receiving chemotherapy, but the therapeutic effects were less certain (Chang & But, 1986).

In 39 patients with cirrhosis of the liver with ascites who failed to respond to other treatment, a modified traditional herbal formula "Wu Ling San," (6-12 grams daily in decoction), was reported to bring about a clinical cure in 17 cases, marked improvement in 7, and significant improvement in 12. The base formula was composed of the following (Bensky and Barolet, 1990):

- ◆ Rhizoma Alismatis Orientalis (ze xie)   4 grams
- ◆ Sclerotium Poriae Cocos (hoelen, fu ling)   2.3 grams
- ◆ Rhizoma Atractylodis Macrocephalae (bai zhu)   2.3 grams
- ◆ Ramulus Cinnamomi Cassiae (gui zhi)   1.5 grams
- ◆ [Sclerotium Polypori Umbellati (zhu ling)   2.3 grams]

Five-peel decoction (Wu Pi Yin) was also given to the volunteers, which consists of the following:

- ◆ Pericarpium Arecae Catechu   15 grams
- ◆ Epericarpium Benincasae Hispidae   6 grams

◆ Pericarpium Citri Reticulae	15 grams
◆ Cortex Poriae Cocos	15 grams
◆ Cortex Zingiberis Officinalis Recens	6 grams
◆ Pericarpium Citri Reticulatae Viride	9 grams

Zhu ling decoction brought good results in five cases of chyluria in 4 of the patients (Chang & But, 1987).

◆ Sclerotium Polypori Umbellati (zhu ling)	3 grams
◆ Sclerotium Poriae Cocos (fu ling)	3 grams
◆ Rhizoma Alismatis Orientalis (ze xie)	3 grams
◆ Talcum (hua shi)	3 grams
◆ Gelatinum Corii Asini (e jiao)	3 grams

Contraindications and Toxicity

G. umbellata was found to be nontoxic in animal studies at the dose of 200-250 mg/kg oral, 500 mg/kg i.p., or up to 100 mg/kg i.p. daily for 28 days (Chang & But, 1987). No negative reactions have been noted in human trials (Zhu, 1987). The LD50 of an acetone extract i.p. was determined to be >0.4 g/kg (Huang et al, 1985). In traditional use, the mushroom is not recommended for people who do not have dampness imbalances, or for long periods of time (Bensky and Gamble, 1993). Used longer than 3-4 weeks it might be too drying (without the addition of other moistening herbs such as marshmallow root).

Uses in Traditional Medicine

In TCM, zhu ling is considered to have a sweet and bland taste; its temperature is slightly cool (Bensky and Gamble, 1993). Zhu ling is used primarily in health imbalances where there is excess dampness—as a diuretic for painful urination, urinary tract infections, edema, diarrhea, jaundice (damp heat in the lower jiao), and leukorrhea (Chang and But, 1987; Bensky & Gamble, 1993). Zhu ling is a major component of the popular Chinese patent formula called Wu Ling San, which also contains other strengthening herbs. This formula is modified from the one given above, and provides a 3-4 week supply:

◆ Zhu ling	180 grams
◆ Hoelen	180 grams
◆ Cinnamon	120 grams
◆ Alisma	300 grams
◆ Atractylodis (stir-fried)	180 grams

Grind the herbs to a powder, blend, and place in capsules (take 2 caps 3 x daily), or stir 6-9 grams into warm water or tea and drink 1 cup morning and evening.

Wu ling san is recommended for invigorating the function of the Kidney, strengthening the Spleen (digestion and assimilation), and increasing urine output. Specific symptoms which indicate the use of zhu ling include water retention, abdominal distention with vomiting, diarrhea, and dry mouth with no desire to drink (Tu, 1988).

Medical Uses
G. umbellata is used to treat lung cancer (Ying et al, 1987). In a clinical report from China, its decoction showed a 92% improvement rate in patients with cirrhotic ascites (Huang, 1993).

Preparation and Dosage
6-15 grams/day as a decoction, extracts in tablet or capsule form, or in soups (Tu, 1988).

Related Species
Grifola frondosa (see above). In the 1940s, low molecular weight antibiotic terpenoids were isolated from what was reported to be *Grifola confluens*, which is probably now *Albatrellus confluens* (Alb. & Schw.:Fr.) Kotl. & Pouz., and named grifolin and neogrifolin by Kubo and Mizuno in 1948 (Hirata and Nakanishi, 1950). Chemically, this compound is 2-trans, trans-farnesyl-5-methylresorcinol and was recently shown to have a cholesterol-lowering effect in rats (Sugiyama, 1992). Grifolin has also shown antibiotic properties against Gram positive bacteria (Hirata & Nakanishi, 1949).

The fruiting body and cultured mycelium of *A. confluens*, known in Japan as Ningyotake, contains polysaccharides which show antitumor activity (Mizuno et al, 1992).

Procurement
Zhu ling is a common component of Chinese prepared products, as mentioned above. It is also available in bulk through Chinese herb dealers.

INONOTUS OBLIQUUS (PERS.: FR.)

(inos=fiber; noton=back and oblique=uneven sides)

PILAT. CHAGA

Synonyms
Poria obligua Bres.; *Polyporus obliquus* Fr.

Other Common Names
Black Birch touchwood, Birch mushroom, Clinker Polypore, tschagapilz, crooked Schiller-porling; kofukisaruno-koshikake (Yokoyama, 1975).

Description and Habitat
The sterile carpophore conk is a hard black, deeply-cracked stalkless growth found on alder, birch, and elm; notable from the appearance of having been burnt. The fertile fruiting bodies are transitory and hard to find. Chaga can attain lengths of 4-5 feet.

Range
Poland, Western Siberia, throughout North America (Kier, 1961; Saar, 1991a).

History
Russian folklore from the province of Olonyets in northwestern Russia tells of a fungus which grows on birch trees being revered for treating a variety of cancers. Folkloric reports also come from Siberia, the Baltic, and Finland. Specifically, only the "abortive" sporophores of the fungus were given to cancer patients as a tea until the cancer improved (Lucas, 1960). In Russia, besides its well-known use against cancer (Grzybek et al, 1983), chaga is regarded as a tonic, blood purifier, and pain-reliever (Hutchens, 1973) and was widely used against cancer in Poland in 1961. It was recommended and approved for public use against cancer by the Medical Academy of Science, Moscow, 1955 (Hutchens, 1973). In 1960, the U.S. National Cancer Institute received a report that a decoction of chaga had been used successfully to treat cancer in Australia (Hartwell, 1971a).

Chemistry
Inooidiol, oxygenated triterpenes, trametenolic acid (Kahlos et al, 1986); tannins, steroids, alkaloid-oramin-like compounds (Piaskowski, 1957); obliquol, (Kier, 1961) along with other trimethylsilyl ethers of lanosterol-type triterpenes, specifically lanosterol; inotodiol (Ludwiczak and Wrzeciono, 1961, 1962); 3-ß-hydroxy-lanosta-8,24-dien-21-al; 3-ß,21-dihydroxy-lanosta-8,24-diene, trametenolic acid (Kahlos and Hiltunin, 1988) and 3-ß,21-dihydroxy-lanosta-8,24-dien-21-oic acid (Kempska et al, 1962). A Pteroiloglatamic acid derivative has also been isolated (Grzybek et al, 1983), as well as the aromatic vanillic-, syringic- and r-hydroxybenzoic acids (Lovyagina et al, 1958).

Pharmacology
Based on its long history of use against cancer, a number of eastern European researchers have tested it in the laboratory for antitumor activity. Gatty-Kostyal et al showed an antitumor effect of the alcoholic extract in 1954, followed by a number of other Polish and Russian researchers who also tested various extracts *in vitro*

and *in vivo* (Jarosz et al, 1990), which lead to the use of the official preparation "Befungin" as an anticancer therapy (Grzybek et al, 1983). Oxygenated triterpenes, particularly Inotodiol, of chaga have shown antitumor activity (*in vitro*) against MCF-7 mammary adenocarcinoma *in vitro* and *in vivo* in mice (Kahlos et al, 1987; Kahlos et al, 1986). In animals, a water extract of chaga at non-toxic doses showed activity against carcinoma (Kier, 1961). The identity of the active compound(s) responsible for the antitumor activity is still under discussion. Some researchers point to the triterpenes, especially obliquol, (Grzybek et al, 1983). However, these compounds occur in very small amounts (less than 0.2%) in the official Russian anticancer remedy Befungin, as does the proven anticarcinogenic compound, a pteroiloglatamic acid derivative (Grzybek et al, 1983). Because of this, Grzybek et al (1983) tested the polysaccharide fraction in the *Allium*-test, which measures the inhibition of the mitotic index. The researchers claim that the test is "predictive of experiments with animal tumor systems." Polysaccharide fraction B from *Inonotus* showed positive activity in the test, prompting a call for further research on chaga polysaccharides, especially since the fraction was found to be contaminated with minerals, proteins, and nucleic acids.

Antitumor activity was only found from extracts prepared by lengthy heating or "decocting," which investigators noted was the means of preparation used in folk medicine. Infusions, prepared by steeping the plant material, were not active against the tumor systems tested (Lucas, 1959).

Chaga showed no *in vitro* activity against *Staphylococcus aureus* and *E. coli* (Broadbent, 1966).

Human Clinical Studies
A study in Poland with 48 patients having third and fourth stage malignancies found chaga injections with cobalt salts to be the most effective form of preparation. In ten of the patients, tumors reduced in size, pain decreased, hemorrhaging occurred less often and became less intense, and recovery was attended with better sleep and appetite and feelings of improvement. Most of these patients were women treated with chaga for cancer of the genital organs or breast cancer (Piaskowski, 1957). Other clinical studies have been conducted in lung cancer patients with an aerosol preparation and in inoperable genital cancer in women with an extract of chaga administered by injection and suppository (Hartwell, 1971a).

Toxicity
No data.

Uses in Traditional Medicine
Chaga is a Russian folk remedy for cancers, including inoperable breast cancer, lip cancer, gastric, parotid gland, pulmonary, stomach, skin, and rectal cancers, and Hodgkin's disease (Hartwell, 1971a). Russians also use chaga to treat ulcers and gastritis and to regenerate organs and glands. To treat the lower bowel, decoctions are applied as colonics (Hutchens, 1973).

In Western Siberia, the Khanty people traditionally prepared chaga and still use the tea to treat tuberculosis, stomachache, stomach disease, liver or heart disease, worms, and as an internal cleansing agent. In the form of "soap water," the fungus is used by women to make a wash for external cleansing of the genitals following or during menstruation; for cleansing new-born infants; for "ritual washing"; and as a soap substitute for washing the feet and hands or the whole body. Soap water is prepared by burning chaga until red and then placing the charred fungus in hot water and stirring until it breaks up, and the water turns black (Saar, 1991a).

Medical Uses
Russian clinicians concluded that in cancer patients chaga is useful in some but not all cancers; that it prevents intoxication and regurgitation, improves appetite, and reduces pain; but that for cancer chaga requires long-term use of at least one year (Larionov, 1965).

Preparation and Dosage
For cancer, chaga has been prepared as a tea, decoction, extract, syrup, injection, suppository, tablet, and aerosol (Hartwell, 1971a).

The tea is prepared by boiling small pieces of the fungus in water for several minutes. Three square centimeters provide 2.5 liters of tea. According to Hutchens (1973), the tea is taken in a dose of three cups per day, 1/2 hour before meals, for 12-20 weeks with intervals of 7-10 days. Hutchens advises that only the middle portion of fungus be used, which is a granulated mass distinguishable from an outer rough part and a soft portion adjacent to the host tree. She suggests a tea be made with warm water (5 parts to 1 of chaga) by soaking the fungus for 48 hours in order not to destroy activity (Hutchens, 1973). However, this method is contrary to methods used by the Khanty (Saar, 1991a), who cut the fungus into small pieces and boiled it for a few minutes (3 cm of the fruiting body/pot of tea). The Khanty drank the tea "until the indispositions were over." And according to antitumor studies, unboiled extracts had no antitumor effect in mice, but boiling apparently activated the antitumor principals, leading to tumor inhibition in mice (Lucas, 1960). It seems that both folkloric and laboratory evidence points towards boiling the grated fungus and administering the tea. An alcoholic extract may also be effective, according to Russian studies.

Related Species
Inonotus sciurinus Imaz., *I. tabacinus* (Mont.) Kavst., and *I. orientalis* (Lloyd) Teng. of China have shown high rates of tumor inhibition against Ehrlich carcinoma and sarcoma 180. The most active was *I. orientalis* with rates of 100% inhibition against both tumor systems. *I. cuticularis* (Bull.:Fr.) Karst. inhibited Ehrlich carcinoma by 100% and sarcoma 180 by 90%. This species occurs on hardwoods throughout the U.S., Canada, and Asia. Medicinal uses include gastropathy, hemorrhages, bromhidrosis, and leprosy. It is considered sweet, smoothing to vital energy, strengthening to mind and spirit, and removing harmful wind (Ying et al, 1987).

Notes
According to Belova and Varentsova (1962), the tincture of chaga should be made 1:10 (weight to volume) preserved with 10% ethanol. The solids content of the tincture should be about 2-2.3%, but that of the decoction made by heating the powdered fruiting body to 80 degrees centigrade for 1 hour is 6-9%. The decoction can be filtered, concentrated under vacuum to 20% solids and then either preserved with 10% ethanol or dried to a powder in a food dehydrator (Yakimov et al,

1961). Andreeva (1961) found that the maximum extraction of a polyphenol mixture was highest at 100 degrees centigrade, but that a self-condensation reaction changed the composition of the extract at higher temperatures. Although the total steroid content of dry chaga was found to be 0.85-0.94% by Loviagina & Shivrina (1962), the authors conclude that the total anticancer effect of the extract must be due to compounds other than inotodiol, the only sterol shown to slow the growth of tumor cells *in vitro*.

Procurement

To my knowledge, chaga is not available in prepared products outside of Russia. It grows on birch and other hosts, especially in the eastern U.S. (I found several in northern Vermont), Alaska, Europe, and other parts of the northern hemisphere.

LENTINULA EDODES (BERK.) PEGLER

(lent=pliable, inus=resembling; edodes=edible)

SHIITAKE

Synonyms
Tricholomopsis edodes Sing., *Lentinus edodes* (Berk.) Pegler. The species name, edodes, means "edible".

Other Common Names
The common Japanese name for *L. edodes*, shiitake, derives from its association with the shiia tree (Willard, 1990). Also known as snake butter, Pasania fungus, or forest mushroom (Liu and Bau, 1980) and Hua Gu in Chinese.

Description and Habitat
These light amber fungi are found on fallen broadleaf trees (Ying et al, 1987). The trees particularly suitable for growing shiitakes are chestnut, chinquapin, beech, oak, Japanese alder, sweet gum, maple, walnut, and mulberry. They have decurrent, even to ragged gills; a central to off-center stem; an inrolled margin when young; and are covered with a delicate, white flocking. They are not found in the wild in the United States but are widely cultivated. Commercial kits which allow one to grow them indoors are available, and outdoor cultivation is also possible (see resource section).

Range
L. edodes is indigenous to Japan, China, and other Asian countries with temperate climates. A very similar species occurs wild in Costa Rica (Arora, 1994).

History
Shiitake has been renowned in Japan and China as a food and medicine for thousands of years. According to historical records, in the year 199 A.D., the Japanese Emperor Chuai was offered the shiitake by the Kyusuyu, a native tribe of Japan. Even older documents record shiitake's use in ancient China, where it was referred to as "ko-ko" or "hoang-mo" (Scientific Consulting Service).

The cultivation of shiitake is probably quite ancient. It is currently the second most commonly produced edible mushroom in the world (Nakamura, 1992). The nascent interest here has been spawned partly because shiitake tastes much more exotic and delicious than the bland *Agaricus bisporus* of supermarket shelves, and partly because of the immense amount of research that has been conducted on its varied medicinal properties.

Constituents
Shiitake has excellent nutritional value, containing proteins (2.22-2.60% fresh and 25.9% dry weight), lipids (primarily linoleic acid), water-soluble carbohydrates (0.45-0.72 g/100 g dry weight), total carbohydrates 67.0% (Terashita, 1990), insoluble (41.6%) and soluble (3.4%) fiber (Horie, 1991), minerals (especially calcium), and vitamins B2 and C (Liu and Bau, 1980; Ying et al, 1987). High amounts of ergosterol, a provitamin which converts to vitamin D in the presence of sunlight (Ying et al, 1987), is also present. In fact, studies have shown that exposing shiitake

to direct sunlight for 3 hours/day increases its vitamin D2 content up to 5 times. Shiitake is an efficient source for this nutrient, containing between 873 and 4,381 IU/100 g of dry mushroom weight (Kobayashi, 1988; Kiribunchi, 1990; Takamura et al, 1991; Takeuchi et al, 1991). Sunlight exposure also increases the free amino acid content which is about 2,180 mg% in the dry fruiting bodies, and it makes them sweeter and less bitter (Kiribuchi, 1991).

The mineral content of cultured shiitake mycelium (on a medium of 90% bagasse, 5% rice bran, 5% wheat bran, and other nutrients) when extracted close to the fruiting stage with boiling water was as follows (in mg/g of dry weight):

K	Ca	Mg	Mn	Cd	Fe	Ni	Cu
15.1	22.0	44-78	1.2	0.96	2.36	52.5	89.1

P	Zn	Ge	Br	Rb	Sr
281-497	282.8	<4	11.4	39.4	164.3

(Iizuka & Maeda, 1988; Ikebe et al, 1990; Lasota and Sylwestrzak, 1989)

As with many vegetables and fruits, the mineral content is highly variable, depending on the substrate where it grows. For instance, shiitake cultured with extra calcium in its culture medium has up to 3 times as much calcium in the fruiting bodies (Sasaki, 1990).

The mycelial cell-saps contain 30 enzymes and more than 10 amino acids, while the fruiting body contains all the essential amino acids, with lysine and arginine being particularly abundant (Liu and Bau, 1980) and methionine and phenylalanine the limiting amino acids (Lasota and Sylwestrzak, 1989). In laboratory analysis it was found that amino acids, protein, glycogen, lipids, ascorbic acid, and total ash contents increased as the fruiting body developed (Fasidi and Kadiri, 1990). Based on these findings, it may be desirable to consume fully mature fruiting bodies for maximum nutritional value. The researchers generally found higher concentrations of nutrients in the cap than the stem of the fungus. Potassium was the most abundant mineral element, followed by phosphorus.

The compounds responsible for the characteristic odor of fresh shiitake have been determined to be 1-octen-3-ol, ethyl acetate, 2-octenol, and octyl alcohol with the addition of 1,2,4-trithiolane in the boiled fruiting bodies. The latter compound—along with 1,2,4,5-tetrathiane—is characteristic of sulfur-containing components (Ahn et al, 1987).

Shiitake is the source of two well-studied preparations with proven pharmacological effects—namely *Lentinula edodes* mycelium extract (LEM) and lentinan.

Lentinan is a cell-wall constituent extracted from the fruiting bodies or mycelium of *L. edodes*. In essence, it is a highly purified, high molecular weight polysaccharide (of about one million) in a triple helix structure, containing only glucose molecules with mostly (1-3)-β-D-glucan linkages in the regularly branched main chain with two β (1,6)-D-glucopyranoside branchings for every five β-(1,3)-glucopyranoside linear linkages (Aoki, 1984b). The configuration of the glucose molecules in a helix structure is thought to be important for the biological activity (Hamuro et al, 1971b). Lentinan is completely free of any nitrogen (and thus protein), phosphorus, sulfur, or any other atoms except carbon, oxygen, and hydrogen (Chihara,1981). It is water-soluble, heat-stable, acid-stable, and alkali-labile (Aoki, 1984b).

Lentinula edodes mycelium extract (LEM) is a preparation of the powdered mycelia extract of *L. edodes* harvested before the cap and stem grow.

LEM's major active constituent is a heteroglycan protein conjugate, that is, a protein-bound polysaccharide. It contains about 24.6% protein and 44% sugars, mostly the pentoses xylose (a wood sugar) and arabinose (a pectin sugar), as well as glucose and smaller amounts of galactose, mannose, and fructose (Iizuka and Maeda, 1988). LEM also contains various nucleic acid derivatives; vitamin B compounds, especially B-1 (thiamine) and B-2 (riboflavin); ergosterol; and eritadenine, an anticholesteremic agent (Sharon, 1988; Breene, 1990). Besides active polysaccharides and protein-polysaccharide complexes, water-soluble lignins were isolated from LEM (Hanafusa et al, 1990). Both lentinan and LEM have been studied extensively for their interesting biological effects, which will be reviewed in the following Pharmacology section.

Pharmacology

It is impossible to consider the pharmacology of shiitake without reviewing its two most important preparations, *Lentinula edodes* mycelium extract (LEM) and lentinan. The chemical nature of these two substances is reviewed in the preceding section. Lentinan and LEM have both demonstrated strong antitumor activity, both orally and by injection in animals and humans. These substances work by enhancing various immune system functions rather than attacking the tumor cells (or viruses) themselves. In the following sections I will review the major published laboratory and clinical work available on their antitumor, immune-regulating, and antiviral effects, as well as their effects on the cardiovascular system.

It must be mentioned here that the immense volume of data available on lentinan alone is overwhelming, and it is not my intention to mention each study. However, a vast majority of the published studies are redundant and only serve to amplify or clarify certain points. In the following sections, I will report on the most characteristic and current studies. Please note that all the studies on lentinan quoted below are performed with test animals (nearly all with mice) by injection—either intraperitoneal (i.p.) or intravenously (i.v.), unless otherwise mentioned.

■ *Antitumor Effects*
To begin with, various polysaccharides extracted from *L. edodes* besides lentinan have shown antitumor (Chihara, 1969) and immunostimulating activities (Cao et al, 1989), for instance, by increasing phagocytotic activity of the peritoneal macrophages (Jiang et al, 1986). In one study, Fuji et al (1978) isolated a polysaccharide containing an a-mannan-peptide complex (KS-2) that strongly inhibited tumor growth when administered to mice both orally and i.p. in doses between 1 and100 mg/kg. Intraperitoneal injections (in mice) of other intracellular polysaccharides increased the phagocytotic function of the reticuloendothelial system (an important defense mechanism composed of highly phagocytic cells), while extracellular polysaccharides showed no effect (Zheng et al, 1985).

Of interest to mushroom-eaters and health-care practitioners is whether lentinan or shiitake in its whole form has any antitumor effect when taken orally as a tea, added to the diet, or used in capsules or tablets, powdered or in extract form. Based on the number of active fractions from shiitake fruiting bodies showing antitumor activity, this would seem likely. Nanba et al (1987) found that powdered shiitake fruiting bodies fed to mice as 10% of their normal diet inhibited the growth of sarcoma 180 and MM-46 tumors by 40%, but not B-16 melanoma, Lewis lung carcinoma, or others. Mori et al (1986) found that if shiitake were made part of the feed (20% a week) after tumor implantation, the tumor inhibition rate was 53.9%. If shiitake feed was given on the same day, the inhibition rate was 72.4%. Powdered whole shiitake fruiting bodies administered orally to tumor-bearing mice at 10% of the normal diet, improved macrophage phagocytosis, which is thought to play a role in its tumor-inhibiting activity (Nanba et al, 1987).

Ikekawa et al (1969) found that an injection (i.p.) of the freeze-dried water extract of shiitake (200 mg/kg/day X10) produced an inhibition rate of 80.7%. Although many early papers (before 1980) on lentinan report that it is not active orally, Aoki (1984b) stated that it is but gave no further details. However, studies in normal mice administered lentinan (1 mg in saline) orally demonstrated that compared to controls, peripheral white blood cell counts showed no significant difference, but that T helper cell and T cell ratios were significantly raised after one month of administration; ratios then fell to normal after eight weeks, thus indicating the development of tolerance to lentinan (Hanaue et al, 1989).

Lentinan was first isolated and studied in 1969 for its anti-tumor effects by Chihara and coworkers of the National Cancer Institute of Japan (Chihara, 1970b). Lentinan's antitumor activity was significantly stronger than polysaccharides from many other fungi, lichens, and higher plants (Arai et al, 1971), but it appears to be active in certain animals for some, but not all, types of tumors (Maeda et al, 1974).

The purified polysaccharide has been shown in animal studies to be nontoxic and enhance the immune response, producing strong tumor regression and even disappearance of tumors by 5 weeks in sarcoma 180 (Maeda et al, 1974b; Togami et al, 1982), ascites hepatoma 134 (Moriyama et al, 1981), and Ehrlich carcinoma (Ying et al, 1987), as well as a number of other experimentally-induced cancers in allogeneic, syngeneic, and autologous hosts as well as preventative activity against chemical carcinogenesis. Injections in mice produced either an 80% reduction in tumor size or complete regression in most of the animals. An intact immune system with a functioning thymus gland was found to be a requisite for the anticancer effect (Maeda & Chihara, 1973; Dennert & Tucker, 1973; Yamada et al, 1981), and when immunosuppressive agents (6-benzylthioguanosine or X-radiation) were given with lentinan, the anti-tumor effect was reduced (Arai et al, 1971). Lentinan has also been found to restore enzyme activity of X-prolyl-dipeptidyl-aminopeptidase, which can be depressed in cancer patients and mice with implanted tumors (Kato et al, 1979).

Laboratory tests seem to point to an important role of the adrenal-pituitary axis and central-peripheral nervous system, including serotonin, 5HT, histamine, and catecholamines in lentinan's antitumor activity (Maeda et al, 1974).

In Japan, lentinan is often used to help support immune function in cancer patients during chemotherapy (for instance cyclophosphamide), often leading to increased survival times (see Human Clinical Trials section). It is well-known that such chemotherapeutic agents can lead to severe immune suppression. A number of animal studies also support this use (Dennart, 1973). Hosokawa et al (1981) report on the importance of timing for the effective administration of combination immunotherapy and chemotherapy. Studies in animals support the use of lentinan in combination with immunobiological agents to treat cancer, such as a combined treatment with IL-2 (Suzuki, 1990; Yamasaki et al, 1989). Against spontaneous lung micrometastases in mice, lentinan or IL-2 alone were ineffective. Used in a combined treatment, pulmonary metastases were significantly inhibited. Thus, IL-2 plus lentinan acted synergistically (Yamasaki et al, 1989).

■ *Immune-Regulating Effects*
As previously mentioned, lentinan does not attack cancer cells directly, but produces its anti-tumor effect by activating different immune responses in the host. This activation was at first thought to occur only in immune-compromised animals, but not in healthy animals (Maeda et al, 1974b) and was called an immunorestorative agent, but recent work has uncovered a true immunopotentiating effect, by showing a clearly augmenting effect on the proliferation of peripheral mononuclear cells (PMNC) from healthy human donors, which is also supported by animal studies (Aoki, 1984b). It is not presently known exactly what molecular interactions take place in the initial stages of lentinan exposure in an animal system; however, there is a transitory but notable increase in several serum protein components in the a- and b-globulin region, namely complement C3, hemopexin, and ceruloplasmin (Maeda et al, 1974a). The following effects have been noted after lentinan administration in animals and humans.

Lentinan can activate natural killer (NK) cells *in vitro* in the same concentrations that can be achieved in the blood plasma of patients clinically-treated with lentinan (Tani et al, 1992; Sendo et al, 1981). NK cell activity is involved in tumor suppression (Herberman & Nunn-Hargrove, 1981) and either does not stimulate T-killer cell activity or only under certain conditions, but it is a strong T-helper cell stimulant (Dennert & Tucker, 1973) both *in vitro* and *in vivo* (Miyakoshi and Aoki, 1984a,b) and can increase their levels (Liu et al, 1988). Lentinan has also shown the ability to stimulate peripheral blood lymphocytes into increased lymphokine-activated killer (LAK) cell and natural killer cell (NK) activity mediated by interleukin 2 *in vitro* from the blood of healthy donors and cancer patients at levels achievable *in vivo* by administration of clinical doses (Arinaga et al, 1992a; Fujimoto et al, 1992; Tani et al, 1993). Intravenous lentinan also significantly increased the capacity of peripheral blood mononuclear cells (PBM) from 10 patients with gastric cancer to produce IL1-a, IL1-b, and tumor necrosis factor (TNF-a) (Arinaga et al, 1992b). It can also inhibit prostaglandin synthesis, which can slow T-cell differentiation in animals and humans (Aoki, 1984b). Lentinan has also been shown to inhibit suppressor T cell activity *in vivo* (Miyakoshi & Aoki, 1984a), and, in addition, increase the ratio of activated T cells, and cytotoxic T cells in the spleen when administered to gastric cancer patients with chemotherapy; this increase in activity of the T cell subpopulation has been associated with decreased immune response in people with certain cancers (Takahashi et al, 1992).

Lentinan can also stimulate Ig production in human cells *in vitro*, as well as interferon in the peripheral blood circulation of cancer patients (Miyakoshi & Aoki, 1984b) and animals and increases the production of lymphocyte-activating factor (Interleukin 1), which is able to enhance the maturation of T cells. Interleukin 6 generation by human monocytes could also be augmented *in vivo* (Sakamaki et al, 1993).

In an *in vivo* study, rats with peritonitis receiving combined lentinan-gentamicin treatment had a significantly better survival rate than controls. Lentinan activated the peritoneal macrophage secretory activity of active oxygen and produced cytokines which thus enhanced the ability of PMNs to produce active oxygen, which possesses a bactericidal ability in PMNs (=polymorphonuclear leukocytes) (Shen et al, 1993). Lentinan could also increase peritoneal macrophage cytotoxicity against metastatic tumor cells in mice, but not against a highly metastatic tumor type (Ladanyi et al, 1993). Of eleven patients treated with lentinan for carcinomatous pleuritis or carcinomatous peritonitis, eight patients improved and in two the malignancy disappeared, while in another two it diminished (Yoshino et al, 1989). Lentinan can activate the normal and alternative pathways in the complement system and can split C3 into C3a and C3b, enhancing macrophage activation (Aoki, 1984b).

When a 2-mg dose of lentinan was administered to twelve patients intravenously twice, the first dose at 3-9 days before and the second the day before surgery, lentinan was effective in increasing the CD4 cell ratios in lymph nodes of twelve gastric cancer patients and strongly increasing the number of tumor-infiltrating lymphocytes (CD4, Leu11, LeuM3) in tumor tissue, but not in those of peripheral blood compared with a control group (Takeshita et al, 1993).

Lentinan's immune-activating ability may be linked with its modulation of some hormonal factors, and it is known that these hormones play a role in tumor growth. For instance, the antitumor activity of lentinan is strongly reduced by administration of thyroxin as well as hydrocortisone (Aoki, 1984b). Lentinan can also restore tumor-specific antigen-directed delayed-type hypersensitivity reaction (DTHR) (Izumi, 1981).

Table 10

IMMUNE EFFECTS OF LENTINAN
IN VITRO AND *IN VIVO* IN ANIMALS AND HUMANS

Activity	Experimental Animal System		Human System	
	In Vitro	In Vivo	In Vitro	In Vivo
Humoral Factors				
Inhibition of immunosuppressive substance production	—	++	—	++
Immunopotentiative substance production	—	++	—	++
C3 splitting activity	—	+	—	—
Antibody production	—	+	—	+

Opsonin production	—	—	—	+
Production of colony-stimulating factor	+	—	—	—
Production of lymphocyte-activating factor (Interleukin 1)	+	+	+	—
Inhibition of prostaglandin release	-	+	—	—
Interferon production	-(?)	+(g type?)	-~±	+(g type)
Cellular Factors				
Natural killer cell activation	-	+	±~+	++
Activation of helper T-cells	—	+	+	—
Activation of killer T-cells	+	+	+	—
Activation of cytotoxic macrophages	-	+	—	+
Delayed-type hypersensitivity reaction	+	+~++		
Mitogenicity	—	—	±~+g	++

From Aoki, 1984b

■ *Antiviral Effects*

Because viral diseases such as HIV are difficult to treat with modern pharmaceuticals, lentinan and LEM's strong inhibitory action against a number of viruses is of great interest, and LEM seems to be the stronger of the two.

Lentinan works through both humoral and cell-mediated immune mechanisms to support host defense against various cancers, bacteria (tuberculosis), viruses (such as the AIDS virus), and parasites (Aoki, 1984b; Mizuno et al,1992). Lentinan has shown antiviral activity in mice against VSV (vesicular stomatitis virus)-encephalitis, Abelson (Chang, 1981), and adenovirus type 12 virus-induced tumors (Hamada, 1981). Lentinan could also stimulate non-specific resistance against respiratory viral infections in mice. Notable protection was induced by lentinan administered intranasally before lethal influenza virus infection which could be confirmed by a reduction of the lung virus titres. Lentinan also conferred complete protection against an LD75 challenge dose of virulent influenza virus, and significantly prolonged the survival time in mice after an LD100 challenge administered by i.v. Enhanced broncho-alveolar macrophage activity was also noted. Measurable interleukin 6 was produced after 6 h, well before IL-6 induced by viral infection alone (Irinoda et al, 1992).

Lentinan was successful in treating a patient positive for HIV but without AIDS symptoms except for low helper-T cell and low lymphocyte counts and low NK cell activity. A drip infusion of lentinan restored these immune cell counts to normal (Aoki, 1984a). Lentinan is particularly active at augmenting helper-T cell activity (Akiyamaet al, 1981). Lentinan may also be useful in clinical practice for strengthening immune and endocrine functions of elderly people and people who are run-down from overwork, as well as the prevention of cancer in high-risk individuals, both orally and by injection (Aoki, 1984b). In Japan, in the treatment of low natural killer cell syndrome (LNKS), a disease which appears to be identical to chronic fatigue syndrome in the West, lentinan was successful in reversing the symptoms of remittent fever, persisting fatigue, and low NK cell activity (Aoki et al, 1987).

LEM may be useful in the treatment of AIDS. It has been shown to inhibit HIV infection of cultured human T-cells (Iizuka, 1990b), and it potentiates the effects of AZT against viral replication *in vitro* (Tochikura et al, 1987c). The mechanism of its action is not known for certain, but the extract was found to activate macrophages and stimulate the production of interleukin 1.

LEM and lentinan are not the only active fractions of *L. edodes*. Water-soluble lignans with antiviral and immunomodulating effects have also been isolated from shiitake mycelium (Hanafusa et al, 1990), and JLS, a new compound recently derived from the mycelium, has shown the ability to block the release of infectious *herpes simplex* virus type 1 in animals (Sarkar et al, 1993). The fungus contains water-solubilized lignin derivatives, such as EP3 and EPS4, which have shown immunological and antiviral activities not only against herpes simplex I and II, but also against equine encephalitis, polio virus, measles, mumps, and HIV (Suzuki et al, 1989, 1990; Sorimachi et al, 1990). In addition, an aqueous extract of the mycelium (known as JLS-18), consisting of 65-75% lignin, 15-30% polysaccharide, and 10-20% protein, has inhibited the herpes virus both *in vitro* and *in vivo* (Koga et al, 1991).

■ *Bacterial and Parasitic Infections*
Another area of research with lentinan is its ability to mobilize the humoral immunity to help ward off bacterial infections resistant to antibiotics. For instance, lentinan was given to 3 patients who were shedding *Mycobacterium tuberculosis* bacilli resistant to antituberculosis drugs. When lentinan was given by IM injection, 1 mg/day, twice a week, titers of specific opsonin toward the bacilli were so elevated that tuberculosis bacillus excretion ceased in one of the patients, and the patient's general conditions improved (Aoki, 1984b). Lentinan is also effective for limiting relapse of tuberculosis infections in the lungs of mice (Kanai & Kondo, 1981) and increasing host resistance to infection with the potentially lethal Listeria monocytogenes (Aoki, 1984b). Lentinan may afford protection against toxic stress from bacterial endotoxin. For instance, when lentinan was administered to rabbits with, or especially before, endotoxin, its clearance was increased (Yokota et al, 1991). Lentinan increased resistance against the parasites Shistosoma japonicum and Shistosoma mansoni, which may have been mediated through T cells (Aoki, 1984b).

■ *Hepatoprotective Effects*
LEM slowed the growth of cancerous liver tumors in rats by injection (Sugano et al, 1982). A polysaccharide fraction from shiitake also demonstrated liver-protective action in animals (Lin and Huang, 1987b; Mizoguchi et al, 1987b), as well as the ability to improve liver function and help produce antibodies to hepatitis B (Amagasse, 1987).

In combination with polysaccharides from the fungi *G. lucidum* and *P. versicolor*, lentinan has improved SGPT and completely restored GPT levels in the livers of mice with toxic hepatitis (Zhang & Luan, 1986).

Crude extracts and/or cultures of the fungus have demonstrated liver-protecting actions (Lin, 1987), perhaps because of their high adenine and choline content (Ying, 1987); anti-inflammatory actions via the inhibition of prostaglandin release from the cell walls of macrophages (Scientific Consulting Service); and the ability to increase interferon production *in vitro* in human umbilical leukocytes (Meng et al, 1987).

■ *Cardiovascular Effects*
Another active compound isolated from shiitake, eritadenine, has been shown to lower blood levels of cholesterol and lipids (Yamamura and Cochran, 1974b). Added to the diet of rats, eritadenine (0.005%) caused a 25% decrease in total cholesterol in as little as one week (Chibata et al, 1969). The cholesterol-lowering activity of this substance is more pronounced in rats fed a high-fat diet than in those on a low-fat diet (Rokujo et al, 1969). Other constituents as well may make shiitake valuable for treating cardiovascular conditions. Recently, two new compounds have been isolated and found to lower serum cholesterol, while the fungus' tyrosinase helps lower blood pressure (Ying et al, 1987). Various other studies have confirmed that shiitake can lower both blood pressure and free cholesterol in the plasma (Kabir, 1987), as well as accelerate accumulation of lipids in the liver, thus removing them from circulation (Kimoto et al, 1976).

■ *Human Clinical Studies*
A number of clinical studies have been conducted on lentinan, less on various other fractions or whole shiitake fruiting bodies. Lentinan was shown to have antitumor activity and to increase the survival time for 3 patients with inoperable gastric cancer (Mashiko et al, 1992; Shimizu et al, 1981), and of women with recurrent breast cancer who have undergone surgical therapy (Kosaka et al, 1985). In a phase II study involving 2 groups of patients with progressive cancer but with no serious liver, kidney, or bone marrow dysfunction and no prior treatment by operation or irradiation within a month of the lentinan administration, lentinan alone did not improve immune parameters or show an anticancer effect. However, lentinan administered once or twice a week with chemotherapy did show a statistically significant difference (<0.01) in immune enhancement and an anticancer effect (Taguchi et al, 1982). A follow-up phase III trial was initiated based on the findings of the phase I and II trials. In this randomized controlled trial, 275 patients with advanced or recurrent gastric cancer were given either one of two kinds of chemotherapy (mitomycin C with 5-fluorouracil or tegafur) alone or with lentinan injections. Statistically, the best results were obtained when lentinan was administered prior to chemotherapy and in the patients with both primary lesion and without prior chemotherapy (Taguchi et al, 1981b). The results were evaluated on the basis of prolongation of life, regression of tumors or lesions, improvement of immune responses, and side effects. In another trial, the relationship between prolonged life span and changes of serum IAP and albumin induced by the therapy of lentinan plus tegafur in inoperable and recurrent gastric cancer was studied. The results were as follows: tumor regression (1 case, 2%), improvement of performance status (PS), appetite, or pain (18 cases, 42%). Cases which showed a decrease of serum IAP from abnormally high levels (more than 500 mu/ml) and an increase of albumin from abnormally low levels (less than 3.5g/dl), had a significantly increased prolongation of life span by comparison with the other cases

(Ishigami et al, 1992). It is important to note that those patients with low protein levels (< 5.9/dl) showed no response to lentinan, whereas those with normal protein levels showed excellent results (Nishihira et al, 1988).

In another group of 16 patients with advanced cancer, lentinan (4 mg/week for 4 weeks) was injected into malignant peritoneal and/or pleural effusions. Eighty percent of the lesions showed clinical responses, and performance status was improved in 7 patients. The survival time for patients who responded immunologically to the treatment was 129 days and 49 days for those who did not respond (Oka et al, 1992).

In another controlled, double-blind study involving 72 cases of chronic persistent hepatitis, lentinan was more effective than danshen (a Chinese herb, *Codonopsis pilosula*) for this condition (Lin et al, 1987). Another study, too, found that a polysaccharide fraction from *L. edodes* was useful for treating chronic viral hepatitis B (Zhu et al, 1985). Forty patients with chronic hepatitis B and seropositive for Hbe antigenemia were given 6 grams of LEM daily (orally) for four months in an unrandomized, uncontrolled clinical study (Amagase, 1987). The study focused on the number of patients seroconverting from HBeAg positive to anti-HBe positive, which was 25% after LEM therapy and was higher in patients with chronic active hepatitis, 36.8%. In addition, 17 patients (43%) became seronegative for HBeAg. Liver function tests showed improvement even in patients who remained seropositive. Only one patient reported side effects—abdominal fullness and loose stools.

As for its effects on infectious disease, in a study of 3 patients with pulmonary tuberculosis who had shed drug resistant *M. tuberculosis* bacteria for 10 years, after treatment with lentinan, the excretion of *M. tuberculosis* ceased (Usuda, 1981). These findings have been supported by several studies with mice (Kanai & Kondo, 1981; Kanai et al, 1980).

Another promising use of *L. edodes* is to boost the immune response in AIDS patients. In one case study, when an extract (LEM) of *L. edodes* was used to treat an HIV+ patient with AIDS symptoms, the T cell count rose from a baseline of 1,250/mm3 to 2045/mm3 after 30 days, and then up to 2,542/mm3 after 60 days. Improvements in symptoms were noted (Iizuka and Maeda, 1988).

After one week on dried shiitake (9 g), 10 young Japanese women showed a decrease in serum cholesterol of 7%. Another group who ate 90 g of fresh shiitake showed a 12% drop in serum cholesterol after 7 days. A further study in young women on fresh shiitake (90 g) for 7 days included butter (60 g) in addition to the shiitake. In a control group of 10 women, only the butter was added to the diet for one week. In this group serum cholesterol increased by 14%, whereas the group on shiitake and the butter showed a decrease in serum cholesterol of 4%. A separate study in people 60 years of age or older found the drop in cholesterol was 9%, whether they had eaten dried or fresh shiitake (Suzuki and Oshima, 1974).

Toxicity
L. edodes is non-poisonous, though some people may experience minor side effects or allergic reactions. For instance, during 17 years researchers have observed numerous cases of shiitake-induced toxicodermia or shiitake dermatitis (Nakamura and Kobayashi, 1985; Ueda et al, 1992). Nakamura (1992) reviewed the clinical

manifestations, laboratory findings, and sources of shiitake dermatitis. It is known that people who work indoors in the cultivation of shiitake are prone to an immune reaction to spores called "mushroom worker's lung." Antibodies to shiitake spore antigens can be demonstrated in people who show symptoms. Protective masks can help, but not entirely eliminate, an eventual reaction to the spores after continued exposure (Van Loon, 1992). A watery extract of the whole fruiting body is reported to lessen the effectiveness of the blood platelets in the process of coagulation, so people who bleed easily or who are taking blood thinners should use caution when chronically using shiitake or its water-soluble fractions (Yang & Jong, 1989).

LEM has shown no evidence of acute toxicity in over 17 years of popular use in Japan, even in massive doses (over 50 mg/day for 1 week), though mild side effects such as diarrhea and skin rashes may occur. Symptoms disappear after a short period, once the body has adapted to the LEM. Likewise lentinan has no known serious side effects (Aoki, 1984b). Patients with allergies may experience some negative reactions due to its histamine sensitizing properties (Chihara, 1981), though this has not been demonstrated in humans. In a phase I clinical trial of 50 patients with advanced cancer, 0.5 to 50 mg/person/day lentinan was given by injection for 2 weeks. Minor side effects such as a slight increase in GOT and GPT liver enzymes and a feeling of mild oppression on the chest were caused at 5 mg/day, but these disappeared after lentinan administration was stopped. In a phase II trial, only 17 of 185 patients with advanced cancer had similar transitory side effects. Skin eruptions were noted in 7 cases, mild oppression on the chest, 6 cases, and mild liver dysfunction, 4 cases (Taguchi et al, 1982). In a follow-up phase III trial by the same researchers, 15 out of 275 patients experienced nausea and vomiting (2), heaviness in the chest (4), heat sensations (2), and one case each of face flushing, a rise in blood pressure, and heaviness in the head (Taguchi et al, 1981b; Aoki, 1984b).

The LD50 by IV injection into mice, rats, dogs, and monkeys is more than 100 mg/kg. Large amounts administered IV chronically for 25 weeks showed definite signs of severe toxicity, but anaphylaxis could not be demonstrated (Aoki, 1984b). In toxicity tests in animals, lentinan caused no antifertility effects in males, and pregnant animals administered lentinan had normal litters with normal offspring (Cozens 1981a, 1981b, 1981c). Lentinan seems to be very safe when given to humans in the dosage range of 1-5 mg/day once or twice a week by IV injection (Taguchi et al, 1982).

Uses in Traditional Medicine
In TCM, shiitake is said to have a sweet taste and be mild in nature. Shiitake is a food that is both strengthening and restorative.

Medical Uses
Shiitake is used medicinally for any and all diseases involving depressed immune function, including cancer, AIDS, environmental allergies, Candida infections (contrary to current fashion in modern western medicine, which holds that fungi only aggravate yeast infections), and frequent flu and colds. It also appears to be beneficial for soothing bronchial inflammation and regulating urine incontinence (Liu and Bau, 1980), as well as for reducing chronic high cholesterol.

According to one prominent Japanese researcher, lentinan is an immunomodulating agent which may be useful both therapeutically, as a general rejuvenative for older persons (no matter what the condition of their health), as well as prophylactically to protect healthy, physically active young people from overwork and exhaustion (Aoki, 1984b). In Japan, lentinan is currently classified as a drug, whereas LEM is considered a food supplement.

■ Shiitake use in Cancer-Prevention

As more clinical research on lentinan is published, the effective range of application is becoming more defined and somewhat broader. The immune mechanisms behind various types of cancer are complex, so lentinan, or any immunostimulant, may or may not be useful for a particular situation or individual. The best results will be realized when "used in conjunction with other therapy under strictly planned timing and schedules, and only when the host-tumor relationship is in good agreement with such treatment" (Chihara, 1981).

In my experience the best results with any immune adjuvants will be realized when one considers the type of cancer (location), the individual's general health and immune and hormonal status, as well as the individual constitutional type. Besides immune adjuvant therapy, it is important to address imbalances in diet and other health habits and attempt to correct any disharmony in other organ systems.

Shiitake mushrooms have cancer-preventive properties and can be a beneficial addition to the diet. Recent statistics show that one out of three people may have cancer sometime in their lives! Compounds that block the formation of carcinogenic N-nitroso compounds from nitrites (which occur in many meats and some vegetables) are produced in shiitake and other mushrooms (such as matsutake and the common button agaric) when they are dried or heated. Uncooked shiitake contains no detectable amounts of the nitrite-scavenging compound thiazolidine-4-carboxylic acid (TCA, thioproline); dried shiitake contains 134 mg/100 g (dry weight basis) of the compound; and boiled shiitake holds 843 mg/100 g (Kurashima et al, 1990).

■ Shiitake and HIV Treatment

Researchers have suggested that LEM may be more effective than AZT in the treatment of AIDS because it inhibits the cytopathic effect of giant cell formation in a cell-free system with MT-4 cells, or a cell-to-cell infection system with MOLT-4 cells, both of which induce multinucleated giant cells very efficiently. LEM may work by blocking the initial stages of HIV infection (Tochikura et al, 1988). AZT inhibits cell-free infection of HIV, but it is ineffective in preventing the formation of multinucleated giant cells. AZT is also expensive and is known to cause severe bone marrow toxicity and a host of other side effects (*Physicians Desk Reference*, 1993). Furthermore, it may become less effective over time or may not offer any long-term survival advantages even with early use (Fackelmann, 1992). LEM is non-toxic and less expensive. It costs $825/kilo (1,000 grams) wholesale, and assuming an average therapeutic dose of 3 grams/day, the cost would be about $2.48/day, or $74.40/month. The dose for prevention or maintenance would be about $.83/day or $24.75/month. See the reference section for suppliers. While products of LEM that are already encapsulated are considerable higher per dose, they do offer convenience, and are readily available from natural food stores and herb shops. However, these products are not suitable for the treatment of ailments where therapeutic doses of LEM are required (over 1 gram/day) because they are too expensive. I recommend encapsulated products mainly for prevention of disease and maintenance of health, as a daily dietary supplement. Of course, more clinical trials will be necessary to assess the long-term benefit of LEM for HIV and AIDS. I also recommend seeking the advice of a qualified health care professional before discontinuing any medications prescribed by a doctor.

Preparation and Dosage

It is important to note that lentinan's anticancer effect is highly dose-dependent. The traditional dose of the whole dried fruiting body in tea, soup, or other dishes is given as 6-16 grams; of the fresh fruiting body, about 90 grams (Liu and Bau, 1980).

According to manufacturer's recommendations and the few clinical trials performed with humans, during the initial stages of AIDS or chronic hepatitis the best dose of LEM may be between 2-6 grams/day in 2 or 3 divided doses orally. Once the disease is more stable, the dosage may be decreased, perhaps to 1/2 -1 gram per day (Sharon, 1988). For lentinan, the optimum dose is 1-5 mg injected IV or IM twice a week and greater doses can cause immune suppression (Aoki, 1984b).

Interestingly, it has been clinically established that smaller doses of intravenous and intramuscular lentinan are more effective than larger doses for cancer patients (1 mg IV injection is considered safe, while 10 mg may produce marked depression in the host immune response). However, it should also be noted that what is considered an excessive dosage intravenously may be a favorable dosage for oral administration (Aoki, 1984b).

Commercial preparations of *L. edodes* are available in the United States in natural food markets. The tablets are usually made from a dried water-extract of the mycelia or fruiting bodies, because drying concentrates the lentinan and other active principles. Standardized extracts are also available, and they are preferred because the amount of lentinan present is certified and clearly stated on the bottle.

Note that for full therapeutic doses, although fresh shiitake can be a valuable dietary supplement, the amount one would need to eat for medicinal doses is so high that it might cause digestive upset. That is why LEM, which is concentrated and easily absorbed, is preferred as medicine.

Related Species

The mycelial extract of *L. cyathiformis*, a species native to Hungary, showed antitumor activity in mice against Ehrlich ascites tumor and sarcoma 180. This fungus was reported to be significantly more active than mycelial extracts of three samples of *L. edodes* collected in the Orient (Korea, Japan, and Vietnam) (Rethy et al, 1983). *L. ponderosus* O.K.M. is found in the western U.S. from August to October (Lincoff, 1981). *L. velutinus* Fr. and *L. crinitus* (L.:Fr.) Fr. are boiled for use as foods by the Sanama Indians of Brazil (Fidalgo and Prance, 1976). *Neolentinus lepideus* (Fr.) Redhead (=L. lepideus Fr.), found from May to September in many parts of the U.S. and in California during winter (Lincoff, 1981), has shown antitumor activity in mice (sarcoma 180 and carcinoma 755) (Espenshade and Griffith, 1966).

Notes

L. edodes shows higher anticomplementary activity than krestin, an immunostimulant extract from Japanese *Trametes versicolor*. It shows more potent anticomplementary activity than *G. lucidum*, *Cordyceps* spp., and *Agaricus campestris*, as well (Jeong, 1990).

Procurement

Shiitake can be found in many markets throughout North America, Asia, and Europe. It is one of the most commonly cultivated mushrooms. I encourage home cultivation, which is an exciting (and certainly one of the most inexpensive) ways to have enough of this fantastic fungus for daily use. See the resources section in the Appendix for sources of mycelium and the books *The Mushroom Cultivator* (Stamets and Chilton, 1983), *The Shiitake Growers Handbook* (Przybillowicz and Donoghue, 1991) or *Growing Gourmet* and *Medicinal Mushrooms* (Stamets, 1994) for more information on cultivation. Shiitake is increasingly popular in prepared products throughout Asia, North America, and Europe, and LEM is available in tablet or capsule form.

(lenz=a German botanist; betul=birch)

GILLED POLYPORE

Synonyms
Agaricus betulinus L., *Daedalea betulina* Fr., *Lenzites ochraceus* Lloyd, *Lenzites varie-gata* Lloyd (Overholts, 1977).

Other Common Names
Kaigaratake.

Description and Habitat
This is an unusual polypore, because it appears to have gills instead of pores. It grows on deciduous and coniferous woods, especially white birch (Liu and Bau, 1980) and looks like a large, thick *T. versicolor* on top, sometimes with a greenish caste. The green color often seen on *L. betulina* is actually a green algal growth which occurs on the pileus as it ages (Overholts, 1977).

Range
This polypore grows throughout most of the United States. I have seen moderate sized patches in California and Oregon, as well as in the eastern United States.

History
No data.

Chemistry
The sterol peroxides ergosterol peroxide and 9(11)-dehydroergosterol peroxide were identified as immunosuppressive compounds in an *in vitro* model (Fujimoto et al, 1994); ergosta-7,22-dien-3β-ol, fungisterol (Yokoyama et al, 1975).

Pharmacology
A water extract of *Lenzites betulina* has demonstrated mild anti-tumor activity against sarcoma 180 in mice (Ikekawa et al, 1968). *L. betulina*, known in Japan as kaigaratake, has shown immunosuppressive activity against lymphocyte prolifera-tion in mice due to sterol peroxides (Fujimoto et al, 1994).

Human Clinical Studies
None.

Toxicity
No data.

Uses in Traditional Medicine
In TCM, *L. betulina* is considered warming; it dispels internal wind and has a mild nature. The mushroom is used to enhance blood circulation, resolving cold and eliminating endogenous wind (Ying et al, 1987), and support the tendons and veins. It is one of the main ingredients in a Chinese patent medicine for leg and tendon pains called "Tendon-Easing Pill" (Liu & Bau, 1980).

Medical Uses
None found.

Preparation and Dosage

1-2 pills twice daily of "Tendon-Easing Pills," or use in tea. To make a tea, simmer 1-2 fruiting bodies in a quart and a half of water for 45 minutes. Strain and add a little sweetener. Drink 1 cup twice daily.

Related Species

None.

Procurement

The birch polypore is common on birch, oak, and other hardwoods throughout North America, Europe, and Asia. There are no commercial products available outside of China to my knowledge.

LEPISTA NUDA (BULL.:FR.) CKE.

(lepista=a drinking vessel or goblet; nuda=naked; blewitt comes from "blue hat")

BLEWIT

Synonyms
Clitocybe nuda, Tricholoma nudum (Bull.) Quél., *Rhodopxillus nuda*

Other Common Names
Purple mushroom.

Description and Habitat
This gilled Basidiomycete is saprophytic and can be cultivated at home. A well-known edible species, it is easy to recognize for the beginner because of its shiny-smooth bright purple cap and purple gills. It grows on the

Lepista nuda from *Text-Book of British Fungi* by W. Delisle Hay, 1887.

ground, either solitary or in groups, and it is firm and has a purple cast, getting lighter as it ages. In California I have seen it frequently under oak trees.

Range
Common throughout the United States, Europe, and Asia.

History
No data.

Chemistry
No data.

Pharmacology
L. nuda has shown pronounced antitumor activity against sarcoma, and the vitamin B1 found in its sporophore makes it effective in regulating carbohydrate metabolism. It is resistant to both Gram positive and negative bacteria (Ying et al, 1987).

Human Clinical Studies
No data.

Toxicity
Although *L. nuda* itself is not toxic, be forewarned that it may accumulate and concentrate heavy metals in contaminated environments. In a study of 60 species of edible mushrooms collected from polluted areas, *L. nuda* was found to contain the second highest level of mercury, after *Calocybe gambosa* (Kalac et al, 1989a). In a later study by the same researcher, eleven species of mushrooms were collected within six km or less from a lead smelter in Bohemia, Czechoslovakia. *L. nuda* showed extensive accumulation of lead, copper, and mercury. All samples had higher concentrations of these metals than mushrooms in any other part of Bohemia, and they far exceeded safe levels. For example, more than 100 mg lead per 1 kg of dry matter were found in *L. nuda*, where the safe limit was established at 5 mg/kg (Kalac et al, 1991a).

Uses in Traditional Medicine
The fruiting body is considered sweet and mild in nature.

Medical Uses
In China, *L. nuda* is used to regulate sugar metabolism and support the nervous system (Liu and Bau, 1980).

Preparation and Dosage
Liberally, as desired, though some people may be sensitive to it, experiencing nausea or digestive upset.

Related Species
There are many related species, but their medicinal properties are presently unknown.

Procurement
The blewit grows commonly throughout North America, Europe, Asia, and other parts of the world, but it is not generally available commercially, at least in the U.S. David Arora reported seeing it on occasion at the Monterey Market in Berkeley, California (1994).

PEZIZA VESICULOSA Bull.:St. Amans

(peziza=mushrooms without a root or stalk; vesiculosa=covered with little bladders or blisters)

BLADDER CUP

Synonyms
None.

Other Common Names
None.

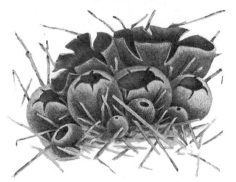

Peziza vesiculosa from *British Fungi and Lichens* by George Massee, circa 1890.

Description and Habitat
This Ascomycete is a round to flattened, cup-shaped denizen of dung.
It is pale brown on top and whitish underneath, and it grows either solitary or in clusters. The Latin vesiculosa, meaning "with bladder (or vesicles)," may refer to the fungus bladder-like shape or to its minutely blistered underside.

Range
Usually found growing in clusters on manure or rotting straw in corrals or around stables and gardens throughout the world (Arora, 1986).

History
No data.

Chemistry
A water-soluble high-molecular weight acidic polypeptide with B-cell mitogen properties called vesiculogen, which is composed of 75-80% protein, 17-19% carbohydrates (Ohno et al, 1986b; Yadomae et al, 1979a), and a β-1,3-glucan polysaccharide (Mimura et al, 1985) have been isolated in addition to various other polysaccharide fractions (Ohno et al, 1985). Another compound, epipentenomycin I, was isolated from the carpophores of *Peziza* spp. (Bernillon et al, 1989).

Pharmacology
The crude extract of *P. vesiculosa* has been shown to act as a B-cell mitogen (i.e., it induces mitosis), and it enhances certain activities of the reticuloendothelial system (RES), especially phagocytosis and inhibition of tumor cells, *in vitro* (Suzuki et al, 1982; Yadomae et al, 1979b). *P. vesiculosa* has also been shown to inhibit sarcoma 180 *in vivo* (Suzuki et al, 1982; Mimura, 1986). A glucan known as PVG (Mimura, 1986) and various polysaccharides extracted from the fruiting body have been implicated in this antitumor activity (Ohno, 1985). The carpophores of *Peziza* spp. demonstrate antimicrobial activity against certain Gram-positive bacteria (Bernillon et al, 1989).

Human Clinical Studies
No data.

Toxicity
According to Arora (1994), it is advisable to cook Ascomycetes (including morels) before ingesting them. I have seen similar fungi from the same genus growing on painted plasterboard, carpets, and other household areas—one should be cautious about using such carpophores because they may pick up heavy metals or other toxic compounds from the substrate.

Uses in Traditional Medicine
It is considered sweet, slightly bitter, and cool in nature.

Medical Uses
In Japan this fungus is used to treat tumors and depressed immune function (Suzuki et al, 1982).

Preparation and Dosage
2-4 g per dose.

Related Species
A number of similar species are common worldwide, including *Peziza domestica*.

Procurement
Available from the wild; in bulk occasionally from Chinese herb dealers; and in China in prepared form.

PHELLINUS IGNIARIUS (L.:FR.) QUÉL.

(phellinus=cork, ignarius= belonging to fire) (fomes, foment=tinder)

FALSE TINDER POLYPORE

Synonyms
Synonyms for *P. igniarius* are *Fomes igniarius* and *Polyporus igniarius* (Gilbertson and Ryvarden, 1987).

Other Common Names
Nisehokuchitake.

Description and Habitat
P. igniarius is a hoof-shaped or semicircular polypore that grows on both living and dead hardwoods, especially birch and aspen. It is brownish, becoming black, furrowed, and eventually cracking (Arora, 1986; Phillips, 1991).

Range
P. igniarius is common in many parts of the world, including the United States, Europe, and Asia.

History
No data.

Chemistry
Ergosta-7,22-dien-3β-ol) and fungisterol have been identified from this species (Yokoyama et al, 1975).

Pharmacology
The mycelium of *P. igniarius* have shown 70% inhibition of sarcoma 180 in mice (Ohtsuka et al, 1977), and water extracts of the sporophore exhibited potent antitumor effects against Ehrlich ascites carcinoma and sarcoma 180 in mice (Ying et al, 1987; Ito et al, 1976).

Human Clinical Studies
No data.

Toxicity
No data.

Uses in Traditional Medicine
According to TCM, *P. igniarius* is bitter and cooling. It is said to detoxify and restore the internal organs (Liu and Bau, 1980). In China, it is a considered a soothing diuretic, digestive tonic, and antidiarrheal agent.

Medical Uses
It may also be used as a styptic, both internally and externally and is used in Traditional Chinese Medicine for treating uterine bleeding and for blood in the urine. *P. igniarius* is also an effective emmenogogue for amenorrhea and for treating leukorrhea (Liu and Bau, 1980; Hanssen & Schädler, 1982; Ying et al, 1987). The powdered fruiting body is taken in liquid or in pill form, and preparations can

also be applied externally for pains in the abdominal region (Hanssen & Schädler, 1982).

Preparation and Dosage

Take 13-30 g of *P. igniarius* or *F. fomentarius* as a decoction 2X/day.

Related Species

P. hartigii shows antitumor activity, as does *P. linteus* (Shibata et al, 1968; Ikekawa et al, 1968; Ying et al, 1987).

Procurement

False tinder polypore is not available in commercial trade but can be picked from the wild in many parts of Asia, North America, and Europe.

PLEUROTUS OSTREATUS (JACQ.:FR.) QUÈL.

(pleur=beside, otus=ear;
ostreatus=oyster-shaped)

OYSTER MUSHROOM

Synonyms
None.

Other Common Names
Hiratake (Japan).

Description and Habitat
P. ostreatus has a fleshy white, brown
or gray, semi-circular capo shaped
like an oyster shell and grows in lay-
ered clusters on deciduous trees
throughout North America, Asia,
Europe, and other areas. This is a
choice edible cultivated in many parts
of the world. It has a pleasant odor,
and inside the cap is a thick, white
flesh. The stalk is usually absent or
small.

Range
North America and most other conti-
nents.

Pleurotus ostreatus from *Our Edible Toadstools and Mushrooms* by W. Hamilton Gibson, 1895.

History
Pleurotus was praised in a poem written during the Sung dynasty (A.D. 420-479)
as "the mushroom of flower heaven" (Y.-C. Wang, 1985). The country people in
France were said to water wild Pleurotus logs to encourage fruitings for the table
(Ramsbottom, 1951).

Chemistry
P. ostreatus contains 8 kinds of amino acids, as well as vitamin B1, B2, and vitamin
P (Ying, 1987), while the dried mycelium is a source of B1, B2, B5 (niacin), B6, and
B7 (biotin), but not B12 (Solomko and Eliseeva, 1988). One analysis of oyster
mushrooms, including *P. ostreatus*, revealed appreciable amounts of all essential
amino acids with the exception of tryptophan. The protein quality was high
enough to nearly equal animal-derived protein (Eden and Wuensch, 1991). Grown
in a medium of peat extract, the mushroom has high protein content and high concentrations of essential fatty acids and minerals (Manu-Tawiah and Martin, 1987).
Grown on wheat straw, *P. ostreatus* contains minerals (7.9%), crude fiber (12.0%),
lipids (4.2%), protein (15.7%), and carbohydrates (54.4%) (Garcha, 1993). The
main fatty acid in the fruit-body is oleic acid (Solomko, 1984), and the saturated to
unsaturated fatty acid ratio is 14 (saturated) to 86 (unsaturated) (Bano &
Rajarathnam, 1988). A lectin has also been described from the fruiting body

(Conrad & Rüdiger, 1994). The major organic acids in the fruiting bodies include formic, malic, acetic (the most abundant at 266 mg/100 g), and citric acids (Bano & Rajarathnam, 1988). See the Nutritional section on p. 56 for further information on this mushroom.

Pharmacology

Antitumor activity of *P. ostreatus* as part of the normal diet was found in a feeding study of the mushroom in mice with sarcoma 180. The tumor inhibition rate reached 79.4%, and against a mammary tumor system (MM-46) there was an 89.7% tumor inhibition rate (Mori et al, 1986). By injection (i.p.), *P. ostreatus* (200 mg/kg/day X10) produced a 75.3% inhibition of tumors (Ikekawa, 1969). An acidic polysaccharide fraction of this mushroom showed a 95% tumor inhibition rate against sarcoma 180 from doses of 5 mg/kg (Yoshioka et al, 1972).

The dried and powdered mushroom fed to hamsters at 2% of a high-fat diet for six months lowered serum very low density lipoprotein (VLDL) in blood plasma as well as cholesterol and triglycerol levels in the liver more than in controls. Serum VLDL decreased by 65-80%, and total serum lipid levels were reduced by 40%. A polysaccharide from the mushroom as part (4%) of a normal diet was found to lower serum and liver levels of cholesterol in hamsters after 2 months' feeding (Bobek et al, 1991b). As 5% of a high-fat diet in rats, *P. ostreatus* lowered serum cholesterol accumulation by 45% in three months (Bobek et al, 1993). Rats with hereditary high cholesterol levels also showed significantly reduced levels of serum cholesterol from feeding on the mushroom as part of the diet (4%). Even with 1% cholesterol added in their feed, these rats showed a nearly 40% decrease in cholesterol levels (VLDL and LDL) (Bobek et al, 1991a). When their diet was supplemented with 2% dried fruiting bodies of Pleurotus, hamsters with a chronic alcohol intake also showed reduced levels of cholesterol and even lower levels than control hamsters not given alcohol. *P. ostreatus* totally negated increases in triglycerol levels and liver cholesterol resulting from chronic alcohol ingestion (Bobek et al, 1991c). Metal-bound proteins, known as carriers of metals in intestinal absorption, were found in *P. ostreatus* (Shimaoka et al, 1990).

Human Clinical Studies

None.

Toxicity

P. ostreatus in Baghdad, Iraq produced toxicity in animals after oral and intraperitoneal administration for 30 days (liver inflammation, hemorrhaging in kidney, liver, intestine, and lung) consistent with local reports of toxicity in people (Al-Deen et al, 1987). The LD50 values for short-term administration were very high, exceeding 3 g/kg. The significance of these findings for potential toxicity from oyster mushrooms in the human diet is not known. I have been eating this wild-harvested mushroom in substantial quantities for a number of years without apparent ill effects.

Uses in Traditional Medicine

It is considered sweet and mild and is used to strengthen veins and relax tendons and to dispel "air and cold" (Liu and Bau, 1980). In Mexico Pleurotus is cooked in stews or fried (Alfaro et al, 1983).

Medical Uses

In China it is indicated for joint and muscle relaxation (Yang & Jong, 1989); when the sporophores are made into "Tendon-easing powder," they are effective in the treatment of lumbago, numbed limbs, and tendon and blood vessel discomfort.

In the Czech Republic, extracts have been made from the fruiting bodies as the main ingredient in dietary preparations recommended for prevention of high cholesterol (Opletal, 1993).

Preparation and Dosage

3-9 grams.

Related Species

Hypsizygus (=Pleurotus) *ulmarius* is used in China to promote the circulation of blood (Yang & Jong, 1989). A freeze-dried water extract of *P. spodoleucus* caused a 72.3% inhibition of sarcoma 180 tumors in mice (Ikekawa et al, 1969). *P. dryinus* was cited by a 12th century Arabian physician as "Gharikoun," a mushroom used to treat tumors of the gullet and throat (Hartwell, 1971). *P. sajor-caju* produced a hypotensive action in rats (25 mg water extract, i.v.) and decreased glomerular infiltration in rat kidneys (Tam et al, 1986).

Notes

Oyster mushroom may be an excellent blood-builder. According to published results, it has up to 19 mg/100 grams (dried) of iron. In animal feeding studies, the addition of *P. sajor-caju* or *P. flabellatus* to the diets of anemic albino rats raised hemoglobin content to 15.5 and 16.2 respectively, which compares with 8.2 for controls, which were fed copper and milk. The value was 14.0 in normal rats (Bano & Rajarathnam, 1988).

P. griseus contains a highly active antibacterial substance named "pleurotin" which is unstable in solution if exposed to heat or light (Brian, 1951).

Procurement

Widely cultivated and sometimes available in markets. I buy them in bulk at my local farmer's market. This is one of the easiest mushrooms for home cultivation (Stamets and Chilton, 1983) and of particular note as a wild species. We pick oyster mushrooms in coastal California starting in early October and continuing through January or even February, though the biggest fruitings are generally in the fall. Not generally found in prepared products.

POLYPORUS TUBERASTER (JACQ.:FR.)

(poly=several, por=pores; tuber=fruit, aster=star)

STONE FUNGUS

Synonyms
Boletus tuberaster Jacq., *Polyporus decurrens* Underwood, *Polyporus mcmurphyi* Murr. (Gilbertson & Ryvarden, 1987).

Other Common Names
Sometimes mistakenly identified as tuckahoe; tuckahoe is *Wolfiporia cocos* (Gilbertson & Ryvarden, 1987).

Description and Habitat
This polypore is short, tough-fleshed, and arises from a black, underground tuber (sclerotium or perhaps pseudosclerotium). Its cap is 4-15 cm in diameter and 0.5-1 cm thick; ochraceous tan to tawny, covered with small scattered scales (Overholts, 1977). Found growing solitary or in two's or three's on the ground in mixed woods and under oak and madrone in the western U.S. (Arora, 1986). Note: the tuber from *Wolfiporia cocos* is white inside; the tuber from *P. tuberaster* is not, as it is heavily mixed with dirt and pebbles (Arora, 1996; Gilbertson & Ryvarden, 1987).

Range
Polyporus tuberaster occurs throughout the eastern United States, western U.S., and Canada, as well as in Europe and perhaps in Asia (Porcher, 1854; Arora, 1986; Overholts, 1977), though whether all the species with a similar appearance occurring with an underground sclerotium are this species is uncertain. Overholts, however, claims that it is widespread.

History
The Native American Indians may have valued this fungus as food, though its identity in the ethnobotanical literature is in question, being confused with the much more edible sclerotia of *Wolfiporia cocos* (tuckahoe). Porcher (1854), a 19th century American doctor, reported that *Polyporus tuberaster* was used in Italy and China for fevers and eruptive diseases. In southern Italy the tubers are still sold in the markets as food, but it is the fruiting bodies that are eaten, not the "tubers." The tubers are sold to be placed in flower pots and watered to produce the edible (when very young and tender) fruiting bodies (Arora, 1994).

Chemistry
No data.

Pharmacology
No data.

Human Clinical Studies
No data.

Toxicity
None known.

Taste & Energy
Bland, cool.

Uses in Traditional Medicine
Stone fungus tastes similar to *Wolfiporia cocos*, which would make it sweet and bland with mild energy, and it may enter the Heart, Spleen, and Lung (Bensky & Gamble, 1993). It has been reported as being used for food by Native American Indians over 150 years ago, though the sclerotium is often riddled with dirt and sand, making it difficult to use, unlike *Wolfiporia cocos* and other sclerotium-producing species (Arora, 1987). The reported use of it as food in Italy may refer to the tender new above-ground fruiting body (Overholts, 1977). Whether this species or other tuber-producing species are similar in action and efficacy to *Wolfiporia cocos* remains to be seen.

Medical Uses
None known.

Preparation and Dosage
9-16 g in decoction, 3X/day.

Related Species
See the entry for *Wolfiporia cocos*, another sclerotium-producing polypore used widely in Asia as a kidney/bladder tonic and diuretic, as well as to treat chronic hepatitis and retard tumor growth. *Polyporus mylittae* also produces edible tubers.

Procurement
Available in the wild only.

PSILOCYBE SPP

(psil=naked, cybe=head)

PSILOCYBE MUSHROOM

Synonyms
Stropharia cubensis (*P. cubensis*), *P. semilanceata*, *P cyanescens* other species.

Other Common Names
Liberty cap, magic mushroom, teonanacatl (flesh of God), etc.

Description and Habitat
Various, depending on the species. Some have a character-istic membraneous pellicle (*P. peliculosa*), and a few show a bluing reaction, especially at the base of the stem—though this should not be taken for an infallible characteristic. Members of the genus have dark purple spores and often grow in cow dung, or rotting grass or wood chips.

Psilocybe mushrooms from *Mushrooms, Russia and History* by R. Gordon Wasson, 1957.

Range
Many parts of the world, including North America, Mexico, South America, Scandinavia, and parts of Asia.

History
As mentioned in the first part of this book, the use of Psilocybe species held an important place among the Meso American peoples, in the context of "mushroom cults," dating back at least 1500 years. Mushroom stones have been found in exca-vations from Mayan sites in Guatemala that are conservatively dated back to 1000 B.C. These cultures were strongly persecuted by the Spanish when they arrived in the new world (Schultes & Hofmann, 1973). See this work for more historical details. It is ironic that some Europeans came to the new world to escape religious persecution, and many delivered to the native people just that from which they were running. Today, the Mazatec Indians are said by Singer (1958) to "have pre-served more of the original Aztec lore about teonanacatl than the people living now in Aztec country, who are at least in part the direct descendants of the Aztecs."

The exploration of the traditional uses of psychotropic fungi, which helped bring this knowledge into the modern collective consciousness, unfolded over the last 100 years or so, but took a giant leap from the work of Schultes, Reko, the Wassons, Heim, Singer, Hofmann, Guzman, and others (Guzman, 1983). In the 50s Valentina and Gordon Wasson organized a number of expeditions to Oaxaca and other parts of Mexico to explore the ethnobotany and ethnophar-

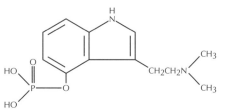

Psilocybin molecule

macology of hallucinogenic mushrooms. These expeditions were interdisciplinary in nature, including scientists from other related fields of research (e.g., the chemist who discovered LSD, Albert Hofmann). Hofmann has given an intriguing account of the group's first experience with the sacramental mushrooms, called Teonanac·tl (meaning flesh or food of the Gods) by the ancient Aztecs, under the guidance of the now renowned curandera, Maria Sabina. The last name Sabina means "wise woman." Because there were no mushrooms growing near the village where the meeting took place at the time, Hofmann offered tablets of pure psilocybin, which Maria Sabina finally declared the same medicine as the mushrooms. After a 1957 article in *Life* magazine by Gordon Wasson, the small village in Mexico where Maria Sabina lived was reported to be "overrun" with hippies wanting to eat mushrooms and meet the curandera (Guzman, 1983).

In the materialism and prosperity of the post war period of the 1950s, it is easy to understand the longing for spiritual exploration which developed during the 1960s.

Hallucinogenic mushrooms may have been used in many parts of the world, including Europe and parts of Asia, as well as the Philippines, Indonesia and Cambodia (Pollock, 1976). A friend of mine who has traveled often to Asia tells me that omelettes and other dishes that include psychoactive mushrooms are on the menu at some eating establishments, especially in Thailand and Bali. This has been reported in other literature (Pollock, 1976). The mushrooms eaten throughout Asia commonly include psychedelic species of Psilocybe and Paneolus.

Chemistry
Four indole alkaloids, hydroxyltryptamine derivatives, related to bufotenin (from toads) and serotonin (a common neurotransmitter in the human nervous system), have been isolated from various Psilocybe spp., in addition to psilocybin, psilocin, baeocystin, and nor-baeocystin (Guzman, 1983; Lincoff and Mitchell, 1977).

Pharmacology
The main active constituent of Psilocybe, is fully water-soluble and relatively stable, though the fruiting bodies may lose up to 50% of their activity after drying. To prevent further degradation of quality, it is important to freeze them immediately after drying. In comparison with unfrozen dried mushrooms from the same batch of Psilocybe, the frozen lots are substantially more potent after 4-12 months. Psilocybin is not soluble in ethanol, but its less abundant isomer, psilocin, is. A mixture of ethanol, diluted acetic acid and water was said to be an effective way to extract psilocybin (Gartz, 1994).

Psilocybin is reported to be 900-1,000 times less potent than LSD but 90 to 100 times more potent than the active alkaloid from peyote, mescalin (Davis, 1981).

About 50% of the psilocybin given orally to rats is absorbed and within 24 hours, 65% is excreted in the urine and about 20% from the bile and feces. The highest concentration in the liver and kidney occurred after 20-30 minutes, and after 40 minutes in the brain. An especially high concentration is found in the neocortex and hippocampus of rats, which may explain its effects on behavior (Aboul-Enein, 1974).

Pharmacological Effects
Psilocybin affects the sympathetic nervous system, especially the sympathetic structures of the brain, and can elicit dilation of the pupils, erection of the hair, rapid heart beat, and an increase of body temperature. Motor control is also affected (Schultes & Hofmann, 1977).

When given to mice and rats, the compound produced an excited state followed by a reduction in motor activity, as well as a marked degree of aggressiveness which was dependent on isolation time, and several other variables. Baboons showed an increase in spontaneous eye movements, but reduced motor activity (Aboul-Enein, 1974).

Human Clinical Studies
See discussion of the use of Psilocybe in clinical medicine on page 27 above.

Toxicity
The known physiological hazards of Psilocybe use are relatively minor (Davis, 1981); true hallucinations are uncommon, except with large doses, but visual distortion and alteration of hearing and other sensory functions are normal (Schultes & Hofmann, 1973).

Psilocybin has very few toxic effects in animals, especially compared to its effective dose. In mice, the LD50 is 280 mg/kg, which makes it 2.5 times less toxic than mescaline and 50 times more potent as a hallucinogen in humans (Schultes & Hofmann, 1973). The acute lethal oral dose of psilocybin was reported by Gable (1993) to be 14,000 mg, the safety margin (between an effective dose and lethal dose) very large and the dependence potential very small.

The most significant danger in the use of psychoactive mushrooms picked from the wild is the possibility of ingesting a toxic species from other genera, such as potentially lethal Cortinarius species (Raff et al, 1992). It has also been reported that psychoactive mushrooms purchased "on the street" may be either adulterated with chemical hallucinogens such as phencyclidine (PCP) or LSD (Schwartz & Smith, 1988). In a screening of 886 samples of alleged psilocybin mushrooms analyzed by Pharm Chem Street Drug Laboratory, 252 (28%) were hallucinogenic mushrooms, while 275 (31%) were other mushrooms adulterated with LSD or PCP, and 328 (37%) were completely inactive.

Uses in Traditional Medicine
Wasson states that the native people of Mexico do not use Psilocybe for pleasure, and Singer (1958) writes that the Nahua Indians consider hallucinogenic fungi "strictly a matter of religious healing, the business of the curandero or curandera". However, he adds that the Mazatec freely talk about their euphoric effects. Among the Mazatec, the mushrooms are often taken either during a divinatory ritual where questions are asked about a sick patient, "about the future, about the stolen money or the missing donkey", or during a long-night vigil of "supplication, chanting and praying." For a complete discussion of the ritual and sacred uses of psilocybe, see the fantastic book *Mushrooms, Russia and History* (Wasson & Wasson, 1957).

Medical Uses

As previously mentioned, psilocybin has been used in psychotherapy, especially in Germany. It was considered more promising than LSD because its effects were milder and of shorter duration, with essentially the same effects (Aboul-Enein, 1974).

Preparation and Dosage

Of the pure alkaloid, psilocybin, between 4 to 10 mg is considered an average dose (Schwartz & Smith, 1988). The amount of psilocybin in Psilocybe sspp. ranges from 2-17 mg/g (Corrigan, 1982), and *P. cubensis* is reported to contain about 10 mg/g of fresh weight.

Related Species

Psilocybe baeocystis, P. caerulescens, P. cubensis, P. cyanescens, P. semilanceata. Only fungi from a few mushroom genera are known to possess a psychoactive effect, mainly Psilocybe (81 species), Conocybe (*C. siligineoides*), Panaeolus (*P. cyanescens, P. subbalteatus*) (+3 species), Gymnopilus (*G. spectabilis*), Amanita (*A. muscaria* and *A. pantherina*), and one of the sac fungi (Ascomycetes), *Claviceps purpurea* (Schultes & Hofmann, 1973).

A species of Russula is reported to be used as a psychotropic agent by the indigenous people of New Guinea but has not been confirmed. The species *Cordyceps capitata* (Fr.) Link, *C. ophioglossoides* (Ehrenb.:Fr.) Link, *Elaphomyces granulatus* Fr., and *E. reticulatus* Vitt. are reported to be used in religious ceremonies among the Nahua Indians from the Nevado de Toluca region of Mexico, but for their "suggestive" testicular shape (Schultes, 1978; Guzman, 1983; Guzman et al, 1976). They apparently do not contain psychoactive substances.

In the following table, I review these genera, their ethnopharmacology and their main active compounds. The information was drawn from Ott (1976, 1978), Schultes (1973, 1978, 1979), Singer (1978), and Wasson (1957, 1968), Lincoff and Mitchel (1977).

Table 11

THE CHEMISTRY AND ETHNOPHARMACOLOGY OF PSYCHOACTIVE FUNGI

Species	Chemistry	Ethnopharm.
Lycoperdon L. marginatum L. mixtecorum	no data	Known as Kalamoto, these species are taken by Shamans in Northern Mexico to increase their powers of divination and to protect them against their enemies
Psilocybe spp.	psilocybin, psilocin, baeocystin, nor-baeocystin	utilized for visionary experience, ritual, spiritual insight, and recreation by native peoples of Mexico, Central and South America; these uses have penetrated into the fabric of modern industrialized countries

Paneolus sp. psilocybin positive: *P. subbalteatus* (Berk. and Br. Sacc. (=*P. venenosus* Murr.) *P. cyanescens* (*P. copelandia*) psilocybin latent (some populations may contain): *P. castaneifolius* *P. foenisecii* *P. sphinctrinus* *P. fimicola* *P. campanulatus* *P. papilionaceus* psilocybin negative: *P. phalaenarum* *P. retirugis* *P. semiovatus*	psilocybin, baeocystin, seratonin (*P. foenisecii,* *P. campanulatus,* *P. semiovatus,* *P. sphinctrinus,* *P. subbalteatus*	use among native peoples of Mexico, Central and South America minor, though Schultes & Hofmann (1973) report that it is used in northern Oaxaca; reported as used by young Americans, Canadians
Gymnopilus *G. validipes* *G. aeruginosus* *G. spectabilis*	psilocybin; no psilocybin was isolated from *G. spectabilis*, rather hispidin and/or bis-noryangonin, psychotropic pyrones similar to those in kava-kava	various reports of intoxication, esp. *G. spectabilis*
Conocybe *C. smithii* *C. cyanopus* sensu Kulmer *C. siligineoides* (not proven)	baeocystin, psilocybin	—
Psathyrella *P. sepulchralis*	none detected	reported used by native people of Oaxaca, but not proven
Amanita *A. muscaria* *A. pantherina*		used for centuries by native people in Siberia; may have been the ancient "Soma," exalted in the Rig Vedas, may have been used in Central or South America

Procurement

Active species of Psilocybe can be picked in the wild throughout the world. Cultivated and dried fruiting bodies, especially of *P. cubensis*, are available on the illicit recreational drug market. They are commonly sold in restaurants and by street vendors in parts of Asia (Thailand), Mexico, and Central and South America. Species of Psilocybe are sometimes grown at home.

Notes

See pages 27-33 for further discussion.

It is interesting to note that up to 24% of undergraduate students at a private southern U.S. university reported the use of mescaline or psilocybin in 1990 (Cuomo et al, 1994).

Amanita citrina and *A. porphyria* are known to produce bufotenine, reported by some to be psychoactive. There is no evidence that the fungi themselves have any activity, and they apparently do not contain toxic amines, being considered only mildly toxic (Tyler & Gröger, 1964).

SCHIZOPHYLLUM COMMUNE FR.

(schizo=split, phyll=gills; commune=common)

SPLIT-GILL

Synonyms
None known.

Other Common Names
S. commune is also known as the "split-fold" mushroom (Liu and Bau, 1980).

Schizophyllum from *American Fungi* by Charles McIlvaine, 1902.

Description and Habitat
These small, whitish fungi have dense hair and no stalk. They grow mostly on dead trees, appearing most of the year. They may be distinguished from look-alikes by their split gills and in-rolled margins.

Range
S. commune grows worldwide, being one of the most common mushrooms known. In fact, the species name, commune, means "common" or "widespread" (Pacioni, 1981).

History
No data.

Chemistry
S. commune contains the amino acids cystine and glutamine (Jung, 1981), as well as schizophyllan, an active polysaccharide (Kikumoto et al, 1970). The dried fungus contains, in mg/100 g, iron (280 mg), phosphorus (646 mg), calcium (90 mg), 0.5% fats, and 17.0% protein (Parent and Thoen, 1977).

Pharmacology
The polysaccharide schizophyllan shows antitumor activity against both the solid (Tabata et al, 1981) and ascites forms of sarcoma 180, as well as against the solid form only of sarcoma 37, Ehrlich carcinoma, Yoshida sarcoma (Komatsu, 1969), and Lewis lung carcinoma (Yamamoto et al, 1981). Schizophyllan has also increased cellular immunity by restoring suppressed killer-cell activity to normal levels in mice with tumors (Oka et al, 1985) and demonstrated protective effects against *Pseudomonas aeruginosa*, *Staphylococcus aureus*, *Escherichia coli*, and *Klebsiella pneumoniae* infections in mice (Komatsu et al, 1973).

Schizophyllan (SPG) activates macrophages (*in vitro* and *in vivo*) which results in augmentation of T cell activities and increased sensitivity of cytotoxic LAK and NK cells to IL-2. Although structurally similar to lentinan, SPG does not directly activate T cells (Shimizu et al, 1992). SPG is distributed in the body in macrophages, tissues next to tumors, and Kupffer cells (in bone marrow, lymph nodes, liver, and spleen) (Mizuhira et al, 1985). In bone marrow cells of mice, SPG inhibited chromosomal damage caused by chemotherapeutic agents (cyclophosphamide, adriamycin, and mitomycin C) and by radiation. Best results against radiation damage were found when SPG was administered shortly after or at the same time as radiation, and SPG restored mitosis of bone marrow cells previously suppressed by anticancer drugs (Yang et al, 1993).

Human Clinical Studies

In recurrent and inoperable gastric cancer, schizophyllan (SPG), combined with chemotherapy (tegafur or mitomycin C and 5-fluorouracil), in a randomized, controlled study in 367 patients, resulted in treated subjects living significantly longer than those on chemotherapy alone. Survival rates were also increased in 323 cases of resectable gastric cancer (Furue, 1985). In randomized controlled studies of SPG in combination with radiation therapy, SPG significantly prolonged the 5-year survival rate of stage II cervical cancer patients, but not stage III patients (Okamura et al, 1985; Okamura et al, 1989). SPG-treated (i.m.) cervical cancer patients show a more "significantly rapid" restoration of T-lymphocyte levels following radiation therapy than control patients (Noda et al, 1992). In cervical patients given SPG prior to surgery, compared to patients not pre-treated with SPG, regional lymph node production of interleukin-2 was significantly higher, suggesting prior helper T cell activation of cervical regional lymph nodes (Shimizu et al, 1992). Intratumoral administration of SPG in advanced cervical carcinoma patients produced increased lymphocyte infiltration in the tumor tissue and in tissue surrounding the tumor and NK cell infiltration in tumor tissue (Gorai et al, 1992). The application of *S. commune* in TCM against gynecological diseases (Yang & Jong, 1989) foreshadowed the current use of SPG against cervical cancer.

In oral carcinoma patients administered SPG (1 mg/kg X 2/week, i.m.), NK cell numbers and NK cell activity in peripheral blood showed a significant increase (Yoneda et al, 1991). There are also indications (*in vitro*) that chronic hepatitis B patients could benefit from SPG, since SPG can enhance immunological responsiveness to the virus, particularly in interferon-g production (Kakumu et al, 1991). In Japan, SPG is also being studied in chronic fatigue syndrome. A clinical report on the experience of a Japanese researcher from Kyoto University was reported in the *Japan Economic Journal* in 1992. Of 11 patients with symptoms of CFS, Uchida found the symptoms of 10 greatly improved, and natural killer cell count increased. The treatment was said to be without side effects.

Toxicity
No data.

Uses in Traditional Medicine
In TCM, *S. commune* is said to have a sweet taste and be mild in nature (Liu & Bau, 1980). It is recommended for general weakness and debility (Ying et al, 1987) and to cure gynecological diseases (Yang and Jong, 1989). In Mexico, *S. commune* is a highly regarded fungus for cooking or frying with sesame seeds and beans. The energetic quality assigned by curanderos who use it is cold (Alfaro et al, 1983).

Medical Uses
In China, the fungus is stewed with eggs to make a preparation used to cure leukorrhea (Ying et al, 1987).

Preparation and Dosage
As a tea, take 9-16 g in decoction, 3X/day.

Related Species
Plicaturopsis crispa (Pers.:Fr.) Reid (Lincoff, 1981).

Notes
This mushroom may be eaten whole raw, as it has a slightly bittersweet taste after mastication. Unfortunately, it is often so small that it is difficult to collect large quantities of this fungus in the wild, at least in California, but not necessarily in all regions (Arora, 1994). In many tropical areas, *S. commune* is a regularly eaten food. The natives of Zaire prepare the fungus by boiling it in water for 1-2 hours with the addition of vegetable salt which tenderizes this tough fungus. They are served drained with peanuts and salt and oil for seasoning (Parent and Thoen, 1977).

Procurement
Review the Notes section above. Schizophyllum is not generally available in North America or Europe in commercial trade, either in bulk or prepared products. In Japan, it is prescribed as an adjuvant to cancer therapy.

(trametes=one who is thin; versicolor=variously colored)

TURKEY TAIL

Synonyms
Boletus versicolor, Polyporus versicolor (Gilbertson and Ryvarden, 1987). *Coriolus versicolor* (L.:Fr.) is often used for *T. versicolor*, but Trametes is now generally accepted as correct (Arora, 1994). Other synonyms less frequently used include *Polystictus versicolor* Fr.and *Polyporus versicolor* (Arora, 1986).

Other Common Names
In Japan, *T. versicolor* is also known as "kawaratake," which means mushroom by the river bank (Namba, 1980). In China, the fungus is called "yun-zhi," meaning cloud fungus (Yang et al, 1993).

Description and Habitat
This common denizen of the woods is true to its name, as the multi-colored cap resembles turkey tails. Its fan-shaped fruiting bodies grow in overlapping clusters on dead logs. The top is zoned, usually in shades of brown, white, grey, or blue (though this is variable), and it sports hairy bands. The underside of the cap is white and shows minute pores which do not discolor after scratching.

Range
T. versicolor is common worldwide. I have seen it growing in many parts of the United States and Europe, and it grows throughout China (Yang et al, 1993).

History
For the year 1987 in Japan, PSK ("polysaccharide Kureha," which is extracted from turkey tail) accounted for 25.2% of the total national expenditure for anti-cancer agents (Fukushima, 1989). Florists in Europe recently adopted this fungus as one of the top species for commercial design (Poppe, 1991).

Chemistry
The lipid fraction from the carpophores of *T. versicolor* amounts to 1.7% of the total weight and contains the lanostane-type tetracyclic triterpenoid ergosta-7,22,dien-3β-ol as the major sterol (common in many other Polyporaceae), along with smaller amounts of ergost-7-en-3β-ol (fungisterol) and ergosterol (Yokoyama et al, 1975; Endo, 1981). They also contain β-sitosterol (Kim et al, 1978) and hydroxymethylquinoline (Abraham and Spaso, 1991). The two principal immunologically active fractions are PSK or "Krestin," a water-soluble, protein-bound polysaccharide that has β-1, 4-glucan as its main component as well as β-1,3 linkages and 38% protein (Sakagami and Takeda, 1993), and PSP, a polysaccharide-peptide consisting of 10% peptides and 90% polysaccharides (Yang et al, 1993). Miyazaki et al (1974) isolated an antitumor polysaccharide that did not contain nitrogen and called it coriolan.

Pharmacology
Pharmacological activities that may be due to the protein-bound polysaccharide PSK include the inhibition of sarcoma 180 (Hirase et al, 1976a; Ueno et al, 1978;

Yan, 1985); improvement in the functioning of blood vessels (Ito and Hidaka, 1980a); support of hepatic function (Ito and Hidaka, 1980b); restoration of serum lysozyme content and normalization of spleen index in irradiated mice (Cai et al, 1987); immune function enhancement (Iwaguchi, 1985), and the possible prevention of liver cancer (Wang, 1989). Against lethal cytomegalovirus infection, the action of PSK appears to be through NK cell activation (Ebihara and Minamishima, 1984). Also, nitrogen-containing polysaccharides extracted from *T. versicolor* mycelia increase antibacterial potency and prolong antibacterial effects of antibiotics and can increase antibiotic sensitivity in antibiotic-resistant bacteria (Kureha Chemical Industry Co., 1978).

Two polyoxygenated ergosterol derivatives showed cytotoxicity (*in vitro*) against hepatoma cells (Valisolalao et al, 1983). *T. versicolor* has been used in the control of the tobacco mosaic virus found on *Nicotiana tabacum* (Asano et al, 1979).

Animal studies have shown that PSK, which is derived from the mycelium, has immune-enhancing activity and a broad antineoplastic scope. It has been shown to prolong the survival time of irradiated mice, stimulate phagocytotic activity of macrophages, and improve the functions of the reticuloendothelial system (Zhu, 1987). In cyclophosphamide-induced granulocytopenia in mice, PSK (i.p.) caused a significant increase in granulocyte production (Mayer and Drew, 1980). PSK (oral) restored antibody (IgG) production in mice bearing sarcoma 180, but not in normal mice (Nomoto et al, 1975).

In regard to PSK's antitumor properties, it acts directly on tumor cells, as well as indirectly in the host to boost cellular immunity. It has shown antitumor activity in animals with adenosarcoma, fibrosarcoma, mastocytoma, plasmacytoma, melanoma, sarcoma, carcinoma, and mammary, colon, and lung cancer (Tsukagoshi et al, 1984). An intriguing feature of this compound is that injection of PSK at one tumor site has been shown to inhibit tumor growth in other sites, thus helping to prevent metastasis (Ebina et al, 1987b). Also, PSK's antitumor activity is enhanced in combination with radiation, chemotherapy, or immunotherapy. Oral administration of PSK as 10% and less of rat feeds suppressed carcinogen-induced cancers of the colon, esophagus, breast, and lung (Tsukagoshi et al, 1984).

PSK has also demonstrated antiviral activity. It may inhibit HIV infection by modifying the viral receptor or by stopping HIV from binding with lymphocytes (Tochikura et al, 1987a). Another mechanism through which PSK is reported to have general antiviral activity is through the stimulation of interferon production (Ebina et al, 1987a).

PSP is an immunostimulant extracted from *T. versicolor* mycelia. Although similar to PSK, which is also extracted from the mycelia, PSP is devoid of the sugar fucose while PSK is without the sugars rhamnose and arabinose. The major sugar in PSP is glucose, and the polysaccharide's main chain is linked by β1-3 and α1-4 glycosides. PSP has shown activity by the oral route and by injection (i.p.). In normal mice, oral doses of PSP (0.5-2 g/kg) caused greatly increased phagocytic activity, comparable to Acanthopanax (300 mg/kg, oral). PSP increased T-cell numbers (*in vitro*), interferon production (*in vitro*), and increased interleukin production in mice (PSP, 1,500 mg/kg/day X5, orally). Co-treatment of mice with PSP and cyclophosphamide resulted in a significant prevention of decreases in white blood cell and IL-2 production. In tumor-bearing mice, PSP stopped thymus atrophy and increased serum IgG values. PSP showed tumor-inhibiting activity in animals with sarcoma 180, P388 leukemia, monocytic leukemia, Ehrlich ascitic tumor, histiocytic lymphoma, human lung adenocarcinoma, and various cancers of the liver, stomach, nose, and throat (Yang, 1993).

A glycoprotein obtained from the mycelia of *Trametes* spp. showed activity (in animal and *in vitro* tests) against experimental hypertension, diabetes, cancer, thrombosis, and rheumatism. The protein inhibits blood platelet aggregation and is analgesic, antipyretic, antihyperlipemic, anti-arrhythmic, anti-inflammatory, and vasodilating. It has also been shown to reverse conditions associated with nephron disorders, improve proteinuria and proteinemia-associated conditions, and regulate prostaglandin formation and degradation (Ikuzawa, 1985).

An extracellular polysaccharide from *T. versicolor* administered to mice (i.p. or oral) challenged with herpes or influenza viruses caused serum interferon induction and inhibited a decrease in phagocytosis (Chen, 1986).

Whole *T. versicolor* has been shown to lower serum cholesterol in animals (Yagishita et al, 1977) and, in combination with the herb *Astragalus membranaceus* Bunge, it has been found to enhance neutrophil function and speed recovery in rabbits suffering from burns (Liu et al, 1985). Finally, a powdered extract (from a 70% ethanolic tincture) of this species was tested in rats by injection in a Hippocratic screening of higher fungi and demonstrated mild tranquilizing and diuretic activity (Malone et al, 1967).

Human Clinical Studies

PSK has been used both orally and intravenously as an immune adjuvant in clinical medicine. Cancer patients given 3 g of PSK per day have shown increased interferon production (Ebina et al, 1987a). In cancer patients, PSK also antagonistically elevates the activity of phosphofructokinase and shows antioxidant activity, working as a superoxide and hydroxyl radical scavenger (Nakamura et al, 1986). PSK has been shown to be effective against many human cancers (Hotta et al, 1981) but seldom with satisfactory results administered alone. In combination with radiation in stage III uterine cervical cancer patients, PSK (3-6 g/day) prolonged the life span and appeared to have enhanced the sensitivity of the cancers to radiation therapy. One study performed at the Department of Gynecology, National Cancer Center Hospital in Tokyo (Kasamatsu, 1982) tested the influence of PSK on the survival rate with cervical cancer patients. PSK was given orally in the dose of 3-6 grams a day in conjunction with radiation therapy. After radiation, patients having no observed tumor cells remaining was 36% with PSK and 11% without. Two-year survival rate was 94% with PSK and 74% without; 3-year survival rate was 85% and 59%, 5-year survival rate 64% and 41% respectively. The rate of cancer deaths within 5 years was 21% with PSK and 52% without.

Improved survival rates have also been reported in gastric cancer patients from PSK (6 g/day) in a combination treatment with the chemotherapeutic agent tegafur following gastrectomy and patients with postoperative stomach cancer. In a randomized, controlled study with 462 curatively resected colorectal cancers, PSK was given orally for over 3 years following mitomycin C (by iv on the day of surgery and 1 day following) and 5-fluorouracil (5-FU) orally for 5 months. At the time of reporting, the average study follow-up was 4 years. The increased disease-free survival curve of the PSK group over the control group (who only received the 2 drugs) was statistically significant (Mitomi et al, 1992). In another similar study, PSK was administered after the same chemotherapeutic regime as the previous study to 56 patients and a placebo to a group of 55 control patients. The rate of remissions and the survival rate in the patients taking PSK was significantly higher than the control group. Enhanced immune functions, including enhanced poly-morphonuclear leukocyte activity was said to be a significant factor in explaining the results (Torisu et al, 1990). PSK was tested as an adjuvant immunotherapy in a group of patients with carcinoma of the nasopharynx (n=21), and found to signifi-cantly increase (35 versus 25 months) the median survival time over the control group (n=17) as well as the 5-year survival rate (28% versus 15%). All patients in both groups had previous radiotherapy with or without chemotherapy (Go & Chung, 1989). Another earlier study with nasopharyngeal carcinoma patients (n=67) reported similar results (Chung et al, 1987). The dose was 1 gram 3 times daily for a minimum of 1 month. Three cases of toxicity were noted.

Other uncontrolled clinical studies have reported enhanced or recovered cellu-lar immunity from PSK in patients with glomerulonephritis, sarcoidosis, and idio-pathic nephrotic syndrome. Symptoms decreased, and relapse was prevented. Improved symptoms and normalization of immunity were reported in systemic lupus erythematosus, and in cases of lupus, chronic rheumatoid arthritis, sclerosis, Beçhet's disease, and dermatomyositis, peripheral lymphocytes showed recovery of blastogenesis. Others have reported that PSK causes a significant decrease in LDL cholesterol in hyperlipidemia (stage IIa) patients, a significant decrease in cyclophosphamide-induced chromosomal damage in children (Tsukagoshi et al, 1984), fewer sick days, and increased immunity in patients with recurrent genital herpes (3-5 g/day) (Kawana, 1985).

A controlled clinical trial of PSP was conducted in 485 cancer patients (211 control patients) treated with the polysaccharide-peptide (3 g/day for 30 days oral-ly) in combination with radio- and chemotherapies. The patients were diagnosed with cancers of the esophagus, stomach, and lung. As a result of PSP, side effects from the conventional therapies most significantly lessened in the categories of pain, poor appetite, tiredness, weakness, and dryness of the mouth and throat. The clinicians noted that in TCM, this indicates an invigorating action on the heart and spleen. Compared to control patients, body weight in the PSP group was sig-nificantly higher, and their T-cell ratio, NK cell activity, and IL-2 levels were also higher. To counteract the decreases in white blood cell, hemoglobin, and platelet levels which accompany chemo- and radiotherapy, batyl alcohol is often given at the same time. PSP in place of batyl alcohol produced comparable results. The rate of remission in the esophageal cancer patients who received PSP plus chemotherapy was 72%, whereas those on chemotherapy alone had a remission rate of 42%. PSP also raised the one-year survival rate for this type of cancer by 11%. The main immunologic pathways activated by PSP to inhibit tumors are through helper T-cell, NK cell, and complement C3 (Yang, 1993). In breast cancer patients treated with 4'epidoxorubicin and cyclophosphamide, PSP stabilized and nearly prevented white blood cell decreases from the chemotherapy (Shui et al, 1992).

Toxicity

Unlike many standard anticancer drugs, the PSK in *T. versicolor* produces few, if any, side effects on the bone marrow or other organs, and it shows no immunosuppressive action. In general, *T. versicolor* has very low levels of toxicity (Su et al, 1987) and produces few or no side effects (Tsukagoshi et al, 1984). The oral LD50 of PSP is reported as 10.0 mg/kg. Negative results were found on the Ames and chromosome distortion tests (Yang & Jong, 1989).

Uses in Traditional Medicine

The taste and energy is sweet and slightly warm; enters the spleen and heart meridians; invigorates the spirit (Yang et al, 1993).

In TCM, *T. versicolor* is used to clear dampness, reduce phlegm, heal pulmonary disorders (Ying et al, 1986), strengthen the physique, increase energy, and benefit people with chronic diseases (Yang & Jong, 1989). In Mexican folk medicine, the fungus is used to cure ringworm or impetigo of the skin (Alfaro et al, 1983).

Medical Uses

In China, it is considered useful for infection and/or inflammation of the upper respiratory, urinary, and digestive tracts, curative to liver ailments, including hepatitis B and chronic active hepatitis, and is used for general immune weakness and tumors (Ying et al, 1987).

Preparation and Dosage

Take as desired in tea, up to 20 g 3X/day. Powder the dried fruiting bodies and take up to 5 grams a day in capsules. For PSP, one gram 3 times daily (Yang & Jong, 1989).

Related Species

T. pubescens has exhibited anti-tumor activity (Shibata et al, 1968), and *T. hirsutus* is also active against sarcoma 180 in mice, and it is a popular folk remedy for benefiting lung diseases, stopping coughing, and promoting the regeneration of muscle (Ying et al, 1987). *Coriolus consors* contains coriolin, an antibiotic that has been shown to inhibit Gram-positive bacteria and *Trichomonas vaginalis* (Takeuchi et al, 1969). In addition, many species of Trametes have shown antibacterial activity (Hervey, 1947).

Notes

T. versicolor is an excellent fungus to collect in the wild, as it is widespread and abundant. To prevent larvae from damaging the fruiting bodies, it should be frozen promptly after harvesting for 24 hours and then dried, or dried soon after harvest in a food dryer at 120 degrees. Trametes number approximately 15 species in the western part of Canada and the U.S. (Lowe and Gilbertson, 1961). The tea is mucilaginous and has a flavor and odor reminiscent of cream of mushroom soup. You may also add a handful of the fruiting bodies to the Wei Qi Soup recipe (page 45), or chew the mushroom raw (it tastes and feels something like mushroom-flavored chewing gum, which is actually more enjoyable than one might first imagine). For the last 10 years, I have often eaten 2 or 3 of the fresh fruiting bodies as

I'm walking in the woods. I also know people who take 4-10 grams of the fungus powder daily as a tonic and cancer preventative. The mild-tasting fruiting bodies can also be used to make soup stock.

Procurement
Review the Notes section above for information on collection from the wild—it is widely available, often in large quantities. PSP and PSK are just beginning to be available in the U.S. and Europe, and are commonly prescribed in Japan for a variety of diseases and as a "health food" as discussed above.

TREMELLA FUCIFORMIS BERK.

(tremell=trembling; fuci=painted, colored; formis=form)

BAI MU ERH (SNOW FUNGUS)

Synonyms
No data.

Other Common Names
T. fuciformis is also known as the "white auricularia," "trembling fungus," or simply the "white fungus" (Zican et al, 1983; Liu and Bau, 1980). In China, the carpophore of *T. fuciformis* is known as "yin er" (Zhibin et al, 1982).

Description and Habitat
Jelly-like, nearly white translucent fruiting body, 5-10 cm in diameter with numerous wavy, leaf-like convolutions. Slightly yellow after drying. Prefers to grow on deciduous trees such as oaks, willows, poplars, chestnut, chinquapin, maple, liquidambar, and even eucalyptus. It is commonly cultivated in Asia (Liu and Bau, 1980).

Range
Grows mainly in the southern United States and warmer climates worldwide; common in Asia (Arora, 1986).

History
T. fuciformis (white fungus) has been used in China since ancient times as a Qi and immune tonic (Zican et al, 1983), as well as nutritive tonic for treating debility and exhaustion (Zhibin et al, 1982). It is said to enhance beauty, gonadal activity, reduce fevers, and heal ulcers. It is recommended in China to be taken for weakness after childbirth, constipation, abnormal menstruation, hemoptysis (blood in the sputum), dysentery, and gastritis. Finally, it is supposed to remove facial freckles if eaten frequently. Despite its gelatinous demeanor, this fungus is obviously a favored delicacy for many Asians. The method of administration is a lukewarm watery preparation made by soaking 3-4 grams of the white fungus for 1-2 hours, then cooking it down into a paste in an earthen pot. If the advice to "add enough crystal sugar to take twice daily" is commonly followed, its popularity might be considerably enhanced in the west (Liu & Bau, 1980).

Chemistry
Various semi-purified polysaccharides have been isolated and characterized from the spores (polysaccharides A and B) (Zhibin et al, 1982) and the fruiting bodies (Kakuta et al, 1979; Ukai et al, 1978). The sterols from the lipid fraction of Tremella consist of 16.8% ergosterol, 28.5% erosta-5,7-dien-3β-ol, and 54.7% ergost-7-en-3β-ol. The fungus also contains the fatty acids undecanoic acid (1.32%), lauric acid (2.37%), tridecanoic acid (1.28%), myristic acid (0.09%), pentadecanoic acid (5.43%), palmitic acid (17.2%), stearic acid (3.11%), palmitoleic acid (2.37%), oleic acid (38.8%), and linoleic acid (27.98%), as well as the phospholipids phosphatidylethanolamine, phosphatidylcholine, phosphatidyl glycerol, phosphatidylserine, and phosphatidyllinositol (Huang & Chang, 1984).

Pharmacology

A number of animal studies have shown that polysaccharides as well as a fermented solution and various extracts from *T. fuciformis* enhance cellular and humoral immune function (Xiao, 1987; Zhu, 1987; Xia & Chen, 1988). The polysaccharides and glycoproteins have been found to increase the effectiveness of interferon induction (Yang et al, 1986); increase splenocyte interleukin-2 (IL-2) production (Ma and Lin, 1992); promote phagocytosis (Zhibin et al, 1982), as well as the size and proliferation (Liu et al, 1994) of peritoneal macrophages. In addition, they protect against the negative effects of radiation (Hu and But, 1987; Xia & Chen, 1988; Zican et al, 1983) by augmenting natural killer cell activity, antibody-dependent cell-mediated cytotoxicity, and production of splenocytes of IL-2 (Zheng et al, 1993). Five polysaccharide fractions isolated from *T. fuciformis*, labeled BI-BV, have demonstrated antitumor activity against HeLa human cervical carcinoma cells *in vitro* (Gao, 1991), and polysaccharides A, B, and C demonstrated antitumor activity (ip) in mice (Ukai et al, 1972).

T. fuciformis polysaccharides and spore extracts have also demonstrated antilipemic (Sheng, 1989), anti-inflammatory (Zhibin et al, 1982; Konishi, 1988), antidiabetic (Xue et al, 1989), liver-protective (oral administration), and antiaging (Zhou et al 1989a) activities, also increasing the SOD activity of the brain and liver and inhibiting brain monoamine oxidase B (Zhou et al, 1989a). One preparation lowered the LDL-cholesterol in rats fed the preparation, which also contained butter, sugar, and egg yolks, by 30% over controls (Nakajima et al, 1989).

The polysaccharides could also increase the rate of survival and prolong the time of survival in mice (pretreated, i.p.) with implanted tumor cells (Liu et al, 1994). They prolonged thrombus formation, reduced thrombus size, reduced blood platelet count, platelet adherence, and blood viscosity, and positively influenced other blood coagulation parameters (Shen & Chen, 1990) and stimulated phagocytotic activity of macrophages (Lin, 1982).

One study showed that administration of *Tremella fuciformis* total polysaccharides (TFTP) has little influence on glycogen metabolism in the livers of mice, whether normal mice or mice in which liver injury was induced by surgery or by carbon tetrachloride, which caused the glycogen content to decrease. Structural protein synthesis in the injured liver was increased by TFTP, whereas synthesis of serum protein levels decreased from TFTP to levels lower than that of untreated controls (Yue & Cong, 1986).

Human Clinical Studies

Two polysaccharides (A and B) and a fermented mixture from *T. fuciformis* have been used in a variety of clinical trials. It is effective treating leukopenia induced in cancer patients by radio- and chemotherapy, and it has also been shown to boost immunological functions and stimulate leukocyte activity (Hu and But, 1987). Other clinical studies have confirmed that extracts of *T. fuciformis* possess antitumor and anti-radiation properties and strengthen immune activity (Zican et al, 1983). In addition, both Tremella spore fermented solution and polysaccharides A and B have increased phagocytosis of macrophages, resulting in improved immunity and resistance to chronic bronchitis in human patients (Lin et al, 1982).

A polysaccharide-containing extract was given to 45 patients with chronic hepatitis, 3 capsules containing 1 gram a day for 3 months (Xiong, H.-Z. et al, 1985). In the 32 patients in the group with chronic active hepatitis, the success rate is reported to be 56.3%, and of the 13 with chronic persistent hepatitis, 76.9%. Ten patients who were HBsAg positive converted to negative, and 13 had a decrease in HBsAg titer. Sixteen patients were said to be clinically cured, and after a follow-up period of 6-36 months, 14 patients were free of further symptoms.

Toxicity
Believed to be non-toxic (Ying et al, 1987; Hu and But, 1987); the LD50 (i.v.) of the Tremella spores fermented solution was 17.87 ml/kg and of polysaccharide A, 380 mg/kg (Lin et al, 1982).

Uses in Traditional Medicine
Taste and energy are sweet and mild (Ying et al, 1987). Therapeutically related to lung and spleen channels (Enquin, 1990;), it is said to supplement the vital energy, promote blood circulation and strengthen the heart, nourish the yin and stomach, and invigorate the brain (Zican, 1983; Bensky & Gamble, 1993).

In TCM, *T. fuciformis* is well known and highly respected in both TCM and folk medicine. It is used as a cough syrup for treating chronic tracheitis and a number of other cough-related conditions, such as asthma, dry coughs, heat in the lungs, etc, especially with yin deficiency (clears yin deficient heat). It is also used to strengthen semen, counteract yin deficiency, lubricate the lungs and intestines, harmonize the blood, stimulate the heart, increase the secretion of saliva, strengthen vital energy, and nourish the stomach, kidneys, and brain (Ying et al, 1987). In China, a number of prepared products are made from this fungus, including "Yin Mi Pian" which includes *A. mellea*. An extract is made by fermentation, a process which may release active high molecular weight polysaccharides and make them available to the body. The extract is then made into tablets, 6-12 of which are taken daily for 4 weeks to enhance the recovery of red-cell production in the bone marrow in cases of "blood deficiency," and enhance immune system functions, such as phagocytosis and levels of lysozyme in bronchial secretions. The tablets are used clinically to benefit lowered white blood cell count after radiation or chemotherapy for cancer, the coughing and phlegm associated with asthma and chronic bronchitis (Yang & Jong, 1989). *T. fuciformis* has shown positive results in treating debility and exhaustion according to TCM practitioners in China (Enquin, 1990; Zhibin, 1982).

Medical Uses
Based on its beneficial effect on the blood and cholesterol-lowering effects in animal studies (see pharmacology section), *T. fuciformis* may be useful when taken daily as a preventative and/or treatment (with other herbs, diet and exercise) for cardiovascular problems, such as arteriosclerosis, atherosclerosis, and abnormal clotting, though there are no clinical studies that support this use. In Japan, a patent was registered for "cholesterol-controlling foods and drinks" containing powdered *Tremella fuciformis*. Clinical trials support its use with chemotherapy and radiation therapy for cancer patients and for patients with chronic infections, to augment immune function.

Preparation and Dosage
3-4 grams twice daily in teas, soups, and other dishes, or powdered and sprinkled on food. *T. fuciformis* is prepared by soaking 3-4 grams of the dried fruit body in water for a couple of hours and then stewing the fungus until it becomes the consistency of a paste, add a sweetener such as honey to taste and take a small amount twice a day (Liu and Bau, 1980).

Related Species
All similar species are usable for food, since none of the jelly fungi are known to be poisonous; not all have been tested for medicinal activity. Two widely used related species are *T. aurantia* and *T. mesenterica* Mart. (Ying et al, 1987; Liu and Bau, 1980). *T. mesenterica*, also known as aureous jelly fungus (Liu and Bau, 1980) or in the west, witch's butter, is bright yellow-to-orange and has a convoluted shape. Commonly seen on logs during rainy weather, it is jelly-like when wet and small and hard when dry. *T. aurantia* has many of the same qualities according to TCM as *T. fuciformis*, namely, it is nourishing, regulates Qi, stops coughing, is used for asthmatic attacks, reduces phlegm, and supports the liver. In addition, it is used clinically in China for hypertension and tracheitis (Ying et al, 1987).

T. mesenterica has been recommended for eye ailments and for palsies in European herbal medicine, especially pungent fruiting bodies, which are thought to be superior to ones that are mild-tasting (Dragendorff, 1898). It is thought to have a sweet taste and cold energy in TCM and is used to relieve inflammation of the upper respiratory tract. It is soothing, demulcent, and slightly expectorant, and it may be taken as tea for colds and flu, asthma, bronchitis, and general debility. To make tea from *T. mesenterica*, use 3-6 g of the fresh fungus, or soak the dried fungus in water to hydrate it before weighing. Simmer the measured quantity in water for 6-8 hours until it becomes a paste. Then add honey and take the preparation continuously for periods of 10 days, resting 2-3 days in between each period (Liu and Bau, 1980). *T. mesenterica* grows on dead hardwoods, especially branches or sticks (Arora, 1986).

A liquid extract from *A. polytricha* and *Flammulina velutipes* was given orally in a study with children and was said to help prevent and treat iron deficiency anemia as well as stimulate weight gains and improve appetite. The preparation was awarded a silver cup at a 1990 international food fair (Ni et al, 1993).

Procurement
Read the Notes section above. Various Tremella species are available in Chinese food stores and herb shops. They are common in the wild, and may be included in some Chinese prepared products.

WOLFIPORIA COCOS (SCHW.) WOLF

(por=pores; cocos=coconut)

TUCKAHOE, HOELEN, FULING

Synonyms
Pachyma hoelen Rumph.

Other Common Names
W. cocos is also known as "hoelen" in Chinese (Narui et al, 1980). "Fuling" is the Chinese name for the sclerotium of this fungus, and other parts of it have names as well. For example, "fulingpi" is the black skin removed from the sclerotium; the inner white portion of the sclerotium is called "baifuling;" and the tuber which encircles the root of the pine tree is called "fushen." There is also a reddish variety of *W. cocos* which is known as "chifuling" (Chang & But, 1986). In Japan, it is known as Matsuhodo.

Description and Habitat
P. cocos grows underground on the roots of pine (Narui, 1980) and other trees. It is often found infecting tree roots and stumps of hardwoods and conifers. There is a rather tough fruiting body arising from a sclerotium. The flesh of the fruiting body is often resupinate on wood, thin and white to tan with the stalk absent (Arora, 1986).

Range
Eastern Asia, Eastern Australia, and especially common in southeastern North America. *Polyporus tuberaster* forms tubers that are riddled with dirt and sand and are much less usable (Arora, 1986).

History
P. cocos is economically important in Nigeria, where it is used as food as well as in traditional medicine (Prance, 1984). In the Eastern and Southern U.S., Indian use of *P. cocos* was primarily for making a kind of bread which the European settlers called "Indian bread." Indian bread, or Indian potato, was also a survival food for slaves running from capture. A single growth could weigh 15-30 pounds and, after baking, it could be ground to produce a flour. Like potatoes, tuckahoes were dug up from the ground and were often found in the same shape and size as sweet potatoes, and they were believed to be poisonous until roasted. In 1821, John Torrey made one of the first analyses of "tuckahoe," finding that it contained a kind of "glutin" made up of a vegetable matter he called "sclerotin," a name genericized in the same year in Sclerotium cocos, a binomial that aptly described both the coconut-like shape of the fungus and its occurrence as a sclerotium (Weber, 1929).

Chemistry
P. cocos contains polysaccharides (Li, 1974), protein-bound polysaccharides such as H-11 (Kanayama et al, 1983), and 0.28% of a mixture of triterpenecarboxylic acids (Iseda & Yagishita, 1956), including the triterpene acids pachymic acid and related compounds, tumulosic acid, and eburica-7-9(11)-dien-20-oic acid (Valisolalad et al, 1980), as well as ergosterol (Li, 1974; Yokoyama et al, 1975); also fungisterol,

eburicoic acid, and other sterols (Yokoyama et al, 1975); and choline, phospho-lipids, and resin (Li, 1974).

Its water-soluble sugars are composed of glucose, sucrose, and a small amount of unknown sugar. No fructose is present (Iseda & Yagishita, 1956). Two new triterpenoids, poricoic acids A (I) and B (II), have recently been isolated from the surface layer of *P. cocos* (Tai et al, 1991). The fatty acids in Korean (white) *P. cocos* have been identified as caprylic acid, undecanoic acid, lauric acid, dodecenoic acid, and palmitic acid, the major ones being caprylic and dodecenoic acids (Moon et al, 1987). According to Suzuki et al (1982), the mineral content (ppm) of *P. cocos* is Na (8.9), K (570), Ca (12), Mg (29), Fe (47), Mn (6.9), Zn (2.2), and Cu (2.2). See the Nutrition section for comparison with other fungi.

Pharmacology

As with many other medicinal fungi, the polysaccharides of *P. cocos* have been reported to inhibit tumors indirectly by stimulating immunological functions (Lou et al, 1988). One such polysaccharide, named pachyman, showed no significant antitumor activity (Narui et al, 1980; Chihara et al, 1970a), but it increased phago-cytosis in the peritoneal macrophages and accelerated recovery from cyclophos-phamide-induced leukopenia in rats (Chen et al, 1987a). However, a protein-bound polysaccharide (H11) isolated from the mycelia of *P. cocos* inhibited sarcoma 180 in mice, apparently through a host-mediated reaction (Kanayama, 1983; Kanayama,1986). H11 was isolated when it was discovered that in large doses (200 mg/kg) a crude fraction of the mycelium produced a tumor inhibition rate of 80% and complete remission of tumors in 10% of animals (Kanayama, 1986). Carboxymethylpachymaran (CMP), a chemically modified form of the polysaccha-ride pachyman in *P. cocos*, increased the effectiveness of interferon induction *in vitro* (Yang et al, 1986), enhanced phagocytic activity of macrophages (Singh et al, 1974), and produced very high rates of tumor inhibition in mice (Hamuro et al, 1971a). Pachyman was found to be effective against original-type, anti-GBM nephritis in rats. This may be due in part to the inhibitory action of pachyman on C3-deposition in the glomeruli (Hattori et al, 1992).

Another compound from *P. cocos* that has been studied in some detail is poriatin, which is said to be a group of low-molecular weight tetracyclic triterpenes (Zhang et al, 1993). It, too, has immunostimulating activities, having demonstrated antivi-ral activity and the ability to activate peritoneal macrophages and increase pinocy-tosis and phagocytosis. It can also improve the production of colony stimulating activity by macrophages, lymphocytes, and other cells, shortening the period of leukocytopenia, and enhance lysosomal enzyme activity "with protein and RNA synthesis" (Ding et al, 1987; Zhong et al, 1993). Poriatin is especially interesting in that it has also demonstrated immunosuppressive activity and is an aldosterone antagonist (Deng and Xu, 1992; Wang et al, 1992a). For instance, in a study on rats with experimentally-induced autoimmune encephalomyelitis, poriatin decreased the severity of the disease. A combined therapy of poriatin and cyclophosphamide (a neoplastic suppressant used in the treatment of lymphomas and leukemias), was even more effective. This not only suggests that poriatin may be useful in treating autoimmune diseases, but also points to the valuable synergis-tic effects that can be obtained by integrating herbal and modern western medicine

(Wang et al, 1992b). *P. cocos* has also shown suppressor action (*in vitro*) against the secretion of cytokines (TNF-Alpha, IL-6, IL-b and GM-CSF), but only from high amounts (Tseng and Chang, 1992).

Finally, *P. cocos* has been shown to have antimutagenic activity (Nunoshiba et al, 1990) and, in combination with other herbs (*Cinnamomum cassia, Paeonia suffruticosa, Prunus persica*, and *Paeonia lactiflora*), to potentiate an increase in the pain threshold, decrease spontaneous locomotive activity, and to produce increased sedative and hypnotic effects in mice given phenobarbital (Xie and Ren, 1987). A methanolic extract of *P. cocos* (as *Pachyma hoelen*) has shown hair growth promoting activity applied topically to mice (Inaoka et al, 1994).

Human Clinical Studies
Reference was made above to the possibilities of integrating herbal and modern western medicine. One such study conducted on humans used a combination of 400 mg metronidazole and a decoction of the roots of *Paeonia lactiflora* and *Angelica sinensis*, plus the sclerotium of *Wolfiporia cocos* (10 g of each herb), to treat viral hepatitis. The cure rate for the combined therapy was 75%, while it was only 40% with the use of metronidazole alone and 36% with the decoction alone. The control group showed 0% cure rate (Wang, 1987). The chemically-modified form of pachyman, carboxymethylpachymaran, which Guo et al (1984) call "carboxylmethyl Poria Cocos Polysaccharide" was reported to produce an "immediate cure" of chronic viral hepatitis in 11 out of 30 patients, while 16 were improved. Following two courses of the polysaccharide (60 mg, i.m.), no side effects were found and a normalization was seen in immune functions (Guo et al, 1984). *P. cocos* has also been used to treat arrhythmia (Ding, 1987).

Toxicity
There has been one case of an allergic reaction to the sclerotium of *P. cocos* which produced systemic pruritus, sore limbs, dizziness, and nausea (Shen, 1985). However, *P. cocos* is generally considered safe.

Uses in Traditional Medicine
According to TCM, it is considered sweet and bland with a mild energy (Chang & But, 1987) and is used to invigorate the Spleen, tonify the Stomach, clear dampness, as a sedative, tranquilizer, and diuretic, and for clearing febrile illnesses and leukorrhea (Tu, 1988). The internal white portion is used as a febrifugal, diuretic, and to strengthen the vital energy, soothe agitation, and lower blood sugar (Ying et al, 1987).

Medical Uses
In China the cortex of the fungus is used as a decoction for coughs, edema, and as a diuretic; the sliced, whole sclerotium is used to treat jaundice and to induce menstruation (Miyasita, 1976; Lee et al, 1977). In Korea, *P. cocos* is used as an antifertility drug to induce menstruation (Lee et al, 1977).

Preparation and Dosage
Usually 9-15 g (Tu, 1988).

Related Species

In the western half of Canada and the U.S. alone, there are approximately 74 species of Poria (Lowe and Gilbertson, 1961).

I have experimented with *Wolfiporia corticola* or look-alikes in the same group and feel that they have potential. These forms of Poria are simply layers of white pores that grow flat on decaying wood. In some years, they grow in thick layers of pores, 1-2" thick on dead alder and oak. I cut them off with a knife, like cutting through honeycombs, and dry the long strips of white pore layers. They make a good-tasting (sweet and slightly bitter) tincture (in 45% ethanol), and the tea is palatable. I have noticed a diuretic effect from it, but I need more clinical experience with it to say more.

Gregory et al (1966) found that *P. corticola* showed strong antitumor activity (Sarcoma 180) in mice, which was supported by Ruelius et al (1968), as well as "considerable antibacterial activity" against a number of bacteria and fungi (Ying et al, 1987). The activity was said to be due to two isolated antibiotic substances, nemotin and nemotinic acid (Kavanagh et al, 1950). Also from this species an antitumor acidic protein was isolated and named poricin (Ruelius et al,1968). In a survey of mushrooms for antibacterial activity, 33 species of Poria showed a strong degree of activity (Hervey, 1947).

Procurement

Hoelen is one of the most commonly used of all Chinese herbs, and is available in Chinese herb shops and some natural food stores in bulk. It is also included in a large number of commercial prepared products in Asia, North America, and Europe. It is difficult to obtain from the wild in North America or Europe, less so in Asia.

ADDITIONAL SPECIES

Brief monographs—for species where there is insufficient data for a full treatment; and table of species

AGARICUS BISPORUS (LANGE) SING.

BUTTON MUSHROOM

It is known that the button mushroom, the most commonly cultivated mushroom in most western countries, contains carcinogenic compounds, most notably agaritine, which is related to a class of chemicals called hydrazines. While these compounds are known to possess carcinogenic properties, tests show that one might have to consume as much as 350 grams of fresh mushrooms daily for 50 years for there to be a significant risk of initiating tumor growth (Toth & Gannett, 1993). It is difficult to correlate this risk with actual human consumption. The researchers also found that during the storage period of commercially-available mushrooms, the carcinogenic hydrazines were reduced up to 47% after 1 week and up to 76% after 2 weeks, and that cooking only reduced them by an average of 25%. This means that cooking does not significantly reduce the risk. Moderate consumption of button mushrooms may not be any more carcinogenic than a number of other slightly risky foods or beverages such as peanut butter or wine. It is interesting to note that a number of other edible mushroom species, including *P. ostreatus*, *F. velutipes*, and *V. volvacea* have been shown to be free of agaritine (Breene, 1990).

Button mushrooms do contain significant amounts of protein, vitamins and minerals, but when one considers the possible carcinogenic effect of their chronic consumption, and the possible trace amounts of malathion that may be present, it is probably wise to eat them no more than 2-3 times weekly in moderate amounts.

CALVATIA GIGANTEA (BATSCH:PERS.) LLOYD, C. SPP.

GIANT PUFFBALL, MA BO

Some authors say that the large fruiting body of this fungus is the largest of all fungi (McIlvaine and Macadam, 1973), though Arora disputes this (Arora, 1994). It has been recorded that specimens of *C. gigantea* have been found as large as 5 ft. and weighing 50 lbs, and one observer has said that from a distance they have sometimes been mistaken for sheep grazing on a hillside (Arora,1986).

One study showed that *C. gigantea* possesses antitumor properties (Roland et al,1960), and the spores of *C. gigantea* contain amino acids, urea, ergosterol, and lipid. They also contain calvacin, a moderately heat-stable mucoid ingredient which effectively inhibits the growth of sarcoma 180 in mice (Hanssen & Schädler, 1982). Externally it is used as a styptic, and internally it is used to reduce fever and internal heat. In TCM, it is said to be effective against chronic tonsillitis, and swollen, sore throats, (Ying et al, 1987) and is applied topically to stop bleeding in oral hemorrhages and nosebleeds (Bensky & Gamble, 1993). Between 1.5-6 grams of the dried puffball is used as a tea internally, or the spore powder is applied externally (Tu, 1988). Pharmacological research in China may support the traditional hemostatic effect of puffball spores. In one study of 467 patients, *C. gigantea* spores was effective in 98% of the cases in stopping traumatic hemorrhage after operations. The spores have also shown activity against a variety of pathogenic bacteria *in vitro*, including *Staphylococcus aureus*, *Pseudomonas aeruginosa*, *Proteus*, and *Streptococcus pneurnoniae* (Bensky & Gamble, 1993).

When preparing the tea, wrap the dried fruiting body in cheesecloth and cook for 20-30 minutes.

Procurement
Available from the wild, or some Chinese herb dealers.

CALVATIA SPP.

Extracts of *Calvatia craniformis* are active against Gram positive and Gram negative bacteria and various fungi. For wounds, it is also used in China to promote granulation of tissue, while relieving inflammation, pain, and swelling (Ying et al, 1987). The antibiotic (effective against gram positive bacteria) and antitumor compound, cavatic acid was isolated from the aerobic culture of the mycelium (Umezawa et al, 1975).

In Chinese folk-medicine *C. gigantea* as well as *C. lilacina* is said to be "soothing and sweet," and is recommended for coughs, hoarseness and sore throats. As with many puffballs, this species is also often used for bleeding of all kinds, for instance, blood in the sputum and nosebleed, but also for hemostasis in patent wounds (Hanssen & Schädler, 1982).

Calvatia bovista, also known as *Lycoperdon bovista* Pers., *C. utriformis* and *C. caelata*, and in pharmacy as *Fungus chirurgorum* has a reputation of stopping nosebleeds and as a general styptic; *Bovista plumbea* Pers. was used likewise (Dragendorff, 1898; Arora, 1986).

Procurement
Available only from the wild.

CANTHARELLUS CIBARIUS FR.

CHANTERELLE

Cibarius comes from the Latin and means "good to eat" (Lincoff, 1981).

C. cibarius is found on the ground near conifers and broadleaf trees. In central and southern California it is often found under oaks, particularly near the edge of pastures (Lincoff,1981; Arora, 1986).

Chanterelles are a beautiful fleshy tubaeform fungi which are bright orange-yellow in color. The common orange-colored chanterelle contains 8 essential amino acids, as well as vitamin A. The frequent consumption of this fungi is beneficial in

Cantharellus from *Esculent Funguses of England* by Charles D. Badham, M.D., 1847.

preventing night blindness, inflammation of the eye (ophtalmia), and dry skin, according to TCM. It also helps tonify the mucous membranes, and may increase resistance against certain infectious diseases of the respiratory tract (Ying et al, 1987).

Studies on mice show ethanol extract of *C. cibarius* sporophore can inhibit the growth of sarcoma 180 (Ying et al, 1987).

Procurement
Abundantly available in some areas of the world, such as the Pacific Northwest of the U.S. Often sold fresh in markets, farmer's markets, and in Europe, they are available canned and dried. On the menus of some gourmet restaurants.

FLAMMULINA VELUTIPES (CURT.:FR.) SING.

ENOKITAKE

F. velutipes is a popular edible mushroom in Japan where a tender cultivated form of the wild version is called "enokitake." It is commonly used in Japanese cooking and increasingly can be found in salads in some gourmet restaurants. If taken on a regular basis, *Flammulina velutipes* may prevent, as well as cure, liver disease and gastroenteric ulcers, according to one Chinese source (Ying et al, 1987; Yoshioka et al, 1973).

F. velutipes contains several types of amino acids including valine, which inhibits the growth of Ehrlich ascities tumour and sarcoma 180 in mice, and lysine, reported to increase body height and weight (Ying et al, 1987).

Polysaccharides of *F. velutipes* show significant tumor inhibition in mice with sarcoma 180 and Ehrlich carcinoma (Ying et al, 1987).

A polysaccharide fraction from this mushroom produced a tumor inhibition rate of 82% with a dose of 1 mg/kg/day against sarcoma 180 in mice (Yoshioka et al, 1973).

F. velutipes contains a cardiotoxic protein (flammutoxin) that is rendered harmless when subjected to heat (100°C) for a period of 20 minutes. The protein also causes the swelling and respiratory inhibition of Ehrlich ascites tumor cells (Lin et al, 1974). I would caution against the chronic use of enokitake raw in salads or other dishes.

Procurement
On the menu in Japanese restaurants and some gourmet restaurants. Enokitake is often cultivated.

KOMBUCHA

Also called kombucha tea, the tea mushroom, *Fungus japonicus*, tea kvass, etc., Kombucha is a tough jelly-like "skin," which is really a complex association or symbiosis of yeasts (which are simple fungi) and bacteria. Over the last 50 years, and probably much longer, Kombucha has enjoyed cycles of popularity in many European countries, throughout Asia and the U.S. and is currently experiencing a reawakening of interest, with numerous reports in the popular press (i.e., Taking the Fungal-Tea Plunge *Newsweek*. January 9, 1995) and on television. Kombucha tea can be considered a traditional fermented food and the Kombucha "skin" is eaten as a dessert delicacy called Nata in the Philippines. As a traditional food and beverage that has been widely used over hundreds of years, Kombucha tea probably has some health benefits, but the fantastic claims that are made for it are undoubtedly overblown. These claims include anti-aging effects, such as restoration of hair and cancer-prevention. A list of other reported uses would place the tea into the realm of the panacea: gout, rheumatism, arteriosclerosis, high blood pressure, irritability, constipation, mental fatigue, and low sex drive. To my knowledge, no studies exist to support such claims. I consider it simply a healthful (when made properly) and to some, a flavorful beverage that is fun to make at home. The social aspect of discussing how our Kombucha is doing, how well it grows on different teas, and sharing the "offspring" with friends and even strangers, is an important part of its allure.

In 1928, Hermann reported on his identification of two bacteria, *Bacterium xylinum* Brown and *B. xylinoides* Henneberg (both are now known to be the same organism, *Acetobacter aceti* subsp. *xylinum* [Brown] comb. nov.), and a second bacterium, *B. gluconicum* Hermann (now *Gluconobacter oxydans* subsp. *suboxydans* [Kluyver and de Leeuw] comb. nov.), named after its ability to form gluconic acid. Researchers have subsequently determined that Kombucha is a symbiotic association of "vinegar bacteria," mainly *A. aceti* subsp. *xylinum*, which produces the pure cellulose mat or pellicle which we associate with the name "Kombucha," *Acetobacter ketogenum* (sic) Walker and Thomas (now *Acetobacter aceti* [Pasteur] Beijerinck), the *G. oxydans subsp. suboxydans* already mentioned, and nest-like masses of yeast cells embedded in the mat, mainly *Pichia fermentans* Lodder, and also

Saccharomyces apiculatus (Reess) (now *Kloeckera apiculata* [Reess Emend. Klöcker] Janke), *Saccharomycodes ludwigii* Hansen, and *Schizosaccharomyces pombe* Lindner (List & Hörhammer, 1973; *Bergey's Manual of Determinative Bacteriology*, 8th ed., 1975). It is entirely possible that other bacteria and yeasts are present in a given batch of Kombucha tea, depending on the type of tea used, the temperature, the starting culture, the percentage and type of sugar used, and other factors.

When the Kombucha organism is grown on a tea infusion which provides nitrogen, vitamins and minerals, other essential nutritive substances, and sugar, its yeasts proliferate. They transform the sugar into small amounts of alcohol, much of which is ultimately changed to acetic acid (up to 3%) by the bacteria, which also thrive on B vitamins produced by the yeast. This process gives the "tea" a sweet and sour smell of fermenting apple cider. The finished tea is reported to contain on average between 0.5 and 1% alcohol, as well as lesser amounts of lactic acid, tartaric acid, malic acid, malonic acid, citric acid, and oxalic acid (List & Hörhammer, 1973). When black tea is used to make the nutrient solution upon which the organism grows, small amounts of caffeine are present, depending on the brewing method and the caffeine content of the original tea. During the fermentation process, the caffeine is not entirely degraded and is still present in the finished tea (Hermann, 1927). Simple sugar content in the finished product, even when table sucrose is used, is minimal, about 3%.

Reports that the tea contains usnic acid, a lichen acid that has antibiotic properties, is simply not true, and I can find no published chemical analysis of kombucha tea or of the organisms in it that identify glucuronic acid as a constituent or metabolic by-product, despite second-hand reports that they do. If it is present, it occurs in minor amounts. Gluconic acid, which is a major component, is chemically distinct from glucuronic acid and is not used by the liver for detoxification of hormones and toxic compounds as is glucuronic acid (Osol et al, 1955).

The infusion of Kombucha is said to have been extremely popular as a folk remedy for thousands of years (Fasching, 1985). The first recorded use of the tea was during the Chinese empire of the Tsim-Dynasty in 221 B.C. (Frank, 1991). It was known as "The Remedy for Immortality" or "The Divine Tsche". The "Tsche" (meaning tea) was said to be introduced in Japan by the Korean doctor *Kombu* in 414 B.C. (Fasching, 1985). Frank (1991) says the name originated from the Japanese name for a seaweed, kombu, and from the word "cha," meaning tea. His contention is that someone may have made the culture from kombu tea, and the name was erroneously transferred to the culture. Kombu tea is still sold throughout Japan and is very popular. Subsequently, Kombucha tea came to be used in India, Russia, and other Eastern countries. It is reported that Kombucha enjoyed wide popularity until World War II when black tea and sugar (with which it is grown) became scarce (Fasching, 1985). In the 1960s a German doctor named Sklenar developed a "biological cancer therapy" using mainly Kombucha, which he had learned about in Russia during the war.

Glucuronic acid, lactic acid, and acetic acid are mentioned with regard to Kombucha's effect on metabolism, particularly concerning its "detoxifying function" through its linkage with D-glucoronate (R. Fashing, 1988; K. H., 1986; H. Korner, 1987; U. Ruckert, 1987). Sklenar theorized that the glucuronic acid causes

Directions for Making Kombucha

A. Pour 34 oz of water into a glass or enamel pan and set on stove.

B. As the water is heating up, add 2 oz sugar and stir until dissolved (if honey is being substituted, add it after the tea has reached room temperature).

C. When the water boils, remove the pan from the heat and add 1-4 teaspoons or 2-5 teabags (to taste) of either black or green tea. Steep 10-15 minutes.

D. If tea leaves have been used, strain through a strainer; if a teabag was used, remove it.

E. Let the mixture cool to lukewarm and then pour it into a glass jar or glazed earthenware jar (to make larger amounts use a large glass cooking bowl or a glass aquarium) (Frank, 1991). Ideally the container should have a wide mouth, and there shouldn't be too much air space above the liquid.

F. Add about 10% Kombucha from the previous batch (if you are making it for the first time, get the extra starter liquid with the culture, or add two tablespoons of boiled vinegar to the tea).

G. Place the culture in the liquid, taking care to not break the layer on the upper surface (the smooth, shiny surface should be face up, with the brown, rougher layer underneath). Sometimes the culture floats and sometimes it sinks to the bottom, which may depend on how soft or hard the water is.

H. Use cheesecloth to cover the mouth of the container and secure with a rubber band.

I. Place in a warm spot (a constant temperature between 64° and 78° F. is optimum) out of direct light and leave without moving for 8-10 days.*

J. Remove the culture after washing your hands.

K. Strain the tea into bottles and store in the refrigerator or in another cool place (Frank suggests not filling the bottle all the way to the top and using corks which can be removed in case pressure should build up). If the cap is tight enough (use an old champagne bottle and tie down the top), the drink can become sparkling, but be cautious when taking the top off.

L. Leave the yeast sediment in the original container, but once a month it should be poured out as well and the container washed with hot water. At this time, wash the culture with cold water and then replace it in the container.

M. Keep approximately 10% of the tea in the fermentation container (unless it needs to be washed, in which case it may be poured back in after the container is washed).

*Some people contend the tea should be poured off after 6 days in winter and after 3-4 days in summer, when it should be allowed to sit in glass containers for another 3 days before drinking. Frank writes that after 12-14 days, the sugar is completely converted and the taste similar to dry wine—and it is easier to digest at this stage. Also, Russian researchers have reported that the antibiotic activity found in Kombucha is at its highest peak on the 7th and 8th days (Frank, 1991).

detoxification, based on its known detoxifying function in the liver. The glucuronic acid forms conjugates with metabolic waste products and harmful substances, such as drugs or poisons, thereby facilitating the detoxification process (Fasching, 1994). This theory has no basis in fact, according to a very thorough search of the scientific literature, but acetic acid and lactic acid may have mild detoxifying effects; they have been widely reported in the literature on fermented foods to retard the growth of harmful bacteria, while promoting the growth of beneficial bacteria in the intestine.

There are no clinical trials to support the effectiveness of Kombucha in cases of cancer, although it is being promoted as an "effective biological cancer therapy."

After careful studies of the available literature, as well as other obtainable information, the Swiss Society for Oncology and the Swiss Cancer Association have not found data that would support Kombucha's use in the treatment of cancer. After my own thorough search, I must come to the same conclusion, though further studies and experience may prove me wrong.

For weakened digestion, Rosina Fasching suggests drinking 1-2 glasses of Kombucha first thing in the morning and after meals at noon and at night. Its taste has been described as thirst-quenching, delicious, and slightly sour. In the 1940s Irion recommended taking about 1/2 cup on an empty stomach in the morning and another 1/2 cup both after lunch and after dinner.

A reduction in the number of colds has been observed by some people taking the tea as a preventive remedy (Fasching, 1994). Also, because of its reputed purifying effects, it is reported to be a good protectant against the daily assault on our bodies from various environmental pollution. Some use kombucha once a year as one would take a spring tonic.

During the 1960s the Waischenfelder Apotheke was recommending Kombucha to be taken daily as a preventative and therapeutic remedy for such diverse ailments as the onset of arteriosclerosis, constipation, physical and mental fatigue, low sex drive, and convalescence. Hans Irion, who was then director of the Brunswick Pharmaceutical Academy, also advocated its use for high blood pressure, nervousness, overweight, sports activities, excessive mental activity, and symptoms of aging (Fasching, 1994).

Hagers Handbuch (List & Hörhammer, 1973) states that "Combucha" is used as a folk remedy for edema, arteriosclerosis, gout, constipation, and stones.

It is reported that Russian, Japanese, and Indian Kombucha afficionados consume approximately 11 oz per day (Frank, 1991). According to this dosage, one would drink 3.5 oz 3 times each day, once upon arising, once either before or after the midday meal, and once before going to bed.

Note: Smoking in the same room where the Kombucha is growing is reported to cause it to mould or dissolve.

Zeller (1924) warned against using alternative mixtures of tea or sugar, as substitutions can disrupt the delicate balance of yeasts and bacteria. The Swiss pharmacist, Bergold, also cautioned against using older fungi, which might be contaminated by various molds. Apparently cultures of dubious origin exist on the market.

Although some critics caution against making the beverage at home or drinking Kombucha tea, it is certainly no more difficult than making yogurt or sauerkraut. Preparing food and medicine with our own hands (just make sure they are clean!) certainly has its merits and eliminates the endless environmentally-unfriendly packaging we are constantly having to deal with. As Gunther Frank points out, the making of Kombucha has been successfully handed down from generation to generation by the Chinese for over 2000 years without any sterile lab techniques.

Several tests for pathological organisms occurring in traditional fermented foods have consistently shown that they are safe (Frank, 1991; Hasseltine & Wang,

1986). Stamets (1994) reports that after experimenting with Kombucha he has observed spontaneous contamination of batches with various green, pink, or black molds. He suggests either throwing the batch out or rinsing a portion of the organism thoroughly with cold water and reintroducing it into a fresh batch of tea and sugar. He mentions that a firm rubbery texture is a good indicator of whether the Kombucha organism has been degraded by infection from potential pathogens. If the organism falls apart when handled, it is best to discard it.

Procurement:
See the Resource Section.

LACTARIUS, RUSSULA SPP.

These two closely-related genera are characterized morphologically by waxy gills and brittle flesh that snaps cleanly like a piece of chalk. Chemically, many contain a series of fatty acid esters produced when an unstable sesquiterpene called velutinal is acted on enzymatically after the mushroom is injured in any way. These compounds include the pungent isovelleral and velleral which have strong antibacterial (against *Escherichia coli*) and antifungal (*Candida utilis*) activity, as well as the less active isovellerol and vellerol, and comprise 80-90% of extracts made more than 5 minutes after grinding (Sterner et al, 1985). It is well-known that a number of species from these two genera have a sharp, biting taste when eaten raw. I have observed that the sharp taste develops a few minutes after putting a piece of the fruiting body in the mouth, the exact period depending on the species. Some species only develop a sharp taste after a minute or two. It is also known that many of the species of Lactarius and Russula that are considered poisonous but are rendered edible when well-cooked (McIlvaine, 1973). According to one group of researchers in Sweden (Sterner et al, 1985), the acrid sesquiterpenes break down over time to ones that are much less biting and toxic.

As mentioned previously, some Lactarius species have been used for treating tuberculosis, a use that is supported because of the strong antibacterial activity present in these mushrooms. Although we have very little experience with these genera in clinical practice, it would seem that for their stimulating and antimicrobial properties, the fungi should be prepared as a tincture about 5-15 minutes after grinding (in a blender) to destroy enzymes that might break down the active compounds. The resulting preparation should have an acrid taste and be used in small amounts (10-25 drops several times daily). With only a few clinical reports from 19th century European medicine and *in vitro* laboratory tests on its antimicrobial activity to go by, it is still impossible to say much about the effectiveness of these genera in clinical practice. I would also advise caution in the use of these fungi for food or medicine unless they are thoroughly cooked.

Procurement
Available only from the wild.

MORCHELLA ESCULENTA (L.) PERS.

MOREL

According to TCM (Ying et al, 1987) as recorded in the *Compendium of Materia Medica, Morchella esculenta* is sweet in taste, cold in property and non-toxic, tonic to intestines and stomach, reduces phlegm, and regulates the flow of vital energy. Studies show that *Morchella esculenta* has 7 kinds of amino acids: isoleucine, leucine, lysine, methionine, phyenylalanine, phreonine, and valine (Ying et al, 1987), as well as the sterol brassicasterol (Yokokawa, 1994).

Procurement
Available from the wild, sometimes in markets and restaurants.

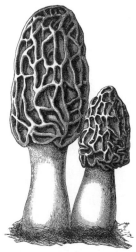

Morel

PHALLUS IMPUDICUS L.: PERS.

STINKHORN

The stinkhorn is aptly named. Both the common and Latin epithets have decided significance, for some species erupt from the earth looking ever so much like a slimy-headed malodorous phallus or horn. Other common names include "wood witch," and "stinking polecat." When young, they often are encased in a white skin or "peridium" which ruptures as the fruiting body expands. Some are ornamented with nets and some are brightly-colored. The spores are produced in the slimy mass that adheres to the "head" of the fruiting body.

The stinkhorns have a reputation throughout history as folk-remedies for various ailments, and even Arora, who mentions little about the medicinal qualities of fungi in *Mushroom Demystified* says of them, "They've been used in countless ointments and potions, e.g., as a cure for gout, epilepsy, and gangrenous ulcers. They've been blamed for cancer and prescribed as a sure-fire remedy for it." A number of references cite stinkhorn as an aphrodisiac.

Porcher (1854) reports that a western doctor had success with a tincture of the fungus as an antispasmodic to relieve pain during attacks of renal colic.

In TCM, the fresh fruiting body is soaked (220 g/500 g of 50 proof liquor) to produce a liquid extract. The preparation is soaked for 10 days and pressed, when it is used for alleviating the pains of rheumatism in the dose of 9-15 grams three times daily (Liu & Bau, 1980).

Although stinkhorn preparations take on an aura of the cure-all, there is some clinical experience and scientific interest in the use of it in ointments for the treatment of cancer. According to a translation of an article in a Latvian newspaper, Laiks, June 19, 1993, the stinkhorn has been a Latvian folk remedy for centuries to heal cuts, wounds, gastric ulcers, asthma, rheumatism, gout, and other ailments. It was used for similar purposes in other parts of Europe (Tyler, 1977). In the 17th century, the German physician Karo successfully used it to treat cancer of the internal organs (*Townsend Letter*, Oct., 1994).

In Latvia, Katzen and Gurvich experimented with an ointment made from 25% fresh juice of the stinkhorn mushroom in the 1960s and 1970s for malignant tumors with promising results. Information from Russia about the stinkhorn mushroom ointment states that its scope of application includes wound healing, benign ovarian cystomas, uterine fibroids, as well as ovarian, uterine, and breast cancers (Tauki, 1994). The author states that if the ointment does not produce a result after 1 month, further use is pointless.

Recent research being performed in Riga, Latvia at the Latvian Medical Academy on the fermented succus of the stinkhorn has shown one active fraction to be a glucomannan called PI-2. Sterols and phenol-carbolic acids were also identified. In laboratory tests with animals, the succus stimulated cytotoxic T-cells, and enhanced the activity of natural killer (NK) cells, demonstrated an anti-stress and adaptogenic activity as well as an antitumor effect with sarcoma 180 and Ehrlich ascites carcinoma and reduced the hemotoxic effects of the chemotherapeutic agent, 5-FU (Kuznetsovs & Jegina, 1993). Studies on the acute toxicity of stinkhorn fermented juice on animals demonstrated an LD50 between 1.5 to 50 ml/kg, depending on the species. Chronic administration of the juice did not lead to demonstrable mutagenic, teratogenic, cancerogenic or allergenic effects (Kuznetsovs et al, 1993).

The related species, *Phallus rugulosus* Fisch. is considered antiinflammatory and is used in Chinese medicine as a scabies remedy (Hanssen & Schädler, 1982), and *P. aurantiacus* Mont. is used to treat leprosy by Yoruba traditional healers in southwestern Nigeria (Tyler, 1977).

Procurement
Available from the wild; prepared creams, and liquid products are available in Eastern Europe.

PIPTOPORUS BETULINUS (BULL.:FR.) KARST

BIRCH POLYPORE

Piptoporus betulinus is a polypore which commonly grows on birch in the northern U.S., Europe, and China. The fresh fruiting bodies are eaten by forest rodents, and they are actually quite palatable when fresh and young, with a slight bitter aftertaste.

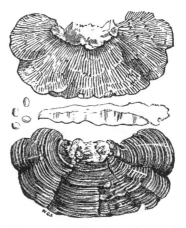

A number of constituents have been isolated from this fungus, including polyporenic acid A, B, which are triterpenes, and a mixture of triterpenes, triterpene C (Efimenko, 1961b); ergosta-7,22-dien-3β-ol, fungisterol, ergosterol, polyporenic acid C, and tumulosic acid. Animal studies have shown polyporenic acid A to have antimicrobial and antiphlogistic activity (Efimenko et al, 1961a), and the fruiting body has

Piptoporus betulinus from *Text-Book of British Fungi* by W. Delisle Hay, 1887.

demonstrated an anti-tumor effect (Ying, 1987). Crude RNA isolated from the fruiting bodies of this fungus induced interferon which had a virus-protective effect when injected into mice (Kawecki et al, 1978).

Pentacyclic triterpenes from the fruiting body have demonstrated antineoplastic effects (Wandokanty & Utzig, 1958). In Poland, the extract was given orally (3 grams/day) to female dogs with Sticker's tumors of the vagina, which were observed to completely disappear after 5 weeks (Utzig & Samborski, 1957). After roasting until black, the powder was applied to wounds to stop bleeding.

Procurement
Not commercially available, but common on birches throughout the eastern U.S., Europe and Asia.

POLYPORUS MYLITTAE COOK. ET MASS.

Also known as *Omphalia lapidescens*, this polypore produces sclerotia that weigh up to 40 lbs. It grows in Australia, where it is called "black-fellow's bread," because of its use as a food by the native Australian people (Arora, 1986).

In Asia, it is used in TCM, under the name lei wan, where it is prescribed in the amount of 6-9 grams in decoction as an anthelmintic, often with Semen Arecae catechu to kill tapeworms, hookworms, and roundworms, and for easing pains in the stomach and intestines associated with worms (Hanssen & Schädler, 1982; Bensky & Gamble, 1986). *P. mylittae* has also been reported to have aphrodisiac properties (Dragendorff, 1898).

The active ingredient is thought to be a proteinase, soluble in water and insoluble in alcohol. The compound is inactivated by heat and is more effective when extracted in a slightly alkaline watery solution. The enzyme destroys the cell nucleus in worms but is harmless to host tissues (Ying, 1987).

An anti-inflammatory and immunostimulating polysaccharide called S4001 has also been isolated from the fungus (Wang & Zhu, 1989).

Procurement
Can be found in the wild in Australia, Asia, Europe, and probably other areas of the world.

PYCNOPORUS SANGUINEUS (L.:Fr.) MURR.

This blood-red colored polypore, also formerly known as *Polystictus sanguineus* Fr. and in China, *Trametes cinnabarina* var. sanguinea (L.:Fr.) Pilát, is popularly used throughout Asia and is recommended in TCM to lower fever, reduce dampness and swelling, and as an antidote for toxins. The decoction is made by simmering pieces of the fruiting body (9-15 grams daily) in water and is recommended for rheumatism, arthritis, gout, and fungus diseases. Externally, the fine powder is applied on wounds to stop bleeding and prevent infections (Liu & Bau, 1980). It is also said to invigorate the body's vital energy, activate the blood circulation, and stop itching (Ying et al, 1987). A cultured mycelium filtrate (called polyporin) (Bose, 1946) and an aqueous extract of the fruiting body (Sevilla-Santos, 1964) has been found to be particularly active against *Staphylococcus aureus, S. albus, Streptococcus salivarius, Pseudomonas aeruginosa, Salmonella paratyphi, E. coli,* and *Shigella paradysenteriae.* The aqueous extract also demonstrated *in vitro* antitumor activity (Sevilla-Santos, 1964). In Malaysia, the fruiting body is used to alleviate pimples and skin ailments when there is a red color, perhaps because of the bright red color of the fungus. In Johore, it is powdered and added to eau de cologne as an application to heal leprous tubercles. The fruiting body is also boiled and used internally as an astringent and applied externally for eczema. In Java, the remedy is used to help with symptoms associated with venereal disease and colic. It is extracted in warm oil and applied to knotty swellings (Burkill, 1966).

Procurement
Outside of China, this species is only available in the wild.

USTILAGO MAYDIS (DC) CORDA

CORN SMUT

Various species of smuts, which are parasitic fungi, attack rye, barley, wheat, corn,
and other grains throughout the world. Smut
was known in Europe at least since the 17th
century, though Gerard does not mention
any therapeutic uses of it. He calls it "burnt
corn" or "blasted corn" and says that it "is
altogether unprofitable and good for nothing, an enemy unto corne, there is nothing
else but blacke dust, which spoileth bread, or
whatsoever is made thereof," and that "burnt
Rie hath no one good property in
phisicke...," though it is unclear which kind
of smut he was describing. The word "corn"
seems to encompass any of the ears of grain,
not simple *Zea mays* L.

Ustilago had a brief period of popularity
among physicians in the U.S., Europe, and
Mexico during the last decade of the 19th
century and early part of the 20th century for

**Corn Smut from *The Vegetable World by
Louis Figuier,* circa 1860.**

enhancing contractions of the uterus during labor. It was considered similar but
weaker (and consequently safer) in action to ergot (Wood, 1890; Shoemaker, 1891;
Martinez, 1959). The recommended dose was 1 to 3 droppersful of the fluid
extract. The fungus is also used in Mexico as a uterine stimulant (Lozoya, 1976).

Corn smut was a favorite remedy of the Homeopaths, who were credited for
introducing it into clinical practice. Ellingwood of the Eclectics was also fond of it
as a uterine tonic and used it extensively before labor, as well as postpartum to control hemorrhage (Felter & Lloyd, 1898). Other indications in the previously mentioned work include ovarian irritation, ovaritis, amenorrhea, dysmenorrhea, pre-
mature menstruation, metrorrhagia, and uterine catarrh. Ustilago was also said to
be useful in "alopecia (abnormal falling of hair), scalp diseases, with dryness,
urticaria, with large, pale welts." The recommended dose of the strong tincture
was 5 to 30 drops (several times daily).

Corn smut is also known in Chinese medicine, perhaps for thousands of years.
Eaten in stir-frys, it is said to have a cold energy, and be a tonic to the liver, stomach, and intestines. When eaten regularly, it is thought to cure hepatic and gastroenteric ulcers, as well as having a mild laxative effect (Liu & Bau, 1980; Ying et
al, 1987).

Despite its monstrous appearance, corn smut is considered a delicacy in Mexico
where it is known as cuitlacoche. Rob McCaleb, director and founder of the Herb
Research Foundation, first alerted me to its popularity in Mexican cooking at an

Iowa herb conference. We were able to locate a small patch of garden corn infected with *U. maydis* with the help of a local herbalist. The fungus upon first appearance seems quite unappetizing. We later stewed the smut with local garden-fresh tomatoes and packed them into corn tortillas. Most of us were pleasantly surprised at the fine flavor, which was like a cross between mushrooms and corn. Corn smut appears to have significant nutritional value, containing sixteen kinds of free amino acids in good quantity (Ying et al, 1987).

A similar species of Corn smut (*U. zeae*) contains ustilagic acid, which is an antibiotic compound that shows *in vitro* activity against *Candida albicans* and other fungi (Windholz et al, 1976). Recently, *Ustilago maydis* has been reported to have antitumor activity in animal studies, and to improve digestion and alleviate constipation (Ying et al, 1987).

Corn smut produces ustilaginic acid, which is a starting material for artificial musk synthesis (Liu & Bau, 1980).

Procurement
Corn smut grows on cultivated corn in many parts of the world. In Mexico it is available dried, canned, and in restaurants.

VOLVARIELLA VOLVACEA (BULL.:FR.) SING.

STRAW MUSHROOM

Commonly called the straw mushroom, this is one of the most widely cultivated edible mushrooms in the world. In China, cultivation can be traced back to the early 1800s, and it was probably introduced throughout other Asian countries in the early 1900s. It contains the cardiotoxic proteins, volvatoxin A, A1 and A2, and flammutoxin, the sterols ergosterol, 24β-methylcholesta-5,7-dien-3β-ol and 24β-methylcholesta-7-en-3β-methylcholesta-7en-3β-0l and γ-ergostenol (Huang, B.-H. et al, 1985). The proteins are heat sensitive, and their toxicity is reduced after the mushrooms are cooked. The Volvariella cardio-active proteins are known to lower blood pressure and inhibit Ehrlich ascites tumor cells (Cochran, 1978).

In Asian countries, it is an important source of protein, and one of the easiest of all mushrooms to cultivate, with a crop completed from spawning to harvest in 10 days (Chang & Chiu, 1993).

Procurement
The straw mushroom is available in markets and restaurants throughout the world, especially in Asia.

The following table lists other species that have been subjected to scientific or clinical research and have a history of traditional use. Literature references are given for those interested in further study.

Table 12

OVERVIEW OF ALL MEDICINAL MUSHROOM SPECIES

Latin Name	Common name	Uses, Properties	Range	References
Agaricus arvensis Schaeff.:Fr.	Horse Mushroom	antibacterial, tumor inhibition	widespread	Arora; Ying
Agaricus bisporus (Lange) Sing. = *Agaricus brunnescens*	Button mushroom	ethanolic extract exhibits antimutagenic activity in vitro, which is heat stable; a decoction of the dried fruiting bodies is reported to be used for diabetes	widely cultivated; also wild	Grüter et al, 1990 Swanston-Flatt et al, 1989
Agaricus campestris L.:Fr.	Meadow Mushroom	antibacterial, tumor inhibition	widespread; sea level to above timberline	Arora; Bo; Ying
Albatrellus confluens (Alb. & Schw.:Fr.) Kotl. & Pouz (=*Polyporus confluens* Alb. & Schw.:Fr.)	Ningyotake	contains polysaccharides which show antitumor activity	widespread	Mizuno et al, 1992
Amanita muscaria (L.:Fr.) Pers.:Hook. (=*Agaricus muscarius* Pers.)	Fly Agaric; Fly Amanita	tumor inhibition, epilepsy, ringworm, visionary plant, *toxic*.	northern hemisphere and in pine plantations in southern hemisphere	Arora; Ying
Armillaria mellea (Vah.:Fr.) Karst. (=*Armillariella* Vahl., *Agaricus mellius* Vahl.), and closely related species	Honey Mushroom	digestive/nutritive tonic	widespread	Arora; Bo; Ying
Astraeus hygrometricus (Pers.) Morg. (=*Geastrum hygrometricus* Pers., *Geaster hygrometricus* Pers.)	Hygroscopic Earthstar	hemostatic, external wounds, chillblains (frostbite)	widespread; sea level to timberline.	Arora; Bo; Chang;Ying
Auricularia auricula (Hook.) Underw. + *A. polytricha*	Wood Ear; Judah's Ear	Qi tonic, pain, blood activating, hemostatic	widespread	Arora; Bo; Ying; Misaki; Xia

			—	Ying
Auricularia mesenterica (Dick.) Pers.	—	tumor inhibition		
Bjerkandera fumosa (Pers.:Fr.) Karst	Smokey-gilled polypore	uterine cancer; simmer slices in water, drink 1 cup 2 x/daily; 1000 g constitutes a treatment; contains lanostane-type triterpenes; t-cell stimulant	widespread; China, North America	Liu & Bau; Yadomae
Boletus edulis Bull.:Fr.	King Bolete, Steinpilz Cep, Porcini	tumor inhibition	northern hemisphere, especially and in southern hemisphere in pine plantations	Arora; Wood & Franklin; Lucas; Ying
Bovista pusilla (Batsch) Pers. (=*Lycoperdon pusillum, B. californica*)	Phusphush	used in India to staunch wounds and promote healing	India, North America	Arora; Rai et al
Calvatia bovista Batsch	Puffball	tumor inhibition, styptic	widespread	Arora; Gregory
Calvatia craniiformis (Schw.) Fr.	—	anti-inflammatory, promotes granulation, tumor inhibition.	southern & eastern N. America; Eurasia	Arora; Gregory; Ying.
Calvatia cyathiformis (Bosc) Morgan	Purple-Spored Puffball, iso-aparo	used in India as an application to wounds; the Yoruba of southwestern Africa blend it with powdered *Daldinia concentrica* and mixed with black soap, to be used as a wash for leucorrhea	Eurasia, North America	Arora; Rai et al, Morgan Oso
Calvatia gigantea (Batsch:Pers.) Lloyd and close relatives (=*Lycoperdon giganteum* Batsch.; *L. bovista* L.)	Giant puffball	tumor inhibition, hemo-static, astringent, anti-inflammatory, lung/throat tonic, emmenagogue, expectorant; formerly thought to have anasthetic properties	widespread.	Arora; Gregory; Lucas; Roland; Draggendorff

Species	Common Name	Uses	Distribution	References
Cantharellus cibarius Fr.	Chanterelle	tumor inhibition; frequent consumption prevents ophthalmia, abnormal eyesight, night blindness, dry skin, excretion of mucous membrane	widespread	Arora; Ying
Claviceps purpurea (Fr.) Tul.	Ergot, Rye Ergot, Wheat Ergot	oxytocic	widespread	Bo; Ying; Tyler.
Clitopilus abortivus (Berk. & Curt.) Sing.	—	tumor inhibition	eastern North America	Lucas
Collybia radicata *see *Oudemansiella radicata*	—	—	—	—
Coltricia cinnamomea (Pers.) Murr. (=*Polyporus cinnamomeus*)	Zimtporling, fairy stool	a liquid extract is made with *Fomes fomentarius* and used in Europe for bladder trouble, dysmenorrhea or hemorrhoids	widespread	List & Hörhammer, 1977
Coprinus atramentarius (Bull.) Fr. (=*Agaricus atramentarius* Bull.)	Inky cap, Tippler's Bane; Tintenschwamm	the amino acid coprine from the fruiting body has "anabuse" activity; in China, preparations of this species are said to be antinflammatory and when applied externally help cure malignant dermatitis, furuncles and various sores; internally, it is considered cold and sweet, and is said to help digestion and reduce phlegm; in Sweden it is applied to sores caused by burns; considered toxic when taken with alcoholic beverages	widespread	Lindberg, 1977; Dragendorff; Ying
Cordyceps ophioglossoides (Ehrenb.) Link	Deer Fungus Parasite	adaptogen, stimulates blood circulation, menstruation regulator, lung tonifier, sedative	eastern N. America, Central America, Asia; rare in California	Arora, Bo, Chang; Gengtao; Jianze, Shih-Chen

Cordyceps sinensis (Berk.) Sacc.	Caterpillar Fungus; Winter worm-summer grass	regulates sexual organs, adaptogen, lung & kidney tonic, Qi tonic	Asia	Bo; Gengtao; Pereia; Ying; Chang;
Coriolus consors (Berk.) Imaz.	—	immune stimulant; antibiotic	—	Wagner & Proksch; Takeuchi
Coriolus hirsutus Wulf.:Fries *see Trametes hirsutus	—	—	—	—
Coriolus versicolor *see Trametes versicolor	—	—	—	—
Craterellus cornucopioides (L.:Fr.) Pers. *Craterellus cibarius*	horn of plenty, black trumpet	ethanolic extract has antimutagenic effects *in vitro*, and activity is heat-stable	widespread	Grüter et al, 1990
Cryptoderma citrinum	—	mitogen	—	Yadomae
Cryptoporus volvatus (Peck) Hubbard	Concealed polypore	according to TCM, stops colon bleeding, benefits carbuncles, hemorrhoids, bronchitis and asthma (anti-inflammatory); whole fruiting body is fragrant when sucked on—small ones given to infants to aid weaning; ergosta-7,22-dien-3b-ol and fungisterol are constituents	widespread; China, North America, Europe	Liu & Bau, 1980; Ying et al Yokoyama et al, 1975
Cyathus stercoreus (Schw.) de Toni *C. limbatus* Tul.	Bird's nest Fungus	The fruiting bodies are ground up in water, filtered and used as eye-drops (2 drops, 2 x daily) for soothing the eyes for such problems as conjunctivitis, redness and swelling	Eurasia; North America (*C. stercoreus*)	Arora, Rai et al
Daedaleopsis tricolor (Bull.:Fr.) Bond. et Sing.	—	tumor inhibition	—	Ikekawa

Species	Common name	Medicinal properties	Distribution	References
Daldinia concentrica (Bolt.) Ces. et de Not.	—	cramps	widespread	
Elaphomyces granulatus Fr.	—	aphrodisiac, galactagogue	widespread	Arora; Shibata
Favolus alveolaris (DC.:Fr.) Quél *syn. Polyporus mori	—	tumor inhibition	eastern North America, Eurasia	Arora; Kamasuka; Maeda
Flammulina velutipes (Curt.:Fr.) Sing.	Velvet foot; velvet stem	tumor inhibition	widespread	Arora; Shibata
Fomes fomentarius (L.:Fr.) Kickx	Amadou	tumor inhibition, indigestion, reduces stasis	circumboreal in the northern hemisphere	Ito
Fomes melanoporus	—	immune stimulant	—	
Fomitopsis officinalis (Vill.:Fr.) Bond and Sing.	Quinine Conk; Quinine Fungus	tumor inhibition, lung tonic, hemostatic, calms vital energy	northern hemisphere	Arora; Ying.
Fomitopsis pinicola (Fr.) Karst.	Red-Belted Conk; Red-Belted Polypore	immune activation, tumor inhibition	common & widely distributed	Arora; Ito; Ying; Shibata.
Ganoderma applanatum (Pers.) Pat.	Artist's Conk	tumor inhibition, immune stimulant, hemostasis, esophageal carcinoma, rheumatic TB	widespread	Arora; Chihara; Ikekawa; Ying
Ganoderma capense Junhua & Ronglan.	—	immune stimulant	China	Zhiyuan & Huiti;
Ganoderma japonicum *see Ganoderma sinese	—	—	—	—
Ganoderma lucidum (Leys.:Fr.) Karst.	Reishi; Ling zhi	tumor inhibition immune activation, Qi tonic, histamine inhibition, anti-oxidant, expectorant, antitussive	widespread	Ying; Chang; Dharmananda; Miyazaki; Hsu; Hikino; Junhua & Ronglan; Huidi & Zhiyuan; Willard.
Ganoderma sinense *syn. G.japonicum	—	adaptogen, Qi tonic, anti-inflammatory, diuretic	Asia	Bo; Junhua & Ronglan.

Species	Common name	Medicinal use	Distribution	Reference
Ganoderma tsugae Murr.	—	tumor inhibition	northern North America and Eurasia	Ying
Geastrum Triplex (Jungh.) Fischer	Saucered Earthstar	throat and lung tonic	widespread	Arora
Grifola frondosa (Dicks.:Fr.) S.F. Gray [=*Polyporus frondosus* (Dicks) Fr.]	Hen of the Woods; Chicken of the Woods; Sheep's head	t cell stimulant, tumor inhibition	eastern North America, Idaho, Eurasia	Arora; Yadomae
Grifola umbellata (Pers.) Pilát [=*Polyporus umbellatus* (Pers.) Fr.]	—	immune stimulant, tumor inhibition, lung cancer, leukemia, diuretic	eastern North America and Asia	Arora; Yadomae; Ito; Miyazaki; Uneo; Suzuki
Hericium erinaceus (Bull. ex Fr.) Pers.	Hedgehog fungus	according to TCM, good for the five internal organs, promotes good digestion, general vigor, strength, and nutrition; inhibits cancer; recommended for gastric & duodenal ulcers and chronic gastritis (in prepared tablet form)	widespread; China, North America	Liu & Bau, 1980 Yang & Jong, 1989
Heterobasidion annosum (Fr.) Bref. [=*Fomitopsis annosa* (Fr.) Karst., *Polyporus annosus* Fr.]	Birch polypore (Sweden)	used as a kind of moxa to burn out (and cauterize) the wounds caused by viper's bites; as a folk medicine for cancer; contains the bacteriocide, fomannosin	common in Europe, North America; also in Jamaica, China	Gilbertson & Ryvarden; Dragendorff; Ying
Inonotus hispidus (Bull.:Fr.) Karst [=*P. hispidus* Bull.: Fr.]	—	formerly known as a drastic purgative in Germany	distributed throughout North America, Europe	Dragendorff; Gilbertson & Ryvarden
Lactarius volemus (Fr.) Fr.	Weeping Milk Cap; Bradley	tumor inhibition	eastern North America, Central America, Eurasia	Arora; Ying
Lampteromyces japonica (Kawam.) Sing.	—	tumor inhibition	Asia and South Pacific	Gregory; Yoshida

Name	Common name	Properties	Distribution	Tu, 1988
Lasiosphaera fenzlii Reich. also used: Calvatia gigantea C. lilacina	Ma bo, puffball	clears heat from the lung, soothes sore throat, stops bleeding; used for hoarseness caused by wind-heat in the lung, eistaxis, and bleeding due to external trauma	widespread	Tu, 1988
Lentinula edodes (Berk.) Sing. (=Lentinus edodes)	Shiitake	adaptogen, tumor inhibition, immune modulation, antiviral	Asia; cultivated in many countries, including U.S.	Arora; Fujii; Saski & Takasuka; Arai; Tabata; Chihara; Togami; Maeda; Nguyen & Stadtsbaeder; Miyakoshi & Aoki; Sugano; Yamamura & Cochran; Fujii
Lenzites betulina (L.:Fr.) Fr.	Gilled Polypore	tumor inhibition; stimulates blood circulation	widespread	Arora; Ikekawa; Ying
Lepista nuda (Bull.:Fr.) Cooke (=Clitocybe nuda)	Blewit	tumor inhibition, antibacterial	widespread	Arora; Ying;
Leucofomes ulmarius	—	tumor inhibition	—	Ikekawa
Lyophyllum decastes (Fr.:Fr.) Sing., Tricholoma aggregatum, Clitocybe multiceps	Fried Chicken Mushroom	tumor inhibition	widespread	Arora; Kamasuka
Morchella deliciosa Fr.	White morel	gastroenteric tonic, expectorant	northern hemisphere	Arora; Bo; Ying
Morchella esculenta (L.:Fr.)	Morel	tumor inhibition, gastro-enteric tonic, expectorant, Qi regulator	mainly northern hemisphere	Arora; Ito; Ying
Oudemansiella radicata (Relhan:Fr.) Sing. [=Collybia radicata]	Beech Rooter	tumor inhibition, lowers blood pressure	eastern North America, Eurasia	Arora; Lucas; Ying.

Panellus stypticus (Bull.:Fr.) Karst	—	tumor inhibition, styptic when used externally	widespread	Arora; Ying.
Penicillium spp.	Bread Mold, etc.	mouldy bread and cereal were used as folk medicines to stop infections; studies show that *Penicillium* organisms in bread and growing on oranges have significant antibacterial activity	widespread	Wainwright et al
Peziza vesiculosa Bull.	Bladder Cup, Common Dung Cup	t cell stimulant, fungal immunomodulator, B-cell mitogen, anti-tumor, enhance function of reticuloendothelial system	widespread	Arora; Suzuki; Ying
Phaeolus schweinitzii (Fr.) Pat.	Dyer's polypore	said to be possibly toxic by Arora; the culture fluids from this species inhibited the growth of *Staphylococcus aureus, Salmonella typhi,* and *E. coli* and was **not toxic to guinea pigs**; contains a carcinostatic polysaccharide	widespread	Bose, 1952; Ohtsuka et al
Phallus impudicus (L.:Pers.)	—	applied to sore limbs	widespread	
Phellinus igniarius (L.:Fr.) Quél	False Tinder Polypore; False Tinder Conk	tumor inhibition, styptic, emmenagogue; diarrhea	circumboreal	Arora; Ikekawa; Ying
Physisporinus sanguinolentus (Alb. & Schw.:Fr.) Pilát [=*Polyporus sanguinolentus* Alb. & Schw.:Fr.]	—	has been prescribed for spitting of blood (hemoptysis)	Widespread in North America, Europe; Brasil	Dragendorff; Gilbertson & Ryvarden
Piptoporus betulinus (Bull.:Fr.), [=*Polyporus betulinus*	Birch Conk; Birch Polypore	tumor inhibition	circumboreal with birch	Arora; Ying; Shibata; Blumenberg & Kessler

Species	Common name	Medicinal use	Distribution	References
Pleurotus ostreatus (Jacq.:Fr.) Quél	Oyster Mushroom	tumor inhibition	widespread	Arora; Ying; Miyazaki
Podaxis pistillaris (L.:Pers.) Fr.	Desert Shaggy Mane	used in China to staunch wounds and for detoxification; in South Africa and Afghanistan to heal cancerous sores	widespread	Rai; Ying
Polyporus rugulosus	—	t cell stimulant	—	Yadomae
Polyporus spp.	—	tumor stimulant	—	Gregory
Polyporus tinosus	—	tumor stimulant	—	Yadomae
Polyporus tomentosus	—	b cell stimulant	—	Ito
Pullularia pullulans	—	tumor inhibition	—	Tabata
Pycnoporus cinnabarina (Jacq.:Fr.) Karst. [= *Trametes cinnabarina* (Jacq.)]	Cinnabar polypore	in China it is used to aid blood circulation, clear heat and damp, to relieve fevers, and to cure rheumatism; this species is also applied as a fine powder on cuts or wounds to stop bleeding, and has demonstrated inhibition against sarcoma 180	Common throughout the Northern Hemisphere	Yang & Jong; Ying; Gilbertson & Ryvarden
Russula virescens (Schaeff) Fr.	Quilted Green Russula; Green Cap Russula	good nutritive value—contains protein, phosphorous, calcium, iron, sulfur, and thiamine; considered sweet, slightly sour in TCM, cools liver fire, increases vital energy; take with ginger to detoxify, moderate use only tumor inhibition, anti-pyretic, improves vision	Eastern North America, Mexico, Eurasi	Arora; Bo; Ying
Schizophyllum commune Fr.	Split-Gill	adaptogen, tumor inhibition, increases vitality	widespread	Arora; Ying; Komatsu; Tabata; Misaki; Kikumoto

				Tabata
Sclerotium glucanicum	—	tumor inhibition	—	
Stereum hirsutum (Willd.:Fr.) S.F. Gray	False Turkey Tail; Hairy Stereum	tumor inhibition, antibiotic against *Micrococcus pyogenes, Diptheria baccilli, Neisseria meningitidis*; contains ergosta-7,22-dien-3b-ol	widespread	Arora; Ying Yokoyama et al, 1975
Stereum membranaceum	—	tumor inhibition	—	Yadomae
Suillus grevillei (Klotzsch) Sing.	Tamarack Jack	tumor inhibition, used in "Tendon-Easing Powder"; benefits tendons, lumbago, leg pain, numb limbs	circumboreal	Arora; Ying
Suillus luteus (L.:Fr.) Gray	Slippery Jack	tumor inhibition	Eurasia; northern N. America, in pine plantations in southern hemisphere	Arora; Ying
Termitomyces microcarpus (Berk. & Br.) Heim	olu-oran	used by the Yoruba of southwestern Nigeria in preparations to cure gonorrhoea.	Africa	Oso
Trametes hirsuta (Wulf.:Fr.) Pil., [=*Coriolus hirsutus*]	Hairy Turkey Tail	tumor inhibition, dispels heat and dampness	widespread	Arora; Ying
Trametes suaveolens L.:Fr. (=*Boletus suaveolens* L., *Daedalea suaveolens, Coriollelus suaveolens*)	anise polypore, Weidenschwamm	night sweats of tuberculosis, lung ailments; aphrodisiac by the natives of Lapland, possibly due to its spicy fragrance	widespread, more southern	Porcher, Dragendorff, Tyler (1977)
Trametes versicolor (L.:Fr.) Pil. (=*Coriolus versicolor*)	Turkey Tail	tumor inhibition, hepatitis, antibiotic	widespread	Arora; Jianze
Tremella aurantia Schw.:Fr.	—	tumor inhibition, regulates chi, hypertension, asthma	—	Ying
Tremella fuciformis Berk.	White Fungus	adaptogen; antipyretic, strenghtens chi, tumor inhibition	Southern United States, Mexico, Asia	Arora; Ito; Ying; Zican; Zhibin
Tremella mesenterica Retz:Fr.	Witch's Butter	expectorant, bronchial inflammation, asthma	widespread	Arora; Bo

				I k e k a w a
Trichaptum fusco-violaceum (Fr.) Ryv.	—	tumor inhibition	—	
Tricholoma gambosum (Fr.) Gill.	St. George's Mushroom	tumor inhibition, improved circulation of body fluids, dispels blood fever, diaphoretic	Europe	Arora; Bo; Ying
Tricholoma matsutake (S. Ito et Imai) Sing.	Matsutake	highly prized as an edible mushroom of great flavor and texture; used as a remedy for difficult labor, acute gastritis, for convulsions, worms, tonsillitis, and to lower fevers		Arora, 1986 Lee, 1966 Han et al, 1984
Ustilago esculenta Henn.	Annual Wildrice Smut; Wildrice Shoot	diuretic, laxative; alleviates reddened eyes, alcoholic toxication, and carbuncle	—	Bo; Ying
Ustilago maydis (DC.) Corda	Corn Smut	uterine tonic, parturition, post-partum bleeding, skin ailments	widespread	Bo; Ying
Wolfiporia cocos (Schw.) Ryv. et Gilbn.	Tuckahoe; Hoelen; Fu-Ling	diuretic, kidney/spleen tonic, sedative, tumor inhibition	southeastern North America, Mexico, Asia	Bo; Arora; Ying; Chang; Narui; Suzuki
Xylaria polymorpha (Pers.) Grev.	Dead Man's Fingers	used as a folk medicine in India to promote lactation after birth; the fruiting body is ground to a powder, blended 1:1 with sugar (substitute brown-rice syrup) and formed into pea-sized pills, which are taken 2 x dialy before meals for five days with milk	Widespread	Arora, Rai et al

Summary of Uses and Doses of Medicinal Fungi

Table 13:

ARRANGED BY SPECIES

Species	Main Uses	Preparations	Dose	Contraindications
Artist's conk	immune stimulant, tumor inhibition, hemostasis	dried, capsules	30 g/day in tea or water-based extract	none
Chanterelle	tumor inhibition	fresh or dried	cooked, *ad lib*	no toxicity
Hoelen	diuretic, antiviral, sedative, fever, spleen/kidney tonic	dried	9-15 g	generally safe
Honey	gastritis, nightblindness, insomnia, "wind-induced" arthritis	fresh or dried powder	fresh, *ad lib* or 30-90 g	no toxicity; may cause mild nausea or diarrhea
Maitake	high blood pressure, tumor inhibition, liver protectant	fresh or dried	3-7 g/day	no data
Oyster	tumor inhibition	fresh cooked, dried, powdered	cooked, *ad lib*	low toxicity
Reishi	immune activation, tumor inhibition, expectorant, hepatitis, hypertension, nervousness, weakness	dried, liquid extract, tablets	tincture, 10 ml 3x/day; tablets, 3 1g tab 3x/day	very low toxicity reported
Shiitake	immune regulator, tumor inhibition, antiviral, antibacterial, liver protectant	fresh, dried, liquid extract, tablets	dried, 6-16 g; fresh, 90 g	no toxicity; some contact dermatitis
Turkey tail	diabetes, antiviral, immune enhancement, hepatitis	dried	20 g 3x/day as tea	no toxicity
Wood ear	immune stimulant, poor circulation	dried	15 g as tea 2x/day	rare allergic reaction

Table 14:

ARRANGED BY SYMPTOM OR CONDITION

Symptom/Condition	Species
Altitude sickness	reishi
Arrhythmia	reishi
Bleeding	false tinder polypore, wood ear, earthstar, puffball
Bronchial inflammation	shiitake, reishi
Cancer, breast	chaga, shiitake
Cancer, esophageal	artist's conk
Cancer, gastric	split gill
Cancer, skin	stinkhorn
Cancer, liver	turkey tail
Cancer preventative	red-belted polypore, maitake, turkey tail, shiitake
Cancer, uterine	chaga
Chemotherapy (to counteract side effects)	maitake, shiitake, turkey tail
Cholesterol, high	shiitake, jelly fungus, oyster mushroom
Colds and flu	shiitake
Coughs	snow fungus, earthstar, hoelen, reishi
Diabetes	turkey tail, maitake, reishi, shiitake
Diarrhea	false tinder polypore
Dizziness	honey mushroom, reishi
Dry skin	chanterelle, honey mushroom
Eye inflammation	tremella
Fever	hoelen
Gastritis	honey mushroom, chaga
Hemorrhoids	wood ear, gilled polypore
Hepatitis	reishi, shiitake, hoelen, turkey tail
High blood pressure	maitake, shiitake, reishi
Immune weakness	maitake, shiitake, turkey tail, reishi
Indigestion	true tinder polypore
Insomnia	reishi, honey mushroom
Low energy	turkey tail
Muscle spasms	wood ear
Muscle tension	oyster mushroom
Nervousness	reishi
Neurasthenia	honey mushroom, reishi
Poor vision, night blindness	honey mushroom, chanterelle
Rhinitis	reishi
Ulcers	chaga, enokitake, reishi
Urinary tract infections	zhu ling
Viruses	shiitake, turkey tail, birch polypore
Wounds, bleeding	earthstar, puffball

Glossary

Alkaloids: any of a group of organic substances containing nitrogen, many of which affect the nervous system; i.e., morphine, caffeine, nicotine, etc.

Basophils: (less than 1% of total white blood cells) non-phagocytic cells that produce chemicals such as histamine; may play a role in allergic and anaphylaxis reactions

Complement: a functional sub-system of the immune system that is composed of a group of heat-sensitive proteins and their biologically active breakdown products that cause the lysis (breaking down) and destruction of antibody-coated cells, such as pathogenic bacteria

Eosinophils: have phagocytic potential (ingests antigen-antibody complexes) and play an important role in anaphylactic and allergic reactions

Erythroid: concerning progenitor cells leading to the formation of red blood cells

Granulocytes: a group of immune cells that have granules in their cytoplasm

Hemostatic: an agent that stops blood flow

Interferon: a class of small soluble proteins released by cells invaded by viruses, which cause non-infected cells to produce an antiviral protein that inhibits multiplication of the virus

i.p.: intraperitoneally; injected into the peritoneum of the abdominal cavity

Krestin: an immune stimulant extracted from Japanese *Coriolus versicolor*; a water-soluble, protein-bound polysaccharide

LD50, LD75: a dose that is lethal to 50% or 75% of the test animals

Leukocytes: the white blood cells, comprising all immune cells mentioned in this book

Lymphocytes: a group of cells involved in cell-mediated immunity (such as the T-helper and T-suppressor cells) and humoral immunity (such as the B-cells that produce antibodies) that play a major role in "specific defenses" against foreign invaders. In other words, they recognize particular chemical markers on virus-infected cells and bacteria (among others) and target their bearers for destruction.

Macrophages: arising from monocytes, these "big eaters" are large, major phagocytic cells, which destroy foreign invaders, toxic chemicals and tumor cells, among other things.

Mycelium: the network of hyphae that form the vegetative part of a fungus

Mycorrhizal: being in a symbiotic relationship between non-pathogenic or weakly pathogenic fungi and the roots of plants; the association benefits the plant or tree because the fungus breaks down organic matter, making nutrients more accessible.

Neutrophils: (50-70% of total white blood cells) a killer cell (by phagocytosis) which plays a major role in protecting the host against infections.

p.o.: an oral dose

PSK: (see Krestin)

Phagocyte: a cell that ingests micro-organisms, other cells, or foreign particles

Phagocytosis: the process of engulphment and recycling of pathogenic bacteria and other foreign particles by our immune cells

Polysaccharides: large molecular weight sugar molecules, some of which are known to activate human immune functions

Reticuloendothilial system (RES): an important component of the human immune system, spread throughout the body, and composed of highly phagocytic cells; its important jobs include protection against microbial infection and removal of worn-out red blood cells

Sarcoma: any malignant tumor of connective tissue

Sclerotium: an underground network of hyphae in certain fungi, which create a hard tuber-like growth

Sporophore: spore-bearing structure; a fruit body of a mushroom

Spore: the reproductive cells of fungi

Sterol: a steroid alcohol, for instance cholesterol or ergosterol

Triterpenes: Chemical compounds containing 30 carbon atoms in a structural skeleton, including steroids

Resources

Bioherb Inc.
P.O. Box 611
Elk Grove, IL 60009
(708) 364-5679
Reishi, Shiitake, Coriolus, and Grifola products in tablets and powder

Mayway U.S.A.
1338 Cyperus St.
Oakland, CA 94607
(510) 208-3113
Chinese herbs in bulk, extracts, and other herbal products

East Earth Herbs
P.O. Box 2802
Eugene, OR 97402
wholesale (800) 827-HERB
retail (800) 258-6878
Reishi liquid extract and products in tablets containing reishi, poria, plus herbs

FS Book Co.
P.O. Box 417457
Sacramento, CA 95841-7457
(916) 771-4203
Mushroom books and spores

Fungi Perfecti
P.O. Box 7634
Olympia, WA 98507
(206) 426-9292
Organically grown, Shiitake, Reishi, Maitake mushrooms and teas

Gourmet Mushrooms
P.O. Box 391
Sebastapol, CA 95473
(707) 823-1743
Suppliers of mycelium to manufacturers

Health Concerns
8001 Capwell Drive
Oakland, CA 94621
(510) 639-0280
Retail and wholesale products containing reishi and other medicinal mushrooms
(this company sells mainly to practitioners)

Great China Herb Company
857 Washington Street
San Francisco, CA 94108
(415) 982-2195
Dried Reishi mushrooms and Chinese herbs

Herb Pharm
Box 116
Williams, OR 97544
(503) 846-6262; (800) 348-4372
Reishi liquid extract

ITM
2017 S.E. Hawthorne
Portland, OR 97214
(800) 544-7504
Ganoderma tablets, Tremella tablets, Lentinan powder

Laurel Farms
P.O. Box 7405
Studio City, CA 91614
(310) 289-4372
Kombucha cultures

Maitake Products
P.O.Box 1354
Paramas, N.J. 07653
(800) 747-7418
Organically-grown Maitake powder in caplets, teas and other Maitake products

Maypro Industries
550 Mamaroneck Ave.
Harrison, N.Y. 10528
(914) 381-3808
Coriolus versicolor (PS-K) in powder form

Min Tong Herbs
4175 Lakeside Drive, Ste. 120
Richmond, CA 94806
(800) 562-5777
Retail and Wholesale Reishi tea and Chinese herbs in powder form

Miracle Exclusives
P.O. Box 349
Locust Valley, N.Y. 11560
(800) 645-6360
Shiitake extract in capsules

Mushroom People
P.O. Box 220
Summertown, TN 38483-0220
(615) 964-2200
Books and supplies for Reishi and Shiitake cultivation

North American Reishi Ltd.
Box 1780
Gibsons, B.C. Von 1VO Canada
(604) 886-7799
Supplier of dried mushrooms, mushroom extracts, and mushroom mycelia to the Natural Foods Industry. Products include Reishi, Shiitake, Maitake, and Cordyceps.

Rainbow Light
207 Macpherson
Santa Cruz, CA 95060
(408) 429-9089
Reishi liquid and products in liquid and caplet containing Reishi and Shiitake

Richter's
357 Hwy 47
Goodwood, ONTARIO
CANADA LOC1AO
(905) 640-6677
Reishi growing kits

Shiitake Far West
24039 Redwood Hwy.
Kerby, OR 97531
(503) 592-4114
blend of organic Shiitake mushrooms and herbs in powder form

Threshold Enterprises
23 Janis Way
Scotts Valley, CA 95066
(408) 438-6851
Reishi, Shiitake, Grifola products in powder and liquid for wholesalers
for retail orders:

Planetary Herbal Products Catalog
P.O. Box 7145
Santa Cruz, CA 95061
(408) 464-2003

Western Biologicals
Box 283
Alder Grove, B.C.
CANADA VOX 1A0
(604) 856-3339
Growing supplies for Shiitake, Oyster, Morels, Maitake, Reishi, etc. plus books on growing mushrooms

Recommended Reading List

GROWING

Manual on Mushroom Cultivation by Peter Oei.
Mushrooms in the Garden by Helmut Steineck.
The Shiitake Growers Handbook by P. Przybillowicz and J. Donoghue.
The Mushroom Cultivator by P. Stamets and J. Chilton.
Growing Shiitake Mushrooms in a Continental Climate by Mary Ellen Kozak and J. Krawczyk.
Cultivating Edible Fungi by P.J. Wuest.

IDENTIFICATION

Psilocybin Mushrooms of the World by Paul Stamets.
Mushrooms Demystified by David Arora.
All That the Rain Promises and More by David Arora.
One Thousand American Fungi by C. McIlvaine and R. Macadam. (plus recipes)
The Audubon Society Field Guide to North American Mushrooms by G. Lincoff.
Peterson Field Guides Mushrooms by K. McKnight and V. McKnight.
Edible Wild Mushrooms of North America by D. Fischer and A. Bessette. (plus recipes)

RECIPES

A Passion for Mushrooms by Antonio Carluccio.
The Edible Mushroom by Margaret Liebenstein.
The New Savory Wild Mushroom by Margaret McKenney and D. Stuntz.

MEDICINAL USES

Icones of Medicinal Fungi from China by J. Ying, et al.
Fungi Pharmacopoeia by L. Bo and B. Yun-sun.
Reishi Mushroom. Herb of Spiritual Potency and Medical Wonder by Terry Willard.

Fungi Bibliography

A Barefoot Doctor's Manual. 1977. Seattle: Madrona Publishers.

Aboul-Enein, H.Y. 1974. Psilocybin: a pharmacological profile. *American Journal of Pharmacy* May-June.

Abraham, W.R. and G. Spasov. 1991. 4-Hydroxymethylquinoline from Polyporus spp. *Phytothera*. 30:317-372.

Abramson, H.A. (ed.). 1960. The use of LSD in psychotherapy; transactions. New York: Josiah Macy, Jr. Foundation.

Abramson, H.A. (ed.). 1967. The use of LSD in psychotherapy and alcoholism. From *International Conference on the Use of LSD in Psychotherapy and Alcoholism.* Indianapolis: Bobbs-Merrill.

Adachi, K. et al. 1987. Potentiation of host-mediated antitumor activity in mice by B-glucan obtained from *Grifola frondosa* (Maitake). *Chem. Pharm. Bull.* 35:262-270.

Adachi, K. et al. 1988. Blood pressure-lowering activity present in the fruit body of *Grifola frondosa* (Maitake). *Chem. Pharm. Bull.* 36:1000-1006.

Agarwal, K.C. et al. 1982. Inhibition of human and rat platelet aggregation by extracts of Mo-er (*Auricularia auricula*). *Thromb. Haemostas (Stuttgart)* 48:162-165.

Ahn, J.S. et al. 1987. Studies on the volatile components of edible mushroom (*Lentinus edodes*) of Korea. *Han'guk Yongyang Siklyong Hakhoechi* 16:328-332. In CA 111:132842w.

Ainsworth, G.C., (N.d.). *Introduction to the History of Mycology.* Cambridge: Cambridge Univ. Press.

Akiyama, Y. et al. 1981. Immunological characteristics of anti-tumor polysaccharides lentinan and its analogues, as immune adjuvants. In *Manipulation of Host Defense Mechanisms*, Aoki, T. et al. (eds.). Amsterdam: *Excerpta Medica* (International Congress Series 576).

Al-Deen, I.H. et al. 1987. Toxicological and histopathologic studies of *Pleurotus ostreatus* mushroom in mice. *J. Ethnopharmacol.* 21:297-305.

Alfaro, M.A.M. et al. 1983. Etnomicologia y Exploraciones Micologicas en la Sierra Norte de Puebla. *Bol. Soc. Mex. Mic.* 18:51-63.

Alleyne, J. 1733. *A New English Dispensatory.* London: Tho. Astley.

AMA Drug Evaluations. 1983. Chicago: American Medical Association.

Amagase, H. 1987. Treatment of hepatitis B patients with *Lentinus edodes* mycelium. Proceedings of the XII International Congress of Gastroenterology, Lisbon, p. 197.

American Pharmaceutical Assoc. 1926. *The National Formulary* (5th ed). Washington D.C.: American Pharmaceutical Assoc.

Anke, H. et al. 1987. Antibiotics from Basidiomycetes: Phlebiakauranol aldehyde an antifungal and cytotoxic metabolite from punctularia atropurpurascens. *J. Antibot.* 40:443-449.

Aoki, T. 1984b. "Lentinan". In *Immune Modulation Agents and Their Mechanisms.* R.L. Fenichel and M. A. Chirgis, eds. *Immunology Studies.* 25:62-77.

Aoki, T. 1984a. Antibodies to HTLV I and HTLV III in sera from two Japanese patients, one with possible pre-AIDS. *The Lancet* Oct. 20:936-937.

Aoki, T. et al. 1987. Low natural killer syndrome: Clinical and immunologic features. *Nat. Immun. Cell Growth Regul.* 6:116-28.

Arai, Y. et al. 1971. Effect of immunosuppressive agents on antitumor action of Lentinan. *Gann.* 62:131-134.

Arinaga, S. et al. 1992a. Enhanced induction of lymphokine-activated killer activity after lentinan administration in patients with gastric carcinoma. *Int. J. Immunopharmacol.* 14:535-539.

Arinaga, S. et al. 1992b. Enhanced production of interleukin 1 and tumor necrosis factor by peripheral monocytes after lentinan administration in patients with gastric carcinoma. *Int. J. Immunopharmacol.* 14:43-47.

Arisawa, M. et al. 1986. Three new lanostanoids from *Ganoderma lucidum. Journal of Natural Products* 49:621-625.

Arora, D. 1986. *Mushrooms Demystified.* Berkeley: Ten Speed Press.

Arora, D. 1991. *All That the Rain Promises and More...* Berkeley, CA: Ten Speed Press.

Arora, D. 1994. Personal communication.

Arthur, H.R. et al. 1958. Isolation of ergosta-7,22-dien-3-one from *Fomes fomentarius. J. Chem. Soc.* 53:2603-2605.

Asano, K. et al. 1979. Agent for combatting plant viruses. (patent). From CA 90:181585w.

Atkinson, N. 1946. Toadstools and mushrooms as a source of antibacterial substances active against mycobacterium phlei and bact. typhosum. *Nature* Apr. 6:441.

Badgley, L.E. and H. Mee. 1986. Improved lymphocyte profiles in AIDS/ARC patients as the result of a natural remedy. Preliminary research report presented at the "Talks on Natural Therapies for Chronic Viral Diseases" in San Francisco, August 23,1986.

Bano, Z. and S. Rajarathnam. 1988. *Pleurotus* mushrooms. Part II. Chemical composition, nutritional value, post-harvest physiology, preservation, and role as human food. *CRC Critical Reviews in Food Science and Nutrition* 27:87-158.

Batchelor, J. and K. Miyabe. 1893. Ainu economic plants. *Trans. Roy. Soc. Japan* 21:198-240.

Barenboim, D. 1986. *Eleutherococcus senticosus.* Moscow: Medexport.

Barron, F. et al. 1967. *LSD, man & society.* R. C. DeBold and R. C. Leaf. (eds.). Middletown, CN: Wesleyan University Press.

Beardsley, G. 1944. Notes on Cree medicines, based on a collection made by I. Cowie in 1892. *Pap. Mich. Acad. Sci., Arts and Letters* 27:483-496.

Beck, D.L. 1988. Hunting the wild mushroom? Be careful. *San Jose Mercury News.* Jan.13.

Belova, O.I. and K.I. Varentsova. Tincture of *Inonotus obliquus. Sb. Nauchn. Tr. Tsentr. Nauchn.-Issled. Aptechn. Inst.* 3:86-93.

Bensky, D. and A. Gamble. 1993. *Chinese Materia Medica,* 2nd ed. Seattle: Eastland Press.

Bensky, D. and R. Barolet. 1990. *Chinese Herbal Medicine, Formulas and Strategies.* Seattle: Eastland Press.

Berkeley, Rev. M.J. 1857. *Introduction to Cryptogamic Botany.* London: H. Bailliere.

Bernillon, J. et al. 1989. First isolation of (+)- epipentenomycin I from Peziza sp. carpophores. *J. Antibiot.,* 42:1430-1432. In CA 112:18862y.

Beverley, R. 1947. *The History and Present State of Virginia.* Chapel Hill: University of North Carolina Press.

Blumenberg, F.W. und F. J. Kessler. 1962. Die Wachstumshemmung des Mäusesarkoms S37 durch den Birkenschwamm (*Polyporus betulinus*). *Arzneim.-Forsch.* 13:198-200.

Bo, L. and Bau Yun-sun. 1980. *Fungi Pharmacopoeia (Sinica).* Oakland: Kinoko Co.

Bobek P. et al. 1991c. Effect on oyster fungus (*Pleurotus ostreatus*) on serum and liver lipids of Syrian hamsters with a chronic alcohol intake. *Physiological Research* 40(3):327-332.

Bobek, P. et al. 1991b. Effect of mushroom *Pleurotus ostreatus* and isolated fungal polysaccharide on serum and liver lipids in Syrian hamsters with hyperlipidemia. *Nutrition* 7:105-108.

Bobek, P. et al. 1991a. Cholesterol-lowering effect of the mushroom *Pleurotus ostreatus* in hereditary hypocholesterolemic rats. *Annals of Nutrition and Metabolism* 35:191-195.

Bobek, P. et al. 1993. The mushroom *Pleurotus ostreatus* reduces secretion and accelerates the fractional turnover rate of very-low-density lipoproteins in the rat. *Annals of Nutrition and Metabolism* 37:142-145.

Boericke, W. 1927. *Pocket Manual of Homeopathic Materia Medica*. Philadelphia: Boericke & Tafel.

Bose, S.R. 1946. Antibiotics in a Polyporus (*Polystictus sanguineus*). Nature 158:292-296.

Bose, S.R. 1952. Antibacterial principles from some higher fungi. *J. Sci. Ind. Research* (*India*) 11B:159-60.

Breene, W. 1990. Nutritional and Medicinal Value of Specialty Mushrooms. *J. Food Pro.* 53: 883-894.

Brekhman, I.I. 1980. *Man and Biologically Active Substances*. New York: Pergamon Press.

Bretschneider, E. 1895. *Botanicon Sinicum. Part III. Botanical Investigations Into the Materia Medica of the Ancient Chinese*. Shanghai: Kelly & Walsh, LTD.

Brian, P.W. 1951. Antibiotics produced by fungi. *Bot. Rev.* 17:357-430.

British Pharmaceutical Codex. 1954. London: The Pharmaceutical Press.

Broadbent, D. 1966. Antibiotics produced by fungi. *Bot. Rev.* 32:219-233.

Burk, W.R. 1983. Puffball usages among North American Indians. *J. Ethnobiol.* 3:55-62.

Burkhill, I.H. 1966. *A Dictionary of the Economic Products of the Malay Peninsula*. Kuala Lumpur, Malaysia: Ministry of Agriculture and Co-operatives, Malaysia and Singapore.

Caldwell, W.V. 1968. *LSD psychotherapy; an exploration of psychedelic and psycholytic therapy*. New York: Grove Press.

Cao, R. et al. 1986. Treatment of 232 cases of Alopecia areata with *Ganoderma capens*. *J. Beijing Med. Col.* 7:217-218. From *Abstracts of Chinese Medicines* 1:547.

Cao, X. et al. 1989. Immunostimulation by polysaccharide of *Lentinus edodes* in mice. *Zhongguo Zhongyao Zazhi*. 14:110-111, 101. In CA 110:205270z.

Ch'u, L.H. 1965. The use of "Wen-Pu Chu-Shui Huan" to treat ascites of late stage schistosomiasis. *Chiang-su Chung-I* 7:38-39.

Chang, H.M. and P. Pui-Hay But. 1986. *Pharmacology and Applications of Chinese Materia Medica*. Vol. 1. Singapore: World Scientific.

Chang, H.M. and P. Pui-Hay But. 1987. *Pharmacology and Applications of Chinese Materia Medica*. Vol. 2. Singapore: World Scientific

Chang, H.M., ed. et al. 1984. *Advances in Chinese Medicinal Materials Research*. Singapore: World Scientific.

Chang, K.S.S. 1981. Lentinan-mediated resistance against VSV-encephalitis, Abelson virus-induced tumor, and trophoblastic tumor in mice. In *Manipulation of Host Defense Mechanisms*, Aoki, T. et al. (eds.). Amsterdam: *Excerpta Medica* (International Congress Series 576).

Chen, D. et al. 1985. Effects of natural Cordyceps and the cultured mycelia of *Cordyceps sinensis* on murine immune organs and functions of mononuclear phagocyte system. *Chinese Journal of Integrated Traditional and Western Medicine* 5:42-44, 50. From *Abstracts of Chinese Medicines*, 1:371.

Chen, D. et al. 1987a. Antineoplastic and related pharmacological effects of pachyman. *Bulletin of Chinese Materia Medica* 12:553-555, 575. From *Abstracts of Chinese Medicines*, 2:295.

Chen, D. et al. 1987b. Effects of Cordyceps and cultured *Cordyceps sinensis* of the formation and ultrastructures of platelets. *Bull. Chin. Mater. Med.* 12:47-49. From *Abstracts of Chinese Medicines*, 2:27.

Chen, H.S. et al. 1986. The antiviral and immunopotentiating activities polysaccharides extracted from *Polystictus versicolor* in mice. *Kangshengsu* 11:390-395. In CA83:37140.

Chen, J. and R. Jiang. 1980. A pharmacognostical study of the Chinese drug Lingzhi (Ganoderma). *Acta. Pharm. Sin.* 15:244.

Chen, K, and W. Zhang. 1987. Advances on anti-aging herbal medicines in China. *Abstracts of Chinese Medicines* 1:309-330.

Chen, R. et al. 1991. Chemical constituents of the spores from *Ganoderma lucidum*. *Zhiwu Xuebao* 33:65-68. In CA 115:131985r.

Chen, X., et al. 1987. Treatment of 19 cases of dermato-myositis and multiple myositis with *Ganoderma Capense. J.Clin. Dermatol.* 16:112. From *Abstracts of Chinese Medicines* 2:187.

Chen, Y. et al. 1986. Clinical effects of natural *Cordyceps* and cultured mycelia of *Cordyceps sinensis* in kidney failure. *Chin. Tradit. Herb. Drugs* 17:256-258. From *Abstracts of Chinese Medicines* 1:547.

Cheng, Z. et al. 1993. Effects of ling zhi on hemorrheology parameters and symptoms of hypertension patients with hyperlipidemia and sequelae of cerebral thrombosis. From Zhu, S. and M. Mori (eds.). 1993. Influence of ling zhi on natural killer cells—Immunopharmacological Study (5). From *The Research on Ganoderma lucidum* (part one). Shanghai: Shanghai Medical University Press.

Cherfas, J. 1991. Disappearing Mushrooms: Another Mass Extinction? *Science* 254:1458.

Chiang, H. and M. Wann. 1986. Improved assay for germanium in crude drugs. *J. Taiwan Pharm. Assoc.* 38:189-198. From *Abstracts of Chinese Medicines* 1:337.

Chibata, I. et al. 1969. Lentinacin: a new hypocholesterolemic substance in *Lentinus edodes*. *Experientia* 25:1237-1238.

Chihara, G. 1981. The antitumor polysaccharide Lentinan: an overview. In *Manipulation of Host Defence Mechanisms*, Aoki, T. et al. (eds.). Amsterdam: *Excerpta Medica* (International Congress Series 576).

Chihara, G. 1992. Recent progress in immunopharmacology and therapeutic effects of polysaccharides. *Dev. Biol. Stand.* 77:191-197.

Chihara, G. et al. 1969. Inhibition of mouse sarcoma 180 by polysaccharides from *Lentinus edodes* (Berk.) Sing. *Nature* 222:637-688.

Chihara, G. et al. 1970b. Fractionation and purification of the polysaccharides with marked antitumor acitivity, especially Lentinan, from *Lentinus edodes* (Berk.) Sing. (an edible mushroom). *Cancer Research* 30:2776-2781.

Chihara, G. et al. 1970a. Antitumor polysaccharide derived chemically from natural glucan (pachyman). *Nature* 225:943-944.

Chihara, G. et al. 1987. Antitumor and metastasis-inhibitory activities of lentinan as an immunomodulator: An overview. *Cancer Detect. Prev.* Suppl 1:423-443.

Chihara, G. 1993. Medical aspects of lentinan isolated from *Lentinus edodes* (Berk.) Sing. From *Mushroom Biology and Mushroom Products*. S.-t. Chang et al (eds.). Hong Kong: The Chinese University Press, 261-265.

Chilton, J.S. 1994. The first international conference on mushroom biology and mushroom products. *Herbalgram* 31:57.

Chone, B. and G. Manidakis. 1969. *Deut. Med. Woch.* 27:1406.

Chung, C.H. et al. 1987. PSK immunotherapy in cancer patients—a preliminary report. *Chung Hua Min Kuo Wei Sheng Wu Chi Mien I Hsueh Tsa Chih* 20: 210-216.

Chung, K. et al. 1991. Mycelial growth of *Ganoderma lucidum* and *Grifola frondosa* in milk whey. *Han'guk Kyunhakhoechi* 19:61-65.

Cichoke, A.J. 1994. Maitake mushrooms: A leap beyond the ordinary! *Total Health* Feb.

Cochran, K.W. 1978. Medical Effects. In *The Biology and Cultivation of Edible Mushrooms*, edited by Chang and Hayes. New York: Academic Press.

Cochran, K.W. 1988. Mushroom Poisoning Case Registry North American Mycological Assoc. 1987-88 Progress Report Cases Reported 1 July 1987 to 30 June 1988.

Conrad, F. and H. Rüdiger. 1994. The lectin from *Pleurotus ostreatus:* purification, characterization and interaction with a phosphatase. *Phytochemistry* 36:277-283.

Cooke, R.C. 1977. Magic mushrooms and hallucinogenic drugs. In *Fungi, Man and His Environment*. London: Longman.

Cooke, W. 1979. *The Ecology of Fungi*. Boca Raton, Fl: CRC Press.

Cozens, D.D. et al. 1981c. The effect of lentinan on the in utero foetal development of the rat and on postnatal development of the offspring. *Toxicol. Lett.* 9:77-80.

Cozens, D.D. et al. 1981b. The effect of lentinan on the in utero embryonic and foetal development of the rat and on postnatal development of F1 offspring. *Toxicol. Lett.* 9:71-76.

Cozens, D.D. et al. 1981a. The effect of lentinan on fertility and general reproductive performance of the rat. *Toxicol. Lett.* 9:55-64.

Crisan, E.V. and A. Sands. 1978. Nutritional value. *Edible Mushrooms*. New York: Academic Press.

Culbreth, D. M.R. 1927. *A Manual of Materia Medica and Pharmacology*. Philadelphia: Lea & Febiger.

Curtis & Tompkins, Ltd. 1981. Analytical report on sample of Shiigen (powder), Reishi & Shiitake. Curtis & Tompkins, Ltd., San Francisco.

Dai, Y. and Y.Yin. 1987. Inhibition of type B monoamine oxidase by Chinese medicinal materials. *Chinese Journal of Geriatrics* 6:27-30. From *Abstracts of Chinese Medicines* 1:513.

Dansereau, P. and V.A. Weadock, ed. N.d. Antibiotics produced by fungi. In *Bot. Rev.* 220-242.

Davis, B.L. 1981. Magic Mushrooms. Technical Report Series A-81-2. Vancouver: Province of British Columbia Ministry of Health, Alcohol and Drug Programs.

Deng, G. and J. Xu. 1992. Poriatin: a potential aldosterone antagonist. *Zhongguo Kangshengsu Zazhi* 17:34-37. From CA 117:62953f.

Dennart, G. and D. Tucker. 1973. Antitumor polysaccharide Lentinan, a T cell adjuvant. *J. Natl. Cancer Inst.* 51:1729.

Dharmanada, S., (N.d.). Commonly asked questions about *Ganoderma*, the herb for the 21st century. *Herb Facts Bulletin*. ITM: Portland, OR.

Dharmananda, S. 1988. Medicinal mushrooms. *Bestways*. July. 54-58.

Dharmananda, S. 1994. Personal communication.

Ding, G. 1987. Anti-arrhythmia agents in traditional Chinese medicines. From *Abstracts of Chinese Medicines* 1:287-308.

Ding, X. et al. 1987. Effects of poriatin on mouse peritoneal macrophages. *Zhongguo Y'lxue Kexueyuan* 9:433-438.

Do, J-H. and S-D. Kim. 1985. Properties of amylase produced from higher fungi *Ganoderma lucidum*. *Sanop Misaengmul Hakhoechi* 13:173-178. From CA 104:2589p.

Do, J-H. and S-D. Kim. 1986. Enzymic properties of a cellulase from *Ganoderma lucidum*. *Han'guk Kyunhakhoechi* 14:79-84. From CA 105:16758u.

Donnelly, D.M.X. et al. 1985. Antibacterial sesquiterpene aryl esters from *Armillaria mellea*. *J. Nat. Prod.* 48:10-16.

Donnelly, D.M.X. et al. 1986. New sesquiterpene aryl esters from *Armillaria mellea*. *J. Nat. Prod.* 49:111-116.

Donnelly, D.M.X. and R.M. Hutchinson. 1990. Armillane, a saturated sesquiterpene ester from *Armillaria mellea*. *Phytochemistry* 29:179-182. From CA 112:155242k.

Dragendorff, G. 1898. *Die Heilpflanzen der Verschiedenen Völker und Zeiten.* Stuttgart: Verlag von Ferdinand Enke.

Ebihara, K. and Y. Minamishima. 1984. Protective effect of biological response modifiers on murine cytomegalovirus infection. *J. Virol.* 51:117-122.

Ebina, T. 1987b. Antitumor effect of PSK. (2). Effector mechanism of antimetastatic effect in the "double grafted tumor system". *Gon to Kagaku Ryoho* 14:1847-1853. From CA 107:108961f.

Ebina, T. et al. 1987a. Antitumor effect of PSK. (1). Interferon inducing activity and intratumoral administration. *Gon to Kagaku Ryoho* 14:1841-1846. From CA 107:108960e.

Eder, J. and A. Wuensch. 1991. Protein quality of oyster mushrooms (*Pleurotus spp.*). *Chem., Mikrobiol., Technol. Lebensm.* 13:25-29. From CA114:227705e.

Efimenko, O.M. 1961a. Polyporenic acid A—An antibiotic isolated from the tinder fungus *Polyporus betulinus. Antibiotki* 6:215-220. From CA 59:21233c.

Efimenko, O.M. 1961b. Triterpenoid acids of *Polyporus betulinus. Kompleksn. Izuch. Fiziol. Aktivn. Veshchestv. Nizshikh- Rast., Akad. Nauk SSSR, Botan. Inst.* 88-94. From CA 66:7717c.

Emboden, W. 1979. *Narcotic Plants.* New York: Collier Books.

Endo, S. et al. 1981. Lipids of five species of polyporaceae (*Pyellinus obustus, Fomitopsis cytisina, Grifola frondosa, Elfyingia applanata* and *Coriolus versicolor*). *Tokyo Gakugei Daigaku Kiyo* 81:13-42. From CA 96:3017282.

Enquin, Z. 1990. *Rare Chinese Materia Medica.* Shanghai: Publishing House of Shanghai College of Traditional Chinese Medicine.

Espenshade, M.A. and E.W. Griffith. 1966. Tumor-inhibiting basidiomycetes. Isolation and cultivation in the laboratory. *Mycology* 58:511-517.

Evans, C.E. 1989. *Trease and Evans' Pharmacognosy,* 13th ed. London: Bailliere Tindall.

Fackelmann, K.A. 1992. No survival bonus from early AZT. *Sci. News* 141:100.

Fadiman, J. 1967. Treatment of alcoholism with Lysergide. Comment on the article by Smart et al. *Q.J. Stud. Alcohol* 28:146-147.

Falch, E. et al. 1984. *Amanita muscaria* in medicinal chemistry. I. Muscimol and related GABA agonists with anticonvulsant and central non-opioid analgesic effects. *Natural Products and Drug Development.* Alfred Benzon Symposium 20:49-54.

Farnsworth, N. et al. 1985. Siberian ginseng (*Eleutherococcus senticosus*): Current status as an adaptogen. In *Economic and Medicinal Plant Research* vol. 1. New York: Academic Press.

Fasching, R. 1994. (1985). *Tea Fungus Kombucha.* Austria: Wilhelm Ennsthaler.

Fasidi, I.O. and M. Kadiri. 1990. Changes in nutrient contents of two Nigerian mushrooms, *Termitomyces robustus* (Beeli) Heim and *Lentinus subnudus* Ber. during sporophore development. *Nahrung* 34:415-420.

Felter, H.W. 1922. *The Eclectic Materia Medica, Pharmacology and Therapeutics.* Cincinnati, Ohio: John K. Scudder.

Felter, H.W. and J.U. Lloyd.1983, [1898]. *King's American Dispensatory.* 2 vols. Portland: Eclectic Medical Publications.

Fernie, W.T. 1897. *Herbal Simples.* Bristol: John Wright & Co.

Fernie, W.T. 1905. *Meals Medicinal.* Bristol: John Wright & Co.

Fidalgo, O. and G.T. Prance. 1976. The ethnomycology of the Sanama Indians. *Mycologia* 68:201-210.

Floersheim, G.L. 1983. Toxins and intoxications from the toadstool *Amanita phalloides.. Elsevier Science Publishers* June:263-264.

Flynn, V.T. 1991. Is the shiitake mushroom an aphrodisiac and a cause of longevity? From *Science and Cultivation of Edible Fungi* (Maher, ed.). Rotterdam: Balkema.

Foster, J.W. 1949. *Chemical Activities of Fungi.* New York: Academic Press, Inc.

Frank, G.W. 1995. (1991) *Kombucha*. Austria: Wilhelm Ennsthaler.

Franz, G. 1987. Structure-activity relation of polysaccharides antitumor activity. *Farm. Tijdschr. Belg.* 64:301-311. From CA 108:31318n.

Freeman, D.X. 1967. Perspectives on the Use and Abuse of Psychedelic Drugs. From *Ethnopharmacologic Search for Psychoactive Drugs* (Proceedings). D.H. Efron et al (eds.). Washington: U.S. Department of Health, Education, and Welfare.

Fu, H. and Z. Wang. 1982. The clinical effects of *Ganoderma lucidum* spore preparations in 10 cases of atrophic myotonia. *J. Trad. Chin. Med.* 2:63-65.

Fujii, T. et al. 1978. Isolation and characterization of a new anti-tumor polysaccharide, KS-2, extracted from culture mycelia of *Lentinus Edodes*. *J.Antibiot.* 31:1079-1090.

Fujimoto, H. et al. 1994. Isolation and characterization of immunosuppressive components of three mushrooms, *Pisolithus tinctorius*, *Microporus flabelliformis* and *Lenzites betulina*. *Chem. Pharm. Bull.* 42:694-697.

Fujimoto, T. et al. 1992. Evaluation of basic procedures for adoptive immunotherapy for gastric cancer. *Biotherapy* 5:153163.

Fukushima, M. 1989. The overdose of drugs in Japan. *Nature* 342:850-851.

Fung, P.-H. et al. 1993. Glycoside inhibitor from *Ganoderma japonicum*. First International Conference on Mushroom Biology and Mushroom Products. Hong Kong, August 23-26, 1993. Programme and Abstracts. The Chinese University of Hong Kong, 1993:103(O-83).

Furue, H. 1985. Clinical evaluation of schizophyllan (SPG) in gastric cancer-randomized controlled studies. *Int. J. Immunopharmacol.* 7:333(23).

Furuya, T. et al. 1983. N6-(2-Hydroxyethyl) adenosine, a biologically active compound from cultured mycelia of *Cordyceps* and *Isaria* species. *Phytochemistry* 22:2509-2511.

Gable, R.S. 1993. Toward a Comparative Overview of Dependence Potential and Acute Toxicity of Psychoactive Substances Used Nonmedically. *Am. J. Drug Alcohol Abuse* 19:263-281.

Gao, B. and G. Yang. 1991. Effects of *Ganoderma applanatum* polysaccharide on cellular and humoral immunity in normal and sarcoma 180 transplanted mice. *Phythother. Res.* 5:134-138. From CA 115:85011v.

Gao, Q. et al. 1991. Polysaccharides and their antitumor activity of *Tremella fuciformis*. *Tianran Chanwu Yanjiu Yu Kaifa* 3:43-48. From CA 116:15461p.

Garcha, H.S. et al. 1993. Nutritional importance of mushrooms. From *Mushroom Biology and Mushroom Products*. Change, S.-T. et al. (eds.). Shatin, Hong Kong: The Chinese University Press, 227-236.

Gau, J.P. 1990. The lack of antiplatelet effect of crude extracts from *Ganoderma lucidum* on HIV-positive hemophiliacs. *Am. J. Chin. Med.* 18:175-179.

Gautier, J.M. 1884. *Les Champignons*. Paris: Librairie J.-B. Bailliere et Fils.

Geng, S. et al. 1985. Treatment of Hyperlipidemia with Cultivated Cordyceps—A Double Blind, Randomized Placebo Control Trial. *Chin. J. Integ. Med.* 5(11), 652.

Gerard, J. 1975 [1633]. *The Herbal, or General History of Plants*. New York: Dover Publications, Inc.

Gilbertson, R.L. and L. Ryvarden. 1986. *North American Polypores*. Oslo, Norway: Fungiflora.

Go, P. and C.H. Chung. 1989. Adjuvant PSK immunotherapy in patients with carcinoma of the nasopharynx. *J. Int. Med. Res.* 17:141-149.

Gong, M. et al. 1990. Molecular structure and immunoactivity of the polysaccharide from *Cordyceps sinensis*. *Shengwu Huaxue Zazl.* 6:486-492. From CA 114:94819w.

Gorai, I. et al. 1992. Immunological modulation of lymphocyte subpopulation in cervical cancer tissue by sizofiran and OK-432. *Gynecologic Oncology* 44:137-146.

Graf, V.E. and H.-J. Winckelmann. 1960. Investigations on the transformation of hydroxy-triterpene acids from *Fungus laricis* [*Fomitopsis officinalis*] to 11-keto-corticosteroids. *Planta Med.* 8:403.

Gray, W.D. 1970. *The use of fungi as food and in food processing.* Boca Raton, Fl: CRC Press. 100-113.

Gray, W.D. 1973. *The use of fungi as food and in food processing.* Part II. Boca Raton, Fl: CRC Press. 205-209.

Gregory, F.J. et al 1966. Studies on antitumor substances produced by Basidiomycetes. *Mycologia* 58:80.

Grof, S. 1980. *LSD psychotherapy.* Pomona, CA: Hunter House.

Grüter, A. et al. 1990. Antimutagenic effects of mushrooms. *Mut. Res.* 231:243-249.

Grzybek, J. et al. 1983. Polysaccharides from *Inonotus obliquus* (Pers. ex Fr.) Pil. and their biological activity in the *Allium* test. *Herba Hung.* 22(2):65-75.

Grzybek, J. et al. 1992. Evaluation of anti-inflammatory and vasoprotective actions of the polysaccharides isolated from fruit bodies of *Boletus edulis. Planta Med.* 58, Supplement Issue 1:A641.

Gu, M. 1986. Three cases of solar dermatitis caused by Muer. *Journal of Clinical Dermatology* 15:158. From *Abstracts of Chinese Medicines*, 1:543.

Guan, H.C. and Z. Cong. 1982. Effects of ling zhi polysaccharide D6 on the biosynthesis of nucleic acid and protein and its preliminary analysis. *Yao Hsueh T'ung Pao* 17:177-178.

Guan, Y.J. et al. 1992. Effect of *Cordyceps sinensis* on T-lymphocyte subsets in Chronic Renal Failure. *Chung-Kuo Cung Hsii Chieh Ho Tsa Chih.* 12(6): 338-339, 323.

Guo, D. et al. 1984. Preliminary observation on carboxy-methyl *Poria cocos* polysaccharide (CMPLP) in treating chronic viral hepatitis. *J. Trad. Chin. Med.* 4:282.

Guo, S. et al. 1992. Determination of sugar components in wild and cultured sclerotia of *Grifola umbellata* at different ages. *Zhongguo Zhongyao Zazhi* 17:77-80. From CA 116:231463h.

Guo, X. et al. 1990. Comparative studies of chemical constituents between Huokesi Chongcao (*Cordyceps hawkesii*) and Dongchong Xiacao (*Cordyceps sinensis*). *Zhongcaoyao* 21:109-110. From CA 112:24036lt.

Guo, Y. et al. 1985. Preliminary study on *Cordyceps barnesii*—comparison of chemical constituents between *Cordyceps barnesii* and *Cordyceps sinensis. Bull. Chin. Materia Med.* 10:129-131. From *Abstracts of Chinese Medicines* 1:18.

Guzmán, G. 1983. The Genus *Psilocybe.* From *Beihefte zur Nova Hedwigia*, vol. 74. Vaduz: J. Cramer.

Guzmán, G. 1976. Psychotropic Mycoflora of Washington, Idaho, Oregon, California and British Columbia. *Mycologia* 68:1267-1272.

Guzmán, G. 1983. The Genus *Psilocybe.* From *Beihefte zur Nova Hedwigia*, vol. 74. Vaduz: J. Cramer.

Habuka, N. et al. 1991. Purification and characterization of two DNA- binding proteins from the basidiomycete *Lentinus edodes. Agric. Biol. Chem.* 55:427-433. From CA 114:138351u.

Hamada, C. 1981. Inhibitory effects of lentinan on the tumorigenesis of adenovirus type 12 in mice. From *Manipulation of Host Defense Mechanisms*, Aoki, T. et al. (eds.). Amsterdam: *Excerpta Medica* (International Congress Series 576).

Hamuro, J. et al. 1971b. The significance of the higher structure of the polysaccharide lentinan and pachymaran with regard to their antitumor activity. *Chem.-Biol. Interactions* 3:69.

Hamuro, J. et al. 1971a. Carboxymethylpachymaran, a new water soluble polysaccharide with marked antitumor activity. *Nature* 233:486-488.

Hamuro, J. et al. 1978a. b(1,3)-glucan mediated augmentation of alloreactive murine cytotoxic T-lymphocyte in vivo. *Cancer Res.* 38:3080.

Hamuro, J. et al. 1978b. b(1,3)-glucans as a probe for T cell specific immune adjuvants: enhanced in vitro generation of cytotoxic T lymphocytes. *Cell Immunol.* 38:328.

Han, D.S. et al. 1984. *Ethnobotanical Survey in Korea.* Proc. fifth Asian symposium on medicinal plants and spices Seoul, Korea, Aug. 20-24. Seoul: Coll. Pharm. Seoul Natl. Univ.

Hanafusa, T. et al. 1990. Intestinal absorption and tissue distribution of immunoactive and antiviral water-soluble [14C] lignins in rats. *Yakubutsu Dotai* 5:661-674. From CA 114:220685q.

Hanaue, H. et al. 1989. Basic studies on oral administration of lentinan I. Influence on lymphocyte subsets in peripheral venous blood. *J. Jpn. Soc. Cancer Ther.* 24:1566-1571.

Hanssen, V. H-P. and M. Schädler. 1982. Pilze als volksmittel in der chinesischen medicine. *Deutsche Apoth.-Zeit.* 122:1844-1848.

Harada, T. et al. 1987. Therapeutic efficacy of LEM against Hbe Ag positive chronic hepatitis B. *Kantansui* 14:327-335.

Harada, Y. 1993a. *Biology in Mushrooms and Molds.* Sasaki, H. ed. Tokyo: Chuo-Koron Sha.

Harada, Y. 1993b. Maitake descends from mountains. Excerpts from "Biology in Mushrooms and Molds", May.

Haranaka, K. et al. 1985. Antitumor activities and tumor necrosis factor producibility of traditional Chinese medicines and crude drugs. *Cancer Immunol. Immunother.* 20:1-5.

Hartwell, J.L. 1971. Plants used against cancer. *Lloydia* 34:386-437.

Hattori, T. et al. 1992. Studies on antinephritic effects of plant components: Effects of pachyman, a main component of *Poria cocos* wolf on original-type anti-GBM nephritis in rats and its mechanisms. *Jpn. J. Pharmacol.* 59:89-96.

Hauser, S.P. 1990. Dr. Sklenar's Kombucha mushroom infusion—a biological cancer therapy. *Schweizerische Rundschan fur Medizin Praxis* 79:242-246.

Hay, W.D. 1887. *An Elementary Text-Book of British Fungi.* London: Swan Sonnenschein, Lowrey & Co.

He, B. and Q. Chen. 1991. Antifertility action of *Auricularia auricula* polysaccharide. *Zhongguo Yaoke Daxue Xuebao* 22:48-49. From CA 115:1028V.

Herberman, R.B. and M.E. Nunn-Hargrove. 1981. Augmentation of natural killer (NK) cell activity by lentinan. From *Manipulation of Host Defense Mechanisms*, Aoki, T. et al. (eds.). Amsterdam: *Excerpta Medica* (International Congress Series 576).

Hermann, S. 1929. Bacterium gluconicum, ein in der sogenannten Kombucha (japanischer oder indischer Teepilz) vorkommender Spaltpilz. *Biochem. Z.* 205:297-305 From CA 23:2738.

Hermann, S. 1927. Über die sogenannte "Kombucha". *Biochem. Z.* 192:176-87. From CA 22:2589.

Hermann, S. and M. Zentner. 1933. Über Substanzen, welche die durch Vitasterin hervogerufene Reststickstofferhöhung bei Katzen beeinflussen. *Biochem. Z.* 266:418-21. From CA 28:1080(8).

Hervey, A.H. 1947. A survey of 500 basidiomycetes for antibacterial activity. *Bull.Torrey Bot. Club* 74:476-503.

Hesseltine, C.W. and H.L. Wang eds.. 1986. Indigenous Fermented Food of Non-Western Origin. *Mycologia Memoir* no. 11, New York Botanical Garden & The Mycological Society of America. Berlin: J. Cramer.

Hibbett, D.S. and R. Vilgalya. 1991. Evolutionary relationships of Lentinus to the Polyporaceae: evidence from restriction analysis of enzymatically amplified ribosomal DNA. *Mycologia* 83:425-439.

Hikino, H. and T. Mizuno. 1989. Hypoglycemic actions of some heteroglycans of *Ganoderma lucidum* fruit bodies. *Planta Med.* 55:385. From CA 111:167128V.

Hikino, H. et al. 1985. Isolation and hypoglycemic activity of ganoderans A and B, glycans of *Ganoderma lucidum* fruit bodies. *Planta Med.* 4:339-340.

Hirase, S. et al. 1976a. Structural studies on the anti-tumor active polysaccharides from *Coriolus versicolor (Basidiomycetes)*. I. Fractionation with barium hydroxide. *Yakugaku Zasshi* 96:413-418.

Hirase, S. et al. 1976b. Structural studies on the anti-tumor active polysaccharides from *Coriolus versicolor (Basidiomycetes)*. II. Structures of ß-D-glucan moieties of fractionated polysaccharides. *Yakugaku Zasshi* 96:419-424.

Hirata, K. et al. 1988. Food analysis by using an enzyme. I. Simple method for the determination of formaldehyde in foods. *Eisei Kagaku* 34:555-559. From CA 110:133808f.

Hirata, A. et al. 1994. Monoclonal antibody to proteoglycan derived from *Grifola frondosa* (Maitake). *Biol. Pharm. Bull.* 17:539-542.

Hirata, Y. and K. Nakanishi. 1950. Grifolin, An Antibiotic from a Basidiomycete. *J. Biol. Chem.* 184:135-143.

Hirose, K. 1985. Cloning of sequences induced and suppressed by administration of PSK, antitumor protein-bound polysaccharide. *Biochem. Biophy. Res. Commun.* 126:884-892.

Hirose, K. et al. 1987. A biological response modifier, PSK, inhibits reverse transciptase in vitro. *Biochem. Biophys. Res. Commun.*149:562-567.

Hiroshi, S. and M. Takeda. 1993. Diverse biological activity of PSK (Krestin), a protein-bound polysaccharide from *Coriolus vesricolor* (Fr.) Quel. From *Mushroom Biology and Mushroom Products*. S.-t. Chang et al (eds.). Hong Kong: The Chinese University Press.

Hirotani, M. & T. Furuya. 1986. Ganoderic acid derivatives, highly oxygenated lanostane-type triterpenoids, from *Ganoderma Lucidum*. *Phytochemistry* 25:1189-1193.

Hirotani, M. et al. 1985. A ganoderic acid derivative, a highly oxygenated lanostane-type triterpenoid from *Ganoderma Lucidum*. *Phytochemistry* 24:2055-2061.

Hirotani, M. et al. 1986. Studies on the metabolites of higher fungi. Part 6. Ganoderic acids T,S and R, new triterpenoids from the cultured mycelia of *Ganoderma lucidum*. *Chem. Pharm. Bull.* 34:2282-2285. From CA105:94209m.

Hishida, I. et. al. 1988. Antitumor activity exhibited by orally administered extract from fruit body of *Grifola frondosa* (Maitake). *Chem. Pharm. Bull.* 36:1819-1827.

Hobbs, C. 1992. *Foundations of Health*. Capitola, CA: Botanica Press.

Hofmann, A. 1967. (Letter) in *Ethnopharmacologic search for psychoactive drugs*. From D. Efron et al. U.S. Public Health Service Pub. No. 1645.

Holland, B. et al. 1991. *Vegetables, Herbs and Spices—The Composition of Foods* (4th Edition). Letchworth, England: The Royal Society of Chemistry.

Hong, J.S. et al. 1990. Alcohols and volatile organic acids as stimulants of rhizomorph production by *Armillaria mellea*. *Han'guk Kyunhakhoechi* 18:158-163. From CA 114:139950a.

Horie, Y. et al. 1991. Dietary fiber in brown algae and mushrooms. *ASIAN FOOD J.* 6:32-33. From CA 115:157467y.

Horii, A. et al.1991. Multidisciplinary treatment for bladder carcinoma—biological response modifiers and kampo medicines. *Urol. Int.*, 47:108-112.

Hosokawa, M. et al. 1981. Importance of timing for combination in immunochemotherapy. In *Manipulation of Host Defense Mechanisms*, Aoki, T. et al. (eds.). Amsterdam: *Excerpta Medica* (International Congress Series 576).

Hotta, T. et al. 1981. Protein-bound polysaccharides. (US Patent); CA 95:185569v.

House, R.V. and P.T. Thomas. 1994. Immunological consequences of in vitro exposure to lysergic acid diethylamide (LSD). *Immunopharmacology and Immunotoxicology* 16:23-40.

Hou, C. et al. 1988. Chemical constituents of the spores from *Ganoderma lucidum*. *Acta Bot. Sin.* 22:837-840. From *Abstracts of Chinese Medicines* 2:145.

Hsu, Hong-Yen et al. 1986. *Oriental Materia Medica, a Concise Guide*. Long Beach: Oriental Healing Arts Institute.

Hu, B. and P. But. 1987. Chinese materia medica for radiation protection. *Abstracts of Chinese Medicines*. 1:475-490.

Huang, B-H.and S-T. Chang. 1984. Constituents of the lipid of *Tremella fuciformis*. *Acta Bot. Sin.* 26:66-70.

Huang, B.-H. et al. 1985. The sterol composition of *Volvariella volvacea* and other edible mushrooms. *Mycologia* 77:959-963.

Huang, C. et al. 1985. Pharmacological effects and diuretic action of polyporus. *Bull. Taipei Med.l Coll.* 14:57-68. From *Abstracts of Chinese Medicines*, 1:45.

Huang, K. C. 1993. *The Pharmacology of Chinese Herbs*. Boca Raton, FL: CRC Press.

Huang, S. et al. 1991. Effects of *Ganoderma lucidum* extracts and their constituents on the spontaneous beating of myocardial cell sheet in culture. *Shoyakugaku Zasshi* 45:132-136. From CA 116:120598m.

Huang, Y. et al. 1987. Toxicological studies on cultured *Cordyceps sinensis*, strain B414. *Zhongchengyao Yanjiu* (10):24-25. From *Abstracts of Chinese Medicines* 2:321.

Huidi, F. and W. Zhiyuan. 1982. The clinical effects of *Ganoderma lucidum* spore preparations in 10 cases of atrophic myotonia. *J. Trad. Chin. Med.* 2:63-65.

Hung-Cheh, C. and W. Mieng-hua. 1986. Improved assay for germanium in crude drugs. *J. Taiwan Pharm. Assoc.* 38:189-198. From *Abstracts of Chinese Medicines* 1:337.

Hutchens, A.R. 1973. *Indian Herbology of North America*. Windsor, Ontario: Merco.

Huxley, A. 1954. *The Doors of Perception*. New York: Harper Bros.

Iizuka, C. et al. 1990a. Antiviral composition extracts from basidiomycetes. Eur. Pat. Appl. EP 464,311. From CA 116: 76351z.

Iizuka, C. et al. 1990b. Extract of Basidomycetes especially *Lentinus edodes*, for treatment of human immunodeficiency virus (HIV). Shokin Kogyo Co., Ltd. Eur. Pat. Appl. EP 370,673 (Cl. 35/84) 30 May 1990, JP Appl. 88/287,316, 14 Nov 1988. From CA 114:95146m.

Ikebe, K et al. 1990. Behavior of several elements in food. IV. Contents of 17 metals elements in food determined by inductively coupled plasma atomic emission spectrometry. Vegetables, fruits, tubers, and mushrooms. *Shokuhin Eiseigaku Zasshi* 31:382-393. From CA 114:246012t.

Ikekawa, T. et al. 1968. Antitumor action of some Basidiomycetes, especially *Phellinus Linteus*. *Gann.* 59:155-157.

Ikekawa, T. et al. 1969. Antitumor activity of aqueous extracts of edible mushrooms. *Cancer Research* 29:734-735.

Ikuzawa, M. et al. 1985. Pharmaceutical preparation containing a glycoprotein. (German patent DE 3,429,551, Feb. 21, 1985). From CA 102:179063.

Imaki, M. 1991. Study on digestibility and energy availability of daily food intake (Part 4. Shiitake mushroom). *Nippon Eiseigaku Zasshi* 46:905-912.

Imazaki, R.Y. and T. Hongo. 1989. *Fungi of Japan*. Yama-kei.

Inaoka, Y. et al. 1994. Studies on active substances in herbs used for hair treatment. I. Effects of herb extracts on hair growth and isolation of an active substance from *Polyporus umbellatus* F. *Chem. Pharm. Bull.* 42:530-533.

Irinoda, K. et al. 1992. Stimulation of microbicidal host defence mechanisms against aerosol influenza virus infection by lentinan. *Int. J. Immunopharmacol.* 14:971-977.

Iseda, S. and K. Yagashita. 1956. Triterpenoids of *Poria cocos*. *Pharm. Soc. Japan* 76:970-971. From CA 2661a.

Ishigami, H. 1992. Relationship between prolonged life span and changes of serum IAP and albumin induced by the therapy of lentinan plus tegafur in inoperable and recurrent gastric cancer. *Nippon Geka Gakkai Zasshi* 93:800-804.

Ito, H. et al. 1972-1973. Studies on antitumor activity of basidiomycete polysaccharides I. Antitumor effect of wild and cultured basidiomycetes on sarcoma 180 subcutaneously implanted in mice. *Mie Med. J.* 22:103-113.

Ito, H. et al. 1973. Studies on antitumor activity of basidiomycete polysaccharides. IV. Antitumor effect of fungal and bacterial polysaccharides on mouse tumors. *Mie Med. J.* 23:117-127.

Ito, H. et al. 1976. Antitumor polysaccharide fraction from the culture filtrate of *Fomes fomentarius*. *Chem. Pharm. Bull.* 24:2575.

Ito, H. et al. 1987. Antitumor effect of pretreatment with polysaccharide from *Agaricus blazei* against solid sarcoma-180 in mice. *Igaku to Seibutsugaku*. 114:259-261.

Ito, K. and H. Hidaka. 1980a. *Coriolus versicolor* polysaccharide for improving hepatic function. (Patent). From CA 94:101304y.

Ito, K. and H. Hidaka. 1980b. *Coriolus versicolor* polysaccharide for improving blood vessel function. Jpn. Kokai Tokkyo Koho (Patent). From CA 94:101303x.

Iwaguchi, T. 1985. Drug evaluation by lymphocyte electrophoresis in tumor-bearing mice. *Recent Adv. Chemother., Proc. Int. Congr. Chemother., 14th*. 2:757-758. From CA 106:68k.

Izumi, T. 1981. Lentinan inhibition of suppressor cell activity in the murine immune reaction. From *Manipulation of Host Defence Mechanisms*, Aoki, T. et al (eds.). Amsterdam: *Excerpta Medica* (International Congress Series 576).

Jain, A.C. and S.K. Gupta. 1984. The isolation of lanosta-7,9(11),24-trien-3b,21-diol from the fungus *Ganoderma australe*. *Phytochemistry* 23:686-687.

James, J.S. 1986. Shiitake, Lentinan, and AIDS/ARC. *AIDS Treatment News* 19:1-6.

Japan Economic Journal, May 1, 1992: Anticancer mushroom agent shows anti-CFS activity.

Japanese N.I.H. 1990, 1991. Anti-HIV Activity, In-Vitro, exhibited by extract from fruit body of maitake mushroom (a preliminary unpublished study). October 29, 1990 and January 23, 1991.

Jaretzky, R. and K. Breitwieser. 1944. Investigations of native [German] plants on their suitability as laxatives. VI. *Polyporus officinalis* and other fungi. *Chem. Zentr.* II: 1295. From CA 42:7673a.

Jarosz, A. et al. 1990. Effect of the extracts from fungus *Inonotus obliquus* on catalase level in HeLa and nocardia cells. *Acta Biochim. Pol.* 37:149-151.

Jeong, H. et al. 1990. Studies on the anticomplementary activity of Korean higher fungi. *Han'guk Kyunhakhoechi* 18:145-148. From CA 115:21814b.

Jetter, A. 1994. Psychedlic cure: Getting off the junkie express. *Globe and Mail* (Toronto), April 30: D5.

Jia, Y. et al. 1993a. Effects of ling zhi on the production of interleukin-1 (IL-1). From From Zhu, S. and M. Mori (eds.). 1993. Influence of ling zhi on natural killer cells— Immunopharmacological Study (5). From *The Research on Ganoderma lucidum* (part one). Shanghai: Shanghai Medical University Press, pp. 254-258.

Jia, Y. et al. 1993b. Effects of ling zhi on hemopoietic system in mice. From From Zhu, S. and M. Mori (eds.). 1993. Influence of ling zhi on natural killer cells— Immunopharmacological Study (5). From *The Research on Ganoderma lucidum* (part one). Shanghai: Shanghai Medical University Press, pp. 284-288.

Jiang, G. et al. 1986. Immunologic basis of the antineoplastic action of the polysaccharides of *Lentinus edodes* and *Tricholoma mongolicum*. *Chin. Trad. Herb. Drugs.* 17:271,281. From *Abstracts of Chinese Medicines* 1:526.

Jingrong, W. 1979. *The Pinyin Chinese-English Dictionary*. Beijing: The Commercial Press.

Johnson, J. et al. 1963. Structure of a new glucan. *Chemistry and Industry.* May 18: 820-822.

Jones, K. 1992a. Reishi (Ganoderma) Longevity Herb of the Orient, Part 1. *Townsend Letter for Doctors* October: 814-818.

Jones, K. 1992b. Reishi (Ganoderma), Longevity Herb of the Orient, Part 2. *Townsend Letter for Doctors* November: 1008-1012.

Jones, K. 1994. Armana Research, Gibsons, B.C.; personal communication.

Jones, W.H.S. 1956. *Pliny: Natural History.* Cambridge: Harvard University Press. Botanical index edited by A.C. Andrews.

Jong, S.C. and J.M. Birmingham. 1992. Medicinal benefits of the mushroom Ganoderma. *Adv. Appl. Microbiol.* 37:101-134.

Josselyn, J. 1860. New England's rarities discovered. *Transactions and Collections of the American Antiquarian Society* 4:105-238.

Jung, J. 1981. Mycelium identification in wood destroying fungi, A. *Phytopathol. Z.* 100:19-38. From CA 94:136143x.

Junhua, C. and J. Ronglan. 1980. A pharmacognostical study of the Chinese drug Lingzhi (*Ganoderma*). *Acta Pharm. Sin.* 15:244.

Junshan, Y. et al.1984. Chemical constituents of *Armillaria mellea* mycelium I. Isolation and characterization of armillarin and armillaridin. *Planta Med.* 50:288-290.

Kabir, Y. and S. Kimura. 1989. Dietary mushrooms reduce blood pressure in spontaneously hypertensive rats (SHR). *J. Nutr. Sci. Vitaminol.* 35:91-94.

Kabir, Y. et al. 1987. Effect of shiitake (*Lentinus edodes*) and maitake (*Grifola frondosa*) mushrooms on blood pressure and plasma lipids of spontaneously hypertensive rats. *J. Nutr. Sci. Vitaminol.* 33:341-346.

Kabir, Y. et al. 1988. Dietary effect of *Ganoderma lucidum* mushroom on blood pressure and lipid levels in spontaneously hypertensive rats (SHR). *J. Nutr. Sci. Vitaminol.* 34:433-438.

Kac, D. et al. 1984. The major sterols from three species of polyporaceae. *Phytochemistry* 23:2686-2687.

Kahlos, K. et al. 1986. Antitumor activity of triterpenes in *Inonotus obliquus. Planta Med.* (6):554 (P109).

Kahlos, K. et al. 1986. Antitumor tests of inotodiol from the fungus *Inonotus obliquus. Acta Pharm. Fenn.* 95:173-177.

Kahlos, K. et al. 1987. Antitumor activity of some compounds and fractions from an n-hexane extract of *Inonotus obliquus. Acta Pharm. Fenn.* 96:33-40.

Kahlos, K. et al. 1987. Preliminary studies on the antitumor activity of polar fractions extracted from Inonotus obliquus. *Acta Pharm. Fenn.* 96:167-174.

Kahlos, K. 1988. Studies on triterpenes in *Inonotus obliquus. Acta Pharm. Fenn.* 97:73.

Kahlos, K. and R. Hiltunen. 1988. Gas chromatographic-mass spectrometric identification of some lanostanes from *Inonotus obliquus. Acta Pharm. Fenn.* 97:45-49.

Kakumu, S. et al. 1991. Effect of schizophyllan, a polysaccharide, on interferon Gama, antibody production and lymphocyte proliferation specific for hepatits B virus antigen in patients with chronic hepatitis B. *Int. J. Immunopharmacol.* 13:969-975.

Kakuta, M. et al. 1979. Comparative structural studies on acidic heteropolysaccharides isolated from shirokikurage fruitbody of *Tremella fuciformis* and the growing culture of its yeast-like cells. *Agric. Biol. Chem.*43:1659-1668.

Kalac, P. et al. 1989a. Contents of mercury, lead, and cadmium in mushrooms. *Cesk. Hyg.* 34:568-576. From CA 112:156890g.

Kalac, P. et al. 1989b. The contents of seven trace elements in edible mushrooms. *Sb. UVTIZ, Potravin. Vedy.* 7:131-136. From CA 111:230841q.

Kalac, P. et al. 1991. Concentrations of lead, cadmium, mercury and copper in mushrooms in the vacinity of a lead smelter. *Sci. Total Environ.* 105:109-119. From CA 115:98270d.

Kamasuka, T. et al. 1968. Antitumor activity of polysaccharide fractions prepared from some strains of basidiomycetes. *Gann.* 59:443-445.

Kanai, K. and E. Kondo. 1981. Immunomodulating activity of lentinan as demonstrated by frequency limitation effect on post-chemotherapy relapse in experimental mouse tuberculosis. From *Manipulation of Host Defence Mechanisms*, T. Aoki et al. (eds.). Amsterdam: *Excerpta Medica* (International Congress Series 576).

Kanai, K. et al. 1980. Immunopotentiating effect of fungal glucans as revealed by frequency limitation of postchemotherapy relapse in experimental mouse tuberculosis. *Jpn. J. Med. Sci. Biol.* 33:283-293.

Kanayama, H. et al. 1983. A new antitumor polysaccharide from the mycelia of *Poria cocos* Wolf. *Chem. Pharm. Bull.* 31:1115-1118. From CA 99:115654c.

Kanayama, H. et al. 1986. Studies on the antitumor active polysaccharides from the mycelia of *Poria cocos* Wolf. I. Fractionation and purification of antitumor polysaccharide Hn. *Yakugaku Zasshi* 106:199.

Kandefer-Szerszen, M. et al. 1979. Fungal nucleic acids as interferon inducers. *Acta Microbiol. Pol.* 28:277-291. From CA 93:37225y.

Kaneko, Y. and G. Chihara. 1992. Potentiation of host resistance against microbial infections by lentinan and its related polysaccharides. *Adv. Exp. Med. Biol.* 319:201-215.

Kanmatsuse, K. et al. 1985. Studies on *Ganoderma lucidum*. I. Efficacy against hypertension and side effects. *Yakugaku Zasshi* 105:942-947.

Kapich, A. et al. 1992. Biosynthesis of prostaglandins catalyzed by enzymes of wood-rotting basidiomycetes. *Dokl. Akad. Nauk SSSR* 322:604-606. From CA 116:169896w.

Kari, P.R. 1977. *Dena'ina K'et'una (Tanaina Plantlore)*. Anchorage, Alaska: Adult Literacy Laboratory, Anchorage Community College:159.

Kasahara, Y. and H. Hikino. 1987. Central actions of *Ganoderma lucidum. Phytotherapy Research* 1:17-21.

Kasamatsu, T. 1982. The radiation of sensitizing effect of PSK in the treatment for the cervical cancer patients. From Yamamura, Y et al. (eds.) Immunomodulation by microbial products and related synthetic compounds. Amsterdam: Excerpta Medica, pp. 463-466.

Kato, K. et al. 1989. Chemical Features of Water-Soluble Polysaccharides in the Fruit Body of *Grifola frondosa*. Gifu Daigaku Nogakubu Kenkyu Hokoku: 199-203. From CA 113:37718t.

Kato, K. et al. 1990. An alkali-soluble a-D-glucan from the fruiting body of *Grifola frondosa*. *Carbohydr. Res.* 198:149-152.

Kato, T. et al. 1979. Reduction of serum X-prolyl dipeptidyl-aminopeptidase activity in tumour-bearing mice and reversal of reduced enzyme activity by lentinan, an anti-tumor polysaccharide. *Experientia* 35:409-411.

Kavanagh, F. et al. 1950. Antibiotic substances from Basidiomycetes V. *Poria corticola, Poria tenius* and an unidentified basidiomycetes. *Proceedings of the Nat'l.Academy of Sciences* 36:1-7.

Kawagishi, H. et al. 1990. Isolation and characterization of a lectin from *Grifola frondosa* fruiting bodies. *Biochim. Biophys. Acta* 1034:247-252.

Kawaguchi, N. and H. Yamada. 1987. Branching frequency of anti-tumor 6-O-branched (1—3)-ß-D-glucan from *Cordyceps ophioglossoides*. *Agric. Biol. Chem.* 51:2805-2806.

Kawai, G. 1989. Molecular species of cerebrosides in fruiting bodies of *Lentinus edodes* and their biological activity. *Biochim. Biophys. Acta* 1001:185-190.

Kawana, T. 1985. Treatment of recurrent genital herpes with PS-K. Proceedings of the International Symposium on Pharmacological and Clinical Approaches to Herpes Viruses and Virus Chemotherapy. Oiso, Japan, Sept. 10-13, 1984. Kono, R. and A. Nakajima, eds. *Herpes Viruses and Chemotherapy: Pharmacological and Clinical Approaches.* Amsterdam: *Excerpta Medica*: 271-272.

Kawecki, Z. et al. 1978. Studies of RNA isolated from *Piptoporus betulinus* as interferon inducer. *Arch. Immun. Ther. Exper.* 26:517-522.

Kaye, G.C. 1984. *Wild and Exotic Mushroom Cultivation in North America.* Cambridge: Harvard University.

Keewaydinoquay. 1978. *Puhpohwee for the People.* Cambridge: Botanical Museum of Harvard University.

Kempska, K. et al. 1962. Investigation of chemical components of *Inonotus obliquus.* VI. 3b-hydroxylanosta-8,24-dien-21-oic acid. *Roczniki Chem.* 36:1453-1457.

Khoda, H. et al. 1985. The biologically active constituents of *Ganoderma lucidum* (Fr.) Karst. Histamine Release-inhibitory triterpenes. *Chem.Pharm. Bull.* 33:1367-1374.

Kier, L.B. 1961. Triterpenes of *Poria obliqua. J. Pharm. Soc.* 50:471-474.

Kiho, T. et al. 1990. Polysaccharides in fungi. XXV. Biological activities of two galactomannans from the insect-body portion of Chan hua (fungus: Cordyceps cicadae). *Yakugaku Zasshi Shigeo* 110:286-288. From CA 113:34550w.

Kikuchi, T. et al. 1985a. Ganoderic acid D, E, F, and H and lucidenic acid D,E, and F, new triterpenoids from *Ganoderma lucidum. Chem. Pharm. Bull.* 33:2624-2427. From CA 103:175028n.

Kikuchi, T. et al. 1985b. Ganoderic acid G and I and ganolucidic acid A and B, new triterpenoids from *Ganoderma lucidum. Chem. Pharm. Bull..* 33:2628-2631 (Eng.). From CA 103:156944s.

Kikumoto, S. et al. 1970. Polysaccharide produced by *Schizophyllum commune*, Part I: Formation and some properties of an extracellular polysaccharide. *Nippon Nogeigaguku.* 44:337-342.

Kim, C. et al. 1990. Studies on constituents of higher fungi of Korea. (LXIV). Constituents of cultured and fused mycelia of *Ganoderma lucidum. Soul Taehakkyo Yakhak Nonmunjip.* 15:38-71. From CA 115:251763p.

Kim, Q. et al. 1979. Studies on the constituents of the higher fungi of Korea. VIII. Sterols of *Coriolus versicolor. Hanguk Kyunhakhoe Chi.* 6:1-4. From CA. 91:35749g.

Kim, B.K. et al. 1993. Antitumor components of *Collybia.* From *Mushroom Biology and Mushroom Products.* S.-t. Chang et al (eds.). Hong Kong: The Chinese University Press, 301-303.

Kim, B.K. et al. 1994. Anti-HIV activities of *Ganoderma lucidum.* From *Fifth International Mycological Congress Abstracts.* Vancouver, BC, August 14-21, 1994.

Kimoto, M. et al. 1976. Effects of "shiitake" mushroom on plasma and liver lipid contents in rats. *Eiyo To Shokuryo.* 29:275-281. From CA 86:42183t.

King, J. and J.U. Lloyd. 1895. *The American Dispensatory.* Cincinnati: The Ohio Valley Co.

King, T. 1993. Mushrooms, the ultimate health food but little research in U.S. to prove it. *Mushroom News* February: 26-29.

Kiribuchi, T. 1990. Study on vitamin D2 contents of various fungi by ultraviolet light irradiation. *Nippon Kasei Gakkaishi* 41:401-406. From CA 113: 148046g.

Kiribuchi, T. 1991. Effective uses of fungi by UV irradiation. 3. Changes of free amino acid composition in fungi by sun or ultraviolet light irradiation. *Nippon Kasei Gakkaishi* 42:415-21. From CA 115:130700g.

Kneifel, H. et al. 1977. Ophiocordin, an antifungal antibiotic of *Cordyceps ophioglossoides. Arch. Microbiol.* 113:121-130.

Kobayashi, T. et al. 1988. Shiitake and vitamin D. *Vitamin* 62:483-490. From CA 109:20988.

Koga, J. et al. 1991. Anti-viral fraction of aqueous *Lentinus edodes* extract. Eur. Pat. Appl. EP 437,346 (Cl. C12pa/02), JP appl. 90/3,818. From CA 115:134197w.

Kohda, H. et al. 1985. The biologically active constituents of *Ganoderma lucidum* (Fr.)KARST. Histamine release-inhibitory triterpenes. *Chem. Pharm. Bull.* 33:1367-1374.

Kojima, M. et al. 1991. Fatty Acid Distribution and Molecular Species of Glycerophospholipids from Maitake Mycellium and Fruiting Body. *Yukagaku* 40:53-57.

Komatsu, N. et al. 1969. Host-mediated antitumor action of schizophyllan, a glucan produced by *Schizophyllum Commune. Gann.* 60:137-144.

Komatsu, N. et al. 1973. Protective effect of schizophyllan on bacterial infections of mouse. *Jpn. J. Antibiot.* 26:283.

Komoda, Y. et al. 1985. Structures of new terpenoid constituents of Ganoderma lucidum (Fr.)Karst (Polyporaceae). *Chem. Pharm. Bull.* 33:4829-4835.

Konishi, H. et al. 1988. Polysaccharides-contg. extracts from Heterobasidiae as antiinflammatory agents. Jpn. Kokai Tokkyo Koho JP 63,183,537 [88,183,537]. From CA 111:9559lr.

Kosaka, A. et al. 1985. Synergistic effect of Lentinan and surgical endocrine therapy on the growth of DMBA-induced mammary tumors of rats and of recurrent human breast cancer. *Int. Congr. Ser.-Excerpta Medica.* 690:138-150. From CA. 104: 81628b.

Kosuge, T. et al. 1985. Studies on antitumor activities and antitumor principles of Chinese herbs. I. Antitumor activities of Chinese herbs. *Yakugaku Zasshi*, 105:791-795.

Kramer, P.D. 1993. *Listening to Prozac.* New York: Viking.

Kretz, O. et al. 1991. Characterization of bolestine, a toxic protein from the mushroom Boletus satanas Lenz and its effects on kidney cells. *Toxicology* 66:213-224.

Kubo, K. et al. 1993. Therapeutic effect of maitake mushroom for diabetes mellitus. From *First International Conference on Mushroom Biology and Mushroom Products, Programme and Abstracts.* The Chinese University of Hong Kong, August 23-26, 1993, Hong Kong. Shatin, Hong Kong: Chinese University Press: 131 (P-2-38).

Kubo, K. et al. 1994. Anti-diabetic activity present in the fruit body of *Grifola frondosa* (Maitake). I. *Biol. Pharm. Bull.* 17:1106-1110.

Kubo, M. 1983. Studies on *Ganoderma lucidum.* IV. Effects on the disseminated intravascular coagulation. *Yakugaku Zasshi* 103:871-887.

Kumari, H. and M. Sirsi. 1972. Purification and properties of laccase from *Ganoderma lucidum. Arch. Mikrobiol.* 84:350-357.

Kumari, H. et al. 1971. Purification and properties of endopolygalacturonase from *Ganoderma lucidum. J. Gen. Microbiol.* 65:285-290. From CA 75:71669j.

Kurashima, Y. et al. 1990. Marked formation of thiazolidine-4-carboxylic acid, an effective nitrite trapping agent in vivo, on boiling of dried shiitake mushroom (*Lentinus edodes*). *J. Agric. Food Chem.* 38:1945-1949. From CA 113: 151069g.

Kureha Chemical Industry Co. 1978. Use of polysaccharides containing nitrogen for promoting the drug-sensitivity antibiotic-resistant bacteria. (German patent 2,816,087); CA 90:12294v.

Kurtzman, R.H., Jr. 1993. Analysis, digestibility and the nutritional value of mushrooms. From *Mushroom Biology and Mushroom Products.* S.-t. Chang et al (eds.). Hong Kong: The Chinese University Press.

Kuznetsovs, S. and K. Jegina. 1993. Experimental and clinical development of *Phallus impudicus* (stinkhorn mushroom). Stockholm: Abstract published in the Proceedings of the 18th International Congress of Chemotherapy.

Kuznetsovs, S. et al. 1993. Studies concerning the effect of stinkhorn mushroom juice in vitro. Pharmex Research Laboratory, Latvian Medical Academy.

Ladanyi, A. et al. 1993. Effect of lentinan on macrophage cytotoxicity against metastatic tumor cells. *Cancer Immunol. Immunother.* 36:123-126.

Larionov, L.F. 1965. *Cancer Chemotherapy*. Translated from the Russian by A. Crozy. New York: Pergamon Press. As quoted by Heinerman, J. *The Treatment of Cancer with Herbs*. Orem: Biworld Pub.

Lasota, W. and J. Sylwestrzak. 1989. Chemical composition of cultivated mushrooms. Part III. Shiitake *Lentinus edodes* (Berk) Sing. *Bromatol. Chem. Toksykol.* 22:167-171. From CA 114:205741m.

Lawson, J.H. 1937, [1714]. *History of North Carolina*. Richmond: Garret & Massie.

Lee, E.B. et al. 1977. Plants and animals used for fertility regulation in Korea. *Korean J. Pharmacogn.* 8:81-87.

Lee, J.W. et al. 1992. Screening of hepatoprotective substances from higher fungi by primary cultured rat hepatocytes intoxicated with carbon tetrachloride. *Korean J. Mycol.* 20:347-353.

Lee, K.S. et al. 1982. Studies on the antibacterial activity of *Poria cocos. Korean J. Mycol.* 10:27-31.

Lee, S.J. 1966. *Korean Folk Medicine*, Monograph Ser. 3. Seoul: Seoul Natl. Univ. Publ. Ctr.

Lei, L. and Z. Lin. 1991. Effects of Ganoderma polysaccharides on the activity of DNA polymerase *a* in spleen cells stimulated by alloantigens in mice in vitro. *Beijing Yike Daxue Xuebao* 23:329-333. From CA 117:62556d.

Li, C. and X. Liu. 1987. Analysis and comparison of amino acid content in fungal mycelia and fermentation broth. *Nanjing Daxue Xuebao, Ziran Kexue*, 23:442-452. From CA 108:74007c.

Li, C.P. 1974. *Chinese Herbal Medicine*. U.S. Dept. of Health, Education, and Welfare. Public Health Service. National Institutes of Health, Washington, D.C., DHEW Publ. No. (NIH) 75-7320.

Li, M. 1985. Review on the studies of antineoplastic fungal polysaccharides. *Jiangxi Zhongyiyao* 59-61, 63. From *Abstracts of Chinese Medicines* 1:444.

Li, S. 1973. *Chinese Medicinal Herbs*. San Francisco: Georgetown Press.

Lin, J. et al. 1974. Cardiotoxic protein from edible mushrooms. *Nature* 252:235-237.

Lin, Y. and G. Wu. 1988. Protective effect of *Polyporous umbellatus* polysaccharide on toxic hepatitis in mice. 9:345-348. From *Abstracts of Chinese Medicines* 2:397.

Lin, Y. et al. 1987. A double-blind treatment of 72 cases of chronic hepatitis with Lentinan injection. *New Drugs and Clinical Remedies* 6:362-363. From *Abstracts of Chinese Medicines* 2:325.

Lin, Z. et al. 1982. Studies on the pharmacology of *Tremella fuciformis*, preliminary research on the fermented solution and polysacchrides of *Tremella fuciformis* spores. *J. Trad. Chin. Med.* 2:95-98.

Lin, Z. and Y. Huang. 1987. Protective action of Lentinan against experimental liver injuries. *Journal of Beijing Medical University* 19:93-95. From *Abstracts of Chinese Medicines* 2:288.

Lin, Z.-B. 1993. Advances in the pharmacology of *Tremella* polysaccharides. . From *Mushroom Biology and Mushroom Products*. S.-t. Chang et al (eds.). Hong Kong: The Chinese University Press, 293-298.

Lin, J.-M. et al. 1993. Evaluation of the anti-inflammatory and liver-protective effects of *Anoectochilus formosanus, Ganoderma lucidum* and *Gynostemma pentaphyllum* in rats. *Amer. J. Chin. Med.* 21:59-69.

Lincoff, G. 1981. *The Audubon Society Field Guide to North American Mushrooms*. New York: Alfred A. Knopf.

Lincoff, G. and D.H. Mitchel. 1977. *Toxic and Hallucinogenic Mushroom Poisoning*. New York: Van Nostrand Reinhold Co.

Lindberg et al. 1977. Isolation and structure of coprine, the in vivo aldehyde dehydrogenase inhibitor in *Coprinus atramentarius*; synthesis of coprine and related cyclopropanone derivatives. *J. Chem. Soc. Perkin Trans.* I:684-691.

Lindequist, U. et al. 1990. New Active Substances from Basidiomycetes. *Zeitschrift für Phyto-Therapy* 11:139-149.

Lindley, J. and T. Moore. 1876. *Treasury of Botany*. London: Longmans.

Lindley, John. 1830. *Introduction to the Natural System of Botany*. London: Longman, Rees, Orme, Brown and Green.

Linnaeus, C. 1749. *Materia Medica*. Holmiae. Laurentii Salvii.

Lipske, M. 1994. A new gold rush packs the woods in central Oregon. *Smithsonian* January:34-45.

List, P.H. and L. Hörhammer. 1973. *Hagers Handbuch der Pharmazeutischen Praxis*, 7 vols. New York: Springer-Verlag.

Liu, B. et al. 1985. A new species of the genus *Cordyceps*. *J. Wuhan Bot. Res.* 3:23-24. From *Abstracts of Chinese Medicines* 1:248.

Liu, C. et al. 1992b. Effects of *Cordyceps sinensis* on *in vitro* natural killer cells. *Chung-Kuo,Chung Hsi I Chieh Ho Tsa Chih* 12: 267-269, 259.

Liu, G. et al. 1979. Comparison of the protective actions of dimethy-lbiphenyldicarboxylate, trans-stilbene, alcoholic extract of Polyporus japonicus and Ganoderma towards experimental liver injury in mice. *Y. Hsueh Hsueh Pao* 14:598-604. From CA 93:542y.

Liu, G.-T. 1993. Pharmacology and clinical uses of *Ganoderma*. From *Mushroom Biology and Mushroom Products*. S.-t. Chang et al (eds.). Hong Kong: The Chinese University Press, 267-273.

Liu, J. et al. 1989. Studies on the chemical constituents of *Cordyceps militaris* (L.) Link. *Zhongguo Zhohgyao Zazhi* 14:608-609. From CA 112:104644k.

Liu, S. et al. 1985. Effects of *Radix Astragali* and *Polystictus versicolor* on the phagocytic and bactericidal actions of leukocytes. *Chin. J. Int. Trad. West.Med.* 5:423-425. From *Abstracts of Chinese Medicines* 1:52-53.

Liu, S.H. et al. 1994. Inhibition effect of *Tremella fuciformis* Berk preparation (TFB) on growth of transplanted mouse tumor cells. *Zhong Guo Zhong Liu Lin Chuang* 21:68-70.

Liu, W.K. et al. 1993. Immunomodulatory activities of mushroom mycelial extracts. . From *Mushroom Biology and Mushroom Products*. S.-t. Chang et al (eds.). Hong Kong: The Chinese University Press, 285-290.

Liu, Z. et al. 1988. Effect of Lentinan on lymphocyte transformation in mice. *J. Lanzhou Med. Coll.* 54-55. From *Abstracts of Chinese Medicines* 2:311.

Locke, S.E. and M. Hornig-Rohan. 1983. *Mind and Immunity: Behavioral Immunology: An Annotated Bibliography 1976-1982*. New York: Institute for the Advancement of Health.

Lou, F. et al. 1988. Natural antineoplastic compounds and their structure-activity relationships. *Abstracts of Chinese Medicines*. 2:484-495.

Loviagina, E.V. and A.N. Shivrina. 1962. Steroids of the chaga fungus. *Biokhimiya* 27:794-800.

Lovyagina, E.V. et al. 1958. Hydrolytic products of the active principle of bracket fungi studied by the method of partition chromatography. *Biokhimiya* (Leningrad) 23:41-46.

Lowe, J.L. and R.L. Gilbertson. 1961. Synopsis of the Polyporaceae of the western United States and Canada. *Mycologia* 53:473-511.

Lozoya, X. 1976. *Estado Actual del Conocimiento en Plantas Medicinales Mexicanas*. Imeplam AC Mexico DF 12, Mexico. From Napralert, K04688.

Lucas, E.H. 1960. Folklore and plant drugs. In *Papers of the Michigan Academy of Science, Arts, and Letters* 45:127-136.

Lucas, E.H. et al. 1957. Tumor inhibitors in *Boletus edulis* and other Holobasidiomycetes. *Antibiotics & Chemotherapy* 7:1-4.

Ludwig, A.M. et al. 1970. *LSD and alcoholism; a clinical study of treatment efficacy*. Springfield, IL: Thomas.

Ludwiczak, R.S. and U. Wrzeciono. 1961. Active substances of *Inonotus obliquus*. *Acta Pharm. Hung.* 31:17-21.

Ludwiczak, R.S. and U. Wrzeciono. 1962. Investigation of chemical components of *Inonotus obliquus*. *Roczniki Chem.* 36:497-502.

Lui, X. 1994. Hepatopathy and uterofunctional bleeding mainly treated with *Ganoderma lucidum*. From Program and Abstracts of the '94 International Symposium on Ganoderma Research. Beijing: Beijing Medical University.

Ma, L. and Z. Lin. 1992. Effect of Tremella polysaccharide on IL-2 production by mouse splenocytes. *Yaoxue Xuebao* 27:1-4. From CA 116:187661v.

Ma, X. et al. 1986. Survey of the ecology of *Cordyceps Barnesii. Bull. Chin. Mat. Med.*11:13-14. From *Abstracts of Chinese Medicines* 1:249.

Madaus, G. 1938. *Handbook of Biological Medicine*, 3 vols. (in German). Reprinted by Georg Olms Verlag, NY.

Maeda, Y.Y. and G. Chihara. 1973. The effects of neonatal thymectomy on the antitumor activity of lentinan, carboxymethylpachymaran and zymosan, and their effects on various immune responses. *Int. J. Cancer* 11:153.

Maeda, Y.Y. and G. Chihara. 1977. Lentinan, a new immunoaccelerator of cell-mediated responses. *Nature* 222:634.

Maeda, Y.Y. et al. 1974a. Unique increase of serum protein components and action of antitumour polysaccharides. *Nature* 252:250.

Maeda, Y.Y. et al. 1974b. The nature of immunopotentiation by the anti-tumour polysaccharide lentinan and the significance of biogenic amines in its action. *Int. J. Cancer* 259-281.

Mahy, W.J. et al. 1972. Inhibition of influenza virus replication by a-amanitin: mode of action. *Proc. Nat. Acad. Sci. U.S.A.*, 69:1421-1424.

Maiwald, L. 1987. Bitterstoffe. *Zeit. f. Phytother.* 8:186-188.

Malone, M.H. et al. 1967. Hippocratic screening of sixty-six species of higher fungi. *Lloydia* 30:250-257.

Manu-Tawiah, W. and A. Martin. Chemical composition of *Pleurotus ostreatus* mycelial biomass. *Food Microbiol.* 4:303-310. From CA 109:91524g.

Martinez, M. 1959. *Plantas Medicinales de Mexico*. Toro de Lazarin, Mexico: M. Leon Sanchez.

Mashiko, H. et al. 1992. A case of advanced gastric cancer with liver metastasis completely responding to a combined immunochemotherapy with UFT, mitomycin C and lentinan. *Gan To Kagaku Ryoho* 19:715-718.

Matsuki, M. et al. 1990. Extraction of antiteratogenic glycoproteins from Basidiomycetes. Kokai Tokkyo Koho Japanese Patent 02 49,732 [90 49,732]. From CA 113:120776f.

Matsumoto, K. 1979. *The Mysterious Reishi Mushroom*. Santa Barbara: Woodbridge Press Publishing Company.

Matsunaga, K. et al. 1987. Restoration of immune responsiveness by a biological response modifier, PSK, in aged mice bearing syngeneic transplantable tumor. *J. Clin. Lab. Immunol.* 24:143-149.

Mayer, P. and J. Drews. 1980. The effect of a protein-bound polysaccharide from *Coriolus versicolor* on immunological Parameters and experimental infections in mice. *Infection.* 8:13-21. From CA 92:209810h.

McDonald, A. 1980. Mushrooms and Madness; Hallucinogenic Mushrooms and Some Psychopharmacological Implications. *Can. J. Psychiatry* 25:586-593.

McIlvaine, C. and R.K. Macadam. 1973 (1902). *One Thousand American Fungi*. New York: Dover Publications.

McRae, M. 1993. Dodging death among the fairy rings. *Sacramento Bee*, Oct. 17:1,6.

Meng, X. et al. 1987. Interferon inducing effect of some Chinese drugs on human umbilical leucocytes. *Shanghai Journal of Traditional Chinese Medicine*. 7:30-31. From *Abstracts of Chinese Medicines*, 2:166.

Merck & Co. 1907. *Merck's 1907 Index*. New York: Merck & Co.

Mikami, Y. et al. 1989a. Plant virucide and its manufacture with Fomes. Kokai Tokkyo Koho Japanese Patent 01,179,691 [89,179,691]. From CA 112:137577u.

Mikami,Y. et al. 1989b. Plant virus-inhibitory high-molecular-weight polysaccharide F-Ab and its manufacture with Fomes. Jpn. Kokai Tokkyo Koho JP 01,1179,692 [89,179,692]. From CA112:137553h.

Miller, D. 1994. Current clinical protocol submitted to the N.I.H. Scientific Director Cancer Treatment Research Foundation, Arlington Heights, IL.

Miller, O.K. 1979. *Mushrooms of North America*. New York: E.P. Dutton.

Mimura, H. et al. 1985. Purification, antitumor activity, and structural characterization of ß-1,3-glucan from *Peziza vesiculosa*. *Chem. Pharm. Bull.* 33:5096-5099. From CA 104:61640w.

Misaki, A. et al. 1981. Studies on interrelation of structure and antitumor effects of polysaccharides: Antitumor action of periodate-modified, branched (1-3)–ß-d-Glucan of *Auricularia auricula-judae*, and other polysaccharides containing (1-3)-Glycosidic Kikurages). *Carbohyd. Res.* 92:115-129.

Mitomi, T. et al. 1992. Randomized, controlled study on adjuvant immunochemotherapy with PSK in curatively resected colorectal cancer. *Dis. Colon Rectum* 35:123-130.

Mitomo, K. et al. 1980. Health food Material from *Coriolus Versicolor*. (Japanese Patent Cl. A61K35/84). From CA 93:44388g.

Miyakoshi, H. et al. 1981. Immunopotentiating activity of Lentinan. From *Manipulation of Host Defence Mechanisms*, Aoki, T. et al (eds.). Amsterdam: *Excerpta Medica* (International Congress Series 576).

Miyakoshi, H., and T. Aoki. 1984a. Acting mechanisms of Lentinan in human - I. Augmentation of DNA synthesis and immunoglobulin production of peripheral mononuclear cells. *J. Immunopharmacol.* 6:365-371.

Miyakoshi, H., and T. Aoki. 1984b. Acting mechanisms of Lentinan in human - II. Enhancement of non-specific cell-mediated cytotoxicity as an interferon inducer. *J.Immunopharmacol.* 6:373-379.

Miyasita, S. 1976. A historical study of Cinses drugs for the treatment of jaundice. *Amer. J. Chin. Med.* 4:239.

Miyazaki, T. 1983. Relationship between the chemical structure and antitumor activity of basidiomycete glucans. *Shinkin to Shinkinsho* 24:95-101. From CA 100:79551v.

Miyazaki, T. and M. Nishijima. 1981. Studies on fungal polysaccharides. XXVII. Structural examination of a water-soluble, antitumor polysaccharide of *Ganoderma lucidum*. *Chem. Pharm. Bull.* 29:3611-3616.

Miyazaki, T. et al. 1974. Chemical structure of antitumor polysaccharide, coriolan, produced by *Coriolus versicolor*. *Chem. Pharm. Bull.* 22:1739-1742.

Miyazaki, T. et al. 1978. Structural examination of antitumour, water-soluble glucans from *Grifola umbellata* by use of four types of glucanase. *Carbohyd. Res.* 65:235-243.

Miyazaki, T. et al. 1979. Relationship between the chemical structure and antitumour activity of glucans prepared from *Grifola umbellata*. *Carbohyd. Res.* 69:165-170.

Mizoguchi, Y. et al. 1987a. Effects of extract of cultured *Lentinus edodes* mycelia (LEM) on polyclonal antibody response induced by pokeweed mitogen. *Gastroenterol. Jpn.* 22:627-632.

Mizoguchi, Y. et al. 1987b. Protection of liver cells against experimental damage by extract of cultured *Lentinus edodes* Mycelia (LEM). *Gastroenterol. Jpn.* 22:459-464.

Mizuhira, V. et al. 1985. Histological and cytochemical studies on the distribution of schizophyllan glucan (SPG) in cancer-inoculated animal: I. Differences in distribution and antitumor activity of ^{3}H-SPG in sarcoma-180 inoculated females between ICR and DBA mice. *Acta Histochem. Cytochem.* 18:221-254.

Mizuno, D. 1981. A possible parameter to classify immunomodulators. From *Manipulation of Host Defence Mechanisms*, Aoki, T. et al (eds.). Amsterdam: *Excerpta Medica* (International Congress Series 576).

Mizuno, T. 1985. Franctionation, structure and anticancer activity of Sarunokoshikake polysaccharide. *Dojin Nyusu* 34:1-11. From CA 106:112985p.

Mizuno, T. and S. Sakamura. 1985. Medicinal and dietary effects of Man-nen-take (Reishi). Antitumor polysaccharides and bitter terpenoids. *Kagaku to Seibutsu* 23:797-802. From CA 104:230280m.

Mizuno, T. et al. 1982. Studies on the host-mediated antitumor polysaccharides. Part VI. Isolation and characterization of antitumor active ß-D-glucan from mycelial cells of *Ganoderma applanatum*. *Bull. Fac. Agric., Shizuoka Univ.* 32:41-58.

Mizuno, T. et al. 1984. Fractionation, structural features and antitumor activity of water-soluble polysaccharide from "Reishi: the fruit body of *Ganoderma lucidum*. *Nippon Nogei Kagaku Kaishi* 58:871-880. From CA 101:226886j.

Mizuno, T. et al. 1986. Fractionation and characterization of antitumor polysaccharides from Maitake (*Grifola frondosa*). *Agric. Biol. Chem.* 50:1679-1688.

Mizuno, T. et al. 1988. Antitumor polysaccharides. XII. Immunostimulative antitumor effects of ß-D-glucans and chitin substances isolated from some medicinal mushrooms. *Shizuoka Daigaku Nogakubu Kenkyu Hokoku.* 29-35. From CA 111:33186d.

Mizuno, T. et al. 1992. Studies on the host-mediated antitumor polysaccharides. Part XVI. Antitumor activity of polysaccharides isolated from an edible mushroom, Ningyotake, the fruiting body and cultured mycelium of *Polyporous confluens*. *Biosci., Biotechnol., Biochem.* 56:34-41.

Moon, S.K. et al. 1987. Studies on the fatty acids in the white *Poria cocos*. *Han Guk Kyunhakhoechi* 15:9-13.

Mooney, J.Y., and F.M. Olbrechts. 1932. *The Swimmer Manuscript* (Cherokee sacred formulas and medicinal prescriptions). *Smithsonian Institution, Bureau of American Ethnology.* 99.

Moore-Landecker, E. 1972. *Fundamentals of the Fungi*. Englewood Cliffs, N.J.: Prentice-Hall.

Mori, K. et al. 1987. Antitumor activities of edible mushrooms by oral administration. From Wuest, P.J. et al. (eds.), *Cultivating Edible Fungi*. Amsterdam: Elsevier:1-6.

Morita, K., *et al.* 1985. Chemical Nature of a Desmutagenic Factor from Burdock (*Arctium lappa* Linne). *Agric. Biol. Chem.* 49:925-932.

Moriyama, M. et al. 1981. Anti-tumor effect of polysaccharide Lentinan on transplanted ascites hepatoma-134 in C3H/He mice. From *Manipulation of Host Defence Mechanisms*, Aoki, T. et al (eds.). Amsterdam: *Excerpta Medica* (International Congress Series 576).

Mottin, J.L. 1973. Drug-induced attenuation of alcohol consumption. A review and evaluation of claimed, potential or current therapies. *Q. J. Stud. Alcohol* 34:444-472.

Murray, F. 1994. Maitake mushrooms, culinary medicine. *Better Nutrition for Today's Living* Feb.:42-43.

Murray, J.A.H. et al. 1933. *The Oxford English Dictionary*. London: Oxford University Press.

Naeshiro, H. et al. 1992a. Skin-lightening compositions containing *Fomes japonicus* extracts. *Jpn. Kokai Tokkyo Koho* JP04,09,314 [92,09,314]. From CA 116:158604y.

Naeshiro, H. et al. 1992b. Skin-lightening compositions containing Ganoderma extract. *Jpn. Kokai Tokkyo Koho* JP 04 09,315 [92 09,315]. From CA 116:158605z.

Naeshiro, H. et al. 1992c. Skin-lightening cosmetics containing culture products of *Fomes japonicus* and their extracts and ginseng extracts, sodium chondroitin sulfate, and hyaluronic acid. *Jpn. Kokai Tokkyo Koho* JP 04 09,316 [92 09,316]. From CA 116:158607b.

Naeshiro, H. et al. 1992d. Skin-lightening cosmetics containing Ganoderma lucidum extract and vitamins. *Jpn. Kokai Tokkyo Koho* JP 04 09,325 [92 09,325]. From CA 116:158610x.

Nakajima, Y. et al. 1989. Foods and drinks containing cholesterol-controlling *Tremella fuciformis*. *Jpn. Kokai Tokkyo Koho* JP 01 20,070 [89 20,070] (Cl. A23L1/28), 24 Jan, 1989.

Nakamura, K.et al. 1986. Suppression of phosphofructokinase (PFK) by sera from cancer patients, and mechanism of antagonistic effect of PSK. *Gan to Kagaku Ryoho*, 13:970-976. From CA 105:35267f.

Nakamura, T. 1992. Shiitake (*Lentinus edodes*) dermatitis. *Contact dermatitis*, 27:65-70.

Nakamura, T. and A. Kobayashi. 1985. Toxicodermia caused by the edible mushroom shiitake (*Lentinus edodes*). *Hautarzt.* 36:591-593.

Nakao, I. et al. 1983. Clinical evaluation of schizophyllan (SPG) in advanced gastric cancer—a randomized comparative study by an envelope method. *Gan To Kagaku Ryoho*, 10:1146-1159.

Namba, T. 1980. *Genshoku Wakanyaku Zukan*. Osaka: Hoikusha:247.

Namba, T. et al. 1981. Studies on dental caries prevention by traditional Chinese Medicines. Part I. Screening of crude drugs for antibacterial action against *Streptococcus mutans*. *Shoyakugaku Zassi* 35:295-302.

Nanba, H. and H. Kuroda 1987. Antitumor mechanisms of orally administered shiitake fruit bodies. *Chem. Pharm. Bull.* 35:2459-2464.

Nanba, H. et al. 1987. Antitumor action of Shiitake (*Lentinus edodes*) fruit bodies orally administered to mice. *Chem. Pharm. Bull.* 35:2453-2458.

Nanba, H. 1991. Report from the Japan Pharmaceutical Conference. October, 1991. From M. Shirota, Maitake Products, Inc.

Nanba, H. et al. 1992. Immunostimulant activity in-vivo and anti-HIV activity in vitro of 3 branched b-1-6 glucans extracted from maitake mushroom (*Grifola frondosa*). From the VIII International Conference on AIDS and the III STD World Congress. Published abstracts.

Nanba, H. 1993. Antitumor activity of orally administered "D-fraction" from Maitake mushroom (*Grifola frondosa*). *J. Naturopathic Med.* 4:10-15.

Nanba, H. 1994a. Power of maitake mushroom. *Explore Professional* (in press).

Nanba, H. 1994b. Activity of maitake D-fraction to prevent cancer growth and metastasis. *J. Naturopathic Med.* (In press).

Nanba, H. et al. 1994c. *Biol. and Pharm. Bull.* 17: Antidiabetic activity present in the fruit body of *Grifola frondosa* (Maitake) I. 1106-1110.

Naoki, T. et al. 1994. Pharmacological studies on *Cordyceps sinensis* from China. From the *Fifth Mycological Congress Abstracts*. Vancouver, BC, August 14-21m 1994.

Narui et al. 1980. Polysaccharide produced by laboratory cultivation of *Poria cocos* Wolf. *Carbohyd. Res.* 87:161-163.

National Cancer Institute. 1991. Developmental Therapeutics Program, In-Vitro Testing Results. NSC: F195001-/ 1. Plate 8283, Lab: 9W. Unpublished test report.

National Institute of Health (N.I.H.). n.d. (ca. 1985). Tryptamine hallucinogens—human neuropsychopharmacology. Crisp Data Base, Washington, D.C.

Nguyen, B.T. and S. Stadtsbaeder. 1980. Comparative biological and antitoxoplasmic effects of particulate and water-soluble polysacchrides, in vitro. *Adv. Exp. Med. Biol.* 121A: 255-68. From CA 92:174295q.

Ni, Z. 1993. Research and application of the product AF31 of edible fungi. Poster P-2-19 from First International Conference of Mushroom Biology and Mushroom Products, 23-26 August, 1993. UNESCO and The Chinese University of Hong Kong.

Nishihira, T. et al. 1988. Anticancer effects of BRM's associated with nutrition in cancer patients. *Gan To Kagaku Ryoho* 4 (Part 2-3): 1615-1620.

Nishitoba, T. et al. 1986. New terpenoids, ganolucidic acid D, ganoderic acid L, lucidone C and lucidenic acid G, from the fungus *Ganoderma lucidum. Agric. Biol. Chem.* 50:809-811. From CA 105:3518g.

Nishitoba, T. et al. 1989. Bitter triterpenoids from the fungus *Ganoderma Applanatum. Phytochemistry,* 28:193-197.

Noda, K. et al. 1992. Clinical effect of sizofiran combined with irradiation in cervical cancer patients: A randomized controlled study. *Japan. J. Clin. Oncol.* 22:17-25.

Nomoto, K. et al. 1975. Restoration of antibody-forming capacities by PS-K in tumor-bearing mice. *Gann* 66:365-374.

Nunoshsiba, T. et al. 1990. Antimutagenic activity of hoelen extracts. *Sci. Eng. Rev. Doshisha Univ.* 30:266-272. From CA 113:1848w.

O'Hearn, E. and M.E. Molliver. 1993. Degeneration of Purkinje cells in parasagittal zones of the cerebellar vermis after treatment with ibogaine or harmaline. *Neuroscience* 55:303-310.

Obuchi, T. et al. 1990. Armillaric acid, a new antibiotic produced by *Armillaria mellea. Planta Med.* 56:198-201. From CA 113:129058f.

Ohmori, T. et al. 1986. Antitumor activity of protein-bound polysaccharide from *Cordyceps ophioglossoides* in mice. *Japan. J. Cancer Res.* 77:1256-1263.

Ohmori, T. et al. 1988a. Component analysis of protein-bound polysaccharide (SN-C) from *Cordyceps ophioglossoides* and its effects on syngeneic murine tumors. *Chem. Pharm. Bull.* 36:4505-4511. From CA 110:128193x.

Ohmori, T. et al. 1988b. Dissociation of a glucan fraction (C)-1) from protein-bound polysaccharide of *Cordyceps ophioglossoides* and analysis of its antitumor effect. *Chem. Pharm. Bull.* 36:4512-4518.

Ohmori, T. et al. 1989b. Isolation of galactosaminoglycan moiety (CO-N) from protein-bound polysaccharide of *Cordyceps ophioglossoides* and its effects against murine tumors. *Chem. Pharm. Bull.* 37:1019-1022. From CA 111:364g.

Ohmori, T. et al. 1989a. The correlation between molecular weight and antitumor activity of galactosaminoglycan (CO-N) from *Cordyceps ophioglossoides. Chem. Pharm. Bull.* 37:1337-1340. From CA 111:49936j.

Ohno, N. et al. 1985. Antitumor activity and structural characterization of polysaccharide fractions extracted with cold alkali from a fungus, *Peziza vesiculosa. Chem. Pharm. Bull.* 33:2564-2568. From CA 103:98397c.

Ohno, N. et al. 1986a. Antitumor activity of a b-1,3-glucan obtained from liquid cultured mycelium of *Grifola frondosa. J. Pharmacobio-Dyn.* (9):861-864.

Ohno, N. et al. 1986b. Chemical Characterization of a Fungal R-cell Mitogen obtained from the Fruit Body of *Peziza vesiculosa. Chem. Pharm. Bull.* 34:2112-2117.

Ohno, N. et al. 1986c. Two different conformations of antitumor glucans obtained from *Grifola frondosa. Chem. Pharm. Bull.* (Tokyo) 34:2555-2560.

Ohno, N. et al. 1987. Conformational changes of the two different conformers of grifolan in sodium hydroxide urea or DMSO solution. *Chem. Pharm. Bull.* (Tokyo) 35:2108-2113.

Ohsawa, T. et al. 1992. Studies on constituents of fruit body of *Polyporus umbellatus* and their cytotoxic activity. *Chem. Pharm. Bull.* 40:143-147.

Ohtsuka, S. et al. 1975. Carcinostatic agent. Japanese Patent 75 32,298 from CA 85:10408h.

Ohtsuka, S. et al. 1977. Polysaccharides. U.S. patent 4,051,314. From CA 87:199194r.

Oikawa, S. et al. 1987. Antitumor Grifolan-N and its production by Grifola frondosa tokachiana. *Jpn. Kokai Tokkyo Koho* (Patent). CA 108:110847n.

Oka, M. et al. 1992. Immunological analysis and clinical effects of intraabdominal and intrapleural injection of lentinan for malignant ascites and pleural effusion. *Biotherapy* 5:107-112.

Oka, T. et al. 1985. Antitumor effects and augmentation of cellular immunity by schizophyllan and bestatin. *Okayama Igakkai Zasshi* 97:527-541. From CA 104:102107y.

Okamura, K. et al. 1985. Clinical evaluation of schizophyllan combined with irradiation on patients with cervical cancer—a randomized controlled study. *Int. J. Immunopharmacol.* 7:333(24).

Okamura, K. et al. 1986. Clinical evaluation of schizophyllan combined with irradiation in patients with cervical cancer. A randomized controlled study. *Cancer*, 58:865-872.

Okamura, K. et al. 1989. Adjuvant immunochemotherapy: Two randomized controlled studies of patients with cervical cancer. *Biomed. Pharmacother.* 43:177-181.

Ono, N. et al. 1988. Antitumor polysaccharide and its preparation with *Grifola frondosa* variety tokachiana. *Jpn. Kokai Tokkyo Koho* JP 63,307,825 [88,307,825] (Cl. A61K31/715), 15 Dec. 1988, 8 pp.

Ooi, V.E.C. et al. 1993. Protective effects of some edible mushrooms on paracetamol-induced liver injury. From *First International Conference on Mushroom Biology and Mushroom Products, Programme and Abstracts*, August 23-26, 1993, The Chinese University of Hong Kong. Shatin, Hong Kong: Chinese University of Hong Kong: 139(P-2-13).

Opletal, L. 1993. Phytotherapeutic aspects of diseases of the circulatory system. 2. The oyster mushroom and its potential use. *Cesk. Farm.* 42:160-166.

Oso, B.A. 1977. Mushrooms in Yoruba mythology and medicinal practices. *Econ. Bot.* 31:367-371.

Osol, A. and G.E. Farrar. 1947. *The Dispensatory of the United States of America*, 24th ed. Philadelphia: J.B. Lippincott Co.

Osol, A. et al. 1955. *The Dispensatory of the United States of America*, 25th ed. Philadelphia: J.B. Lippincott Co.

Ostrom, N. 1992. Another mushroom miracle? *New York Native* June 29:34-35.

Ott, J. 1976. *Hallucinogenic Plants of North America*. Berkeley, CA: Wingbow Press.

Ott, J. 1978. Recreational use of hallucinogenic mushrooms in the United States. From *Mushroom Poisoning: Diagnosis and Treatment*. Rumack and B.H. Rumack and E. Salzman (eds.). Boca Raton: CRC Press.

Ousley, Y. 1993. University of Miami is Ready to Test Ibogaine on Humans. *Miami Herald*. August 28.

Overholts, L. 1977. *The Polyporaceae of the United States, Alaska, and Canada*. Ann Arbor: University of Michigan Press.

Pabst, G. 1887. *Kohlers Medizinal-Pflanze in Naturgetreuen Abbildungen Mit Kurz Erläuterndem Texte*. Gera-Untermhaus: Verlag von Fr. Eugen Kohler.

Pacioni G. 1981. *Simon and Schuster's Guide to Mushrooms*. New York: Simon and Schuster.

Parent, G. and D. Thoen. 1977. Food value of edible mushrooms from Upper-Shaba region. *Econ. Bot.* 31:436-445.

Parish, R.C. and P.L. Doering. 1986. Treatment of *Amanita* mushroom poisoning: a review. *Vet Hum.Toxicol.* 28:318-322.

Paxton, J. 1844. *A Pocket Botanical Dictionary*. London: Bradbury & Evans.

Penman, S. et al. 1970. Messenger and heterogeneous nuclear RNA in HeLa cells: Differential inhibition by cordycepin. *Proceedings of the National Academy of Sciences* 67:1878-1885.

Pereira, J. 1843. Summer-plant-winter-worm. *N.Y. J. of Med.* 1:128-132.

Perrot, Em. 1943-1944. *Matieres Premieres Usuelles Du Regne Vegetal.* Saint-Germain: Libraires De L'Academie De Medecine.

Pettit, G.R. and J.C. Knight. 1962. Steroids and related natural products. XII. *Fomes applanatum. J. Org. Chem.* 27:2696-2698.

Pfister, J.R., (n.d.). Identification of 2-Aminouinoline as the *Leucopaxillus Albissimus* chemical defense system. *Institute of Organic Chemistry, Syntex Research.* 746:1-6

Pharmaceutical Society of Great Britain. 1934. *The British Pharmaceutical Codex.* London: The Pharmaceutical Press.

Phillips, R.1991. *Mushrooms of North America.* Boston: Little, Brown and Company.

Physicians Desk Reference. 1993. Montvale, N.J.: Medical Economics Data.

Piaskowski, S. 1957. Preliminary studies on the preparation and application of preparations from black birch touchwood in human cases of malignant tumors. *Sylwan* 101:5-11.

Platonova, E.G. and A.N. Shivrina. 1965. Higher fungi as sources of provitamin D2. *Kormovye Beiki i Fiziol. Aktivn. Veshchestva dlya Zhivotnovodstva, Akad. Nauk SSSR, Botan. Inst.* 73-79 (Russ). From CA 65:10962b.

Pollock, S.H. 1974. A novel experience with *Paneolus,* a case study from Hawaii. *J. Psychedelic Drugs* 6:85-89.

Pollock, S.H. 1975. The *Psilocybin* Mushroom Pandemic. *J. Psychedelic Drugs* 7:73-83.

Pollock, S.H. 1976. Psilocybian mycetismus with special reference to *Panaeolus. J. Psychedelic Drugs* 8:43-57.

Pope, J. and K. Heungens, 1991. First commercial growing of ornamental mushrooms and its use in floristry. From *Science and Cultivation of Edible Fungi,* 2. Maher, M.J., ed. Rotterdam: A.A. Balkema: 821-830.

Porcher, P. 1854. On the Medicinal and Toxicological Properties of the Cryptogamic Plants of the United States. *Transactions of the American Medical Association. Vol. 1.*

Prance, G.T. 1976. The ethnomycology of the Sanama Indians. *Mycologia,* 68:201-210.

Prance, G.T. 1984. The use of edible fungi by Amazonian Indians. *Ethnobotany in the Neotropics.* 1:127-139.

Priestley, J. 1993. Current clinical research, reported by M. Shirota, Maitake Products, Inc.

Protiva, J. et al. 1980. Triterpenes and steroids from *Ganoderma applanatum. Collect. Czech. Chem. Commun.* 45:2710-2713.

Qiu, G., and A. Wu. 1986. Chinese materia medica with anti-atopic effect. From *Abstracts of Chinese Medicines.* 1:119.

Raff, E. et al. 1992. Renal failure after eating "magic" mushrooms." *Can Med Assoc J* 147 (9) November 1:1339-1341.

Rai, B.K. et al. 1993. A note on ethno-myco-medicines from central India. *The Mycologist* 7:192-193.

Ramsbottom, J. 1951. *A Handbook of the Larger British Fungi.* London: The British Museum.

Ramsbottom, J. 1953. *The New Naturalist Mushrooms & Toadstools. A Study of the Activities of Fungi.* London: Collins.

Read, B.E. 1936. *Chinese Medicinal Plants from the Pen Ts'ao Kang Mu...A.D. 1596. of a Botanical, Chemical and Pharmacological Reference List.* (Reprinted by Southern Materials Center, Inc., Taipei).

Redwood, T. 1857. *Supplement to the Pharmacopeia.* London: Longman & Co.

Reinhold, L. et al. (N.d.). *Progress in Phytochemistry. Vol. 7.* Oxford: Pergamon Press.

Remington, J.P. and H. Wood. 1918. *The Dispensatory of the U.S.* (20th ed.). Philadelphia: J.B. Lippincott.

Rethy, L. et al. 1983. The host's-defense increasing (anti-tumor) activity of polysaccharides prepared from *Lentinus cyathiformis*. *Annales Immunologiae Hungaricae* 21:285-290.

Reuter News Service. 1994. Swimming-China to pass on World Cup in Hong Kong. (Beijing, Dec. 30, 1994).

Reynolds, J.E.F., ed. 1982. *Martindale, The Extra Pharmacopoeia* 28th ed. London: The Pharmaceutical Press.

Reynolds, J.E.F., ed. 1993. *Martindale, The Extra Pharmacopoeia*, 30th ed. London: The Pharmaceutical Press.

Richard, C. 1971. Sur l'activite' antibiotique del' Armillaria mellea. *Can. J. Microbiol.* 17:1395-1399.

Richards, L.G. 1969. *LSD-25: a factual account; layman's guide to the pharmacology, physiology, psychology, and sociology of LSD*. Washington, U.S. Bureau of Narcotics and Dangerous Drugs (U.S. Printing Office).

Ripperger, H., and H. Budzikiewicz. 1975. Phytochemical reports: Steroide aus *Ganoderma Applanatum*. *Phytochemistry* 14:2297-2298.

Rjarathnam, S., and Z. Bano. 1989. *Pleurotus* Mushrooms. Part III. Biotransformations of Natural Lignocellulosic Wastes: Commercial Applications and Implications. *Critical Reviews in Food Science and Nutrition* 28:31-113.

Rokujo, T. et al. 1969. Lentysine: A new hypolipemic agent from a mushroom. *Life Sciences* 9: 381-385.

Roland, J.F. et al. 1960. Calvacin: A New Antitumor Agent. (N.p.).

Rold, J.R. 1986. Mushroom Madness. *Postgraduate Medicine* 79:217-218.

Rolfe, R.T. and F.W. Rolfe. 1925. *The Romance of the Fungus World*. London: Chapman & Hall, Ltd.

Roy, S. and N. Samajpati. 1988. Free amino acid composition in the cell pool of three Indian edible mushrooms. *Sci. Cult.* 54:135-136.

Ruelius, H.W. et al. 1968. Poricin, an acidic protein with antitumor activity from a basidiomycete. I. Production, isolation and purification. *Arch. Biochem. Biophys.* 125:126-135.

Saar, M. 1991a. Fungi in Khanty Folk Medicine. *J. Ethnopharmacol.* 31:175-179.

Saar, M. 1991b. Ethnomycological data from Siberia and North-East Asia on the effect of *Amanita muscaria*. *J. Ethnopharmacol.* 31:157-173.

Sakagami, H. and M. Takeda. 1993. Diverse biological activity of PSK (Krestin), a protein-bound polysaccharide from *Coriolus versicolor* (fr.) Quel. Proceedings of the First International Conference on Mushroom Biology and Mushroom Products, August 23-26, 1993, The Chinese University of Hong Kong, Hong Kong. *Mushroom Biology and Mushroom Products*. Chang, S.-T. et al. (eds.). Shatin, Hong Kong: Chinese University Press: 237-245.

Sakagami, H. and Y. Kawazoe. 1991. Pharmaceutical compositions containing lignin for virus infection prevention. *Kokai Tokkyo Koho* JP (Patent). From CA 115:263495r.

Sakai, Y. et al. 1986. Antimutagenicity of extracts from crude drugs in Chinese medicines. *Mutation Research* 174:1-4.

Sakamaki, S. et al. 1993. Individual diversity of IL-6 generation by human monocytes with lentinan administration. *Int. J. Immunopharmacol.* 15:751-756.

Sarkar, S. et al. 1993. Antiviral effect of the extract of culture medium of *Lentinus edodes* mycelia on the replication of herpes simplex virus type 1. *Antiviral Res.* 20:293-303.

Sasaki, T. 1990. Preparation of calcium-high edible mushroom. *Jpn. Kokai Tokkyo Koho* JP 02,119,720 [90,119,720] (Cl. A01G1/04) (Patent). From CA 113:210491p.

Sasaki, T. and N. Takasuka. 1976. Further study of the structure of Lentinan, an anti-tumor polysaccharide from *Lentinus edodes. Carbohyd. Res.* 47:99-104.

Sastri, B.N., ed, et al 1950. *The Wealth of India. V.II.* New Delhi:Publications & Information Directorate, Council of Scientific & Industrial Research.

Sato, H. et al. 1986. Ganoderiol A and B, new triterpenoids from the fungus *Ganoderma lucidum* (Reishi). *Agric. Biol. Chem.* 50:2887-2890.

Sawada, T. and K. Endo. 1989. Distribution of RNA, nuclease and phosphatase in Shiitake and their changes during the growth of fruit body. *Nippon Kasei Gakkaishi* 40:347-353. From CA 111:171224r.

Scates, K. 1975. Mushroom Bargain. *Pacific Search.* March:44.

Schillings, R.T. and H.W. Ruelins. 1968. Poricin, an acidic protein with antitumor activity from a basidiomycete. *Arch. Biochem. Biophys.* 127:672-679.

Schmid, F.L. and H. Czerny. 1953. Chemical investigation of *Polyporus pinicola Scientia Pharm.* 21:258-264. From CA 50:6982a.

Schultes, R.E. 1978. Plantae Mexicanae II. From Teonanacatl, Hallucinogenic Mushrooms of North America. Extracts from the 2nd Int. Conf. on Hallucinogenic Mushrooms, 1977. Ott, J. and J. Bigwood. Seattle: Madrona Publishers, Inc.

Schultes, R.E. and A. Hofmann. 1973. *The Botany and Chemistry of Hallucinogens.* Springfield, IL: Charles C. Thomas, Pub.

Schultes, R.E. and A. Hofmann. 1979. *Plants of the Gods.* Maidenhead, England: McGraw Hill.

Schwartz, R. and D. Smith. 1988. Hallucinogenic Mushrooms. *Clinical Pediatrics* 27:70-73.

Scientific Consulting Service, Inc. (undated). Len-Shii® - Immunopotentiator. (Shiitake/Cellulase). Typescript. Oakland, CA.

Sekizawa, N. et al. 1988. Edible mushrooms. I. Analytical method for 5'-nucleotides and their contents in mushrooms. *Iwate-ken Jozo Shokuhin Shikenjo Hokoku* 130-134. From CA 110:6467a.

Sekizawa, N. et al. 1989. Processing of Edible Mushrooms. II. Differences in 5'-mononucleotide Content Depending on Kinds of Mushroom and Drying Methods. *Iwate-ken. Jozo Shokuhin Shikenjo Hokoku*: 85-89. From CA 112:20159t.

Senatore, F. 1990. Fatty acid and free amino acid content of some mushrooms. *J. Sci. Food. Agric.* 51:91-96.

Sendo, F. et al. 1981. Augmentation of natural cell-mediated cytotoxicity by administration of Lentinan in mice. . From *Manipulation of Host Defence Mechanisms*, Aoki, T. et al (eds.). Amsterdam: *Excerpta Medica* (International Congress Series 576).

Sershen, H. et al. 1994. Ibogaine reduces preference for cocaine consumption in C57BL/6By mice. *Pharmacol. Biochem. Behav.* 47:13-19.

Sevilla-Santos, P. 1964. Oncostatic and bacteriostatic activities of a Philippine strain of *Polyporus cinnabarinus. J. Philippine Pharm. Assoc.* 50:133-139.

Sharon, T.M. 1988. Personal Observations: *Lentinus edodes* (shiitake) mycelial extract. Typescript.

Shen, L. and Y. Chen. 1985. Treatment of 18 cases of chronic nephritis mainly with cultivated *Cordyceps. Liaoning Journal of Traditional Chinese Medicine.* 9:32-33. From *Abstracts of Chinese Medicines* 1:198.

Shen, S.C. et al. 1993. The Ability of Polymorphonuclear Leukocytes to Produce Active Oxygen in a Model of Peritonitiis in Rats. *Surg. Today.* 23:603-608.

Shen, Z. A report of 3 cases of allergy to Chinese herbal drugs. *Chin. Pharm. Bull.* 21:354-355. From *Abstracts of Chinese Medicines*, 1:394.

Sheng, J. and Q. Chen. 1987. Anticoagulant effect of polysaccharides from *Auricularia auricula, Tremella fuciformis,* and *Tremella fuciformis* Spores. *Zhongguo Yaoke Daxue Xuebao.* Q. Chen. 1989. Antilipemic effect of polysaccharides from *Auricularia auricula, Tremella fuciformis,* and *Tremella fuciformis* spores. *Zhongguo Yaoke Daxue Xuebao.* 20:344-347. From CA 112:132234v.

Sheng, J. and Q. Chen. 1990. Effects of polysaccharides from *Auricularia auricula, Tremella fuciformis* spores on experimental thrombus formation. *Zhongguo Yaoke Daxue Xuebao.* 21:39-42. From CA 112:210752d.

Sheng, Z. 1986. 18:137-140. From CA 107:109109w.

Shiao, M.-S. et al. 1989. Natural products in Cordyceps. *Proceedings of the National Science Council, Republic of China, Part A* 13:382-387.

Shiao, M.-S. et al. 1994. Natural products and biological activities of the Chinese medicinal fungus *Ganoderma lucidum.* 342-354. From *Food Phytochyemicals II: Teas, Spices, and Herbs.*Tawain:Amer. Chem. Society..

Shibata, S. et al. 1968. Antitumor studies on some extracts of basidiomycetes. *Gann.* 59:159-161.

Shibata, S. et al. 1964. *List of Fungal Products.* Tokyo: University of Tokyo Press.

Shiio, T. and Y. Yugari. 1981. The antitumor effect on Lentinan and the tumor recognition in mice. From *Manipulation of Host Defence Mechanisms,* Aoki, T. et al (eds.). Amsterdam: *Excerpta Medica* (International Congress Series 576).

Shimaoka, I. et al. 1990. Preparation of therapeutic metal-bound proteins from mushrooms. *Jpn. Kokai Tokkyo Koho* JP (Patent). From CA 114:325040z.

Shimizu, T. et al. 1981. A combination of regional chemotherapy and systemic immunotherapy for the treatment of inoperable gastric cancer. From *Manipulation of Host Defence Mechanisms,* Aoki, T. et al (eds.). Amsterdam: *Excerpta Medica* (International Congress Series 576).

Shimizu, A. et al. 1985. Isolation of an inhibitor of platelet aggregation from a fungus, *Ganoderma lucidum. Chem. Pharm. Bull.* 33:3012-3015.

Shimizu, Y. et al. 1992. Augmenting effect of sizofiran on the immunofunction of regional lymph nodes in cervical cancer. *Cancer* 69:1188-1194.

Shin, H-W. et al. 1986. Studies on constituents of higher fungi of Korea. Part XLIII. Studies on inorganic composition and immunopotentiating activity of *Ganoderma lucidum* in Korea. *Saengyak Hakhoechi* 16:181-190. From CA 105:29874k.

Shiozawa, S. et al. 1991. Schizophyllan augments development of immunoglobulin-secreting cells upon costimulation with Staphylococcus aureus Cowan I. DICP Ann. Pharmacother. 25:101-102.

Shirota, M. 1994. Personal communication with the National Cancer Institute and others.

Shiu, W.C. et al. 1992. A clinical study of PSP on peripheral blood counts during chemotherapy. *Physiotherapy Research* 6:217-218.

Shivrina, A. et al. 1965. Vitamin B12 contents of Polyporaceae and Agaricus strains. *Kormovye Belki i Fiziol. Aktivn. Veshchestva dlya Zhivotnovodstva:* 88-91.

Singh, P. and S. Rangaswami. 1965. Chemical examination of *Fomes fomentarius. Indian J. Chem.* 3: 575-576. From CA 64:14240f.

Singh, P.P. et al. 1974. Scleroglucan, an antitumor polysaccharide from *Sclerotium glucanicum. Carbohy. Res.* 37:245-247.

Singer, R. 1958. Mycological investigations on teonanacatl, the Mexican hallucinogenic mushroom. Part I. The history of teonanacatl, field work and culture work. *Mycologia* 50: 239-261.

Singer, R. 1978. Hallucinogenic Mushrooms. From *Mushroom Poisoning: Diagnosis and Treatment.* Boca Raton: CRC Press.

Smart, R.G. et al. 1967. *Lysergic acid diethyamide (LSD) in the treatment of alcoholism; an investigation of its effects on drinking behavior, personality, structure, and social functioning.* Toronto: Addiction Research Foundation (University of Toronto Press).

Smith, F.P. and G.A. Stuart. 1911. *Chinese Materia Medica. Vegetable Kingdom* (reprinted by Georgetown Press, SF, 1973).

Smith, H.A. 1949. *Mushrooms in their Natural Habitats.* Portland: Swayer's Inc.

Solomko, E.F. and G.S. Eliseeva. 1988. Biosynthesis of vitamins B by the fungus *Pleurotus ostreatus* in a submerged culture. *Prikl. Biokhim. Mikrobiol.* 24:164-169.

Solomko, E.F. et al. 1984. Lipid content and fatty acid composition of the higher edible fungus—oyster mushroom *Pleurotus ostreatus* (Fr.) Kummer. *Prikl. Biokhim. Mikrobiol.* 20:273-279.

Solomko, E.F. et al. 1986. Mineral composition of some cultivated and wild Basidiomycetes. *Mikol. Fitopatol.* 20:474-478. From CA 106:116529r.

Song, C.H. et al. 1989. Growth stimulation and lipid synthesis in *Lentinus edodes. Mycologia* 81:514-522. From CA 112:4697m.

Sorimachi, K. et al. 1990. Antiviral activity of water-solubilized lignin derivatives in vitro. *Agric. Biol. Chem.* 54:1337-1339. From CA 113:52122n.

Soskin, R.A. 1973. The use of LSD in time-limited psychotherapy. *J. Nerv. Ment. Dis.* 157: 410-419.

Stamets, P. 1994. *Growing Gourmet and Medicinal Mushrooms.* Berkeley: Ten Speed Press.

Stamets, P. 1994. My Adventures with the Blob. *Mushroom the Journal.* Winter 1994-95.

Stark, A. et al. 1988. Lentinellic acid, a biologically active protoilludane derivative from Lentinellus species (Basidiomycetes). *Z. Naturforsch.* 43:177-183.

Stavinoha, W. et al. 1990. Study of the anti-inflammatory activity of *Ganoderma Lucidum.* Research paper presented at the Third Academic/Industry Joint Conference in Sapporo, Japan on Aug. 18-20, 1990. From CA 113:52122n.

Sterner, O. et al. 1985. The sesquiterpenes of *Lactarius vellereus* and their role in a proposed chemical defense system. *Journal of Natural Products* 48:279-288.

Su, C.H. et al. 1993. Hepato-protective triterpenoids from Ganoderma tsugae Murrill. Proceedings of the First International Conference on Mushroom Biology and Mushroom Products, August 23-26, 1993. Chang, S.-T. et al. (eds.). *Mushroom Biology and Mushroom Products.* Shatin, Hong Kong: Chinese University Press: 275-283.

Su, X. et al. 1987. Antineoplastic activity, immunological action and toxicity of compound muji infusion. *Journal of Shenyang College of Pharmacy.* 4:41-45. From *Abstracts of Chinese Medicines* 2:169.

Subramanian, S.S. and M.N. Swamy. 1961. Ergosterol from *Ganoderma lucidum. J.Sci. Ind. Research* 20B:39. From CA 16677h.

Suga, T. et al. 1985. Effect of Lentinan against allogeneic, syngeneic and autologous primary tumors, and its prophylactic effect against chemical carcinogenesis. *Int. Congr. Ser.- Excerpta Med.* 609:116-128. From CA 104:81371n

Sugai, A. et al. 1986. Pyrophosphatidic acid in mushrooms. *Lipids.* 21:666-668.

Sugano, N. et al. 1982. Anticarcinogenic actions of water-soluble and alcohol-insoluble fractions from culture medium of *Lentinus Edodes* mycelia. *Cancer Letters* 17:109-114.

Sugano, O. et al. 1985. Anticarcinogenic action of an alcohol-insoluble fraction (LAP1) from culture medium of *Lentinus Edodes* mycelia. *Can. Lett.* 27:1-6.

Sugiura, M. et al. 1980. Studies on antitumor polysaccharides, especially D-II, from mycelium of *Coriolus versicolor. Jpn. J. Pharmacol.* 30: 503-513. From CA 93:230733r.

Sugiyama, K. et al. 1992. Isolation of plasma cholesterol-lowering components from ningyotake (*Polyporus confluens*) mushroom. *J. Nutr. Sci. Vitaminol.* 38:335-342.

Suzuki, A. et al. 1982. Elution of metals from crude drugs. *Shoyakugaku Zasshi.* 36:190-195.

Suzuki, H. et al. 1986. Immunological activities of high-molecular-weight fractions purified from *Lentinus edodes* mycelia extract (LEM)-macrophage-activating effect and mitogenic activity. *Igaku no Ayumi* 138:441-442. From CA 106:60905r.

Suzuki, H. et al. 1989. Inhibition of the infectivity and cytopathic effect of human immunodeficiency virus by water-soluble lignin in an extract of the culture medium of *Lentinus edodes* mycelia (LEM). *Biochem. Biophys. Res. Commun.* 160:367-373. From CA 110:205157t.

Suzuki, H. et al. 1990. Structural characterization of the immunoactive and antiviral water-solubilized lignin in an extract of the culture medium of *Lentinus edodes* mycelia (LEM). *Agric. Biol. Chem.* 54:479-487. From CA 112:171824g.

Suzuki, I. et al. 1982. Antitumor activity of an immunomodulting material extracted from a fungus, *Peziza vesiculosa. Chem. Pharm. Bull.* 30:1066-1068.

Suzuki, I. et al. 1984. Antitumor activity of a polysaccharide fraction from cultured fruiting bodies of Grifola frondosa. *J. Pharmacobiodyn.* 7:492-500.

Suzuki, I. et al. 1989. Antitumor and immunomodulating activities of a beta glucan obtained from liquid-cultured *Grifola frondosa. Chem. Pharm. Bull.* (Tokyo) 37:410-413.

Suzuki, M. et al. 1990. Induction of endogenous lymphokine-activated killer activity by combined administration of lentinan and interleukin 2. *Int. J. Immunopharmacol.* 12:613-623.

Suzuki, S. and S. Ohshima, 1974. Influence of Shi-Ta-Ke (*Lentinus edodes*) on human serum cholesterol. Mushroom Science IX (Part I). *Proceedings of the Ninth International Scientific Congress on the Cultivation of Edible Fungi,* Tokyo: 463-467.

Swanston-Flatt, S.K. et al. 1989. Glycaemic effects of traditional Europoean plant treatments for diabetes studies in normal and streptozotocin diabetic mice. *Diabetes Res.* 10:69-73.

Swanton, E.W. 1915. Economic and folklore notes. *Transactions of the British Mycological Soc.* 5:408-409.

Tabata, K. et al. 1981. Ultrasonic degradation of Schizophyllan, an antitumor polysaccharide produced by *Schizophyllum commune* Fries. *Carbohyd. Res.* 89:121-135.

Taguchi, T. et al. 1982. Clinical Trials on Lentinan (Polysaccharide). In Yamamura, Y. et al (eds.). *Immunomodulation by Microbial Products and Related Synthetic Compounds*, pp. 467-475. New York: Elsevier Science Pub. Co.

Taguchi, T. et al. 1981. Phase I and II studies of Lentinan. From *Manipulation of Host Defence Mechanisms*, Aoki, T. et al (eds.). Amsterdam: *Excerpta Medica* (International Congress Series 576).

Tai, T. et al. 1991. Triterpenoids from *Poria cocos. Phytochemistry* 30:2796-2797. From CA 115:275725d.

Takahashi, M. et al. 1992. Two-color flow cytometric analysis of splenic lymphocyte subpopulations in patients with gastric cancer. *Surg. Today* 22:35-39.

Takamura, K. et al. 1991. Determination of vitamin D2 in shiitake mushroom (Lentinus edodes) by high-performance liquid chromatography. 545:201-204. From CA 115:27819d.

Takeshita, K. et al. 1993. Effect of lentinan on lymphocyte subsets of peripheral blood, lymph nodes, and tumor tissues in patients with gastric cancer. *Surg. Today* 23:125-129.

Takeuchi, A. et al. 1991. Effect of solar radiation on vitamin D2 contents in shiitake mushrooms (*Lentinus edodes*). *Bitamin.* 65:121-124. From CA 115:134542e.

Takeuchi, T. et al. 1969. Coriolin, A New Basidiomycetes Antibiotic. *J. Antibiot..* 22:215-217.

Takeyama, T. et al. 1988. Distribution of grifolan NMF-5N 1-B, a chemically modified antitumor beta glucan in mice. *J. Pharmacobio-dyn.* 11:381-385.

Tam, S.C. et al. 1986. Hypotensive and renal effects of an extract of the edible mushroom *Pleurotus sajor-caju*. *Life Sciences* 38:1155-1161.

Tamura, T. et al. 1987a. Fermentation product as food additives for patients with hyperlipidemia. *Jpn. Kokai Tokkyo Koho* (Patent). CA 108:110854n

Tamura, T. et al. 1987b. Fermentation product as food for patients with Alzheimer's disease. *Jpn. Kokai Tokkyo Koho* (Patent). From CA 108:110852k.

Tamura, T. et al. 1987c. Fermentation product as food for patients with diabetes. *Jpn. Kokai Tokkyo Koho* (Patent). CA108:110855p

Tamura, T. et al. 1987d. Fermentation product as food for patients with liver failure. *Jpn. Kokai Tokkyo Koho* (Patent). CA108:110853m.

Tamura, T. et al. 1987e. Fermentation product as food for patients with mental diseases caused by environmental stress. *Jpn. Kokai Tokkyo Koho* (Patent). From CA 108:110851j..

Tanaka, S. et al. 1989. Complete amino acid sequence of an immunomodulatory protein, Ling zhi 8. An immunomodulator from the fungus *Ganoderma lucidum* having similarity to immunoglobulin variable regions. *J. Biol. Chem.* 264:1632-1637. From CA 112:229432w

Tang, R. et al. 1986. Pharmacology of natural Cordyceps and cultured mycelia of *Cordyceps sinensis*. *Chin.Tradit. Herb. Drugs.* 17:214-216. From *Abstracts of Chinese Medicines*, 1:529.

Tang, W. and Eisenbrand, G. 1992. *Chinese Drugs of Plant Origin*. Berlin: Springer-Verlag.

Tani, M. et al. 1992. In vitro generation of activated natural killer cells and cytotoxic macrophages with lentinan. *Eur. J. Clin. Pharmacol.* 42:623-627.

Tani, M. et al. 1993. Augmentation of lymphokine-activated killer cell activity by lentinan. *Anticancer Res.* 13:1773-1776.

Tarlo, S.M. et al. 1979. Human sensitization to Ganoderma antigen. *J. Allergy Clin. Immunol.* 64: 43-49.

Tasaka, K. et al. 1988. Anti-allergic constituents in the culture medium of *Ganoderma lucidum*. (I) Inhibitory effect of oleic acid on histamine release. *Agents and Actions* 23:153-156.

Tauki, Z. 1994. Stinkhorn Mushroom Ointment. *Townsend Letter for Doctors* 139:1059.

Tebbett, I.R. 1984. Mushroom Poisoning. *The Pharmaceutical Journal* September 8:270-271.

Teow, S.S. 1994. The therapeutic value of *Ganoderma lucidum*. From *Fifth International Mycological Conference Abstracts*. Vancouver, BC, August 14-21.

Terashita, T. et al. 1990. The proximate components, free and protein-bound amino acids in protein and 5'GMP in fruiting bodies of Lentinus edodes Singer (shiitake mushroom) grown on artificial bed-blocks. *Nippon Shokuhin Kogyo Gakkaishi* 37:528-532. From CA 114:80243a.

Terashita, T. et al. 1984. Proteinase of basidiomycetes. Part IV. Streptomyces pepsin inhibitor-insensitive carboxyl proteinase from *Ganoderma lucidum*. *Agric. Biol. Chem.* 48:1029-1035. From CA 101:50548j.

Tochikura, T.S. et al. 1987a. A biological response modifier, PSK, inhibits human immunodeficiency virus infection in vitro. *Biochem. Biophys. Res. Commun.* 148:726-733.

Tochikura, T.S. et al. 1987b. Inhibition of replication and cytopathic effect of human immunodeficiency virus by the extract of culture medium of *Lentinus edodes* mycelia In Vitro. *First Symposium on AIDS*. Dec. 21, 1987.

Tochikura, T.S. et al. 1987c. Suppression of human immuno-deficiency virus replication by 3-azido-3-deoxythymidine in various human haematopoetic cell lines in vitro: augmentation by the effect of lentinan. *Jpn. J. Cancer Res. (Gann)*: 78:583.

Tochikura, T.S. et al. 1988. Inhibition (in vitro) of replication and of the cytopathic effect of human immunodeficiency virus by an extract of the culture medium of Lentinus edodes mycelia. *Med. Microbiol. Immunol.* (Berl) 1988;177(5):235-244

Toda, S. et al. 1988. Effects of the Chinese herbal medicine "Saiboku-To" on histamine release from and the degranulation of mouse peritoneal. *Shoyakugaku Zasshi* 43:142-147.

Todd, R.G. 1967. *Martindale, Extra Pharmacopeia*. London: The Pharmaceutical Press.

Togami, M. et al. 1982. Studies on Basidiomycetes. I. Antitumor polysaccharide from bagasse medium on which mycelia of *Lentinus edodes* (Berk.) Sing. had been grown. *Chem. Pharm. Bull.* 30:1134-1140.

Tominaga, T. 1985. Combined effect of PSK and adriamycin on rodent tumors. *Recent Adv. Chemother., Proc. Int .Congr. Chemother., 14th.*, 2:836-837. From CA 106:308p.

Tomoda, M. et al. 1986. Glycan structures of ganoderans B and C, hypoglycemic glycans of *Ganoderma Lucidum* fruit bodies. *Phytochemistry.* 25:2817-2820.

Torisu, M. et al. 1990. Significant prolongation of disease-free period gained by oral polysaccharide K (PSK) administration after curative surgical operation of colorectal cancer. *Cancer Immunol. Immunother.* 31:261-268.

Toth, J.O. et al. 1983a. Chemistry and biochemistry of Oriental drugs. Part IX. Cytotoxic triterpenes from *Ganoderma lucidum* (Polyporaceae): structures of ganoderic acids U-Z. *J. Chem. Res., Synop.*:299. From CA 100:117512t.

Toth, J.O. et al. 1983b. Les acides ganoderques T`a Z: Triterpenes cytotoxiques de *Ganoderma lucidum* (Polyporacée). *Tetrahedron Letters.* 24:1081-1084. Translated by S. Yao, *et al.* Singapore: World Scientific.

Toth, B. and P. Gannett. 1993. *Agaricus bisporus:* An assessment of its carcinogenic potency. *Mycopathologia* 124:73-77.

Trestrail, J.H. 1991. Mushroom poisoning in the United States—An analysis of 1989 United States Poison Center data. *J. Toxicol. Clin. Toxicol.* 29:459-465.

Trinci, A.P.J. 1991. 'Quorn' mycoprotein. *The Mycologist* 5:106-109.

Tseng, J. and J.G. Chang. 1992. Suppression of tumor necrosis factor-alpha, interlukin-1 beta, interlukin-6 and granulocyte-monocyte colony stimulating factor secretion from human monocytes by an extract of *Poria cocos. Chin. J. Microbiol. Immunol.* 25:1-11.

Tsukagoshi, S. et al. 1984. Krestin (PSK). *Cancer Treatment Reviews* 11:131-155.

Tu, G. 1988. *Pharmacopoeia of the People's Republic of China* (English Ed.). Beijing: People's Medical Publishing House.

Turner, N.J. 1973. *Ethnobotany of the Thompson Indians of British Columbia*. Steedman, E.V. (ed.). Facsimile reproduction, 1973. Extracted from 45th B.A.E. Annual Report, Wash., D.C., 1930:503-504.

Turner, N.J. et al. 1980. Ethnobotany of the Okanagan-Colville Indians of British Columbia and Washington. *Occasional papers of the British Columbia Provincial Museum* No. 21. Province of B.C., Victoria, B.C.:16-17.

Tyler, V.E. and D. Gröger. 1964. Investigation of the alkaloids of *Amanita* species. I. *Amanita muscaria. Planta Med.* 12:334-339.

Tyler, V.E. 1965. Recent studies of the chemical constituents of the Agaricales. In *Beiträge zur Biochemie und Physiologie von Naturstoffen*. Jena: Gustav Fischer Verlag.

Tyler, V.E. et al. 1976. *Pharmacognosy*. Philadelphia: Lea and Febiger.

Tyler, V.E. 1979. Folk uses of mushrooms—medicoreligious aspects. In *Mushrooms and Man: An Interdisciplinary Approach to Mycology*. Albany, OR.

Tyler, V.E. 1994. Personal Communication, Sept. 26, 1994.

Ueda, A. et al. 1992. Allergic contact dermatitis in shiitake (*Lentinus edodes* (Berk) Sing) growers. *Contact Dermatitis* 26:228-233.

Ueno, Y. et al. 1978. Nitrogen-containing polysaccharides. (Patent). From CA 88:91357c.

Ueno, Y. et al. 1982. An antitumor activity of the alkali-soluble polysaccharide (and its derivatives) obtained from the sclerotia of *Grifola umbellata* (Fr.) Pilát. *Carbohydr. Res.* 101:160-167.

Ukai, S. et al. 1972. Antitumor activity on sarcoma 180 of the polysaccharides from *Tremella fuciformis* Berk. *Chem. Pharm. Bull.* 20:2293-2294.

Ukai, S. et al. 1978. Polysaccharides in fungi part 4. Acidic oligosaccharides from acidic heteroglycans of *Tremella fuciformis* and detailed structures of the polysaccharides. *Chem. Pharm. Bull.* (Tokyo) 26:3871-3876.

Ukai, S. et al. 1983. Polysaccharides in fungi. XIII. Antitumor activity of various polysaccharides isolated from *Dictyophora indusiata, Ganoderma japonicum, Cordyceps cicadae, Auricularia auricula-judae,* and *Auricularia* species. *Chem. Pharm. Bull.* 31:741-744. From CA 99:17195x.

Umezawa, H. et al. 1975. Calvatic acid. Japan. Kokai 75 52,290 (Cl. C07G, C12D, A61K) 09 May 1975. From CA 83:162178e.

Uphof, JC. Th. 1968. *Dictionary of Economic Plants.* New York: Verlag von J. Cramer: 152.

Urdang, G. *Pharmacopoeia Londinensis of 1618* Reproduced in Facsimile with a Historical Introduction. Madison, WI: State Historical Society of Wisconsin.

Usuda, Y. et al. 1981. Drug-resistant pulmonary tuberculosis treated with lentinan. In *Manipulation of Host Defence Mechanisms.* T. Aoki et al. (eds.). Amsterdam: *Excerpta Medica* (International Congress Series 576):50.

Utzig, J and Z. Samborski. 1957. Effect of triterpenes present in *Polyporus betulinus* on Sticker's tumors. *Med. Weterynar.* 13:481-484. From CA 52:3173i.

Valentin, J. and S. Knütter. 1957. The contents of purging agaric. *Pharm. Zentralhalle* 96:478-484.

Valisolalao, J. et al. 1983. Steroides cytotoxiques de *Polyporus versicolor. Tetrahedron* 39: 2779-2785.

Van Loon, P.C. 1992. Mushroom worker's lung. Detection of antibodies against Shii-take (Lentinus edodes) spore antigens in Shii-take workers. *J. Occup. Med.* 34:1097-1101.

Vetter, J. 1993. Chemische Zusammensetzung von acht eßbaren Pilzarten. *Z. Lebensm. Unters Forsch.* 196:224-227.

Vogel, V.J. 1977. *American Indian Medicine.* Norman: University of Oklahoma Press.

Wagenfuehr, A. et al. 1988. Enzymic pretreatment of wood. Ger. (East) DD 271,078. Patent applied 314,149. From CA 111:58581n.

Wagenfuehr, A. et al. 1989. Enzymic chip modification for use in the production of wood-based materials. *Holztechnologie.* 30:62-65. From CA 111:25182j.

Wagner, H. 1983. Immunostimulants of fungi and higher plants. In *Natural Products and Drug Development.* Proceedings of the Alfred Benzon Symposium 20. Edited by P. Krogsgaard-Larsen, et al. Copenhagen: Munksgaard.

Wagner, H. and A. Proksch. 1985. Immunostimulatory drugs of fungi and higher plants. *Economic and Medicinal Plant Research.* New York: Academic Press.

Wainwright, M. et al. 1992. The scientific basis of mould therapy. *The Mycologist* 6:108-110.

Wallace, R. A. et al. 1991. *Biology, the science of life,* 3rd ed. New York: HarperCollins.

Wan, F. and D. Huango. 1992. Anti-inflammatory and analgesic actions of artificial and fermentative *Ganoderma sinense* (AFGS). *Chung Kuo Chung Yao Tsa Chih* (10): 619-622, 640.

Wandokanty, F. and J. Utzig. 1958. Effect of pentacyclic triterpenes obtained from *Polyporus betullinus* on malignant neoplasms. *Med. Weterynar.* (Poland) 14:148-151.

Wang, B. et al. 1989. Protective effect of plant polysaccharides against radiation injury. *Zhonghua Fangshe Yixue Yu Fanghu Zazhi.* 9:24-26. From CA 111:73916y.

Wang, D. et al. 1983. Some pharmacological effects of Grifola polysaccharide. *Zhongcaoyao* 14:267-268. From CA 99:133348k.

Wang, G. et al. 1992a. Effect of poriatin on mouse immune system. *So. Chin. J. Antibiot.* 17:42-47.

Wang, G. et al. 1992b. Effect of poriatin on the induction of experimental autoimmune encephalomyelitis in Wistar rats. *So. Chin. J. Antibiot* 17:38-41.

Wang, G. et al. 1993. Antitumor active polysaccharides from the Chinese mushroom Songshan lingzhi, the fruiting body of *Ganoderma tsugae. Bioscience, Biotechnology and Biochemistry* 57:894-900.

Wang, J. et al. 1985. Study of the action of *Ganoderma lucidum* on scavenging hydroxyl radical from plasma. *J. Trad. Chin. Med.* 5:55-60.

Wang, N. et al. 1989. Carcinogenic course of rat liver cancer induced by aflaxtoxin B1 and effect of *Polyporus versicolor* polysaccharide on carcinogenic action. *Tianjin Yiyao*, 17:534-536. From CA 112:93657p.

Wang, S.Y. et al. 1994. The role of *Ganoderma lucidum* in immunopotentiation: effect on cytokine release from human macrophages and T-lymphocytes. From Program and Abstracts of the '94 International Symposium on Ganoderma Research. Beijing: Beijing Medical University.

Wang, Y.-C. 1985. Mycology in China with emphasis on review of the ancient literature. *Acta Mycol. Sin.* 4:133-140.

Wang, W.J. and X.Y. Zhu. 1989. The antiinflammatory and immunostimulating activities of S-4001 - a polysaccharide isolated from lei wan (*Polyporus mylittae*). Yao Hsueh Hsueh Pao, 24:151-154.

Wang, X. 1987. Treatment of 100 cases of viral heptatitis with Compound 370. *Shanghai J. Trad. Chin. Med.* (4):5. From *Abstracts of Chinese Medicines* 2:223.

Wang, Z. and H. Fu. 1981. Treatment of hereditary cerebellar ataxia with *Ganoderma capense* (Report of 4 Cases). *J. Trad. Chin. Med.* 1:47-50.

Wasson, V.P. and R.G. Wasson. 1957. *Russia, Mushrooms and History*. New York: Pantheon Books.

Wasson, R.G. 1961. The hallucinogenic fungi of Mexico: an inquiry into the origins of the religious idea among primitive people. *Bot. Mus. Leafl., Harv. Univ.* 20:25-73c.

Wasson, R.G. 1968. *The Divine Mushroom of Immortality*. New York: Harcourt Brace Jovanovich.

Watanabe, N. et al. 1990. A novel N6-substituted adenosine isolated from Mihuanjun (*Armillaria mellea*) as a cerebral-protecting compound. *Planta Med.* 56:48-52. From CA 113:52337m.

Watson, G. 1966. *Theriac and Mithridatium, A Study in Therapeutics*. London: The Wellcome Historical Medical Library.

Watt, J.M. & M.G. Breyer-Brandwijk. 1962. *The Medicinal and Poisonous Plants of Southern and Eastern Africa*. Edinburgh & London: E. & S. Livingstone Ltd.

Weber, G.F. 1929. The occurrence of tuckahoes and *Poria cocos* in Florida. *Mycologia* 21: 113-130.

Wei, B. et al. 1991. Chemical structures of water-soluble a-glucan in the fruit body of Grifola frondosa. *Denpun Kagaku* 38:263-265. From CA 116:3314e.

Wei, Q. et al. 1983. Effects of *Polyporus umbellatus* polysaccharides on liver carbohydrate metabolism and adrenocortical function of mice bearing hepatoma H22. *Zhongguo Yaoli Xuebao* 4:52-54. From CA 98:209687.

Wei, Y., and C. Zheng. 1986. Effects of *Tremella* polysaccharides on synthesis of protein and on glycogen content in normal and injured livers of mice. *Acta Pharm. Sin.* 7:364-367.

Whang, J. 1981. Chinese traditional food therapy. *Journal of The American Dietetic Association* 78:55-57.

Willard, T. 1990. *Reishi Mushroom. Herb of Spiritual Potency and Medical Wonder*. Issaquah: Sylvan Press.

Winder. 1846. On Indian Diseases and Remedies. *Boston Medical and Surgical Journal* 34:13.

Windholz, M. et al, eds. et al. 1976. *The Merck Index. Tenth Edition.* Rahway: Merck & Co., Inc.

Won, S.-J. et al. 1992. *Ganoderma tsugae* mycelium enhances splenic natural killer cell activity and serum interferon production in mice. *Jpn. J. Pharmacol.* 59:171-176.

Wood, G.B., and F. Bache. 1834. *U.S. Dispensatory.* Philadelphia: Grigg & Elliot.

Wood, H.C. 1890. *Therapeutics: its Principles and Practice.* Philadelphia: J.B. Lippincott Company.

Worthen, L.R. et al. 1962. The Occurrence of indole compounds in *Corpinus* species. *Econ. Bot.* 16:315-318.

Wu, S. and D. Zou. 1994. Therapeutic effect of grifola polysacharides in chronic hepatitis B. From International Symposium on Production and Products of Lentinus Mushroom, Program and Abstracts. Mushroom City, Qingyuan, China: International Society for Mushroom Science.

Xia, D. and Z. Lin. 1989. Effects of Tremella polysaccharides on immune function in mice. *Zhongguo Yaoli Xuebao* 10:453-457. From CA 111:187102k.

Xia, D. et al. 1990. Effects of the polysaccharide isolated from mycelium and fermentation fluid of *Schizophyllum commune* on immune function in mice. *Yaoxue Xuebao* 25:161-166. From CA 113:150585k.

Xia, E. and Q. Chen. 1988. Isolation, analysis and biological activities of the polysaccharide of *Tremella Fuciformis. ACTA Mycol. Sin.* 7:166-174. From *Abstracts of Chinese Medicines* 2:397.

Xia, E. and Q. Chen. 1989. Biological activities of polysaccharide from *Auricularia auricula,* Underw. *Zhonqquo Yaoke Daxue Xuebao,* 20:227-230. From CA 111:224835.

Xia, E. et al. 1987. Effect of polysaccharides from *Auricularia auricula, Tremella fuciformis* and *Tremella fuciforms* spores on DNA and RNA biosynthesis by lymphocytes. *Zhongguo Yaoke Daxue Xuebao* 18:141-143. From CA 107:109014m.

Xie, D. et al. 1985. Effects of *Ganoderma* polysaccharide BN3C and matrine on mouse T lymphocytes. *Chin. J. Microbiol. Immunol.* 5:8-13. From *Abstracts of Chinese Medicines* 1:185.

Xie, J. and S. Ren. 1987. Effects of Guizhi Fuling pill on the central nervous system. *Zhongchengyao Yanjiu* 29-30. From *Abstracts of Chinese Medicines* 2:175.

Xiao, L. 1987. Progress in the studies on Chinese drugs with immunological actions. *Zhongchengyao Yanjiu.* 3:25-27. From *Abstracts of Chinese Medicines* 2:228.

Xiong, H-Z. 1985. Clinical observation on 45 cases of chronic hepatitis by the treatment with *Tremella fuciformis* polysaccharide. *Chin. J. Antibiot.* 10:363-365.

Xu, J. et al. 1985. Effects of *Ganoderma* extract on mouse immunocytes. *Acta Acad. Med. Sin.* 7:301-304. From *Abstracts of Chinese Medicines* 1:39.

Xu, N. and B. Zhang. 1987. Effect of Cordyceps on plasma lipids in normal, stressed and hyperlipemic rats. *Chin. J.Pathophysiol.* 3:215-219. From *Abstracts of Chinese Medicines* 2:317.

Xu, R. and X. Peng. 1988. Effects of *Cordyceps sinensis* on natural killer cell activity and formation of Lewis lung carcinoma colonies. *Bull. Hunan Med. Coll.* 13:107-111. From *Abstracts of Chinese Medicines* 2:412.

Xu, R. et al. 1992. Effects of *Cordyceps sinensis* on Natural Killer Activity and Colony Formation of B16 Melanoma. *Chin. Med. J.* 102(2):97-101.

Xu, W. et al. 1988. Effects of Cordyceps mycelia on monoamine oxidase and immunity. *Shanghai J. Trad. Chin. Med.* (1):48-49. From *Abstracts of Chinese Medicines,* 2:394.

Xue, W. et al. 1987. Antiulcer effects of the polysaccharides from *Tremella fuciformis* and *Auricularia auricula. Journal of China Pharmaceutical University,* 18:45-47. From *Abstracts of Chinese Medicines* 1:532.

Xue, W. et al. 1989. Prevention and treatment of alloxan-induced diabetes in mice by polysaccharides isolated from *Tremella fuciformis* and *Auricularia auricula*. *Zhongguo Yaoke Daxue Xuebao* 20:181-183. From CA 111:126794r.

Yadomae, T. et al. 1979a. A B-lymphocyte mitogen extracted from a fungus *Peziza vesiculosa*. *Microbiol. Immunol.* 23:997-1008. From CA 92:108941w.

Yadomae, T. et al. 1979b. Examination of the mitogenic activity of materials from fungi on murine lymphocytes *in vitro*. *Microbiol. Immunol.* 23:815-819.

Yagishita, K. et al. 1977. Effects of *Grifola frondosa*, *Coriolus versicolor*, and *Lentinus edodes* on cholesterol metabolism in rats. I. *Nihon Daigaku No-Juigakubo Gakujutsu Kenkyu Hokoku* 34:1-13. From CA 87:21138.

Yakimov, P.A. et al. 1961. Working up *Inonotus obliquus* to medicinal products. *Kompleksn. Izuch. Fiziol. Aktivn. Veshchestv. Nizshikh Rast. Akad. Nauk SSSR, Botan. Inst.*, 129-138. From CA 57:4759d.

Yamada, H. et al. 1984a. Structure and antitumor activity of an alkali-soluble polysaccharides from *Cordyceps ophioglossoides*. *Carbohydr. Res.* 125:107-115.

Yamada, H. et al. 1984b. Structure of a galactosaminoglycan from *Cordyceps ophioglossoides*. *Carbohydr. Res.*134:275-282.

Yamada, Y. et al. 1981. Antitumor effect of lentinan on the mouse system. From *Manipulation of Host Defense Mechanisms*, Aoki, T. et al. (eds.). Amsterdam: *Excerpta Medica* (International Congress Series 576).

Yamada, Y. et al. 1990. Antitumor effect of orally administered extracts from fruit body of *Grifola frondosa* (Maitake). *Chemotherapy* 38:790-796.

Yamaguchi, N. et al. 1990. Augmentation of various immune reactivities of tumor-bearing hosts with an extract of Cordyceps sinensis. *Biotherapy* 2:199-205.

Yamamoto, H. 1977. *Nihon Daigaku No-Juigakubo Gakujutsu Kenkyu Hokoku* 34:1-13. From CA 87:211390.

Yamamoto, T. et al. 1981. Inhibition of pulmonary metastasis of Lewis lung carcinoma by a glucan, schizophyllan. *Invasion Metastasis* 1:71-84.

Yamamura, Y. and K.W. Cochran. 1974a. A Selective inhibitor of myxoviruses from Shii-Ta-Ke (*Lentinus Edodes*). *Mushroom Science*. IX (Part 1): 495-507. From The Proceedings of the 9th- International Scientific Congress on the Cultivation of Edible Fungi.

Yamamura, Y. and K.W. Cochran. 1974b. Chronic hypocholesterolemic effect of *Lentinus Edodes* in mice and absence of effect on scrapie. *Mushroom Science*. IX (Part I):489-493.

Yamasaki, K. et al. 1989. Synergistic induction of lymphokine (IL-2)-activated killer activity by IL-2 and the polysaccharide lentinan, and therapy of spontaneous pulmonary metastases. *Cancer Immunol. Immunother.* 29:87-92.

Yan, R. et al. 1987. Treatment of chronic hepatitis B with Wulingdan Pill. *Journal of the fourth Military Medical College*. 8:380-383. From *Abstracts of Chinese Medicines* 2:188.

Yan, Y. et al. 1985. Anticarcinogenic effect of the polysaccharide from Laoshan polystictus versicolor. *Medical Journal of Chinese People's Liberation Army*. 10:183-185. From *Abstracts of Chinese Medicines* 1:59.

Yang, J. and P. Cong. 1988. Mass spectrometric studies on the sesquiterenol aromatic esters from the mycelium of *Armillaria mellea*. *Huaxue Xuebao* 46:1093-1100. From CA 110:132206w.

Yang, J. et al. 1984. Chemical constituents of *Armillaria mellea* Mycelium I. Isolation and characterization of armillarin and armillaridin. *Planta Med.* 50:288-289.

Yang, J. et al. 1986. Stimulatory effect and kinetics of carboxymethylpachymaran on the induction of interferon by lymphoblastoid cell culture. *Chin. J. Microbiol. Immunol.* 6:157-159. From *Abstracts of Chinese Medicines* 1:515.

Yang, J. et al. 1989a. Chemical constituents of *Armillaria mellea* mycelium: Part 2, Isolation and structure elucidation of armillaricin. *Planta Med.* 55:564-565. From CA 113:37701g.

Yang, J. et al. 1989b. Chemical constituents of *Armillaria mellea* mycelium. Part IV. Isolation and structures of two new sesquiterpenoid aromatic esters: armillarigin and armillarikin. *Planta Med.* 55:479-481. From CA 112:95519u. .

Yang, J. et al. 1990b. Chemical constituents of *Armillaria mellea* mycelium. VI. Isolation and structure of armillaripin. *Yaoxue Xuebao* 25:353-356. From CA 113:148923a.

Yang, J. et al. 1990a. Chemical constituents of *Armillaria mellea* mycellium. V. Isolation and characterization of armillarilin and armillarinin. *Yaoxue Xuebao* 25:24-28. From CA 113:3243u.

Yang, J. et al. 1990c. The structure of armillarizin, a new protoilludane sesquiterpenoid aromatic ester from *Armillaria mellea*. *Chin. Chem. Lett.* 1:173-174. From CA 115:110168m.

Yang, J. et al. 1991b. Two novel protoilludane norsesquiterpenoid esters, armillasin and armillatin, from *Armillaria mellea*. *Planta Med.* 57:4787-4800. From CA 116:102296g.

Yang, J.et al. 1991a. Chemical constituents of *Armillaria mellea* mycelium. VII. Isolation and characterization of chemical constituents of the acetone extract. *Yaoxue Xuebao* 26:117-122. From CA 115:89082s.

Yang, J.J. and D.Q. Yu. 1990. Synthesis of Ganoderma alkaloid A and B. *Yao Hseuh Hseuh Pao* 25: 555-559.

Yang, Q.Y. and S.C. Jong. 1989. Medicinal mushrooms in China. *Mushroom Science.* XII (Part I): 631-643. Proceedings of the Twelfth International Congress on the Science and Cultivation of Edible Fungi. From K. Grabbe and O. Hilber (eds.). 1989. Braunschweig - Germany: Institut für Bodenbiologie, Bundesforschungsanstolt für Londwirtschoft.

Yang, Q.Y. et al. 1993. A new biological response modifier - PSP. From *Mushroom Biology and Mushroom Products.* S.-t. Chang et al (eds.). Hong Kong: The Chinese University Press, 247-259.

Yang, W. et al. 1985. Treatment of sexual hypofunction with *Cordyceps sinensis. Jiangxi Zhongyiyao* 5:46-47. From *Abstracts of Chinese Medicines* 1:401.

Yang, Z.-B. et al. 1993. Inhibitory effects of sizofiran on anticancer agent- or X-ray-induced sister chromatid exchanges and mitotic block in murine bone marrow cells. *Japan. J. Cancer Res.* 84:538-543.

Yeung, H. 1985. *Handbook of Chinese Herbs and Formulas.* Los Angeles: Institute of Chinese Medicine.

Ying, J. et al. 1987. *Icones of Medicinal Fungi From China.* Translated by X. Yuehan. Beijing: Science Press.

Yokokawa, H. and Y. Takahashi. 1990. Contents of vitamin D2 in edible mushrooms. *Tachikawa Tandai Kiyo* 23:35-38. From CA114:5076m.

Yokokawa, H. 1994. Sterol compositions of the fruit-bodies of higher fungi. From *Fifth International Mycological Congress Abstracts.* Vancouver, BC, August 14-21, 1994.

Yokota, M. 1991. Endotoxemia is masked in fungal infection due to enhanced endotoxin clearance by beta-glucan. *Int. Surg.* 76:255-60.

Yokoyama, A. et al. 1975. Distribution of tetracyclic triterpenoids of lanostane group and sterols in the higher fungi especially of the polyporaceae and related families. *Phytochemistry*, 14:487-497.

Yoneda, K. et al. 1991. Immunoregulatory effects of sizofiran (SPG) on lymphocytes and polymorphonuclear leukocytes. *Clin. Exp. Immunol.* 86:229-235.

Yoshida, J. et al. 1989. Antitumor activity of an extract of Cordyceps sinensis (Berk.) Sacc. against murine tumor cell lines. *Jpn. J. Exp. Med.* 59:157-161.

Yoshida, T.O. et al. 1962. A Tumor inhibitor in *Lampteromyces japonica. P.S.E.B.M.* 3: 676-679.

Yoshino, S. 1991. Effects of intraperitoneal administration of lentinan on rats with carcinomatous peritonitis. *Yamaguchi Igaku* 40:133-142. From CA 115:41561v.

Yoshino, S. et al. 1989. Effect of intrapleural and/or intraperitoneal lentinan therapy on carcinomatous pleuritis with special reference to immunological evaluation. *Nippon Geka Hokan* 58:310-319.

Yoshioka, I. and T. Yamamoto. 1964. Constituents of *Polyporus umbellatus*. 2-hydroxytetracosanoic acid. *Yakugaku Zasshi* 84:742-744.

Yoshioka, Y. et al. 1972. Studies on antitumor activity of some fractions from basidiomycetes. I. An antitumor acidic polysaccharide fraction of P. ostreatus (Fr.) Quel. *Chem. Pharm. Bull.* 20:1175-1180.

Yoshioka, Y. et al. 1973. Studies on antiumor polysaccharides of Flammulina velutipes (Curt. ex Fr.) Sing. I. *Chem. Pharm. Bull.* 21:1772-1776.

Youngken, H. 1925. The drugs of the North American Indian (II). *Am. J. Pharm.* 97:257-271.

Yu, C. et al. 1985. Effect of *Grifola* polysaccharide on HBsAg production by human hepatoma cells PLC/PRF/5. *Beijing Med. J.* 7:158,187. From *Abstracts of Chinese Medicines* 1:175.

Yu, H. 1985. Treatment of arrhythmia with *Cordyceps Sinensis. J. Zhejiang Trad. Chin. Med. Coll.* 9:28. From *Abstracts of Chinese Medicines* 1:204.

Yu, J.G. et al. 1990. Studies on constituents of *Ganoderma capense* IV. The chemical structures of ganoine, ganodine and ganoderpurine. *Yao Hsueh Hsueh Pao* 25:612-616.

Yu, L. et al. 1993. Combined traditional Chinese and Western medicine: Effect of *Cordyceps sinensis* on erythropoiesis in mouse bone marrow. *Chinese Medical Journal* 106:313-316.

Yu, L.A. and Q.L. Xu. 1989. Treatment of infectious hepatitis with an herbal decoction. *Phytother. Res.,* 3:1314.

Yue, W. and Z. Cong. 1986. Effects of *Tremella* polysaccharides on synthesis of protein and on glycogen content in normal and injured livers of mice. *Acta Pharm. Sin.* 7:364-367.

Zang, M. and D. Ji. 1985. Notes on Phallaceae from the eastern Himalayan region of China. *ACTA Phytotaxon. Sin.* 4:109-117. From *Abstracts of Chinese Medicines* 1:87.

Zhang, G. and Y. Li. 1987. Determination of nucleosides and nucleotides in *Cordyceps sinensis. Chinese Journal of Pharmaceutical Analysis.* 7:6-9. From *Abstracts of Chinese Medicines* 2:142.

Zhang, J. et al. 1993. Pharmacokinetics and metabolic fate of tritiated poriatin in rats. *Chin. J. Antibiot.* 18:149-153.

Zhang, L. 1987. Polysaccharides from *Fomes pinicola*. I. Isolation and characterization of FP1 and FP2. *Journal of Northeast Normal University.* (4):85-91. From *Abstracts of Chinese Medicines* 2:275.

Zhang, L. and M. Yu. 1993. Influence of ling zhi on Natural killer cells—Immunopharmacological study (5). From From Zhu, S. and M. Mori (eds.). 1993. Influence of ling zhi on natural killer cells—Immunopharmacological Study (5). From *The Research on Ganoderma lucidum* (part one). Shanghai: Shanghai Medical University Press, pp. 246-253.

Zhang, L. et al. 1993. Effects of ling zhi on the production of interleukin-2 (IL-2). From From Zhu, S. and M. Mori (eds.). 1993. Influence of ling zhi on natural killer cells—Immunopharmacological Study (5). From *The Research on Ganoderma lucidum* (part one). Shanghai: Shanghai Medical University Press, pp. 259-265.

Zhang, S. et al. 1985. Activation of murine peritoneal macrophage by the natural Cordyceps and the cultured mycelia of *Cordyceps sinensis. Chinese Journal of Integrated Traditional and Western Medicine.* 5:45-47. From *Abstracts of Chinese Medicines* 1:371.

Zhang, S. et al. 1986. Preliminary study on the growth condition of *Cordyceps sinensis. Microbiology.* 13:56-58. From *Abstracts of Chinese Medicines* 1:570.

Zhang, S. et al. 1987. Effects of Cordyceps and cultured *Cordyceps sinensis* on mouse Lewis lung cancer. *Bull. Chin. Mater. Med.* 12:117-118. From *Abstracts of Chinese Medicines* 2: 29.

Zhang, S. et al. 1991. A phamacological analysis of the amino acid components of *Cordyceps sinensis* Sacc. *Yao Hsueh Hsueh. Acta Pharm. Sin.* 26:326:330.

Zhang, X., and H. Luan. 1986. Effects of some fungal polysaccharides on experimental hepatitis in mice. *Journal of Northeast Normal University.* 4:101-108. From *Abstracts of Chinese Medicines* 1:527.

Zhang, Y. et al. 1985. Effect of the ethanol extracts of *Tremella fuciformis* and *Armillariella mellea* on the cardiovascular system. *J. Beijing Med. Coll.* 17:97-100. From *Abstracts of Chinese Medicines* 1:183.

Zhang, Y.H. et al. 1991. Effect of *Polyporus umbellatus* polysaccharide on function of macrophages in the peritoneal cavities of mice with liver lesions. *Chinese Journal of Modern Developments in Traditional Medicine* 11:225-226 (Chinese).

Zhao, Y. 1991. Inhibitory effects of alcoholic extract of Cordyceps sinensis on abdominal aortic thrombus formation in rabbits. *Chung-Hua Hseuh Tsa Chih* (Chinese Medical Journal) 71:612-615.

Zhao, J.-D. and X.-Q. Zhang. 1994. Resources and taxonomy of lingzhi (Ganoderma) in China. From Program and Abstracts of the '94 International Symposium on Ganoderma Research (October 24-26, 1994). Beijing: Beijing Medical University.

Zhen, F. et al. 1992. Mechanisms and therapeutic effect of *Cordyceps sinensis* (CS) on aminoglycoside induced acute renal failure in rats. *Chung-Kuo, Chung Hsi I Chieh Ho Tsa Chih*, 12:288-291, 262.

Zheng, S-Z. et al. 1993. Study of protective effect of *Tremella fuciformis* Berk preparations TFB on immunity of irradiated tumor-bearing mice. *Chin. J. Clin. Oncol.* 20:451-454.

Zheng, X. et al. 1985. Immune function of the extracelluar and intracellular polysaccharides of *Lentinus edodes in normal mice. Zhongcaoyao.* 16:494-7. From CA 104:107523r.

Zhiyuan, W. and F. Huiti. 1981. Treatment of hereditary cerebellar ataxia with *Ganoderma capense. J. Trad. Chin. Med.* 1:47-50.

Zhong, J. et al. 1993. Screen of inducer of CSFs: I. Inducers of CSFs from poriatin - 10150 and 10152. *Chin. J. Antibiot.* 18:243-249.

Zhou, A. et al. 1987. Antineoplastic effect of the polysaccharides of *Tremella fuciformis. J. Beijing Med. Univ.* 19:150. From *Abstracts of Chinese Medicines* 1:537.

Zhou, H. et al. 1989b. Antihepatitis and antimutation effect of polysaccharide from *Tremella fuciformis* and *Auricularia auricula. Zhongguo Yaoke Duxue Xuebao* 20:51-53. From CA 110:185434a.

Zhou, H. et al. 1989a. Antiaging effect of the polysaccharides from *Auricularia auricula* and *Tremella fuciformis. Zhongguo Yaoke Daxue Xuebao* 20:303-306. From CA 112:132431g.

Zhou, L. et al. 1990. Short-term curative effect of cultured *Cordyceps sinensis* (Berk.) Sacc. mycelia in chronic hepatitis B. *Chung-Kuo Chung- Yao Tsa Chic* (China Journal of Chinese Materia Medica) 15:53-55, 65.

Zhu, D. 1987. Recent advances on the active components in Chinese medicines. *Abstracts of Chinese Medicines.* 1:251-286.

Zhu, J.L. and C. Lin, 1992. Modulating effects of extractum semen Persicae and cultivated Cordyceps hyphae on immuno-dysfunction of inpatients with posthepatitic cirrhosis. *Chung-Kuo Chung Hsi I Chieh Ho Tsa Chih* 12:207-209, 195.

Zhu, X. et al. 1985. Treatment of chronic viral hepatitis B and HBSAG carriers with polysaccharides of *Lentinus edodes. Jiangxi Zhongyiyao.* 5:20,25. From *Abstracts of Chinese Medicines* 1:400.

Zhu, X.Y. and H.Y. Yu. 1990. Immunosuppressive effect of cultured *Cordyceps sinensis* on cellular immune response. *Chung Hsi I Chieh Ho Tsa Chih Chinese Journal of Modern Developments in Traditional Medicine* 10:485-487,454.

Zhuang, J. and H. Chen. 1985. Treatment of tinnitus with Cordyceps infusion: A report of 23 cases. *Fujian Medical Journal.* 7:42,53. From *Abstracts of Chinese Medicines* 1:66.

Zican, W. et al. 1983. Studies on the effects of *Tremella fuciformis* berk preparation on immunity and blood formation in rhesus monkeys. *J. Trad. Chin. Med* 3:13-16.

Zurich, D.B. 1993. *Physicians' Desk Reference*. Montvale, NJ: Medical Economics Data.

Index